A Life, A Sail,
A Changing Sea

by

Robert Arthur Balfour,
The Right Honourable
The Lord Riverdale of Sheffield

Hutton Press
1995

Published by

The Hutton Press Ltd.,
130 Canada Drive, Cherry Burton,
Beverley, East Yorkshire HU17 7SB

Copyright © 1995

Printed by
Image Colourprint Ltd.,
Grange Park Lane,
Willerby, Hull
HU10 6EB

ISBN 1 872167 76 4

DEDICATION

I have no hesitation in dedicating this book to Christian and
memories of her participation in my sailing life. For nearly sixty
years she backed me to the full in every venture; during an initial
trek round the west of Ireland, suffering seasickness and some
trepidation, she told me that she was on the verge of giving up
and coming home but realising that if she did this she would lose
contact with me over an important section of my life. She
decided to stick it and was rewarded by coming to thoroughly
enjoy the cruising and the ship life. What she had to put up with
in the times when I was designing or building a yacht is difficult
to imagine, it must have been horrific. Though she did passages
of more than a thousand sea miles, she preferred the cruising
life, particularly the islands, the coasts, the people and the
languages rather than crossing the great oceans. She also had to
put up with my absences on those occasions when I went off to
sail in other yachts to gain experience. She made a marvellous
job of the children's holidays in 'Bluebird' for about five years;
she became expert in provisioning a yacht for a voyage. She
sailed thousands of miles, playing her full part and taking
watches night and day in any weather and I think one of the
highlights of her life was a voyage in 1971 round the Pacific
Islands when she was voted : "O A P First Class Tasman Tested";
it was a proud moment. Finally, and those who sailed with us
would agree without hesitation, the life on board gained
something extra when Christian was present and I now feel that
without her participation in my sailing life, this book could not
have been written.

Contents

Page

Acknowledgements 4

Foreword by Hammond-Innes 5

Introduction 6

Chapter One   **How Far the Sea
- Early Days 1912 -18** 7
- The 'Nancy Belle'
- I built a cruising dinghy
- The Mad Major
- Water Skis

Chapter Two   **A Blinding Flash of Inspiration
and Trials 1922-25** 25
- Invention
- Trials
- The first twin keel yacht
- The Humber to Portsmouth
- Alterations and Improvements

Chapter Three   **Adventures and Achievements
1925-29** 38
- The bi-ped rig
- Comrade D
- Divinely Mad
- 'Bluebird' completes a
circumnavigation
- The Wrath to come

Chapter Four   **Experience of Other Yachts,
Other Places 1931-39** 62
- Spanish cruise avoiding Spain
- The East and the Antipodes
- 'Dunlin' a sailing canoe
- 'Curlew of Walney'

Chapter Five   **First 'Bluebird of
Thorne' 1939-46** 72
- Design and building
- The trial cruise

Chapter Six   **A Cruise Round
Ireland 1946 -61** 80
- RCC award the Romola
Cup 1946

Chapter Seven   **Fifteen Years of Family
Cruising** 86
- Storm in the Irish Sea
- Biscay

Chapter Eight   **Nine Years of Baltic
Cruising** 100
- Welkomm to Finland
- So near the Midnight Sun

Chapter Nine   **Design and Building the
Second 'Bluebird of
Thorne' 1961-63** 118

Chapter Ten   **Now We Know 1963-64** 130
- The first Atlantic passage
- Caribbean
- This vast America

Chapter Eleven   **Hurricane off Bermuda** 144
- The voyage home

Chapter Twelve   **So This is Mare Nostrum
1965-67** 156
- Malta
- Eastern Mediterranean
- Skipper's Rhapsody

Chapter Thirteen   **Half This Our World** 175
- Grenada/Panama
- Galapagos Islands
- Galapagos/Marquesas
- An Epic Trek
- Storm in the Tuamotues

Chapter Fourteen   **My Sailing Life
- 1970 to date** 194
- Three simple questions
- Preparation for a voyage
- A circuit of islands
- A catalyst
- The world of twin keel 'Bluebirds'
- Where do we sail from here?

Acknowledgements

The Royal Institute of Naval Architects - A paper, 'The Design and Development of Twin keel Yachts' - September 1967.

The Royal Cruising Club Journal and Roving Commissions - 1936 to date.

The Humber Yawl Club Year Book - 1922 to date.

The Yachting World Magazine - in particular 18 articles from January 1926 to date.

The Yachting Monthly Magazine, Yachting USA, magazines in many lands including, Scandinavia, Germany, France, South Africa, Canada, Australia, New Zealand.

Lord Stanley of Alderley - Merlin cruises.

The late Arthur Robb MBE - for design in collaboration.

Richard and Michael Dunston - for invaluable and friendly help during the building of two 'Bluebirds'.

The Berthon Yacht Yard at Lymington - I shall always be grateful for an almost lifelong connection with this excellent yard and their help at various stages with all my 'Bluebirds'.

My friends of the Nicholson family in Antigua - for their hospitality, welcome and help.

Phil and Plat Allen - Talulah cruises.

My friend the late Thomas J Watson Jnr. - for reference to and photographs from his work, 'Log Book for Helen'.

My long time friend Ralph Hammond-Innes - for encouragement at all times and his foreword to this book.

My thanks to Dorothy Clarke - who typed the whole of the original manuscript for this book.

My thanks to my friend Nigel Greenstreet - for the frontispiece of the book and for the many illustrations.

My thanks to Charlotte Ann Smith - who edited it and then put the result onto computer.

My friend Tony Watts - not only for independent editing but help and encouragement at all times.

Foreword
by Hammond Innes

Robin Riverdale is about the same age as the century. In a sense he has been to the Royal Cruising Club what Owen Aisher was to the Royal Ocean Racing Club but Robin is interested in going places rather than racing. He has that rare quality, an inventive mind that has never quite lost the youthful zest for seeking out and discovering.

Just the chapter headings of this book tell you a great deal about the man. Born into the Balfour family, he was twenty-two and just coming out of the dinghy stage; the voyager in him seeking the means to sail out of the estuaries and enclosed waters, out into the sea proper.

To what extent he was influenced, as so many of us had been, by Erskine Childer's account of the cruise of the 'Dulcibella' I do not know but the conception of a twin-keeled hull came to him as a 'blinding flash' after discarding the idea of a drop keel as being too dangerous in tidal waters where a small yacht can be rammed up against sand or mud banks. Twin keels would enable him to take the ground, thus opening up innumerable inlets, harbours and waterways where those with mono-hulls hesitate to venture. He never ceased to emphasise that his prime objective was a seaworthy cruising yacht, not just a shallow draft yacht, that would take the ground upright.

The result was his first 'Bluebird' - referred to now as 'Little Bluebird'. He designed and built her himself with a reckless expenditure of energy; his design capabilities and craftsmanship became evident when he built the first twin-keel yacht to his own design with diagonal teak-planking construction.

It seems hard to believe now but apparently nobody had then thought of a twin-keeled yacht until Robin started experimenting with model boats. Two years later, in 1924 when 'Little Bluebird' was finished, he was playing around with what he called a 'bi-ped' rig.

Not for twenty years after that did he build another yacht. 'Bluebird of Thorne' was completed just before World War II. By then he was married and bringing up a family. He had also sailed quite a few miles, some of it hard cruising, exploring much of Scandinavia.

Finally he built a second and larger 'Bluebird of Thorne', working this time in collaboration with one of our best-known yacht designers, the late Arthur Robb MBE. Whereas with 'Little Bluebird' he had been content to test the hull with model yachts, now he was into tank testing. "Oh yes, we did consider centreboards, swing keels and lifting ballasted keels". But the twin keels won, comparing sufficiently well with other forms and needing no cradle, they can pitch like other forms but tend to roll less and have direction stability. In 1963 he drove this new boat slap through a hurricane offshore of the Caribbean.

He is fascinating to listen to, his enthusiasm for his twin-keel conception knowing no bounds. Occasionally he breaks into what Bernard Ferguson would have classed as doggerel: "If you've ever had the notion (to go to sea in a twin-keeled boat) to sell your farm and cross the ocean; take time before urge vital passes, work is the curse of the cruising classes".

Nevertheless, I think of him as very much in the mould of the traditional steel masters - tough, shrewd, innovative and businesslike. Once, when Dorothy and I were staying with him and his wife Christian at Ropes, a ranch house he designed and euphemistically called a bungalow, he took us round one of the Balfour Steelworks. Not the Skipper of a yacht then but a man with a built-in enthusiasm for the special steels for which his firm were world famous. Both the first and second 'Bluebirds of Thorne' were steel construction and here his knowledge of steel and metallurgy must have been invaluable.

Way back in 1925, several members of the RCC interested in racing, split off to form a club of their own. Unhappily the success of this highly-motivated group caused some resentment amongst the RCC traditionalists. To his great credit, Robin, elected Commodore in 1962, started the slow process of healing the breach. Looking back down the list of post 1925 Commodores I think he was probably the only one of them who could have done it.

Energy and the channelling of it is the chiefest hallmark of outstanding personalities. Robin Riverdale has always had an abundance of energy and readers of this sailing side of his life may wonder how he managed to fit in all his other activities.

Introduction
A Life, A Sail, A Changing Sea

I well remember that throughout my early years, my mother was particularly fond of and would often quote from Robert Louis Stevenson: "This be the verse you grave for me, here he lies where he longed to be, home is the sailor home from the sea and the hunter is home from the hill". At some point I must have thought that this was on the gloomy side and I produced my own parody: "When time runs out, no grief for me, I lived much as I wished to be. Life but a sail on a changing sea, with peace to be found on the hill". And it was from this that the title of this book came to the surface. As sailing has been the most important part of my life second only to my industrial career, one might imagine that this book would come first. However, I first produced the book, "Squeeze the Trigger Gently' for my ninetieth birthday and I have explained how that came about. No sooner was this accomplished than all my friends came in and said, why not a sailing book? Why not indeed. As will appear, it has been a major preoccupation for 80 years; I live with the phrase: "No one can take away your memories". It would give me enormous pleasure if some part of this can be passed on for the enjoyment of others. I also feel that it is a tribute to all the splendid men and women who shared my exploits, enabled me to carry them out and enriched my life with their friendship. A tribute also to Christian, my wife, who not only became competent herself with the special skills in provisioning the yacht for a voyage but also always backed me to the hilt and herself got great rewards from the sailing life. I close this introduction with a verse:

> If you perhaps have had the notion
> To give up all and cross an ocean,
> Act now ere urge that's vital passes,
> Work is the curse of the cruising classes.
> Just sell your farm and go to sea,
> The life is healthy, wind is free.
> Learn navigation, use your hands,
> Explore the world, see foreign lands;
> On distant shores find rich rewards
> With memories your log records,
> But if enthusiasm wanes,
> Take heart, there may be other gains
> Your motivation may increase
> When you find your taxes cease.

It would be difficult to find a more unpromising start for a man who was to become dedicated to sailing and yachting; born and brought up in Sheffield, my father ran a crucible steel manufacturing business, my mother was occupied with a young family. Far from the sea there were no uncles, relatives or even friends with any seafaring connection. My parents' attitude to the sea which could have been and indeed to some extent was a powerful influence ran as follows: My mother had a purely romantic attachment to the sea, not backed up by any practical experience. I think this was not unconnected with the picture of seeing young men in uniforms; she loved uniforms and they did something for her throughout her life. There were no forebears with any seagoing attachments though I did remember my mother saying of her father: "He once said that he had tried a Rob Roy canoe and you had to part your hair in the middle to stay up in one of those things". She was a member of the Navy League, then pressing the Government for a bigger and better Navy to match the ambitions of the Kaiser in Germany.

My father's attitude to the sea was very different; to him it was an obstacle that had to be overcome to do business in other countries, it took time which was undesirable, it cost money which was unwelcome and it could make you sick which was horrible, but his real condemnation of the sea was that nobody seemed to be able to manage it or organise it. I can imagine him arriving at Dover bound for a meeting in Paris to be told that owing to a great storm the ferry could not sail. His reaction to such an occurrence might well have been: "It is intolerable, I must attend that meeting, is there some fisherman or something that will take me across?" (This was of course before the days of flying). But from this background, my mother's diary records that as soon as I could hold a pencil I drew nothing but ships; as soon as I could read I wanted sailing stories. I was not officially allowed a knife but when I managed to get one with a swop at school, I immediately started to try and make ship models and one or two examples of these were still in my mother's display cabinet when she died in 1959.

It seems that people of all sorts may have the urge to go to sea. A friend of mine in Norway, Erik Asker, sent me a lovely letter in fractured English, "I think I have uncovered your originals". He had found a place called Balsfiord in northern Norway a thousand years ago and was convinced that via the Shetland Islands this was the origin of the name Balfour, backed up by the fact that the Orkneys and Shetlands are stiff with Balfours. In my mother's romantic mind, this gave her immense pleasure as she could say I was descended from the Vikings.

Chapter One
How Far The Sea – Early Days 1912-18

In 1912, my father bought a property 'Ropes' at Fernhurst in Sussex. The life that opened up for me at 'Ropes' was a revelation and a new departure. It had a profound effect on my life and future development in every field. For the first time I had a workshop, this was a little corner room opening from the house to a secluded corner of the garden where we could do what we liked. I had a bench, a vice and I quickly built up a set of woodworking tools and some basic metal working tools. I even had a little lathe which had come down to me from my maternal grandfather who had been an engineer. Almost subconsciously I have said 'we' not 'I' and the reason for this is that Jack Hope, the son of Linton Hope, the yacht designer, retired and in poor health, was living in a house on the property. Jack Hope, nearly two years older than me, became an inseparable friend and partner in every venture.

The first effort was a crude sort of punt, little more than a packing case affair, made waterproof with difficulty. We had not even a pond until we dammed the small stream and made one. The punt was little more than a bit of fun, the sort of thing that we tried to get our sisters into and listened with delight to their screams as the water crept up on them. The next adventure was both strange and significant; somehow the idea came up in my mind: "Why not put sails in bicycles?" This was not a, 'no sooner said than done' job, a considerable amount of ingenuity, construction and experiment was required. One memory intrudes on this; Jack and I had worked a whole morning making a socket for the mast on the bicycle, my younger brother Francis, four years younger at eight years old, was frankly more a nuisance than a help; as was natural he would tag along with us whenever possible. He had been watching this procedure and at the very moment when we found that our construction was not strong enough and would have to be redesigned and made again, he came up with this remark: "I could do it if I want but I don't want". Naturally we 'scragged' him and he fled howling to his mother and we duly received dire punishment for bullying brother Francis. Life could be quite complicated even in those days.

When we did eventually succeed and had two bicycles rigged with sails, we were able to try them out on a large double tennis court with a surrounding grass area, high up in the garden with a good unobstructed wind. They worked. Rather surprisingly the balance against the wind pressure was no problem, achieved instinctively and automatically by leaning the bicycle towards the wind as required. Of no use to windward, of little use at 45° or 50° to the wind, definitely helpful to progress with the wind astern. It was with the wind abeam that our sailing bicycles really came to life. They were of little service on the road until we could find a good straight, level stretch with a free beam wind; there was an enormous thrill and satisfaction and life became quite exciting. Remember in those days there was still considerable horse traffic and the sailing bicycles caused consternation; horses confronted with these two strange and terrifying objects, the like of which they had never seen before, were apt to shy and attempt mayhem.

This was not the end of the story; I wrote an article with a crude photograph and some sketches and sent it in to 'The Boys Own Paper' which was then the most prestigious magazine of its sort. The article was accepted, published and I was paid a modest fee. Perhaps fortunately there was no great excitement about this. My parents both extremely busy in different ways, took an attitude which might be described thus: "What a strange idea but then he has always been interested in that sort of thing, the article seems to have made a good impression, quite well done really". It is only in retrospect that I realise that this venture was far more important than that. I had at the age of twelve invented something, created something, made it work and written an article which had been paid for. Unrealised at the time, this had started a trend which has persisted throughout my life, trying to think with originality, create things, make things and sometimes write about them or give lectures on them. An odd thought; perhaps I should not be writing this chapter for this book if I had not invented 'sailing bicycles'.

About a year later, up came the next venture; in one way more ordinary, in another more difficult to achieve and finally more dubious in its result. I built a sailing canoe; there was no formal design only sketches because the design was dictated by the difficulty in finding materials for its construction, thus a keel might be cut out of an old plank, the longitudinals, if suitable timber were not available, made up by 'scarphing' shorter lengths together, the sides of the centreboard case were made from the discarded top of an old table but the stem and the ribs were quite a different story. Here I went out into the woods, selected suitable young ash trees, felled them, trimmed them and dragged them

Boy on bicycle.

home. I then cut from the trunks by hand, the strips I wanted. Alas I had not then penetrated the mysteries of steam heating wood to make it bend readily without breaking. The pliable green ash strips bent well but not quite well enough and so the design suffered, the bilges being slacker than I had intended. I had nothing available which would serve for planking. Fortunately in a loft I found some thick paper-like sheets which were waterproof and it had I think been intended for roof lining. This would have to serve instead of planking. As it was rather too flexible, there was what might be called 'a hungry dog look' as it sagged slightly between the ribs. Copiously treated with linseed oil and then with paint, the job was completed, centreplate, mast and sails and rudder but where could we try it? Exploring the countryside on our bicycles, we found Lugashall Mill Pond, a fine sheet of water about six miles away and the kindly farmer gave us access and free use of his land around the lake. How to get the canoe to the water? We lashed it between two bicycles and pushed, Jack on one side, I on the other. All this was far too crude so we made a trailer from two bicycles' wheels and then hitched the nose of the canoe up behind the saddle of one bicycle. On the level or downhill you could now ride, uphill you still pushed but a great improvement. The first trials and a bitter disappointment. The slack bilges resulted in minimal stability, the mast was too big and heavy, the sail too large and the craft was soon flat on its side. A much smaller and lighter mast, much smaller and lighter sails and means to prevent the craft flooding when laid down flat until at last I had a canoe that would sail. It was controllable, it would go about, it would beat to windward but it lay over on its side in any sudden squall; and the verdict? I had learned a lot, I had only achieved limited success and I didn't write an article about this one. There was however to be a useful little sequel. In 1937 when my son Mark was about ten years old, he discovered this canoe in a loft. He got it out and we patched it up. He repainted it, blue this time, and using it as a kayak canoe with a double-bladed paddle, had a lot of fun with it on local ponds. "I call her 'Bluefine' because she's blue, because she's fine and because she's mine". Fair enough and this in turn was the start of his maritime adventures.

The Nancy Belle
They called her 'The Nancy Belle'
And she made our life a hell;
With a lot of dirty water in her bilge.
Her best days were long since past
But as long as she would last,

Though leaky, nail sick and thin,
She could sail so flashing fast
And she turned like a fly on a pin.

It would be in 1916 that Jack discovered that there was a small yacht belonging to Linton Hope and the family. He found this and we got it up into working order with some difficulty. It was an 18 ft day boat, designed of course by Linton Hope, built about 1900 of a type rarely seen twenty years later but contemporary with the splendid sailing canoes which were a feature of the yachting scene in the 1890's. She was light and fast, the verse gives more information and as centreboard, she had a long, narrow, deep dagger plate. She was entirely decked with the exception of a cockpit space about 6 ft long 4 ft 6 inches wide with quite high combings. Initiated by Linton Hope, her rig was also typical of his work. A foresail and a 'Gunter' lug mainsail with a long, curved yard, the bottom third of which was vertical and close behind the mast. Jack kept her on moorings at the creek at Gosport opposite Portsmouth. By this time he had a motorcycle and we used to go 'ponk, ponk, ponk' over the Downs to sail away in the 'Nancy Belle' by the day or occasionally for the weekend. On such occasions, we might anchor for the night in, for example, a creek off the Lymington river, sleep on the floor, sometimes losing the battle with the rising bilge water; in the cockpit with no bed, cold food, no cooking facilities and protection only by the mainsail draped over the boom. It was rugged stuff but we were young and we were tough and we enjoyed these expeditions.

I shall always be grateful to the 'Nancy Belle' because I gained experience and I learned something important, the sailing performance that was possible from a small, fast yacht, designed by a master hand. Jack, two years older than I, went off into the Royal Naval Air Service and became what we called, "a man who smashed aeroplanes". Crashes were all too common in those days and it was said that a good crash was one that you walked away from. I even had an illicit flight with him from a farmer's field which created another interest in my life which developed later. So we come to 1918, the end of World War One, I was technically in the Royal Flying Corps but never really served as the Armistice was signed before I completed flying training. A very different life now lay ahead.

Top: Transporting the sailing canoe.

Above: Sailing Canoe 1916.

Left: Mark aged 8 with 'Bluefine'.

Below: Sailing canoe - Mark using 'Bluefine' as a caique.

I Built A Cruising Dinghy

In 1920 at the age of 19, I was working in a Sheffield steelworks. The war to end all wars had ended but times were bad and a land fit for heroes to live in was failing to provide a living for many of them. The great Coal Strike and General Strike were still to come. The lower paid adult worker earned fifty shillings for a fifty-two hour week, coal was 8s.6d a ton at the pit head, there was plenty of muck in the air and on the ground in the Sheffield of those days. There were few cars and the cheapest was beyond the dreams of avarice for a young man. City transport was the clang of the tram but the country was covered by a network on which steam trains ran with quite admirable regularity. There had been inflation during the war but compared with today the pound in your pocket still had a distinct kinship with the golden sovereign. The length of the working week included working to 12.00 noon on Saturdays while any study was in your own time which made leisure and hobbies pretty limited, but I had built a dinghy.

'Seamouse' was a 10 ft dinghy chosen as a safe craft with no claim to speed. Her lines were developed from another design and her construction, worked out to suit my purposes, used the Ashcroft double skin, diagonal planking system. This was to be a cruising dinghy and if two men are to sleep in a 10 ft dinghy, there can be no permanent centre thwart. A special construction with bent frames inside the longitudinal ribbons supported a small side deck and the centreboard case. 'Seamouse' was decked over forward as far as the mast. There was a useful built-in stowage locker at the stern, christened by a small boy as the "crew's booze locker". A tent cover fitted over the boom, a camping primus, paraffin lamp and a galvanised bucket were provided with a few other bits and pieces to make a floating home.

I shall now refer more than once to the influence of materials on design and compare the early days with the facilities taken for granted today. It is much easier to list what one had not got in the 1920's; there were no cars, no trailers, few clubs or launching ramps, outboard engines were very primitive and little known. There was no marine plywood that would stand the sea, no adequate glue, no synthetic rope, cloth fibre, no GRP, no Tufnol, no stainless steel or sea water resisting light alloy. What remains? There was wood, galvanised iron, copper, brass, manila and cotton. It was not possible to buy a building kit with a set of plans, the amateur had to work out every piece of wood

'Nancy Belle' - a surviving Linton Hope day boat.

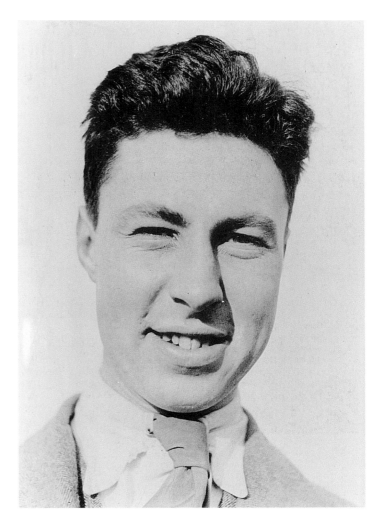

Jack Hope - my greatest friend. He married my second sister and was killed flying a fighter over France in the Second World War.

required, list and order it and similarly decide the right sizes of copper nails, rooves and screws. The need for special tools was learned the hard way and so were techniques of the boat building craft. Despite all this, 'Seamouse' was built and she was strong and good, though she would be considered impossibly heavy today. She gave years of useful service until after I sold her and I do not know where and when she met her end.

Learning to sail was no easier than building. I do not think there were any sailing schools or tuition, I had only experience with a very cranky sailing canoe and one or two sails with Jack Hope in a Linton Hope day boat. 'Seamouse' went by train to Lymington to connect with a family holiday in that area and one day she was rigged with the kindly help of the Berthon yard. That was the start of an association that was to endure to this day with three generations of men in charge.

I stepped aboard, pushed off, hauled in the sheet and sailed away down the river to the Solent. I shall never forget the delirious thrill of that first time at sea under sail and in command of my own yacht. Surely the Solent can be regarded as a sea and a 10 ft dinghy as a yacht if you have produced it with your own hands. In the ensuing weeks I gained experience; I capsized an uncle, an unpopular exercise but luckily without loss of uncle! I cruised, and I think it may be regarded as cruising, between the limits of Christchurch and Langston harbour. Disaster must have been avoided many times by beginner's luck or just by instinct.

I next had experience on the Humber, the Trent and the Yorkshire Ouse. The creek at Brough on the upper Humber was my base, and there, and at Hessle, I was welcomed by that fine old club the Humber Yawl Club. In 1933, I decided to bring 'Seamouse' to these waters nearer home. She came by train to Goole. Going over by myself one weekend, I got her ready, hoisted sail and set off down the Ouse just before the top of high water. My knowledge of the river was nil, my experience was slight indeed, the wind, generally favourable, was far, far too strong. Trouble threatened; with the risk of overturning under full sail at maximum speed I dared not round-up; I had no experience of the little, short seas that build up in these waters. In one squall, my bow went under, I just retained control but we should have been swamped but for the decking and coaming forward for this was a cruising dinghy and we had indeed a small deck aft, a very broad gunnel and a slight coaming, all of which helped to avert

disaster and of course we had to gybe on the bends of the river. Every gybe was hair-raising and each might have been our last. Progress was rapid with wind and tide and time passing. We rushed past Brough, I didn't know the entrance, I could see my way in and in those conditions I did not like the look of it. So down the Humber and to Hessle. There, closer in, a little shelter; I could see the entrance and feeling rather dispirited I made one last gybe and sailed up the Haven with just enough water remaining to make fast to Snippet.

It was Sunday morning, George Holmes, after church, was having a yarn with Stanley Knowles on board. Alerted, they came up and with a look of some incredulity, saw a young man in a strange 10 ft dinghy alongside. I think they had both decided that they were not sailing that weekend on the weather forecast. I was cold, wet, tired, hungry and I had been very frightened. They knew just how to deal with this situation, received me on board, welcomed me and restored me. I didn't realise it at the time but I had literally gybed myself into membership of the Humber Yawl Club - that was sixty-five years ago. At last I was in contact with men who knew about boats and yachts. Dear old George Holmes took me on a weekend cruise in 'Snippet' and in that short space taught me much of the tides and river lore of that rugged environment. He was a disciple of Albert Strange, the Artist/Designer who had developed the Humber canoe yawls. Many years later, one of them, 'Sheila', made an epic single-handed voyage to New Zealand.

The Humber was a fine training ground if your enthusiasm could survive the discouragement and I would put mud right at the head of the list. If your seamanship could survive disaster, then you might be better prepared to tackle new experiences at sea. By such processes the day came when I planned a circumnavigation of Lincolnshire in two weekends. I tremble when I recall the care with which I prepared for this venture, when ignorance could trip me at every step, but I did take thought and navigation was involved and to deal with this I had one general chart and Bartholomews half inch to the mile, land maps. They showed some of the contours and if your draught was 6 inch with the plate up, you might well be more concerned with objects ashore than many fathoms at sea. A church steeple (conspicuous) on a chart was far easier to identify from perhaps three other churches, two chimneys and a water tower from Bartholomews, than from a chart. There was a boat compass, a cockpit cover as well as the tent, an anchor and plenty of rope.

The oars were good, not the toothpicks called dinghy sculls. The primus was in a biscuit tin with tested ventilation, Kapok sleeping bags doubled as life saving equipment. Quite a list of other things with a few tools was supposed to deal with all emergencies. I had thought about more dire possibilities and provided a sea anchor. In bad weather I intended to lie to this at sea or if the worst happened, to run her on the beach. 'Seamouse' was light enough for two men to haul up, if she smashed and the men were not impaired in the process, at the worst, I hoped that the men would crawl up the beach. Rocks might be nasty but there were few rocks on our intended route. I do not now remember whether I had ignored or put out of my mind the possibility of grounding on banks in bad weather far from the coast; faith and hope were not listed in the inventory but they must have been all present and correct.

On Saturday 6 July, we arrived at Brough by train at 2.30 pm. Dick had been for one weekend in 'Seamouse' and was prepared to come again. Throwing the gear aboard we made sail and left Brough creek. It was high water but not a strong tide. We changed and stowed our gear and as we started down river, the whole sail breeze against the tide caused the short hollow waves, inevitable in those parts and horrible in a small open boat. As we could neither point high nor move fast and were shipping water, progress was slow and it was the tide that took us to windward and down river. For this reason we kept to the main channel where the stream was strongest, though the seas were worst. Off Hull, with the tide at full strength, the seas were larger but not more difficult as we began to rise to them. The wind increased and we reduced sail. We had passed Paull Creek at 8.15 pm but the tide was spent, we could not leave the Humber that night and there was no refuge for many miles before Grimsby. We entered Paull Creek and secured to one of two small fishing craft known locally as 'blobbers'. We had a meal and dried out slightly as everything was wet - so were we. The oilskins in those days were heavy, clammy stiff and only too frequently sticky as well, imposing such a handicap to movement that we seldom wore them. We went ashore and went up to Hedon, now well inland up a drainage ditch. It had been a port before Kingston-upon-Hull but like many another, larger craft and change of channels had left it to memories. On our return the two boats had lifted with the returning tide and a forbidding leap across a dark gap was necessary to regain 'Seamouse'. The floorboards were hard but we slept.

At 3.00 am we were under way just before high water, the wind had changed and we could hold our course to Grimsby on the starboard tack. A tremendous thunder storm developed, there appeared to be three centres, the largest right above us with magnificent lightning and continuous thunder crashes. The rain was so blinding that only by the lightning could we see the buoys. A culminating flash and with an ear-splitting crash we were struck and both received a shock strong enough to be nasty. Perhaps the all pervading wet, as we were practically sitting in the river, had saved us from injury. The water was over the floor boards, we baled with the half round galvanised pan, equally useful for the two P's, one of which is paddle. There were no dinghy pumps, self balers, transom flaps or plastic scoops. The storm passed on and did a lot of damage in Lincolnshire. Behind it the wind was light and freer. We set our small sail (our trysail) on a boat hook as a spinnaker; murky weather with showers ensued until we had passed Grimsby at 7.00 am. Conditions were good enough for a cooked breakfast. The spinnaker came in as we rounded Donna Nook; we had left the Humber, this was the North Sea. The water lost its chocolate hue, the sun came out, there was an uplift of spirit and we made our maximum speed until the wind came ahead and grew lighter so that we were becalmed off Mablethorpe.

We had sailed as if racing, losing no chance to gain a yard, we now rowed in to close the coast and cheat the tide. At 1.45 pm a head wind came off the land and we sailed long and short legs. At St Leonards it was glorious sailing with smooth water and as much wind as we could handle but against the tide progress was slow and we did not reach Skegness until 5.00 pm. The wind came right ahead and though light, the tide was against us. We considered anchoring but as the wind was offshore we sculled towards the beach and towed, adjusting the line so that 'Seamouse' steered herself as we enjoyed a leg stretch by turns. The tide was due to turn at 9.30 pm as we were entering the Wash and we had a meal with the boat just moving in light airs. It was a fine evening and a beautiful sunset. On one of the banks to seaward, we heard appealing noises like a child crying with an occasional groan as though a man in pain. We thought it was a stranded porpoise but could do nothing about it. The night closed in and a light mist came down. We were rowing and sailing, sometimes together, well clear of the land and steering by compass. At 12.30 am, a cluster of lights showed ahead and we closed them at 2.00 am to find coastal steamers anchored awaiting the tide. Needing rest, we secured to a buoy on the shore

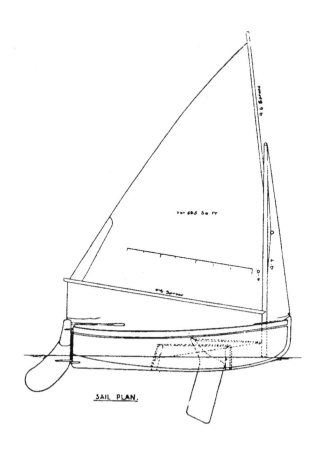

SAIL PLAN.

'Seamouse' - a 10ft cruising dinghy 1918.

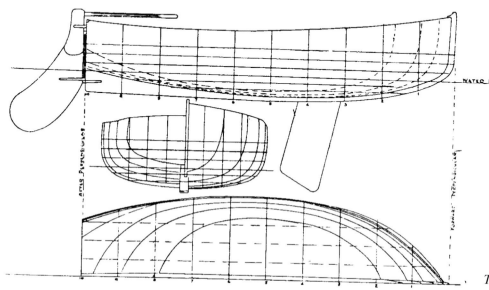

The design of 'Seamouse'.

side of the channel until 4.00 am. The light was making and we were glad to find ourselves in the Boston channel and only a mile from the entrance to the River Whitham. We had ten miles still to go. We sailed into the river and met the fishing fleet coming out. The boats made a magnificent picture against the sunrise with Boston Stump showing behind them with a band of mist across it like a veil. The heat was rising to a fine, hot day. Progress in the river was only possible by towing and this was heavy as it involved some mud, some ditches and occasionally fences. The last mile was only achieved by rowing flat out against wind and current.

We secured by the ferry at Boston on a shelf of mud at 08.00 am, 105 miles had been made good in 41 hours; 36 under way. I think we were a little pleased with the performance but I am sure we did not realise how lucky we had been. The plan for the second weekend was simple. The Trent must be reached by canal and river, passing through Lincoln and that Saturday if we were to have any chance of returning to Brough by working tides on Sunday. Man proposes! On the chosen Saturday, I arrived at Boston with another friend but it was 6.30 pm before we started up the River Whitham. The wind was ahead, the channel was narrow and sailing was difficult. We rowed until 8.30 pm. The primus valve failed, it flared up and melted out. We alternated sailing and rowing until 1.30 am and then slept. We were under way at 4.00 am and rowed for four hours. Impelled by hunger, we repaired the primus by a wooden plug with a packing washer made from green duck weed. A head wind howled down the river and whistled in our teeth. The tow path was now lined with anglers, each to his peg about 15 yards apart for a fishing match. The river was straight as a sword of vengeance as far as the eye could see. We reefed down and tried to sail, but impeded by the fishermen we could only make a few yards on each tack. Again we had to tow. We were not popular and heard more than the four letter words, sometimes with unpleasant hints as to our future! The line had to be flicked over each fisherman and his rod; in turn we grew hoarse with request and apology. Occasionally an almost friendly character asked us why we had no engine. Our jaundiced view of their proceedings registered about five small fish, a lot of empty beer bottles and enough ground bait to poison the Cut. Averaging two miles an hour, we reached Bardney Lock at 12.30. It did not work on Sundays; we had to empty 'Seamouse', remove the centreplate and carry her up and round the lock and then re-rig and restow all the gear.

At this point we were beaten. It would be impossible to reach Torksey in time. The head wind was now a gale. We rowed on and into Lincoln. Slums and bridges led to another lock, this time there were unbroken railings on each side, almost insuperable but we were able to recruit help and lift her bodily on end. An hour and a half later we reached Brayford. The day was done and so were we. We slept until 5.00 am and then tackled the job of cleaning ourselves up and returning to work by train. This weekend had no rewards, the friendship survived but he never came again.

For the third weekend, I was single-handed and left Lincoln at 4.00 pm on Saturday, sailing on the wind and keeping off the bank by pulling a lee oar when necessary. This was a fairly acrobatic exercise, simultaneously steering and tending the sheet as required. It rained steadily and at Saxilby the mast had to be struck for a bridge. After an hour, a welcome bend in the canal enabled me to sail to Torksey and with twelve miles done, I looked out into the Trent, secured to an old Lighter. It was a dirty night of wind and rain and I had to rig the stern line through a block and to a cleat at hand so that I could tend it as I slept, more or less.

Sunday produced a beautiful morning with a strong fair wind. I had deliberately chosen a spring tide; high water at Torksey would be 11.00 am. The bore or 'aegir' came up with a roar at 8.30 am. It was an extraordinary sight and not without danger to small craft. Here 80 miles from the sea, in the middle of a country scene, salt water comes charging up with a line of breakers licking hungrily at the land. I was under way as soon as I could, a pretty but winding and tree-blanketed stretch of river gave tricky sailing and a turn or so to windward brought some spray aboard. With the water still high and the reeds almost submerged, there was a good view over the surrounding country and no worry about running aground on the bends. We passed Gainsborough and its bridge at 12.30 and the ebb running strongly made short miles to Owston Ferry. The river was now well known to me as I had cruised this area before and this was helpful. The wind increased but I was carrying rather too much sail to make all speed and with the ebb tide, I was covering the ground at ten miles an hour. The view had gone, the reeds towered high and with anxious care, I followed the deep water at the bends, gybing constantly with even more anxiety as there was every risk of a capsize. Burton Stather provided all the thrills. It was almost low water at 4.30 pm as I left the Trent and entered the Humber. At 5.00 pm, the flood made and a sea kicked up at once but, just holding my own, I edged into the Lincolnshire shore at maximum speed. Glorious sailing but hazardous. The bows threw wings of spray shining in the sun. The whole dinghy quivered and constantly threatened to broach or gybe. I had to work every eddy and it was touch and go at times as I had to go out into the current on the points. Two steamers bound for Goole came up and their wash almost flooded me. I reached a Keel aground at 6.30 pm and secured to her, being made welcome with a mug of tea. I had been unable to leave the helm even for a moment for 8 hours. An hour later with the flood now slacker, I made the remaining distance to Brough without further difficulty by 8.00 pm. 'Seamouse' was back in the familiar creek, its mud so soft that a scull could be plunged to its depth with no resistance. I had the horrors at the thought of a fall head first into certain suffocation. The circumnavigation of Lincolnshire had been completed in three short weekends with a total of 250 miles covered. Though I failed to do it in two as intended, for all I know the record stands to this day for a 10 ft dinghy and possibly for much more able vessels.

I had now learned enough to make an assessment and realised that I had made the mistake which I afterwards found to be a classic one. 'Seamouse' was too small. The effort I had put into building her could have produced a 14 ft or even 16 ft craft at little extra cost. Speed and performance were entirely governed by her 10 ft length as also the seas in which she could live, while when stowed for cruising, there was neither room nor comfort. The decking had saved her many times from capsize and twice I had driven the bow under but recovered. The construction had stood up yet it was impossible to keep anything dry. We had no plastic bags or containers. In ignorance risks had been taken; there was no built-in buoyancy, no life jackets or harnesses, neither were available in modern form. There was only cork and kapok and we should have had flares and a powerful torch but I had gained experience and I must have covered about 1000 miles during my ownership of 'Seamouse'.

I had gained even more experience in human contacts and already realised how unique an approach is provided by the sailing life. The tough men in the Keels and Sloops never failed in help and courtesy though they could not understand what we were trying to do or why and if ever a yacht club gathers a genuine body of enthusiasts it is the Humber Yawl Club. In that environment they have to be keen! There was also much knowledge of the past within the lifetime of men who talked to me; salmon still ran the Trent and Ouse, sturgeon were caught in

the Humber and punt guns were in regular use for commercial wild fowling. This must have been deadly dangerous in those waters. Whalers sailed from Hull and I had seen Keels and Sloops under sail though they were at the end of their days.

"Selby was a sea port town
When Goole was still a marsh;
Now Goole it is the sea port grown
In Selby life is harsh".

Barges once came down the River Idle from the wharf at Bawtry to load sailing coasters on the Trent with manufactures from Sheffield and iron ore was imported from Norway for the Crucible furnaces. There were then no bridges at Goole and Keadby on the River Trent, and the water was still used. It was fresh at low water and standing overnight an inch of silt settled. When we grounded there we bathed of necessity and we said, "It is not so much that we mind a dead dog, it is the constant expectation of meeting one".

Not often in this life is one given the opportunity to correct mistakes, I had the chance to create what 'Seamouse' should have been. Ken Flather came to me and it transpired that he wanted to do what I had done with 'Seamouse'. That was on Saturday - and the poor chap never had a chance! In the early hours of Monday morning, exhausted and dizzy, he got away clutching a roll of plans. I had designed 'Sparrow', a 14 ft cruising dinghy and I had made a sailing companion and friend for life. Ken built 'Sparrow' using a similar construction and the experience I had gained from 'Seamouse'. I could not help a great deal as I was engaged on other projects. When she was completed, I had eight cruises in 'Sparrow' with him including the more ambitious passages from Brough to Scarborough and return to the Humber. 'Sparrow' was a success and proved what 'Seamouse' should have been. She could be handled single-handed and was much faster, safer and more seaworthy, there was room to live and she was drier. The rig with a normal foresail and later with a large foresail on a temporary bow-spit and also used as a spinnaker, was a great improvement. Ken learned to sail as I had done. Inevitably we reached the limits of 14 ft and I then designed a 2 ft extension astern. With this we had more power and speed and at last some built in buoyancy, fore and aft. I must have sailed 750 miles in 'Sparrow' and though this bridged other exploits it is included here as invaluable experience before I graduated to keel and decked yachts.

In the early 1920's, there were many racing dinghies often

'Sparrow' - a 14ft cruising dinghy designed for Ken Flather, later extended to 16ft and the first experimental bi-ped rig.

associated with the name Morgan Giles but in 1927 Uffa Fox produced 'Avenger', a 14 ft National and with this the planing dinghy was born and a break through in design as well. His success in this year rivalled that of 'Kismet' thirty years before. His feat in racing and winning at Cowes, sailing to Cherbourg, racing and winning there and sailing back to Cowes for another race, fired the imagination. The racing dinghy was not intended for cruising but who could then in their wildest dreams imagine Frank Dye and his companion sailing a 16 ft 'Wayfarer' dinghy to the Faroes and on to Norway? The development, the technique and the expertise in all branches of the game, with the courage and physical endurance, though aided by all the materials of another thirty years, showed as much advance in the sailing game as climbing the north face of the Eiger in another sport. Thousands can now have pleasure and recreation in modern dinghies with increasing leisure and affluence which brings this sport within the reach of all whether it is racing, cruising or just 'messing about in boats'. While the car, the trailer and the outboard have brought navigable water within reach or every city, sails are seen on every reservoir or old gravelpit.

The Mad Major

At this time I began to realise how little I knew. This was probably an improvement in my outlook. I was seeking knowledge and information from any source and I was reading everything I could get hold of.

Dick was responsible for two different experiences during the summer of 1923.

There was a well known character in Sheffield who owned a yacht. He was a kindly man but of rather ferocious aspect. His best friends would admit that he was excitable, others would have said irascible or worse. When in action under a full head of steam he was apt to foam at the mouth - a daunting spectacle for the young. He had a fluttering of attractive daughters and it was rumoured that he had them all well broken in and trained as crew on his vessel. I knew that Dick was attracted by one of these daughters. He did not know that I knew this or even that I knew the girl, but I did and I thought she was pretty smashing myself! A yacht crewed by a bevy of beauties was a new conception. Dick managed to get himself invited for a long weekend and he included me, feeling possibly that he needed nautical support and still under the illusion that I knew enough about things maritime to prevent father foaming too much or attract ridicule from the expert daughter! I jumped at this and I swear that the chance to sail in a Watson lifeboat yacht conversion was more important than the beauty chorus! The yacht 'Chaperon' was stationed at West Mersea and this tempts another digression. I then owned a motor cycle, my pride and joy, ranking almost level with 'Seamouse'. It was a 500cc Sunbeam, the single cylinder 85 x 85 millimetre with side valves, an enduring machine of good quality on which you sped high up in the air in a 'sit up and beg' attitude, over very narrow tyres. Road holding was minimal anyway but roads were rough. There were still greasy cobble stones in Sheffield and there were tramlines. If these were entered incautiously you either fell off or proceeded to the tram shed! I had so many falls that I claimed to have covered the distance from my home to my work at one time or another on my hands and knees. Two up on my 'magic carpet', Dick and I joined ''Chaperon' at West Mersea. The weekend was a huge success though confined to the back water. There was a Morgan Giles 10 ft sailing dinghy and the opportunity to see other types of yacht, while 'Chaperon', a skillful conversion by G U Laws, was excellent and gave a very good impression, sailing well, though slow to windward. She had a good engine well installed but it was temperamental as was then the accepted state. Running down the back water the owner ordered us to set the square sail. I was thrilled to handle gear I had only seen in books, but it took all hands more than an hour. The wind promptly changed and another hour was required to hand it and stow the gear away. All this had been achieved with a little froth but no foam! Everything worked well, the yacht was competently handled and I learned as much as I could have expected. Dick was pretty silent on the way home. I don't think he had made much progress.

Whether the same urge was responsible or not, Dick answered an advertisement for a crew which resulted in Dick and I with his younger brother John, joining the yacht 'Cerise' at Exmouth for a fortnight's cruise. Our motives were somewhat different. John, I think, imagined a gay and exciting time on the *plage* in Brittany; Dick may have had the same or other thoughts; I hoped to learn some navigation and handle a yacht at sea. 'Cerise' was a real yacht. She was an excellent example of her day and type, 43 foot overall, lean with 10 foot beam and deep with 8 foot draught. An almost straight stem carried an enormous bowsprit. The stern was a long flat counter, the keel was straight, the gear simple and heavy. I shudder to think what the displacement

might have been but her ballast was reputed to be 12 tons, mostly in curiously shaped lumps of lead lying at random in a cavernous bilge below the floors. She was almost the plank on edge type with heavy construction of grown oak frames, pitch pine planking, yellow pine decks and teak trim. She was rigged as a gaff yawl. There was an engine 12/15 horse, four cylinder Kelvin. This had been installed at an unknown date in a cupboard to port between a companionway and the side of the ship and drove a wing propeller. We were to learn more of this later.

The owner, a Major, struck us as very old, but remember the axiom; at any age an old man is ten years older than yourself! He might have been sixty-five but this could have been very wrong. After long service in India he was also a bit shrivelled. In the Kipling idiom when every family had some member serving the British Raj, he was a Pukka Sahib. There was a paid hand, Etienne Galliot, a tough and rather attractive Breton fisherman, speaking no English, who lived in the fo'c'sle, while the Major had a two berth cabin opening from the cockpit over a bridge deck. A separate companionway from the deck descended vertically to the companionway and a deep dark dungeon type of saloon with two sofa berths and an enormous heavy ballasted swing table. John was to sleep in a hammock above this. Cooking was by two primus stoves at the aft end of the fo'c'sle to starboard with a primitive bucket type W C opposite them to port.

The weather was glorious. Our hopes were high though we were stale and tired from an overnight journey.

I asked the Major to show me round the gear and introduce me to the engine. I was told that the deck was Etienne's department and that the engine ran sweetly! We made sail and got the anchor. As no-one knew the gear this took time. There was a nice breeze and we should have sailed out without difficulty, but no, after a small rainstorm we were in irons in the narrows at the harbour entrance and I was ordered to start the engine. The starting handle worked in the saloon through a hole in the bulkhead and had a bare two inch clearance for the knuckles at two points in its swing. It was at those points that the handle chose to come off when the engine fired. The machine started. It ran on two cylinders only but I managed to get way on the yacht by easing the clutch in and out to avoid stalling. Just clear of the entrance the engine died.

What joy to sail peacefully to Torquay. I was revelling in this and nothing could destroy the beauty of the scene. Next day a session with the engine revealed dud plugs on cylinders one and four, which could be cured and an exhaust valve seized in cylinders one and three. We removed one of these valves by packing up over the tappit but number three defeated us. A trial confirmed that we now had three cylinders. All parts of the engine likely to need attention were inaccessible between the main body of the engine and the side of the ship. We shut the cupboard door. I was the engineer.

The Major returned from friends ashore and announced that we would sail for France forthwith as the wind and weather were favourable. Enthusiastic confusion ensued, with no direction, until with all plain sail set and the cable hauled short, something had to happen soon. Port tack? I said hopefully, passing the cockpit from the mizzen and the Major agreed. A few moments later 'Cerise' paid off on the starboard tack and slowly gathered way; her formidable bowsprit aimed at the steps on the quay where several dinghies were made fast. "Out on the bowsprit", was the Major's comment to John and he obeyed. Theirs not to reason why. I can picture the scene to this day. The gay harbour and the sunshine, the Major at the helm, white and still, John, young and fair, at the very end of the bowsprit apparently prepared for symbolic sacrifice with the faces of the onlookers faintly pleased, as onlookers are, at the prospect of disaster. Etienne, who never spoke, waved his hand and said' "La Barre" in a firm voice. The Major jerked from paralysis and put the helm down. "Cerise' at best had a slow and stately sweep. John missed doom by feet. The enormous weight just carried her into the wind. Etienne backed the jib and I attended to the foresail. Very slowly we went on to the port tack and were able to clear the harbour entrance. "You see, Balfour," said the Major, "You never know what tack it will be".

An ancient chart was produced on which to lay off a course. I hovered around this operation as I did want to learn but after some awkward fumbling the Major said, "Go away! I can't do this with you watching me". We were given a course and I was told, "You find out about the leeway afterwards Balfour". I was clearly going to learn but not in the manner I had expected! It was a lovely evening, a relaxed atmosphere developed, we were young, this was the life and we were going foreign. The Major was kind and amiable and more expansive than he had been. With five of us aboard, life should have been easy, but who did what and when? We had our own discussion. Dick, who was said to know the Major best, as he

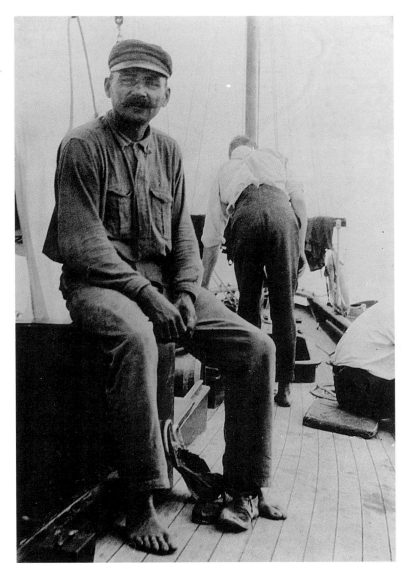

Etienne Galliot - a fine Breton seaman.
He wanted me to marry his daughter.

had made the arrangements, would be our spokesman and act as steward and storekeeper. I was already engineer and expected to double on deck and communicate with Etienne as I had the better smattering of French. John was cast as cook but that was soon to be modified by seasickness. The Major kept no watches and did not cook or wash up, which was entirely reasonable. He washed frequently with both fresh and salt water. Etienne did what he was told, no more and no less and this was less as he seldom received an order! He did not cook or wash up and he never washed!

The three beginners slept in the saloon. Night fell with no watches set. We sat and talked until late. The binnacle light failed. Later I took over and sent Etienne below. It was my first night watch, out of sight of land in a yacht. A sense of awe came over me at this marvellous feeling. I shall never forget that night as I experienced some magic transformation of the spirit that has never left me. The silence, the feeling of power in the wind and propulsion without effort, the swing of the ship, the water sliding past and the tiller alive under my hand. But above all the stars, by which I had to steer, with the gaff rig tracing an uneven but rhythmic course across the heavens. I was unconscious of time until the dawn, a slow growing light as objects aboard became visible, the changing shade and then the colour of the sea, until at last the sun rose with the splendour of a new day. I turned out Dick and went below quite dazed as well as tired. It was a slow calm passage and we eventually picked up the light of Les Sept Isles. It was never revealed whether this had been intended or was pure chance but Peroz Guerec was mentioned as a possible destination. Another day of calm and another night passed. Drifting back and forth on the tides with Les Sept Isles and Tragoz all too adjacent, at times a morning breeze and providential high tide enabled us to make Roscoff after sixty-eight hours on passage from Torquay, but that Roscoff was our destination may not be unconnected with the fact that this was Etienne's home port.

I look back over the years with many passages, many landfalls, in the ports of many countries but it does me good to recall that first arrival in Brittany. Sailing in made it all different and emphasised the colours, the sights, the sounds and the very potent smells of France. Good meals and good wine. The fun of marketing in a strange language. The fishing craft of strange designs and types, then mainly under sail, were fascinating. It was a delight. We remained three days as all was not so well aboard 'Cerise'. The first day was a free for all. There was talk

of Dourenez. The second day was devoted to the engine. The third we did not sail because Etienne was drunk but we visited St. Pol de Lecon, bathed and frolicked around. Soon after our arrival a truly enormous jar of strong red wine appeared on a hand cart. It had been ordered by the Major and was stowed, as he directed, under Etienne's berth in the fo'c'sle. Thereafter he was never sober but only occasionally completely drunk. He produced his family and this I suspected had influenced our course far more than the Major's navigation. It was proposed that I should marry his eldest daughter. I hope neither of us considered this a fate worse than death. She was a pleasant and comely wench. His wife, obviously accustomed to a fuddled Etienne, handled the whole situation with great dignity. That evening a row developed between the Major and Etienne. It was more amusing than serious and without effect as the Major's French gave out in splutters of rage and Etienne was in any case too drunk to care!

The engine overhaul was an epic and involved stripping down the whole engine and removal of the cylinder blocks. Obviously sea water had come back up the exhaust. There was rust everywhere but the sticking valves were the final cause of failure. We lashed the cylinder blocks to dinghy sculls and with these over our shoulders we made our way through the town to the blacksmiths, where heat, large wrenches and dangerous risks with hammers eventually removed all valves which were then in a shocking state. Quite undeterred we straightened stems, heads were filed to an approximate fit and ground in for hours and hours. Reassembly of the engine in its cupboard was completed by 1.30am. Rust in the engine raised not the flicker of an eyebrow with the Major but two or three spots of oil on the deck caused a major brain storm. He would not let us test our handiwork because he did not like the smell of petrol, though this could not compete with the sewer discharge into the harbour right under our noses. Next day we tried the engine. It ran on all four cylinders and took us out of the harbour to anchor outside to wait our tide before sailing to Peroz Guerec. The last mile or so through the rocks was taken under power as the wind had gone and then only did it transpire, quite casually in conversation that the propeller dropped off the year before and that the Major had replaced it with a second hand one, very cheap, but the wrong size! No wonder that poor machine could only cough along at half throttle, knocking badly.

Surrounded by rocks it stopped again but this was more routine. The whole fuel system was blocked up with dirt, fluff and matchsticks. This was rectified mere seconds before we hit the rocks. We secured to the quay in Peroz Guerec. Etienne and I, separately at different times, without seeing the other, took a halyard ashore to a bollard to list her inward. The Major ordered both of us to bring it back aboard and wandered off returning with two men staggering under a large spar which he had hired to lash as a leg in the outboard rigging. He took us ashore and stood us a good dinner. On our return Etienne was drunk in his bunk. 'Cerise was precariously balanced leaning slightly outward on the spar and the 30 foot tide so near low water. I again tried the halyard but unfortunately the Major came up at that moment for another purpose and had a brain storm. We turned in. A loud crack woke us, 'Cerise' tilted outwards and fell. It was a major crash as the gunwale described an arc or 12 foot on to sand and rock so that she lay with the masts horizontal. Two men, the hammock and the table with its heavy lead weights, torn from its fastening, landed on top of the third man in the bottom berth. It is a mystery that nobody was hurt but before we could heave the table away, disentangle ourselves from the hammock and grope our way upright, water was streaming into the angle of the berth. The saloon doors, both fore and aft, were jammed solid and the skylight was smashed. Using the table weight as a battering ram we burst out the remains of the skylight and, using a blanket over the broken glass, we got on deck. It was a dark night and that was not a good moment. Etienne emerged shaken and fuddled. I got a candle and took it to the Major. He had been on the low side but was unharmed. I could see that it was doubtful whether 'Cerise' would lift or fill. The tide rose fast.

First, a bucket chain. Second, cover the cockpit with old sails to increase chances. Third, though rather a forlorn hope, try to find and stop any major leak. When I went below with knife and wedges on this last task I found the Major standing in his nightshirt on the side of his ship, his face close to the starboard berth and with the candle, which I had used to find him, was busy taking coins from his trouser pockets and carefully sticking them, with candle grease, one by one onto the bunk board. I could not help remembering Kipling - "If you can keep your head when all about you ..." I felt better when I had him dressed and, with a borrowed dinghy, got him to the steps and onto the quay with a blanket. I did manage to wedge some leaks. The 'bucket gang' were doing their best. Time passed. 'Cerise'

My friend Dick Colley with the Mad Major.

quivered and started to lift just as the water lapped over our defences into the cockpit. Bailing continued and then the pump began to draw. Hours passed before we were able to move her up the quay so that she had only a foot or two under her at high tide. The port came to life. It was Regatta day in Peroz Guerec. We had to salvage all the wet gear and spread it out on the quay and clean up the worst of the mess below before we could muster anything for breakfast. Etienne was sober more or less. The Major was himself more or less. We rigged a defiant string of flags as our part in the Regatta.

When the tide fell it was possible to inspect outside and in. As I had feared from the bulging bulkheads, there had been such distortion that some of the heavy grown frames had cracked and broken. Plank butts had started and caulking spewed out. No help could be had on holiday and Regatta day, but I managed to beg, borrow and steal some bits of copper, some canvas and some nails. With these I tingled up the worst places. When 'Cerise' rose on the next tide she was tight enough to avoid continuous pumping and we could enjoy the Regatta. That evening I got the Skipper of a neighbouring yacht to tend her as she took the ground. Etienne had passed out and it was better to take the Major away for a shore dinner. We were tired but when he was aboard we went to the dance and a good time was had by all. Then we passed out! The disturbance of the ballast had stirred up the filth in the bilge, unseen for many years. A noisome yellow scum, stinking like a sewer, floated up and made us wake in the morning with headaches and sore throats. A shipwright came and made a more permanent job of my patches but the major, now in buoyant mood, was convincing himself that there was no damage and any trickling noises within were explained as 'drips coming out of the cupboards'. The shipwright and I shook our heads together. He agreed that we might get her home but she would then demand a major refit and repair.

We had an hour or two on a neighbouring *plage*. This was what John and Dick had come for and it was good value. Of course the society, though interesting, was not permissive in those days. A plan emerged. We were to sail for Guernsey in the morning. We did our shopping; we tried the engine and it still ran. The Major would not allow us to get any petrol or oil. We moved out of the harbour and anchored; eventually buying petrol and oil ourselves and smuggling it aboard in the dinghy. It had been instructive to walk out of the harbour at low tide, as instead of sea or horizon, there was a veritable Himalaya of rocks through

and over which we had entered and must pass to reach the sea. At 6 am next morning it was blowing hard. We took a big reef in the mainsail and put to sea. Close hauled we could just lay the course for Guernsey. The Major ordered us to set the jib topsail but when we cleared Le Sept Isles, 'Cerise' lay over, her lee rail under and plunged heavily and sluggishly, shipping a lot of water. The canvas over the smashed skylight did not prevent much of it going below. The saloon was again a shambles. Breakfast was prepared under difficulties. We then had to hand the jib topsail. This was another 'first' for me. Dumped into the seas at the end of that bowsprit I was sick but still thought that this was the life. Etienne, a splendid chap when once at sea, was working well and he and I were now in complete accord. Under this stress, 'Cerise' was leaking badly and we had to pump continuously. The pump was the old fashioned type, working in a hole in the deck with the pull on the up stroke and nothing to hold on to. It was difficult and exhausting. We made up to Guernsey and smoother water. The Major ordered the engine to enter port. We handed the mainsail and the gaff jaws broke. The motor failed, this time the working bulkhead had jammed the fly wheel. Under mizzen and headsails we were lucky to enter and anchor without fouling anything, but had to shift berth later and with difficulty. 'Cerise' still leaked.

My time was up. I left for England by the Southampton boat that day and I was down to my last shilling when I reached home. Dick and John followed two days later. 'Cerise', after being slipped and further repaired in St. Peter Port, was sailed to England by a runner crew who encountered heavy weather in which they nearly lost her. The Major wrote me a very nice letter when he reached home, in effect thanking me for saving his yacht at Peroz Guerec. I had learned so much from him that I was grateful. Negative knowledge may be as valuable as positive. How many things there are that one must not do! I think he had previously sailed with a competent paid crew or competent family and friends. Dick formed the base suspicion that he had advertised and we had fallen in with him because nobody who knew him would sail with him again and he earned the title of, 'Mad Major'. What a magnificent opportunity it had been to weigh up the virtues and defects of 'Cerise'. It added up to a conclusion: That type was not for me. There was also a new ambition; one day I would sail my own yacht on that fascinating coast. In spite of everything, I still liked the old boy; he might have been the Mad Major but he was still a Pukka Sahib.

Water Skis

The ideas factory was working at full blast and the workshop was never out of use. A sailing Sharpie was built. This was to be used for sailing for fun on an inland lake and also for fishing and as a gun punt. The first role demanded a simple rig and a shallow centreboard. The second, no obstruction with the mast lowered and stability with all round seating. The third, a low profile, grey camouflage and a propelling rudder to creep up to wild fowl. The propelling rudder deserves special mention. While not an invention, I had never seen one and so I had to design one from scratch and construct it myself. It was not highly efficient but it did work and we did actually creep up to wild fowl lying flat and peering over the gun barrels while gently waggling the tiller with one hand behind your back. I think I give myself a good mark for this effort. This craft had to be cheap and constructed quickly and easily. As I was overseas a lot of the time, my younger brother Francis virtually built this craft. Always helpful and in support, his skills were not high and the whole design was influenced by this. One innovation was the use of reinforced cement at the stem to avoid complicated carpentry. This was successful and the Sharpie did all that was intended for some years.

I then made water skis. Rather typical for the way my mind ranged and I now forget where this came in chronological order, but I had the idea of walking on water and designed and built a pair of water skis. Very simple, very easily done, plywood with a canvas hatch and footboard and a canvas tube which laced up round your legs. Propulsion was by a self-actuating flap on each ski and yes, we walked upon the waters but only just. I found a basic necessity, each ski had to be capable of carrying more than the total weight of the man by a considerable margin otherwise it was an acrobatic feat to stay upright and even with increased displacement, the weight of the standing man was so far above the means of flotation that there was little stability so after one or two brief trials, this idea was abandoned and the water skis went on the scrap heap. It had become obvious that a kayak canoe was a better proposition in every way but the idea was later patented and some character made a Channel crossing some years later. I think this indicates that I had in fact invented something without realising it.

A Catamaran followed. There was nothing very odd about this, in retrospect it was quite a competent design, it would have worked and there was nothing wrong with it except of course that at 15 foot it was rather too small. I was trying to evolve a construction something like that later supplied by fibreglass plastic. The frames and longtitudinals were aluminium and for the planking, I found a celluloid like substance, black in colour, which was called Erinoid. This craft was never finished and tried and I cannot now remember whether it was because I went off on a foreign voyage or whether it was overtaken by the blinding light of the twin keel idea.

Above: Experimental catamaran construction aluminium frames, a type of celluloid skin with my friend Edwards 'Moses'.

Above: 'Sharpie' - a duck punt with self-propelling rudder, stem construction ferro cement.

Chapter Two

A Blinding Flash of Inspiration and Trials 1922-1925

Invention

Way back in the 1920's - 1921/22, I was nudging twenty-one years in age and working in a Sheffield steel works learning my trade and attending courses in metallurgy at Sheffield University. Remember that in those days it was long hours, I think sixty a week and one worked on Saturday mornings. I had not many pennies, a worker in a steel warehouse in Sheffield in those days would be earning 25 shillings a week. I lived in a room in my parents' house so my living was free, my mobility was assured by a Sunbeam solo motorcycle, rather sit up and beg, with narrow tyres which were deadly in the numerous worn tram lines of those days. You might well think it extremely unlikely that any serious time or attention could be given to seafaring or the production of a yacht but the desire for my own yacht never ceased. Somehow I had managed to get experience of a turn of the century, plank on edge, deep draught, heavy displacement yacht and also about ten other different sizes and types of yacht including a very nice eight ton Albert Strange type canoe-yawl on the Humber.

This then was the situation when quite suddenly I had a 'Blinding Flash of Inspiration' when pondering the difficulties I had encountered with the types that I have mentioned. Suddenly there it was in the mind. "Why not twin keels?' When I came down to earth, I set about serious investigation of the possibilities and did research on resistance, whetted surfaces, stability and so forth; I found nothing adverse. I gave considerable and anxious thought to the question of a self-draining cockpit; on the one hand it would have had to be so small and so high up that it was no more than a little footwell in the deck. The crew would have had to sit higher up, exposed and unprotected and in those days with no lifelines or guardrails, they were very likely to have been thrown or washed overboard by a breaking sea. Any considerable volume of water at cockpit level and position would have crippled so small and light a yacht and so I decided to have a small but adequate cockpit that would just seat two men. In practice, the two men on the weather side

kept out a great amount of water in bad weather and if a breaking sea came over their heads and shoulders at the considerable angle of heel at which 'Little Bluebird' would be sailing, much of it would go right over the cockpit and overboard to leeward. I now consider that this feature was one of those in which I cannot say that I was right but the fact that 'Little Bluebird' has survived so many perils of the sea for seventy years, at least shows that I was not far wrong.

Trials

I then built 2 models, one a twin keel design of my own, the other a normal comparable single keel design. I sailed these and tested them. In the light of today's knowledge, they were too small but they still gave me some useful comparisons and if I look back now with later knowledge, I can see that the characteristics that later became apparent were present in those early designs and tests. The only way in which I could achieve a yacht would be to design it and build it myself. My next task was to produce the final lines and plans for the projected new yacht; a formidable task when I consider my then limited knowledge and experience.

The First Twin Keel Yacht

Real thought was now devoted to my next yacht. Now that I had experienced 'Cerise', the Mad Major's yacht, a centreboard type would have been logical but I was not satisfied. It had been delightful to see an expert like George Holmes using his intimate knowledge to sound his way delicately across banks, lifting his centreplate a little when necessary and dropping it when possible but I had also seen a craft, forced beam on to the hard sand by the awesome pressure of the Humber tide. It was impossible to raise the plate against the side pressure which also imposed enormous stresses on the yacht's structure while the angle of heel might be so great that the yacht would be flooded by water flowing in on the leeward side. The strain threatened to bend the plate or strain the whole structure of the centre case. The eddies round bow and stern dug a hole in the sand into which the boat was forced in shuddering jerks and this torment continued until there was enough depth of water to take her upright over the bank or enable her to stream to an anchor, but on a falling tide you were left high and dry. From this experience, a logical objection to the centreplate was that when it was most needed to make to windward it might be most risky to use it.

I was lucky enough to have experiences of leeboards. I had seen these in use on the Humber Sloops but not in a yacht. A weekend with E B Tredwen in the barge yacht 'Pearl', was instructive. I did not realise at that time that a Thames barge could capsize, though rarely did so owing to her weight, while this risk was real with a similar design scaled down to 10 tons. The conclusion was decisive; the performance was dim and the hull seemed to me a specialised adaptation for use in shallow estuaries. Even from my inexperience, it did not seem a good thing at sea. If I had been introduced to sailing in a normal way, I should have gone out and bought the most suitable yacht I could find or adapted within the modest limits of my purse. If it had been 1964, I should have had an ample choice of craft, well designed, in any size and suitable for a wide range of use. But it was the early 1920's and I was on my own; I would have to design and build it myself. A pretty formidable undertaking and you have already seen how little spare time I had but I had a brother and a friend who would help. My parents were co-operative, my mother romantically favourable in spite of the fact that I should make an awful mess of her garden. My mother gave me the mast and spars, no aluminium in those days, they were from the McGruer Hollows Spar Company, a splendid construction which proved almost everlasting. My father, full of doubt and no doubt thinking, "I don't want him to take his mind off his work". He did however give me the engine.

In those days there were no such thing as kits of parts for a yacht. You had to work out for yourself the dimensions and requirements for every single piece of timber, decide the sizes and types of copper nails, rooves and screws that you wanted, the quantities required and find out where to order them. I was determined not to make the mistake of building too small. Racing was impracticable and living and working as I did I had already proved that I must be able to live aboard; I wanted to be able to cruise anywhere in Europe. At that time I did not think of crossing oceans. I had sailed single handed but preferred sailing with a friend. I never thought of more than one other companion nor of the future or of family needs. My limit for building, lifting and transport was 3 tons. There were no big lorries, no portable cranes or massive trailers. Another limitation was the standard crane in a railway siding and the ordinary flat car in railway rolling stock. This would take an all up lift weight of 3 tons and so would dockside cranes or ships' derricks. I envisaged both means of transport and of course no cradle would be necessary with twin keels. The building site was on the lawn against the side of the house under a temporary shed with canvas cover. I decided to build the hull upside down (this proved a good solution) and substantial stocks had to be constructed but were there difficulties. They showed up at every turn. I had a large basement room as my workshop but not easily accessible. Low timbers had to be threaded in and out of this through a window at one end. I was determined to draw the lines of the yacht full size to ensure the accuracy of my moulds but where could I do this? Believe it or not the only solution was to do it upside down on the ceiling of my workshop with the added difficulty of an interrupting beam in the middle. So I had to devise, invent and construct a whole system of splines, props and wedges to enable me to do this but it worked and the moulds were accurate.

As my construction for a twin keel yacht differed from the conventional, I also had problems of bending large timbers and had to construct a steam box and steam boiler. To illustrate the scale of this difficulty, my largest timbers were the twin keels in the bilges of the yacht and these were 8 inches x 3 inches at the centres, tapering down and extending the whole length of the yacht. The keels themselves were not so difficult. This was Sheffield and a friendly firm offered to cast them for me in steel if I provided the moulds and to these keels, lead ballast bulbs had to be attached. Oh yes, I bought scrap lead, found a way of melting it, made the moulds and cast these myself. I didn't choose the easy method of construction, far from it! I wanted the best teak planking, double diagonal (this was a system then used for constructing lifeboats), a lot more work was involved, but again I invented gauge gadgets to assist the fitting of the planks which were fastened to the frames and to each other by innumerable copper nails, riveted over with rooves. My brother was the champion at this and must have clenched up thousands. After deep thought I had decided to fill the spaces between the timbers and the bottom of the boat with cement. This would add some intrinsic strength and provide a smooth surface that could easily be cleaned. An elderly widow neighbour started lodging complaints at noises in the night but I managed to bring her round, showed her what was afoot and somehow charmed her into becoming a supporter. There was other voluntary labour, sometimes helpful, sometimes rather a handicap; there was a balancing point at which overseen, unskilled labour was less productive than doing the job myself. Somehow or other, in the middle of these proceedings, I acquired the name, 'The Master Builder' and thereafter I was always referred to as such. The design of 'Bluebird' shows the answer. My job, without realising it, had

Design of Little 'Bluebird'.

BLUE BIRD

By R. A. BALFOUR

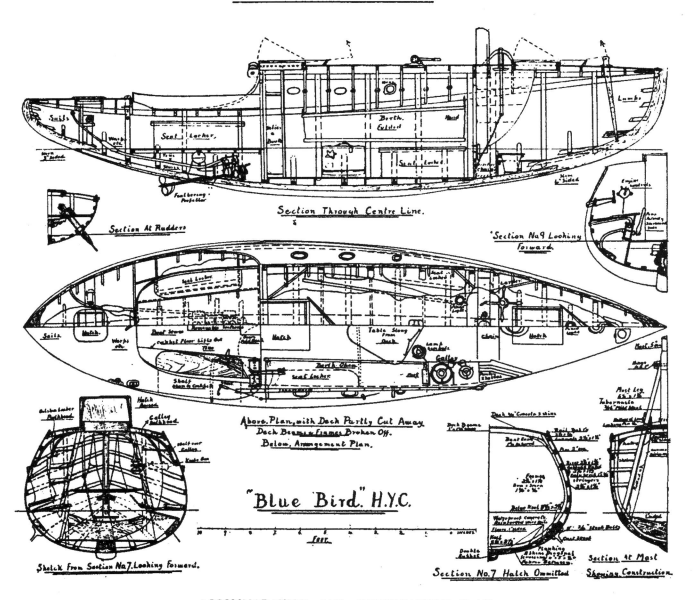

Section Through Centre Line.

Section At Rudders

Section No 9 Looking Forward.

Above. Plan, with Deck Partly Cut Away
Deck Beams & Frames Broken Off.
Below, Arrangement Plan.

"Blue Bird." H.Y.C.

Sketch From Section No.7. Looking Forward.

Section No.7 Hatch Omitted

Section At Mast Showing Construction

ACCOMMODATION AND CONSTRUCTION PLAN

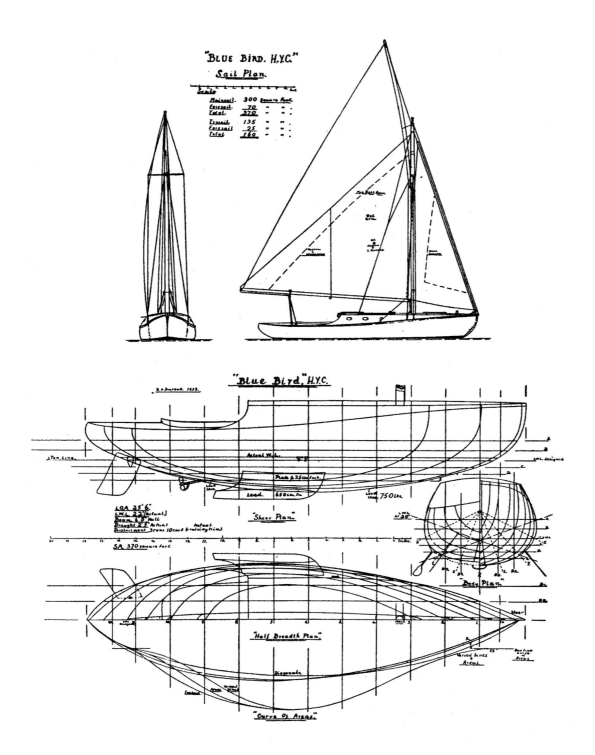

Design of Little 'Bluebird'.

Top: Little 'Bluebird' - full size lines were drawn on the ceiling, the only available place.

Above: The frames on which Little 'Bluebird' were built.

built up engineering knowledge, added metallurgy and I knew a good deal about the use of machines and the making of tools. I had reached a rather dangerous stage; I remember thinking, "If I wish, I could now make anything in wood or metal. If I have need of a tool I can make one. If I do not know how to do some task, I can invent a method". I had developed an ability to work any tool with either hand, realising how useful this could be particularly in working wood with and against the grain. I found that family and friends positively enjoyed being involved and I had more help than I had expected. When I look back, I wonder how it was possible to do the volume of work as a spare time effort. Something must have suffered and at times I did also; did I ever sleep? But a reckless expenditure of energy with the resilience which is simply youth in eruption, can achieve the almost impossible.

After an ocean of difficulties, lasting about eighteen months and involving thousands of hours of labour, we had to rush the final stages to get her afloat before the end of the season and we were also threatened by the forthcoming closure of the canal for lock repairs. Somehow or other on the deadline day in August 1924, we had, with difficulty, loaded her onto a flat float, borrowed from the works. The yacht started its first voyage, horse drawn, through Sheffield in the early hours of the morning to the canal at Tinsley where it was launched as planned by the standard dockside crane. There was very little ceremony, the whole thing was practical and depressing rather than exhilarating but we had got a name and when she went into the canal, this was announced I think by my uncle Bertram Balfour. 'Bluebird', and where did this come from? I am almost certain that I had it from my mother and that she had announced, 'Bluebird of Happiness'. I have since discovered that a Belgian author called, Maeterlink, had written a book, 'Bluebird and Bluebirds', published in 1924. So many people have asked me why I decided upon this name and this rather scattered explanation is the best I can do.

The Humber to Portsmouth

In due course we took 'Bluebird' down the Sheffield canal, working on her as we went and at Thorne, making contact with my friend, Richard Dunston who ran the shipyard there. This was to have repercussions later. So eventually through the lock and out into the river Trent where we encountered one or two yachts of the Humber Yawl Club.

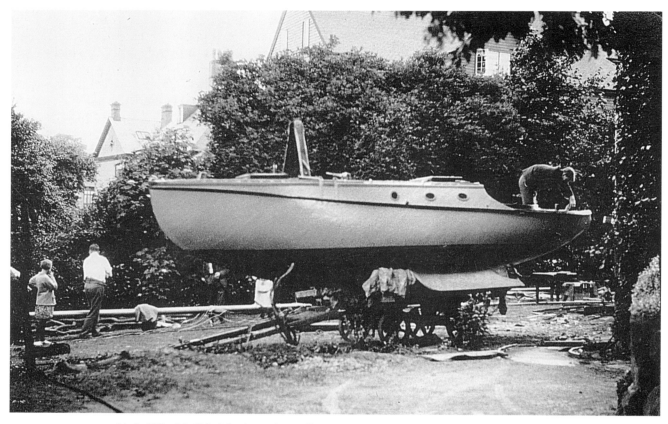

Little 'Bluebird' finished, on the trolley prior to launching on the canal at Tinsley.

There were moments such as the discovery, at this point, that one of the rudders could not be moved to a sufficient angle but under sail for the first time we proceeded down the Trent into the Humber and to a berth at Brough. I never had any intention to keep 'Bluebird' on the Humber even for the first winter but rather to take her to Portsmouth. I want to avoid a detailed description of these passages and I am aided in this by what I called 'Graphic logs', which I produced for the Humber Yawl Club. Reference to these may enable you to gather enough information to reconstruct the details of the passages. Why Portsmouth? I think it was memories and experience from the 'Nancy Belle' but as things transpired I could not have done better than choose this location. When I left the Humber and went to sea, it ought to have been one of the most thrilling moments of my life but alas it was a complete anticlimax. I was worn out, 'Bluebird' was not properly finished, we were woefully unprepared and I had with me two companions, neither of whom had ever sailed before. Both of them were slightly seasick, both were appaled at the living conditions but the fates, however were kind and we had no untoward difficulties or bad weather. Both went thankfully ashore at Harwich and neither ever sailed again.

We sailed next morning, the wind quite strong and the motion excessive on our way to Ramsgate. The Master Builder was in optimistic mood and from time to time burst into song or verse: "A life on the ocean wave is better than going to sea". Or a new song. "Ashes to ashes, dust to dust and everything else to the bilge". He declaimed this at frequent intervals and the slogan, though we knew it not, was fated to persist in its apposite significance throughout the whole trip. Nearing the South Foreland, things were beginning to happen. We had to dodge steamers, one close to us was invisible from the hollows, we started bailing with a bucket and it was badly needed. The

Little 'Bluebird' on the canal.

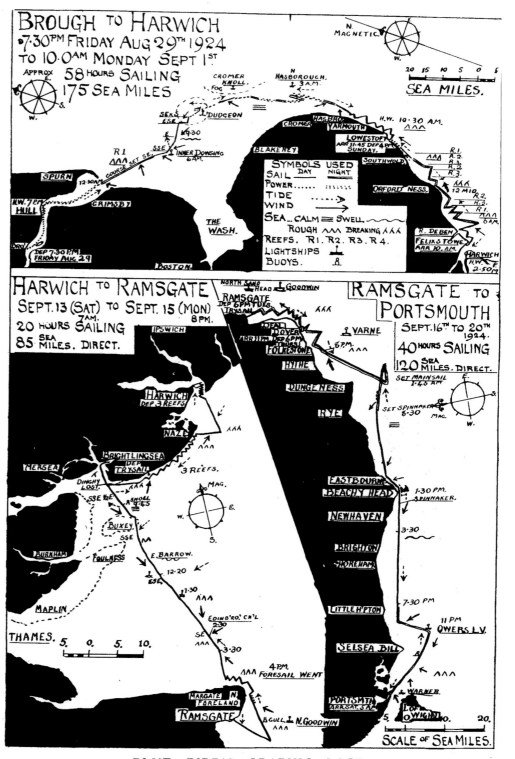

Graphic chart.

BLUE BIRD'S GRAPHIC LOGS

cockpit was like bathing in a heavy surf and a bucket of water hurled straight at the helmsman from the cabin door was blown away like smoke, long before it reached him. We could hardly speak without taking a mouthful and life was very wet. An extra large one hit us and Jack bawled into the Master's ear, "Very wet waves they keep round here". 'Bluebird' kept punching along and although we had fearful trouble with the foresail sheets, we put her about, time after time in the worst of it. In that wind we could not haul the foresail sheet in but this was partly due to the cleats themselves and the position in which they had been placed. We had no time to worry about Susan (the pram dinghy) beyond noting from time to time that she was still there but she must have been a fearful drag and she was to cause trouble later.

The Master Builder attempted later to put the feeling into words:

Out, beating up to windward with the wind against the tide
We should not have an earthly chance without the friendly tide.
There is trouble with the crockery,
And comfort is a mockery:
The water swishes to and fro across the cabin floor.
The seas are growing larger, steep,
The hollows very deep,
A long, slow climb up each dark hill, the turn upon the crest;
The swoop adown the rushing airs
Like falling down the stairs.
'Till buried in the trough, we snatch a hurried second's rest.
The roaring crest is torn by wind and capped with hungry white.
It breaks aboard, a mighty crash
With a pause before the smash.
As the solid weight of water hits us clean across the spine,
Time to blink and gasp and spit
Or shift our feet to fit.
The coaming down below us where the floor boards ought to be;
Hard work, bailing with a bucket -
Wishing we could chuck it
But we are up to windward and a nasty, breaking sea,
Man becomes just nature's tool
Mere elemental fool,
Smashing up to windward with the wind against the tide.

The wind was still increasing as we approached the eastern entrance to Dover harbour, we missed the windward or outer side of the opening by as small a margin as we dared, a moment later, wind, tide and sea threw us across like a blown leaf and the Master Builder saw the inner pier looming up uncomfortably close to leeward. "Very narrow these entrances," observed Jack. The Master Builder finds a curious after effect of such a trip is that he cannot visualise how bad conditions were. Others have told him that they find the same thing. Sometimes he thinks that it was all imagination and that it was relatively calm and peaceful. Again he recollects some circumstance which seems to prove that it must have been blowing fairly hard, when actually out in it the impression created is surprisingly small as one has very little time in which to observe and the chances of observation, especially at night, are very limited. One is, moreover, so occupied that little thought is given to the matter. The truth is that the impression left after such an experience is bound to be untrustworthy and well-nigh impossible to describe adequately. Mere adjectives and superlatives failing to do justice and laying the writer open to the loathsome charge of grossly exaggerating the facts. It is quite amazing that in that first year with the passages from the Humber to Portsmouth, that we did not meet with disaster; the yacht was barely complete, not properly fitted out or worked up and to add to my relative inexperience, we had no knowledge as to how this new and experimental type of yacht would actually behave.

There were, however, two incidents which should perhaps be recounted as in both of them 'Bluebird' might have been wrecked and destroyed and we might indeed have lost our lives.

The first of these was when we made the passage from Ramsgate to Dover, we had a strong headwind which was increasing to gale but were making good progress and a swift tide was with us but wind against tide was kicking up a short and ugly sea and we were as usual over-canvassed. There was a lot of ship traffic and at that moment I discovered that my companion was colour blind and could not distinguish whether ships' lights were red or green. As we approached the east entrance to Dover harbour, a wave almost capsized and half filled the pram dinghy which we were towing. Handicapped by this drag astern, we staggered through the entrance and then, attempting to go about, we missed stays and hit the outer mole. Thank God we were inside! Had we been outside the harbour, 'Bluebird' would have been lost. As it was in smooth water and almost motionless, we drifted on to the wall when we missed stays, suffering no damage. We were able to go forward and with our combined full weight on the boat hook, we managed to push her bows off the wall, far enough for the wind to catch the backed foresail on the port side so that we were able to stagger off the wall and managed somehow to work up the harbour until we could anchor in shelter. A near shave if ever there was one. I think we might record this as the first time 'Bluebird' survived.

The second incident was approaching the Solent from the Owers, again at night, again in a strong and increasing wind that was sufficiently on our port bow to enable us to hold our course to our objective which was Portsmouth. The wind eventually increased to the point where we must reduce sail but when we at last attempted to reef, disaster struck. The wire halliard came off the sheath at the mast head and jammed solid between the side of the sheath and the mast; we could neither reef nor lower sail and with the gale we were now laid over far on our side but we had a dramatic discovery and illustration of a hitherto unknown characteristic of 'Bluebird', with her twin keels and twin rudders. Though perhaps laid over to 50° or 60°, she was spilling enough wind to reduce the pressure but still had some forward propulsion and we found that we still had some measure of steering control. An ordinary, small centre keel yacht under such conditions would simply have blown away to leeward and have been wrecked. Two things indicated that conditions were indeed serious; I heard afterwards that a 6 ton yacht was lost in the Solent that night and though I went forward to do some necessary job on the foredeck, I did so on the side of the yacht aided by the tumblehome rather than on the deck. The only thing we could possibly have done, though I did not think of it at the time, would have been to lash a knife to a boat hook and slash the mainsail so that it blew away in shreds but that desperate remedy would again have left us totally out of control.

It could be said that two rather hardy and determined men could exist in what the Americans called the 'accommodations' of 'Little Bluebird'; they were absolutely basic, sanitation was by 'bucket and chuck it', cooking was by one primus stove on a low shelf, lighting was an Aladdin pressure paraffin lamp which also served as heater in the tiny cabin. Sleeping was on canvas soft berths later to be known as the 'Roots' type. A small cabin table, semi-swinging, was lowered from the cabin roof by rods and on this any primitive chart work was done. There was little storage space, none of it really dry. Water was a 6 gallon tank with a 2 gallon filling can. Engine fuel was 4 gallons of petrol, paraffin was a few pints, there were no electrics whatsoever unless somebody brought a torch but remember, this was the height of luxury in comparison to my cruising in open dinghies. There was

sitting headroom only and well bent crouching to move about below; you could stand up only with your head and shoulders out through the forehatch (to pull up your trousers at the bucket) or at the main hatch. This prompts another mention connected with design and seaworthiness; the flush, raised deck with no deep openings undoubtedly contributed to this, while the considerable tumblehome reduced weight and windage and gave the midsection a nearer approximation to the intrinsically strong circular form compared with the multiple right angle joins of a normal deck, coach roof and/or doghouse. You could not go out and buy a winch in those days, I designed and made myself, two neat little wire drum winches for the peak and throat halliards, anything else needing more power meant block and tackle. Finally, instrumentation, we had a basic compass without light; you judged your speed, wind force and direction you calculated from the feeling on the back of your neck. Depth in shallow water you prodded over the side with a boathook, in deeper water a mine leadline to five fathoms.

In spite of all the difficulties and everything that was unfinished or wrong during that first season, it is only fair to report the Master Builder realised that he had created a yacht that could and would sail and was intrinsically a good sea boat.

Alterations and Improvements

When we arrived at Portsmouth at the end of 1924 after the October voyage from Brough, it was time for assessment. I had a yacht, it had great potential; 'Bluebird' could sail fast. She was a good sea boat and could survive but what next? What had we learned - some good , some not so good and some bad. It was when I started to write this that I realised there would be duplication. It would be better to describe what we did by way of alteration, improvement and finishing the job rather than first describe what we had learned. That winter, the first and the most serious problem was the stability. Whatever the theory, and this was impeccable, one keel in the air like a flying trapeze, you sail on the sea with the greatest of ease. With the keel in the air at one stroke you'd removed a considerable amount of wetted surface and resistance and with the keel in the air you had added stability, it acted in exactly the same way as men sitting out to windward. So far so good but, and it was a very big but, we realised that at 20° angle of heel you could live. At 30° angle of heel, life below became pure hell and almost impossible. How were we to deal with this? Obviously we had been under ballasted and over canvassed and this must be dealt with. I had kept about 3 hundredweight of ballast in lead slabs in the bilge for trimming if necessary. Trimming had not been required and I now took this lead, added about another 3 hundredweight and made a shoe which was bolted on externally; this increased the ballast ratio and lowered its centre of gravity. As far as the rig was concerned, I took a length off the long gunter-yard and several feet off the boom, removing 75 square feet of sail, this made the mainsail much smaller, a more efficient shape and all inboard easier to reef and in better proportion with the foresail. I designed and made two cunning little wire reel winches at the forward end of the cockpit to deal with the throat and peak halliards. The next problem was the rudders. I shall always be thankful that in that first season I had left the two rudders disconnected, each with its own separate tiller. In practice one steered with the lever tiller, the windward rudder feathered itself, the only trouble being that in a sea-way. The tiller would bang about a bit and bang you on the knuckles from time to time. When I coupled the tillers of the two rudders, I used to borrow a word form the motor world - Ackerman Linkage. The single central tiller was so pivoted and linked that it subtended a considerably smaller angular movement than the rudders thus, while giving ample power, its normal movement from full helm port, to full helm starboard, was well within the width of the cockpit. This may sound rather complicated, in practice it was extremely simple and the result worked perfectly. But one did learn exactly what happened. I also concluded that the rudders which were what were called spade rudders, slightly balanced, were rather too light-hearted in their work and so I added skeggs in front of the rudders, gave them a bottom bearing and removed the balance. This made them much more serious in their work and also delayed the point at which they would stall.

Another feature of 'Bluebird's' design, and not her most pleasant characteristic, was that there was no central hollow point and water had to be collected by the pump from the bilges through a flexible, large diameter inlet hose. It also followed that in really bad weather this bilge water would slosh up the sides right to the deck and fall into the berths or anything else so that there was not a dry stitch in the ship. The best memorial to this feature was much later when a Dutch owner and friend, Jan den Boer, wrote to me saying, "My wife is complaining that 'Little Bluebird' is too often soiling her tresses. I love her dearly but I fear we shall have to part". I have always admired the lovely ambiguity enshrouding his love for his wife and his love for his yacht. I know not how much trauma resulted but it was 'Little Bluebird' who finally departed.

This feature did lead to another equally important necessity, a large capacity, unblockable pump and the answer was a Beck pump, a solid bronze affair developed for use in the trenches and dug-outs of the 1914/18 War. Its valves, easily expelled, were large, lead balls covered with rubber. It shifted a bucketful in about three strokes, it demanded the undivided and hard working attention of one man.

Then there was the dinghy situation. We had learned you need a dinghy when you are cruising. You cannot effectively tow one, it is bound to get you into trouble sooner or later and on a yacht of this size, it is difficult to stow a dinghy; in those days there were no inflatable dinghies. What to do! The answer, I designed and built a very special lightweight, 6 foot dinghy which stowed upside down, nose outwards on the stern, its bow decked and about 18 inches outboard. This also had an extending section 2 foot long, which stowed inside it in the manner we had learned from 'Sparrow'. This worked extremely well and it might almost be said afterwards that the yacht had been designed to house the dinghy as much as the dinghy had been designed to stow on the yacht.

But what about the engine; this a Saunders, five horse power, portable inboard, was under the cockpit floor. It's a clever design, well made, solid bronze, two cylinder, two stroke and the propeller which was feathering and adjustable with its integral shaft, passed through a slot no bigger than 15 inches by 3 inches, in the bottom of the yacht. The engine was bolted down by eight bolts on a rubber gasket over the slot. The engine was rated 5 horse power but with a small fast-running propeller, those horses in effect were no more than Shetland ponies and the realistic speed was not more than 4 miles per hour in a flat calm with no sea and no wind. As wind and sea rose, the performance rapidly fell away to nothing so that you could not, for example, depend on the engine to drive you out of harbour against a force 4 wind or sea. You had to sail out using the engine only to give some assistance when you went about and make sure you did not stay. At sea when the weather was bad, the engine was quite useless anyway as it could not be started. Hand starting and temperamental as two strokes are, it was attended to and started by removing a section of the cockpit floor and you had to kneel down and reach down to the engine from above and it was always drenched with seawater when the weather was bad. The only thing we could do to mitigate this situation was to provide a waterproof removable cover and we also thermal insulated this with asbestos. This was an enormous improvement but did not remove the inherent defects.

We had no anchor winch but I now improved the stowage of the anchors and added a stout pawl above the chain roller at the stem head. This made getting the anchor both safer and easier and prevented the chain taking charge and running free. A metal capping was added to the pitch-pine rubbing band to take the 'sair dunts' that a cruising life was sure to provide. The reefing of the mainsail was now properly engineered on the roller system and the foresail was on what was known as the Wyckham Martin furling foresail gear. This was a crude revolving system with the luff of the sail on a large wooden roller - not very efficient. I substituted a 1 inch monel metal tube and this worked extremely well and was considerably more efficient. Camper and Nicholson's excellent craftsmen tackled all the joinery, everything that was not well done, unfinished or skimped was properly attended to and down below. The main improvement was deep ledges and fiddles on all shelves and the table. They also effected a few hand-holds and the removal of some sharp corners. The whole rig was attended to in the same way; sheaves, leads, cleats were all made workable and the stays and rigging made adequate and properly adjusted. We even considered a self rigging cockpit which could be rigged when required but discarded this as being too clumsy and unworkable in practice. Little else was done below but the vital bucket now had a proper stand in the fo'c'sle even with a fitted seat and cover. Finally a really proper and thorough painting and varnishing job was done, finishing up with anti-fouling. I shall always be grateful to Camper and Nicholson, their patience and collaboration and understanding were invaluable. The whole list of little jobs which must have been more nuisance than benefit to them, however essential they were to me and 'Bluebird', were impeccably executed by their excellent craftsmen.

The experience of the first season might well have reduced my enthusiasm but this had not happened. I found that I was now keener than ever. I had a yacht, at last I could go to sea, I could sail properly and I could start cruising as I had originally intended and so we faced a summer season of 1925 with great hope and great expectation. All this cost a pretty penny, even in terms of those days the bill was £125; one quarter of what I said it had cost me to build 'Bluebird' but I did not then realise that this was exactly the fee that I was going to earn from my articles in the Yachting World in 1926.

Jack Giles

You would not expect professional designers to rush into print or going about saying what they thought of a new idea like twin keel yachts. One exception, Robert Clark who was really coming from amateur to professional, did produce an interesting design called 'Buttercup'. She was so clearly 'Bluebird' designed.

Jack Giles later told me after many years, that he had done some model experiments on twin keel yachts but he did not tell me what his findings or conclusions were. He later designed a twin keel yacht for the Westerley Company which was well received and successful. The Westerley Company was started by one, Fred Rayner and while I couldn't possibly claim to have had anything to do with the launch of this successful company, it may be true that if Fred Rayner had not happened to meet up with me and 'Bluebird' at Beaumaris, where he was quite fascinated and had extensive discussions on the design, he might not have started the Westerley Company and I well remember his successful twin keel design 'Centaur', which was one of their early models. He did tell me that he had in fact a dilemma. Westerley were marketing centre keel yachts and these included their fastest and more sporty, racing types. Whilst the twin keel yachts were intended to be for cruising and rather more sedate, Jack Giles found however, that in some conditions that his twin keel design was beating their more sporting versions.

Jack Giles designed one other twin keel yacht, this because he was heavily leaned upon by a friend who wanted to try some experiments. As I remember it the yacht had experiments with rig, hull and keels which contained complicated plates intended to maintain the same centre of lateral pressure whether they were down or half up. Alas as others before him have found, it is a mistake to try too many experiments at once and this character died before he got it all sorted out.

The yacht came into the hands of a retired Group Captain whom I had met. He came to me and told me that he was dissatisfied with the yacht but felt it had potential and what did I advise. Could I resist such a challenge - oh no! Scrap the plates, redesign solid twin keels. The rudder was an ugly, narrow, hoisting blade affair. Scrap this and as the yacht had considerable weather helm, I stuck my neck out and advised twin angled and asymmetrical rudders. This brave experiment worked well; the rig and other questions he sorted out for himself and so at the end of the day he had a useful yacht that satisfied him and was a worthwhile member of the twin keel society.

Above: Lumstrum rig - Little 'Bluebird' dinghy.
Left: A 6ft dinghy extending to 8ft 6inch, stowed on the stern -
it also sailed.

Chapter Three

Adventures and Achievements

For all these reasons, it was June 1925 after hard working weekends, when Ken and I left Portsmouth for the west. A sail to windward in the day took us to Poole Harbour. There we were entertained by Frank Cowper, now an old man, his yarns fascinating and his experience unrivalled. One of a small band of amateur seamen, he had handled most unsuitable craft single-handed under the nickname of 'Jack all alone' and he had written, 'Cowper's Sailing Tours' and other books. He sailed 'Bluebird' on a day out from Poole and raised our morale by his verdict, "Bluebird' is fit to go anywhere", which he told us as he bade us farewell when we sailed from Poole. We now kept proper watches and were well equipped by comparison with previous experiences and 'Bluebird', in her new trim, developed a capacity to sail herself; a tremendous cruising asset.

This year we had a big foresail, also used as a spinnaker and boomed out with a spar on which the sail could be set as with a short bowsprit. We found that we could gybe this sail and set it singlehanded at night. For Ken this was his first experience of a yacht at sea. He was an altogether admirable companion, shortish and rather square, about my age, he had a tough and rather inexpressive face and said little but he was a born seaman and developed an uncanny instinct for keeping a plot in his head. When he was with me I never had to worry where the other watch had put us. He claimed that he was descended from a well known buccaneer, no less than Captain Kidd and one could easily picture him in the pirate's rig of those days with cutlass and pistols. This made me wonder again whether ancestry had been responsible for my love of the sea. The passage went well until it blew hard and suddenly from the north when we were past the Eddystone Light and we had to reef right down and had a hard beat on and up to Fowey with the spray flying until we closed the land and beat into the squalls at the entrance to anchor thirty-four hours out from Poole. We made expeditions up the river and the inlets in our dinghy, explored the town and walked the hills. Drifting on the tide one evening, we found a Japanese boat propelled by the yuloh. Aboard her were figures in kimonos, talking a strange language with weird music from a one string fiddle (a samishen). This contact with the east fitted the magic mood as

the moon rose over the hills. Fowey is a lovely place from which to begin or end a voyage. The welcome I received was to bring me back again from long voyages in distant years ahead.

Falmouth was equally charming though less intimate and that was where we made careful preparation before sailing out past the Manacles to make our departure from the Lizard. That night with the big foresail set, we were sailing easily about 3½ knots. Over a long swell from the west, a Barquentine under full sail slid mysteriously into the path of the moon and without a sound, her sails moved in glorious curves against the silver light until she passed slowly and steadily into the shadows of the night. In the dawn, 'Bluebird' tramped out at 6 knots with her full sail of 500 sq ft and still steering herself. What a passage! And with Ushant the objective, we awaited landfall. In thick haze, a lighthouse was sighted and then lost again. Ushant was assumed and we altered course to the west against a strong tide. When the evening closed in, we bore away to pick up the lights when they came on. Strange, a noise like a train. There could be no trains on Ushant. Lights on the starboard bow. That could only have been Ushant and we realised the lighthouse we had seen must have been a different one. We were at the northern entrance of the Chenal du Four, with the wind and tide we were bound to go through. "Now we know where we are, I wish we weren't here", said Ken. I remembered the Major - "You find it afterwards, Balfour". We later found that our compass, previously checked, had shifted slightly on its mounting but we were busy studying lights and bearings and reefing down to have 'Bluebird' well in hand for any manoeuvre.

The chart blew overboard! It was a tense moment and Ken dug out sailing directions while I sailed 'Bluebird' northward in short tacks. This, the opposite to our direction, was to reduce the speed over the ground as the tide bore us backward and to give us more time to see rocks astern and sheer away from them across the tide. Buoys and rocks loomed up and grew prodigiously like a nightmare. We eluded them with a dreamlike feeling of almost automatic but unavailing flight. I told Ken that the strength of the tide would take us round and not over any rocks dangerous to us with our 3 ft draught, only hoping that this theory was correct as ominous boils and eddies passed beneath us. I don't remember how long the passage took but we emerged and taking a deep breath, shook out a reef and turned to windward towards the Goulet de Brest, our destination and still quite a long way away. It was my watch; how could I keep awake as 'Bluebird' sailed herself? Study the new chart, check the lights, time to put her about. The tiller came away in my hand; another crisis but 'Bluebird' hove to on a safe course by herself with the rudders loose. Ken turned out and together we found the bits and pieces with the torch and made the repair. When coupling the rudders, the filter had not put on lock nuts or split pins - and I had not checked! We both had the same thought - what if this had happened in the Chenal du Four! My watch below - oblivion.

Three hours later with 'Bluebird' still steering herself to windward and going fast in the growing dawn with the land about us, we passed the entrance to the Naval Harbour. There was a warship with a magnificent ram designed no doubt with a gallic flourish to deal the foe a dirty blow beneath the belt. We entered the Port du Commerce; the smells of France! And this was the achievement of the ambition formed at Roscoff all those years before; 33 hours from Falmouth, 130 miles made good, all France was ours to explore. The harbour was teeming with interest. All local traffic appeared to be under sail and a variety of craft of all sizes and types, many with huge lug sails which made lovely curves as they were hoisted and sheeted to the stiff breeze. They entered and departed, magnificently handled and the quay was a sight to be remembered with the crews, the cargoes, the horse and cart traffic and the women in picturesque Breton costumes. We cleared customs with the crew of 'Otter', a 9 ton cutter from Falmouth and Green, her owner, could not have been kinder. The ages of his crew of two friends, was 160 years, Ken and I totalled well under 50. They lent us charts and told us of the coast to the south, never hinting at our obvious inexperience or, as they must have considered, 'Bluebird's dubious innovations. We sailed up the Chateaulin River; every hour a new scene, a new delight. A suspension bridge was under construction; a fleet of cutters and luggers were plying from Brest with materials for the work and made a grand sight as they came crowding up the curving river on the flood tide.

We had been so successful in forgetting everything that we now found with surprise that it was Friday. Both of us were due back next week and I was involved in Brussels a few days ahead. Our mood ignored any difficulty in returning to England, it seemed a sad waste of an opportunity. Here we were fit and keen, 'Bluebird' had found herself, the weather was good and we were on the threshold of a new world. Given time we realised what we might have done. Concaneau, La Rochelle, "Why not Spain", we said. The temptation was strong. I look back on this moment

with the thought that had we played truant for a fortnight it would have been worthwhile and would not have mattered much in a lifetime. We made the most of our remaining day before sailing to Point St Matthieu. How easy the Chenal du Four now appeared with a Great Thonnier giving us a lead, as reefed down with the wind, we splashed and thrashed to the northward against a 6 knot tide. An easy passage ensued, mainly with light head winds, a little engine in some calm but we had fresh mackerel straight from the sea to the pan and life was pleasant. The passage ended as it began. We sailed to windward right up Restronguet creek where Green and the 'Otter' arrived almost simultaneously and he helped us to put 'Bluebird' to bed so that we could catch the night train at Truro to return to work.

A few weeks later, I returned with Jack Hope, intending to take 'Bluebird' up to Liverpool during the August Bank Holiday. I wonder why I was prepared to leave the delights of Cornwall but there was the desire to explore and the Commander of the Training Ship 'Conway', then at Rockferry, had offered help in maintaining 'Bluebird'. He was one Harvey Broadbent, a family friend and honourary uncle. From that base I could make more use of 'Bluebird' and have weekends in the area.

At Restronguet, with help from Green, 'Bluebird' was made ready for sea with surprising speed and in the afternoon, tired by this effort and the overnight journey, we went up the hill for a sleep in the shade on the kindly earth with the swelling contours of the hills and the harbour below where boats and sails were crossing aimless wakes. Across the creek, they were reaping a field of wheat; the clatter of the binder came faintly on the breeze as turn by turn the nodding gold became neatly spaced bundles awaiting the crawling figures stacking up four rows at once. Near at hand were the soft, tearing sounds of grazing cattle, the rustle of wind in the hedge, the buzzing of the insects and the smell of summer growth and flowers under the warm air. When we awoke, the cornfield was finished, the workers gone, the sun far round and 'Bluebird' floated on the tide, for we could see reflected sunlight off the ripples on her topsides. It was an interlude that stayed in our minds and we little knew what contrast would follow in the days ahead.

In those days there was no radio or weather forecasts. You used your own weather lore, watched the barometer and took much heed of local knowledge from fishermen. We sailed with a fresh south westerly breeze which took us out to the Lizard, where, with the all important tide in our favour, the race was formidable. Starting out into this, both of us were seasick. Jack had the sea in his blood but he was always apt to suffer, though he had never been ill in aircraft; I was usually ill at the start of a rough passage. There was a seasickness remedy in those days called 'Mother Sills'. As I remember it , you took two pills, one red and one blue. I gave these to Jack although it was obviously too late. Later when he had recovered I asked him whether they had done any good. His reply was to point at two holes in the bulkhead at the foot of the berth, "I think that's where they went", he said. 'Bluebird' behaved well; she was so small that she could rise even to these steep seas. The crests were breaking and as they rose to grow thin above us, they loomed so high that in the sunlight they were translucent and bright green. We shipped some water and we might well have been swept but each time with what seemed a convulsive wriggle, 'Bluebird' rose until the breakers collapsed in creaming disorder alongside and astern. It became dull with hurrying clouds but with the race astern the motion became easier and we could check sheets a trifle. Jack reappeared and took the helm while I sat on the companion step to rest. A horrible feeling jerked me out of a doze. The bottom of the boat was moving under my feet. Jack, seasick, had not kept the water down and it had burst the floorboards from their securing cleats. We made great speed to the end of the land, passed inside the Longships and gradually worked behind a weather shore. It was blowing harder and we were not in good shape for a long passage, so we beat into St Ives, where 'Bluebird' could dry out for a quiet night.

Early on Saturday morning, the day was fair and the barometer steady with a gentle breeze south east, we sailed with the spinnaker to starboard for a passage of about 100 miles. The land faded out on the starboard quarter as we made 4 knots, apparently to open sea but in reality at the mouth of the notorious Bristol Channel. In the afternoon, the wind backed easterly, the sky thickened, the barometer fell sharply and the wind rose steadily. We reefed and reefed again as it did so. The seas were rising and steering began to need care. We prepared for a dirty night, dressing up in turns and securing all the gear. Discussing plans we determined to continue our course to Milford Haven as long as possible and if it then seemed advisable, to run off to the west and out into clear water. If the weather became too much for us we would heave to or lie to a sea anchor; this we had rigged and ready. We had no experience of either manoeuvre in really heavy weather and we judged the wind as already force 6;

a yachtsman's gale for 'Little Bluebird'. I reefed to the normal maximum, "Can you take more off her?' Jack asked. I lowered the jaws to the boom, got in the leech and lashed it, topped the boom well up and eased the peak slightly before turning to the foresail. This demanded foredeck work and in those days we had no pulpits, no life lines and no harness. Jack said, "Don't go overboard". I said, "Try not to gybe her", and started the first crawl forward. 'Bluebird's' foredeck seemed like a naked tooth pick in violent motion. It was not easy to get the foresail secured so that only a scrap of clew remained. We were down to about 40 sq ft; it was more than enough. I managed to light the binnacle and the cabin lamp which made things more cheerful and would have helped to warn other shipping, as we had seen some steamers. Jack refused to be relieved, he did not know the gear so well and he was afraid he would be seasick. There was more wind and sea, we were near the limit. "Wait half and hour", I said. "If this gets worse we must get the main off and stream the sea anchor". The runners were now a danger but I had made them to fail safe and rigged an extra shroud well aft. The half hour was up, there was no change and we carried on. A light ahead. Eventually we could confirm Milford Haven but conditions were so bad that we decided not to close the lee shore but carried on, edging westward.

The seas became worse with the tide and we had them more on the quarter. The dinghy had remained secure and appeared to prevent us being pooped but we were shipping water regularly. I pumped and Jack steered. We used to call his trade, 'making smashed aeroplanes', it must have been a good training. I had time for reflection in the short intervals between pumping and that night, in a way that had not happened before, I came to terms with fright. I had often been frightened, not with panic fear but the mounting anxiety as to what might happen and also how one would cope with it. Jack had a matter of fact approach which was a great help. He was about two years older than I and, without realising it, had passed through the same stages earlier in his career, flying under all conditions with the aircraft of those days in the Royal Naval Air Services. I was to be frightened in the future but it never had the same effect again. I had rationalised this once and for all and whatever the anxiety, I had conviction that I should not lose my judgement and that I could carry on. Slowly the dawn grew out of the smother and slowly the darkness tattered into light. The sea looked far worse in the morning light and Skokholm Island showed almost abeam. Jack looked back and forth as he watched the seas, he looked grey and tired yet how well he was handling her. 'Bluebird' staggered, twisting into the hollows then stood on her nose and swooped, as the ugly ones picked up her stern. I pumped and pumped; we had both had enough of it. A banana and a stick of chocolate was breakfast. An hour or so later the sky began to clear, the wind eased slightly as we worked round into St Brides Bay. Here, it was relatively smooth water and the barometer began to rise. I made more sail and then I took the helm. Jack stripped and went through the bedding, fastidiously looking for the drier bits. There weren't any dry bits but he turned in. He had been at the helm for ten hours. The entertainment was over. Rather dazed and using the smoother water, I stood in rather too far and then out again to run through St David's Sound as wind and tide served. We continued to Fishguard, taking short watches and anchored at 4.30 pm. It had been 30 hours from St Ives; it felt longer and we had made good 120 sea miles.

Early next morning, feeling restored by food and sleep, we sailed for Bardsey Island, still with the big reef in the mainsail. The wind decreased until, with the island looming like a volcano in the haze, we were almost becalmed and started the engine to save our tide through the Sound. At 9.30 pm, it was almost full dark and we were in the Sound, when a backfire and silence brought us to an abrupt halt. We had fouled a crab pot line; so securing to it, I went overboard with a knife to free the propeller. It was a clammy job; diving, hanging on first and then tearing at the rope, bouncing up and out to breathe and then down again. A ragged length of rope came away and we were free. There was still no wind and the engine would not start. We guessed that the timing had slipped. It was not an easy job to re-time an engine by feel, upside down, through a hole in the cockpit floor but to our surprise the engine started until a breeze filled in and we sailed to the entrance of the channel into the Menai Straits. With our draught, we smelt our way up the channel, sounding with a pole and passed three buoys before we met a fishing boat. With our slight draught, we could do things like this in the dark and with the fisherman's directions, we carried on. The light found us anchored at the threshold of the Straits close to Conway on a foul tide.

Early on Tuesday (this was a bank holiday), we sailed into the Straits. There were yachts and it was civilised, while we felt pretty sea stained and shabby. We sailed through the bridge and the Swellies. We had been prepared and told to keep to the starboard hand but we had not realised that the rocks were so close to the bridge. Making a cross in the flukey breeze, we scraped into the main channel by a few feet and whizzed down a young waterfall, still under sail but spinning out of control. Once again that business about the current taking us round rocks held good and we spewed out into calm water at the other bridge. "Shooting the rapids under sail", we said and with a stiff breeze astern and four rolls in the mainsail but the spinnaker set, we drove her hard out of the Straits and right up to the Horse Channel into the Mersey which we entered at 8.00 pm, four and half days from Falmouth. It was inch by blasted inch to Rockferry where we came to anchor on the edge of the mud, close to the Conway. As usual we were overdue and rushed away as soon as possible. We and 'Bluebird' had been tested and emerged the stronger from this affair.

What were the reactions to all this from the cognoscente (a nice word that) of those days? They usually came up with something like this: "Interesting, indeed praiseworthy, but of course bilge keels have been tried before and we all know that adding bilge keels to a yacht, merely results in a disappointing performance". Others said, "Of course there are grave constructional difficulties in supporting the stresses of bilge keels". Both absolutely missed the point that this was not a yacht with bilge keels, it was a twin keel yacht, designed and constructed as such. There were also those who said, "Of course it is an unusual way of achieving shallow draught and a yacht that will take the ground upright". They were also wide of the mark: these advantages, if desirable attributes, were purely incidental. I was then and I have ever since been trying to produce a good, seaworthy, all-round cruising yacht. And finally, those with not much knowledge would say, "Of course with shallow draught, you must have ample beam". They again were wrong because all the 'Bluebirds' have been on the slim side rather than the beamy side. There is one man and one only to whom I pay tremendous tribute and to whom I am eternally grateful; that great sailor-man, E G Martin, famous for his yacht, 'Jolie Brise' which was derived from a French pilot cutter and the early ocean racing. He was then editor of 'The Yachting World' magazine and I am sure motivated by the desire to help a young man, he encouraged me, paid handsome tribute, accepted and published a series of articles on the design and building of 'Little Bluebird' and paid me £125 for this. (There were 18 articles appearing between January and May 1926). Believe it or not, that was one quarter of the cost of my yacht in those days; what would that be today?

The Bi-ped Rig

I first thought of the Bi-ped rig in connection with Sparrow and Ken Flather, always willing to have a go at any of my ideas, constructed it. On Sparrow it was extremely simple. Just 2 slim poles mounted and hinged in the mast position at the gun-whales and joined at the apex by a sort of wooden hoop. The luff of the mainsail was hoisted with hanks on a wire stay exactly like a normal foresail and the objective; my reasoning was that the foresail was apt to be more efficient than a mainsail because it did not suffer from the wind disturbance of a mast and spars in front of its leading edge. With the bi-ped rig the mainsail should surely be as efficient as the headsails and if you wished to lower the mast what could be simpler? This proved so successful that Ken Flather retained it on Sparrow until he sold her, when the new owner, deeply suspicious, reverted to the normal rig. When I sold 'Bluebird' to Alfred Gallimore, he also discarded the bi-ped rig. I have not heard of any other examples.

When 'Bluebird' was in the Mersey I thought, why not apply the Bi-ped rig to 'Bluebird'. In this case there were additional objectives and possible advantages. If you raked the mast aft about 10° with every reef, you maintained the proportion of mainsail and foresail, you maintained the position of the centre of effort and it was reduced in height progressively while the angle of the leading edge would provide more lift when reefed which might be an advantage and improve the sea-keeping qualities of the yacht. Also, when anchored in a gale, if the bi-ped mast were lowered aft to an angle of say 60°, not only would its windage be greatly decreased but it would ensure that the yacht streamed true to the wind from her anchor without shearing about. I duly constructed this one winter and it was fitted at Bond's Rockferry yard. Alas, when I sailed in the Spring, I had not gone far down the Mersey when in some squall the mast started to buckle, swivel and collapse. "Bluebird" went back to the Bond's yard and I went back to the drawing board. I had run up against a nasty gremlin that attacks the unwary engineer; it is known as "The scale effect". A simple explanation is that a construction which worked perfectly may be over-stressed and fail if enlarged without total redesign. I set about doing this, slightly larger solid poles for the two masts, two struts between them, three wire stays and suitable arrangement of the hanks on the mainsail gave support to the luff at four points instead of two. A fore and aft stay at mid-mast height completed the stiffening of the whole structure. I hoped that even with this mild complication both weight and windage might still be less

The bi-ped rig.

than that of a normal mast, spars, struts and stays. Thus modified it worked and its exploits appear in sailing chapters, but I realised that on 'Bluebird' the idea had reached its limit and I should not have tried to apply it to a larger yacht. By pure chance I noticed that a model of a nile boat in Tutankhamun's tomb had a sort of Bi-ped rig mast, not I think associated with sail. I doubt whether had I applied for a patent, Tutankhamun would have opposed this on the grounds of 'prior user', some 3,000 years earlier. And the epitaph - a good idea, perhaps an invention, it worked, it was a worthwhile experiment but it was unnecessary as better alternatives were just over the horizon.

Comrade D

'Bluebird' had visited the north east coast of Ireland but this had not been explored in detail. Ireland became a challenge and I started out determined to sail right round it and thus add the circuit of the British Isles to 'Bluebird's' achievements; I realised that this endeavour was to cover two seasons and involve a winter laid up in Ireland. Even less did I expect the special experiences and the enormous impression Ireland would make on me. I certainly did not realise what I should encounter on the west coast. We sailed from Conway at dawn with hopeful hearts; I had Alfred Forest with me. He was a cousin of Ken Flather, a long, thin man wearing glasses. Ken must have talked him up pretty considerably as, without experience, he was prepared to try the sailing game. The first passage was not auspicious but only too accurate a presage of the cruise. We spent about four hours hove to near the Skerries which involved both mental and physical distress for the crew. A wild beat to Holyhead followed; the third and last reef came down for the first time since 'Bluebird' had the 'bi-ped' rig and it was with thankfulness that we reached port after 14 hours. A pot of marmalade had spilt and spread itself over the galley and all objects within. We spent two days removing marmalade, repairing damages, restoring morale and awaiting a lesser wind.

The passage to Wicklow started with one reef and a head wind but degenerated into clam fog and a slow passage. An enormous shark followed us for twenty minutes; it was uncomfortable to see the great form clearly visible and at least the length of 'Bluebird' herself. The dorsal fin made a bow wave of its own and the slow sweep of the great tail, propelled the shark without effort so that it kept an exact station half a ship's length astern. We made a magnificent landfall after twelve hours 'blind'. In Wicklow we saw an old schooner, 'The Pride of the West',

eighty-five years old but beautifully maintained. She had been built for the Newfoundland Salt Cod trade and was now kept as a family heirloom by the family whose fortune she had initiated. The following day we made Arklow but only after a wild passage. The entrance can be unpleasant and was a case of "only just" with a freshening north east wind. During the next three days, it blew and it rained. We walked, we said, as many miles as we had sailed and fully appreciated the ghastly nature of the coast for navigation in a small boat under these conditions.

In Arklow, Tyrell and the ship yard were a great attraction. I was to sail later in a yacht built by his yard but Arklow was full of relics of the past. It was sad to see such a collection of small sailing vessels; ketches, cutters and sloops which had carried on the coastal trade of the past under sail. Steam had taken over; changing trade, declining population and the development of road transport had pushed them into dereliction; uneconomic to run, not worth repair, unsaleable and so well constructed that even to pick them to pieces was too laborious. And so in such small ports as this, they slowly gave way in the long battle between time, the fibres of the enduring oak and the shipwright's skill. We escaped and sneaked down to Rosslare on a day with some sunshine. It did not last and we battled our way past the Tuskar with head winds, hard winds and reefs the order of most days. Nearly always it rained. Always there was a large sea running with evil in it at the headlands, frequent bad visibility and a motion that might have soured the water in the tanks. We smelt our way into Fethard in thick fog. This little tidal basin with five fishing boats had a quay and a ruined storehouse. We were to find this typical, these were the places where the sailing trade of the past had come and wherever there was such a quay and storehouse, there was likely to be shelter for 'Bluebird'. The knowledge was useful.

We sailed up the inlet in the dinghy, an amusing expedition, meeting people and talking with everyone we met. It was here that we began to appreciate the atmosphere of Ireland. So different and so foreign in a way and yet so close. There were the soft accents and the habit of saying, "Look at it" and "I know" and also an inconsequential cautiousness, a mixture of the unexpected and the contradictory, so that we never knew what would happen next. It was as well to relax and enjoy it. We heard the legend of the lost city of Bannow and a discussion on this and its cause was followed by a vivid account of the appearance of the devil at Lofhus Hall and there, visible on the headland, was the ruin of the Hook Tower. We were to find the force of the saying, "By hook or by crook" for we had a struggle seven miles out and only just made it against a horrible sea. We had one day running to the west and this was not without incident. The wind was strong and the sea enormous. The spinnaker pulled me over the side when it tore a fastening out and then, while Alfred was on the foredeck clearing up the mess, we hit a shark with a thud that fetched us up all standing from a speed of 5 knots. I rushed below expecting damage but there was no leak and we must have left one shark wondering who was handling a blunt instrument. Examination later showed marks under the bow like scores made by a giant piece of sandpaper.

Thus we came to Helvick, port for the silver Hake of Dungarvan and here we were told of sharks up to 40 foot long and occasionally stranded whales. There was lamentation over the fishing. The season was already a month late and now made impossible by the weather. It was typical we thought that a poster said, "Only dead English", while we were treated like long, lost brothers and an incongruous touch was provided by an old man who said, "The fishing had never been the same since the English went". And another spent an hour telling us a tale of grief and desolation which we had first thought was his own personal experience, only at the end of the tale did we realise that it was the sorrows of 400 years ago! Alfred had now become competent. He could steer well and had almost overcome seasickness from which I had not been immune myself. In all this the engine had been little used. The moment there was wind, 'Bluebird' sailed. In hard winds, the engine was powerless. Even entering or leaving harbour, we might run it as a precaution against missing stays but if it blew, we always had to sail in or out and dare not depend on the engine alone. This was splendid in developing seamanship but it had its awkward moments.

The following day found us off the old head of Kinsale where we decided to turn back in a fog so thick that it was difficult to find our way up the river to Kinsale. Our time was up, I had enjoyed it, Alfred had not. He was one of the ones who got away. He had decided quite definitely that this life did not suit him. For me it had been a magnificent introduction to Ireland and experience of new coasts in spite of almost continuous rain and bad weather.

I went back to Kinsale later that year by myself, very undecided about my plans. I found 'Bluebird' in good order. A delightful man had taken both of us into the bosom of his family. Nothing was too much trouble, in another world he would have been "a boost for Birdsberg" but this was Ireland and his enthusiasm for Kinsale was quite different. I asked about local charts and was referred to the Town Hall. I ascended the stairs and was assailed by a pack of spaniels and found an old man in his office; I think he was the Town Clerk. "Certainly", he said with surprised enthusiasm when I asked for charts. "We have some very fine ones. Very interesting. Let me show you one from James I". Rallying smartly from a discussion of ancient charters and connecting our needs with the sea, he then came up with, "There is a relief model of the port made by one of my predecessors". We parted great friends and I had been adopted by the spaniels. With a little encouragement I am sure I could have taken one of the pups away with me. Kinsale Regatta was an eye opener. I sailed with a friend's son and we came in first. 'Bluebird' participated and was a grandstand during the greasy pole and the ducking episodes. The glorious muddle and the pitch of enjoyment could not have been surpassed. Arguments everywhere and a few fights but that was to be expected. The evening festivities lasted all night and at the dance I met another of the charms of Ireland. Introduced by my friends was one of the most beautiful girls I had ever seen. About 18 years of age I suppose, she might have been a beauty queen in figure and movement, with a voice so low that it raised vibrations. Her complexion only Ireland could produce with the dark colouring, the blue/black hair, combined with the most striking violet eyes. This memory had not faded but I never met her again and I cannot even recall her name! Much later when the serious drinking started, I somehow met D; half an hour later my plans were made. I had found a crew and abandoned the idea of sailing back to England single-handed which had been my most likely possibility. The weather in complete contrast with the last cruise was now fair and there was even some ease in the wind. A circumstance that could not be wasted. Throw caution to the winds, I would go west and take my chance. How simple it had all been at Kinsale, already I had faith in how things happened in Ireland.

Next day in a more sober mood I wondered what I had done but prepared 'Bluebird' for sea. I then went to look for D. It was not easy to track him down and when I found him he was so much the worse for wear that he had not surfaced at all. What to do? If I waited, I feared that he and his friends would settle in to another night of drinking, so I collected one or two of the more sober characters and, suitably primed and rewarded, they promised to deliver D to 'Bluebird'. Two hours later, a rather shaky little procession arrived at the quay, my volunteers, staggering slightly, as they supported a very sagging D. He was manoeuvred aboard. Two brown paper parcels followed, one containing a borrowed sweater and the other a pair of sand shoes (deck shoes with nonslip treads were not available in those days). I put to sea down the river out to the old Head of Kinsale and sailed away to the west with a good fair wind. D crawled up into the cockpit and surveyed the scene with bloodshot eyes. I stared at him more clearly but with an equally dubious gaze. He was a little man, about 5 foot 3 inch, fairly thick set and tough looking, about forty years of age, I suppose and there were the beginnings of a belly. His hair was dark, turning grey at the temples and his expression, somehow Irish, chubby but weatherbeaten. His hands looked hard and I knew from the night before that he spoke well. He was wearing a serviceable blue serge jacket, rather nautical in style, with socks and battered shoes. There was no other luggage other than an old cap and some oddments in his pockets and the parcels I have mentioned. "Ye wouldn't have a drink, for the love of God?" He said. "I would not", I replied firmly, quite decided that my one hidden bottle of whisky was not, repeat not going to be produced. "Bloody lime juicer", he remarked bitterly, but with more resignation than I had expected. "Take her", I said, "and I will get something to eat". He settled himself at the helm and I could see at once that he knew this business. A mug of soup and a sardine sandwich was my guess but he only managed the soup. I left him to it and took a watch off.

Over a cup of tea, the atmosphere relaxed. The night before, if he remembered it, I had told him something of the outfit. I knew nothing of him but those who had led me to him said that he knew the sea. "Do you own this yacht?" He asked and I agreed. "You must be a bloody capitalist". I agreed but added, "We are at sea now". After a long pause he came up again, "I am what you would call a communist, do you mind if I call you Comrade in accordance with my principles?" I said, "You can call me anything you like provided you behave yourself and do your full share while we keep afloat". A pact had been made, we were comrades and neither of us ever regretted it. The days that followed were an education and a delight, enlivened by Irish happenings so that sailing was almost secondary in importance, though making it all possible. Comrade D really did know the sailing game and he soon got the hang of 'Bluebird'. We lived well, not only was he a good cook but he caught fish with

practiced skill and knew exactly how to wheedle supplies out of the most remote and unlikely place. He knew the coast intimately and so we had sheltered anchorages that I might not have discovered. He was also an introduction to a rich fund of contacts ashore. I strictly controlled the purse so that drinking was just enough for introduction and enough to loosen his astounding command of language, but not enough to get him involved in embarrassing sessions. To start with he was critical and suspicious of 'Bluebird' but he developed, first tolerance and then appreciation until finally he was convinced. This had astounding results. He confessed that he would like nothing better in this world than such a craft and the freedom of her. To others he might have been the owner and waxed lyrical in her praise. I was convulsed with laughter as he appealed to me for corroboration of the wildest feats. At times he would talk about her as if she was a favourite horse that he had ridden for years.

The weather was kind and Ireland was as beautiful as could be imagined. We sailed and drifted westward as far as Crookhaven in almost calm seas with light winds and it was so hot that clothes were hardly necessary. This gave D a chance to wash his scanty garments which he did religiously, borrowing a pair of my old pyjamas while his shirt and smalls were drying in the rigging. I quickly came to know him better and he gradually expanded. I formed a picture of the surprising son of rather strict and proper parents, not on the breadline of the slums but in a middle level where every shilling was hard earned. He had probably become wild and uncontrollable, unsatisfied and adventurous, breaking away from family ties. He particularly remembered and valued expeditions along the coast with a few companions in a rowing galley. There he had first learned seamanship, followed by sailing experience, camping, fishing, shooting, poaching and no doubt drinking. I could see how the life he pictured had suited him and how he had developed. In and out of every sort of job and every sort of scrap or scrape, he had drifted all over Ireland. Girls of course but not the most important thing in life, quite incidental. I never discovered if he had married but probably he had valued freedom too much to risk restriction. How and where he had acquired more than adequate education was a mystery but I was sometimes left behind as he quoted books and recited poetry. His own descriptions could be impressive: "Sure it's a marvellous day. The weather, the sky and those little clouds drop in from above and the sun casting dark shadows on the sea where the waves are just rocking us, while the tops are winking at 'Bluebird' and tickling the rudder so that the tiller is alive with desire in my hands. Look at the colour on the land and the spray on the rocks with the patterns on the strand. What more could a man want on such a day?" A pause and then remembering his other self, "Except to weep for the suffering of the world - or any other bloody thing".

The legends and the folklore of Ireland he could quote by the hour. I liked the one about the Sack of Baltimore by Algerian pirates, "She never smiled O'Driscoll's child but wept for Baltimore". I gathered that the poor girl had probably met a fate worse than death before stabbing her captive well and truly in the midriff, so that one fears her last state may have been worse than the first! Comrade D was happy sitting in the sunshine in his trousers and braces with his body turning pink in the sun and as for me the complications of life had been shrugged off, I was free with no distractions, no plans and at last I was a part of Ireland. There was a sort of Irish efficiency in our doings which meant that everything happened sooner or later and every task got done somehow but don't for God's sake try to hurry anything or expect anything on time: "There are things that would be happening that could not be 'deschcribed'".

We beat out round the brow of Mizzen Head and crossed the mouth of Bantry Bay - 'The strand of the women' to Castletown, Berehaven. This passage was sterner stuff. The weather threatened to deteriorate with a falling barometer. Comrade D enjoyed this sail, hard day though it was and became even more impassioned as he told the tale that night. He had now left the waters he knew intimately and we were heading into the unknown. Next day we tackled Dursey Sound and missing our tide as it had taken us so long to beat out, we had a struggle to make the passage. In the midst of this we hooked a fine rock cod with the line we had forgotten, weighing 10 lbs or so. It was a fight to haul in and land him while handling 'Bluebird' in the narrows. We bashed our way across the Kenmare river and night came down with vicious squalls. The Irish Pilot known to us as 'The Green Terror' was not encouraging: "Derrynane Harbour inaccessible except in quiet water and covered by outlying rocks on which, as well as on the foul ground between them and Hog Island, the sea breaks furiously in unsettled weather, rendering the approach to this shore and the channels dangerous". I now know that Derrynane is not easy for the first time by day unless your are 'acquaint'. The following hours were a unique experience, never have I seen such phosphorescence.

'Bluebird's' keels and rudders glowed in silvery light as if the hull was a filament drawing cold current from the passage of the sea. Running, beating and fighting the squalls in the blackness of that night, we sought the entrance to Derrynane. Probably the phosphorescence saved us as by that light alone could we see the sea breaking on reefs and rocks while we entered what might have been the harbour but proved to be a cul de sac. 'Bluebird' was superb and only when, as we afterwards confirmed, we had twice entered the opening to the harbour without being able to see a way through, did we retreat to smell our way round Abbey Island. This is what we should have done in the first place and there we anchored, safe at last, in three fathoms on sand, only a stone's throw from the ruins. We lay to two anchors as the squalls were wicked. Warm and fed, Comrade D confessed that this had been a new experience: "With my life in my hands and the ship preserving my soul, the way she could be felling the stags of stone with her turbines as she twisted in the night".

Derrynane is the most enchanted fairyland I know and we explored outward from the harbour itself the next day. The dazzling white sands with cowrie shells and palms ashore, almost gave a feeling of the tropics. There was the ancient Abbey and the richness of the fuschia growing as large as the thorn hedges in England and in the woods, moss dripping from the trees. There is a profusion of birds and always the sea thundering on the rocks outside. Strong north winds now said, "Go back" with an effort we could not dispute. We couldn't reach the Shannon or even Valentia. We swooped at speed round Dursey Island and the Mizzen Head, round the Fastnet to take a photograph there, then on to Cape Clear and, hauling our wind, we beat in to Baltimore the home of many ships and where they are building them still. In England, the Fastnet Race was just starting; ill fated that year by storm and the loss of Colonel Hudson from 'Maitenes II', which was nearly overwhelmed and lost. The American 'Dorade' won, a great victory, and came within an hour of 'Patience' and 'Highland Light', the leading vessels which were much larger and lucky as they were in before the gale struck. Conor O'Brian and his exploits vied with the old legends on that coast. His 'Saoirse' had been built here and they were proud that she had sailed the world; she was still going strong in 1970.

As straight as the mast of his galleys,
As wild as the waves of the sea.

When we enquired about the tide in a narrow channel, one man told us, "Sure it would be running 12 knots against you", but another old man contradicted this, "I would be rowing up against it with a pair of paddles". The currents are like the Irish miles - just what you wish to believe.

In these last days, Comrade D told me that he had been in Russia for a prolonged stay and that he had returned to Ireland being landed on the coast on a dark night from a Russian submarine. I did not take all his tales as gospel but the majority stood some tests and had at least a substantial foundation. What he had to say in this case about life in Russia and particularly his opinion on the elimination of the family life with free love, free marriage and free divorce, the children going to the care of the State etc., was convincing together with his prophesy that this theory would not work and was already likely to be abandoned. This left me in no doubt that he had been in Russia, but why? From another story it would appear that he had been there for training in communist theory and industrial sabotage, as he also talked of fermenting grievances and causing strikes. There had recently been a bad strike at the Ford factory near Cork with troubles, pickets and bloodshed. This factory was eventually closed down, uneconomic and a failure. True or false? And what was to be claimed by or attributed to saboteurs? He strongly hinted that he had started all this and it had suited him very well to lie low for a time. What better way to disappear than in 'Bluebird's' trip to the west; but he received news by mail and he read me a passage from a friend's letter - What is this man, a Count, Maxim or Christopher Columbus? And what is this boat that sounds like a cross between a shark and a catamaran with fins above and below and sails set on wires without masts? So the tale had not lost in the telling.

With a good wind behind us, we ran back along the coast enjoying sparkling conditions. Comrade D gave a rendering of, "The pleasure of the world is on the waters", swiftly followed by, "Be sure the great God never planned for slumbering slaves a better land - or any other bloody thing". The miles rolled fast behind us with the bow wave lifting high and the hissing wake astern. "Give waves to fools and gold to knaves or rank to the bended knee". There was no class consciousness at sea. It was a hard beat into the land and into Cork harbour to anchor at Crosshaven. We had covered 63 miles at 5.3 knots on the last day. In the morning we went up river to the little yard at Carrigloe and I demonstrated 'Bluebird's' trick of sailing up a river by touching the mud before going about on each tack, well knowing that this would start another legend. Swiftly I made arrangements to leave 'Bluebird' for the winter. I found I could get passage on a boat to Liverpool if I could catch a bus within the hour. Comrade D put me ashore in the little dinghy and we said goodbye. "I would steal 'Bluebird' from you with the greatest of pleasure", were his parting words. I ran for the bus with my kitbag, leaving 'Bluebird' in his hands with complete confidence. This was not misplaced, he put her to bed for the winter with meticulous care, the job has never been better done and though he was not out of pocket, I never paid him a penny. We were comrades! The day came when I had no reply to my letters and I often wonder what happened to Comrade D, philosopher, idealist, communist and a good seaman. Only Ireland could produce such a man.

Divinely Mad

In May of the next year, Ken and I went out to Cork by ship to fit out 'Bluebird'. This task was made easy by the way in which she had been put to bed. We had a short but not an easy sail the first day away, anchoring in Ringabella Bay. A walk ashore under a blue sky, a warm sun and the tearing wind did us good. The colours were wonderful; the green so vivid it could hardly be grass and the gorse in dense masses of gold like a flame against the hill with the scent borne everywhere on the wind and pursuing us back to 'Bluebird'. We started out at 5.00 am next day to use the tide and soon passed the old Head of Kinsale, making our way along the coast I now knew so well. The Seven Heads showed up, there was now more wind and sea. Ken lost interest in the proceedings while I took 'Bluebird', keeping well clear of the Dhulac, a horrible flat topped rock awash at low tide, surrounded by foul ground on which the sea might break. It seemed prudent to make for Glandore, steering was exacting but again I felt the old thrill as the little ship dealt cleverly with a nasty sea. Some large fishing vessels like ourselves were seeking shelter and together we passed between Adam and Eve Islands. The fishing boats went up to Union Hall and we made the little boat harbour of Glandore. I had been steering for 7 hours though it was only 2.00 pm. Ken soon recovered.

The depression arrived with pouring rain, high winds and a low barometer. Next morning was no better so we walked to Union Hall and returned with purchases including a large cabbage. Ken said I looked like 'the return from the allotment' with this clasped to my bosom. In the afternoon we sailed, though with much misgiving, finding conditions bad but possible. We had a most interesting sail to Castle Haven where we anchored near a green lobster boat called, 'Fear Nought'. We badly needed a meal and a chance to change out of sodden clothing. A dinghy came alongside with a message inviting us to the Castle for coffee after dinner. In due time we landed, walked up through the village, took directions and came to a gateway. As we turned in off the road, I might well have turned pale for I had seen the scene in a dream three days earlier. Ken, though knowing about the dream, did not realise that I had recognised the place and proceeded placidly up the drive to the castle - an imposing building. And there was the door I had seen, massive, forbidding and covered with hand-forged nails. Ken rang the bell. The door swung open and before me, just inside, stood a little brass cannonade I had also seen. Then, and next day, we were received and treated as members of the family by the hospitable Townshends. They had arrived in Ireland as Townends in the reign of Edward III, settled here and married the Fitzgeralds and the name had been twisted to become Townshends. There were now guests in the castle with ten languages represented, ranging from Arabic to Erse. Fun and games followed and next day welcome baths but I never told them about the dream. Why? I don't know.

It was quite impossible to sail next day so we went for a long walk out to Toe Head. The sea was terrible. "Indaid it is a wild day, a wild day entoirely", was a typical greeting. We visited the green lobster boat whose old owner named Callahane, with his son, came from Hare Island, the home base of many lobstermen. The boat was thirty-two years old and everything had an austere look of well used working simplicity. Accommodation was a bit of hay under a canvas, rigged over a scull. There was a turf fire on a stone and clay hearth and on this they were baking soda bread. The bilges were stuffed with heather to keep out the smaller crustaceans, the simple gaff sloop rig was low and practical. Two tons of iron ballast gave power; the boat would be able but the large open well, a danger in bad weather. Their traditional season started on June 1st. They had sailed early and for a week had done no work, held in port by bad weather. Their return visit made us realise how luxurious 'Bluebird' must seem to them though pretty spartan for us; everything is relative. Callahane was fascinated by our bi-ped rig and after prolonged study, produced the best description yet - "Be God, it's bloody strong shrouds ye have on a thin mast". Only Ireland could have thought of this. Next day the wind, while still strong, was not so

vicious but still unpleasant with rain. Influenced by similar passages which had been justified, we reefed down and prepared to sail. As we got our anchor, a hail came from the 'Fear Nought', "maybe we will meet you in Baltimore or it might be Schull but it might be that I'll meet you in Heaven. There is a sea off the Stags that you will not be passing". The day needs no description. Callahane was very nearly right. There was a moment when we should have returned but it passed in a squall so heavy that we could hardly breathe for the rain and spray and the pump was in action. The smaller the yacht, the larger the pump, was one of our mottos.

We made Baltimore and we were rewarded. The sun broke, the wind eased and for the first time in four days, we could dry clothes and bedding. We shopped quickly and sailed on, dodging through the islands by intricate channels to find smooth water, past Hare Island and the entrance to Schull, to anchor in Croagh Bay. There was something enchanting in the stillness, we spoke in whispers. It was the absence of wind; for days the air had been tearing past us, dragging at our clothes and carrying away our voices. The eye could delight in the reflections where we had become accustomed to the constant movement of windswept water. After a short night, we resumed the wetter life but now we had changed to a truly horrible sea with no wind. So far we had not used the engine at all but Ken and I gave each other one look, the only question was, who was to do repairs and make it run? Triumph at last, with greasy hands we were able to make our way over the enormous but now harmless swell. It was not long before we had wind again that took us to Castletown Bellhaven but the approach was not rapid. Only by watching closely could we see that a distant mountain was actually creeping out from behind the shoulder of a nearer hill. Ken was surprised when milk and eggs came from a milliners and lime juice from the grog shop; not for nothing had I sailed with Comrade D.

An impression may have been given that we never turned back but we did so from Blackball Head. It was not so much the conditions as fatigue and we said that a sort of 'wakeness' or 'slackeen' had overtaken us. The wind just played with us until we gave up. At the next attempt, it was rain and squalls and though Dursey Sound was not dull, it was much easier than last year. As we rushed across the Kenmare River, I told Ken about the battle of Dursey Island. A bloody revolt against some Government impost caused the authorities to send for reinforcements from Cork. It was a Saturday night when the

Above: Little 'Bluebird'.
Right: Robin Balfour, his friend Ken Flather (Left).

force of policemen assembled in the tug, 'Stormcock' without enthusiasm. The weather was bad and the ballad runs - "The gulls were drinking porter when the 'Stormcock' sailed and weakened by seasickness, the forces of law were temporarily defeated by the rebels".

Derrynane by day and now "acquaint" was easy and Ken was introduced to its delights. We had to make arrangements for Gray to join us and eventually after difficulty and delay, organised a car to take us over to the cable station at Waterford which was the only hope after we had walked to Cahir Daniel and failed. We noticed that here shop signs were in Erse only and our driver barely spoke English. He said that the direct road back to Derrynane was, "too high for car" and "made him fear". While even the road over Koomakista Pass, "was too much tall". There was the 'Glen of the Treasure' where the crew of a Spanish galleon, wrecked in that bay of wicked rocks, were reputed to have brought ashore and buried their valuables when the stricken Armada had been scattered. Now we had announced a rendezvous it was Valentia or bust. We fought our way out and sped across Ballinskelligs Bay, we lost shelter and it became almost tack and tack to the entrance to the Portmagee channel, the back door and nearer way to Valentia. 'Bluebird' reached a new set of limits that day and we had an unpleasant experience. There are patches shown on the chart where the sea-bed rises perhaps to 10 fathoms and on these the sea could break. We had rather ignored it thinking that the 'Green terror' was referring only to the great seas of winter gales but wind and sea were now rising over an already enormous swell and 'Bluebird' could only just bear to windward because she was knocked flat on the crests, yet we could not reduce sail as we were almost becalmed in the hollows and the wind came in squalls more dangerous than a steady blow. A little more and we should have been completely overpowered, unable to go back because of tide and sea or forward because of sea and wind - bound then to end up on the rocks. Then the unexpected danger, half an acre of sea ahead of us reared up and broke rapidly so close that the edge of the break swept our foredeck. There was nothing we could do. We sailed on and we sailed over. The patch did not break again until we were clear by 200 yards, there was a distinctly impressed look on the usually impassive face of Ken Flather. A fishing boat, looking like a dinghy in that sea, altered course to close us. Here the Skipper signalled to the mouth of the Portmagee channel and clearly indicated, "make for shelter boys". It was high time we got out of this but we were already doing our best and it seemed

a long slow haul until we reached some shelter where we should again have been defeated by the squalls had it not been for smoother water. We drove 'Bluebird' to the limit for the 9 miles up the channel to Valentia and secured to the wharf with a damaged sail, a mess below and water everywhere. No matter, we arrived and later went up to Cahirciveen. The anchor and the dinghy went over together and I ran for the station still in my oilskin and encrusted with salt as the train was due.

It was not long before someone said, "She's there", pointing to a tiny black worm crawling along the immense flank of the mountain by Macgillycuddys reeks. Ten minutes later, they came in. Gray was relieved to see us as we were to meet him. We dined ashore and then pooled bedding. I slept on a layer of sails on the saloon floor, Ken departed by the midday train next day, while Gray and I cleared up the ship and settled in. He had not sailed with me before; another brother-in-law. He was an artist and had not long returned from a voyage round the Horn, returning from Australia in the grain ship, 'Olive Bank'. This venture was partly for experience and partly to see one of the sailing ships from an artist's eye. The fishing boat that had seen us outside had passed the word around and we were welcomed by the fishing fraternity. One of the drifters on the quay asked us to go out with them for a night's fishing. Gladly we accepted and reported at 6.30 pm in oilskins and sea boots. Before long, the two paraffin engines were thrusting the heavy hull into a lump swell in Dingle Bay. The light was dropping down to the western horizon and our bow rose and fell against the dark sea with the rugged outline of the Blaskets beyond and an occasional drift of light spray clearing the rail and pattering across the foredeck. Gray and I wedged ourselves in the tiny wheelhouse with the Skipper. There was not room for us and we had to make ourselves thin to miss the spokes of the wheel as it swung. Around our heads were various little cards tacked on to the beams. They were mainly religious and encouraging in tone. The Skipper's blue eyes twinkled and snapped in a manner which made his seventy-one years ridiculous as he explained many mysteries; the ways of fish-buyers, the ancestry of the drifter, the running of the ship, the ridiculous price of spares for his engine, the bad luck of the season - a good deal of this, and his cow.

So far, fortune had not smiled upon them. In a fortnight they had only managed three nights fishing. I remarked inwardly that 'Bluebird' had been at sea most of the days and that weather bad enough to stop their fishing is getting tough for a three tonner;

they had worked for empty nets. The day before, they had decided to leave and the Skipper had bought a cow. They had rigged up a pen on deck and were away for Baltimore and home to take a week's rest before starting for the Isle of Man. This last night was a last fling, an afterthought made in the nature of a gamble. As he explained, we marvelled at the matter of fact way in which risks were faced and taken, daily or nightly, in this strange trafficking with nature. Uninsured and without money to lose, they risked £300 worth of nets every time they shot. No wonder the Skipper explained in answer to a question I put as to the consequences of fouling another boat's nets, "There's things that would be happening to you that could not be deshcribed", and he wagged his head solemnly. We were not alone on the sea. Sail and power, brown lugs and black hulls showed here and there; the engineer put his head in the doorway and pointed out the position of some vessel. Other members of the crew joined in. A discussion followed well nigh unintelligible to us but momentous to them. We admired the free way in which they all took part, without discipline yet without slackness. It was more like that rare thing, a large family in complete harmony. The Skipper went forward to look around. I shall not forget the picture of the three of them braced against the motion and silhouetted against the last of the light, while astern the mountains turned to velvet dark. The motion had been horrible with a wallowing quickness that made 'Bluebird' seem preferable. The nets were shot, the boy went down forward to tend the warp; he had confided to us that this was his first trip and that he was ill every night. I do not wonder, his place in the bows with the smell of the engines and the warp would have finished me in a few minutes.

It was grand to watch the rhythm with which the net went overside as the warp slid out and the stoppers were caught and bent on with lightning dexterity as they went past with a flick over the head of the man at the foot rope. Over two miles of nets to go but it did not take long. The lamp was lit, the engines died into silence and the wallowing motion became the unmistakable inert roll of a ship without steerage-way. The wind had increased and with flurries of rain, was cold and cheerless. The temperature was only 43°F, although it was nearly June, in the warmest corner of the British Isles. We went below and it was warm enough down there. I had heard the expression, "like a drifter's boiler-room", denoting something rather sticky. There was no exaggeration. The triangular space with the lockers on the sides and the bunks above, held nine men. At one end there

was a coal stove roaring away and on it the cook was preparing a meal. Alongside this was a vertical boiler and this was being stoked up to raise a head of steam for working the capstan. It was innocent of lagging as the cabin was innocent of ventilation and the heat seemed almost audible as the pressure gauge hissed and bubbled, the feed pump ran with a syncopated clank and the water level in the gauge glass rose and fell as the ship rolled. The faces and forms cast strange shadows in the glow from the oil stove and the dim light of the oil lamp. Boiled herring with a lump of bread, butter, a mug of tea and condensed milk. The ingredients were simple and the tools also. There was a shortage of plates, a shortage of knives, no forks and our fingers. We started yarning. Talk turned to song and back to talk again. We had shanties from Gray and the Skipper; all the others did a turn. I well remember those songs, one of them 'The Galway Hooker', came from the days when the hookers were trading on the whole of that wild coast:

When the wind is in the west
And the wild waves rise together;
Not a drop she took aboard her
That would wash a fly away.

Chorus:

Oh, she's neat, oh she's sweet
She's a beauty every line;
The pride of Connemara is this bounding
Barque of mine.

There's a light shines out afar
Just to keep us from dismaying
And if we can but follow
It will lead us safely home

There were many, many verses.

There was another song - 'The Bosuns's Dream' in which the old Bosun foretells the day, then far ahead, when steam ships would be large and fast and replace sail:

Crossing o'er the western ocean
30,000 tons was she,
Steady, scarcely any motion
Though there was a heavy sea.

And the Bosun, old sea rover,
Leaned upon her rail and dreamed.

Days of sail now long forgotten
Pages turned in times-old log,
Cargoes of spice, silks and cotton
Fearing nothing else but fog.

Then there was a hale from for'ard,
Fastnet light came, now abeam,
40 fathoms sure and over
Broke the grey, old Bosun's dream.

Again, many more verses to the conclusion.

Meanwhile, the needle of the pressure gauge had quivered higher and higher; the heat had become almost unbearable. It was time to haul nets. We struggled into oilskins and hauled ourselves clumsily on deck. The work started. I hauled on the foot rope as long as my hands would stand it and Gray and I continued to sing. "We must change your luck", we said, "and sing the fish to the nets". The first few fathoms of net came in blank, then there was a gleam of silver and this steadily increased until a rising number of fish were spread over the deck and the crew grew more cheerful. The Skipper said that if this continued, they would stay for a few more days. It looked as if we had changed their luck. We returned to port in the early morning light with wonderful colours on the hills and over the sea. Back alongside with all senses working, tired but with the rhythm of accustomed toil, a good catch went ashore. The gulls screamed and fought for damaged fish, occasionally a gannet would make its dive so close that its path could be followed below the surface of the clear water. The big gulls could take half a dozen fish while the gannets appeared to be insatiable. We returned to 'Bluebird' for a quiet day, doing useful jobs. Life was real and we could not forget that time was getting shorter and we had anything up to 500 miles to sail, while we had already proved that it was impossible to forecast progress on this coast.

A long and varied day took us across to Blasket Sound and onward making the best course we could to a north west wind with the Aran Isles a possible objective. We were out of sight of land and the weather was deteriorating. We were beyond Loop Head at the northern entrance to the Shannon estuary. Life was no longer pleasant. We managed a meal and then took in a reef. It was near dusk and we had been on passage for 20 hours. Gray was ill; he was at times subject to some trouble that was not seasickness but laid him low (obviously the appendix was playing up). Had it not been for this I might have carried on but goodness knows whether we should have made the Aran Isles. Now I realised a point of no return would soon be reached and that this could be dangerous. Without further hesitation, I laid a course back to the Shannon, travelling now at maximum speed and hating every hard won mile so swiftly thrown away. We should have reefed again but Gray was beyond helping and it was difficult to leave the helm and 'Bluebird' swooped and staggered for three hours until I could see the lighthouse and we slid into shelter and beat up into Kilbaha Bay, the nearest anchorage. The weather justified our return. Gray slowly recovered and here for the first time I saw the curraghs in action. I could see how well adapted they were to make use of the materials on hand for construction and, like the cobles of the Yorkshire coast, deal with the special beaching problems and the menace of the Atlantic seas, but again, like the cobles, they surely demanded skilled seamen brought up to handle them.

At this point, we had a last choice; we could have returned to the south or entered the Shannon to take 'Bluebird' later through to Dublin by river and canal. I cannot remember that either of us hesitated as we were determined to carry on. The passage, of about forty miles in that dangerous area, was not very different from the day I had turned back but we started fresh and Gray was better. We made Aran in eight hours with the wind forward of the beam, a reef as usual and a sea that had come all the way from America. The Aran Isles have their own atmosphere and we wished that we had had more time. To me the particular interest was the hookers carrying turf and produce to and from the mainland; they were fine craft and quite distinctive. I could detect no derivation in their design, it appeared to be a purely local and instinctive development for local conditions. We sailed again and suddenly everything had changed. After beating for so long, we could hardly believe it when a really fine day developed with hot sunshine and a fair wind. Out came all our gear to dry, up went the spinnaker and we boomed up the coast at speed, taking watches. I had not allowed for Gray's still incomplete adaptation to 'Bluebird', very different was this from a trick at the wheel of a 3,000 ton sailing ship with a steel shelter behind the helmsman. He handled 'Bluebird' without difficulty but as I slept, the wind increased and it never occurred to him that it was becoming dangerous. I should have been warned. I surfaced with a crash. The sheet had carried away, the spinnaker boom had smashed and the outer end, made into a club by the flogging sail, had carried away the forestay and roller gear. We cleared up the mess, rigged a forestay from a spare halyard, reefed the main well down and intended to carry on with the passage but this was the west of Ireland. Within an hour, we were off Slyne Head, a notoriously nasty area. We again had a head wind and the sea that developed was soon too much for the temporary forestay and the mast came down. With the bi-ped rig, this was not the smash-up we might have had with a normal rig, but still! There was nothing we could do except execute the old naval order of the first wooden wall frigates that had auxiliary steam, "Up funnel, down screw".

The little two stroke alone stood between us being blown out into the Atlantic, out of control and dismasted. With the spars down, windage was so reduced that the little motor was more effective. Before we had lost the mast, we had skated along and closed the coast somewhat; everything possible must be done to help the engine. All windage was taken off and knowing that the cooling system was a limiting factor, I disconnected the outlet pipe from the cylinder block so that the pump was under positive sea pressure and could deliver more than normal flow. The discharge ran to the bilge through the fog horn acting as a funnel and of course it had to be hand pumped overside at intervals. We made for shelter in Clifton with the engine opened up to its small maximum. It was touch and go; there were times when the squalls stopped our way and put her out of control, the bow paying off before the wind. At such times, I still used sail to keep control. Gray was the sail. Wearing a big oilskin coat, he crawled from stem to stern at my command, setting the coat with extended arms so that I could bring her back into the wind and hold her there when course permitted. We made Clifton; we had been lucky. We had not escaped unscathed but had everything on hand necessary for repairs, mainly a new strut and some wire splicing with which went naughty words! We sailed when repairs were completed with the happiest memories of Clifton and wondering whether the beauty of the islands and the mountains here was greater than in Kerry. It was a lovely sail to Inishboffin, the fishing was good; we caught many mackerel and passed curraghs on every hand. Gray was particularly attracted by this island in the west and shortage of time was again a tragedy.

After a dawn start, it was a race to make Achill Sound, inside the Benmullet Peninsular. I had looked forward to this as promising an interesting change and a useful distance to be gained in shelter. But here we were pressing on at sea outside the Benmullet Peninsular. I cannot remember what reasoning lay behind this but in view of the next happenings, it would almost appear that some fate had taken us in hand. Meanwhile we had other troubles. The flat-out run with the engine had finished the stern gland packing and we had a leak - not serious but annoying. We pumped enough in 'Bluebird' without this addition and I had a curious unease and apprehension. This time there was no obvious cause, conditions were not too bad. True, there was a long way to go to make the next advantageous shelter but we were not unduly tired. A night passage lay ahead but this did not dismay us. Why did I suddenly grab the chart and make a critical examination of a coast I had thought unapproachable? Spotting French Port, a very small inlet, I headed in. It was a lee shore and an inexplicable decision. When we had closed, there seemed to be no entry and we had to sail right along the rocks which were spouting spray, until we found the diagonal passage from which the reefs overlapped, leaving a narrow lane of clear water. We sailed in an opening to a safe and pleasant bay, shallow at the head with sand bottom. The anchor went down and we went below for a meal.

Before we did so, I saw a man with a dog. He was in a white Bainin wool coat and he was sitting on a rock above the sand opposite to us. He had been there when we entered. After a meal we agreed to launch the dinghy and take a turn ashore. As we stepped out on to the beach, the man rose, came slowly towards us and, ignoring Gray, came directly to me, made a formal gesture and said in halting English, "You'll be wanting to see your castle". This had no significance whatsoever but he turned and we followed, perhaps two miles across a desolate land with rock everywhere, bog pools and scant vegetation and we came to a castle, not large, looking fairly old and fairly in ruin. Our guide led in through a gateway to a sort of courtyard; this was open to the sky and in one corner was a little lean-to dwelling. He invited us in and made us a cup of tea but said little. "What is this place?" I asked. "You'll be knowing", he replied, "It's Bingham Castle". Then I started thinking. My mother was a Bingham and there was a family legend of a daughter of the Nottinghamshire Binghams who, without her family's consent, had run away and married a distant cousin of the same name from Ireland. From that union, my mother's branch of the family had come. There was little more to learn. The old man was fairly inarticulate, he expected me to know. There was a real and larger Bingham Castle at Binghamstown in Block Sod Bay. How can one explain that this man apparently expected us and that he was patiently waiting for us at the strand as we sailed almost to his feet, that he could distinguish me from Gray - but this is Ireland! I began to wonder whether these Binghams had married the Townshends, to put another question mark behind the dream. On my return, my mother filled in as much as she knew and then traced and invited to stay a Bingham who was living in Guildford. He was the last of the Binghams in those parts. The place I had visited had been his home. Impoverished and in the troubles, he had abandoned the place and pulled off the roof to avoid taxes, the cruel fate responsible for so many Irish ruins. The old man who had waited for us was probably the last of those who had served him. He brought some family records which fascinated my mother and confirmed the legend. In particular, there was the miniature of a beautiful girl, this was a duplicate of one my mother owned and may have been the original girl who ran away from her home in Nottinghamshire. How fantastic can your ideas become. Nothing like this had ever happened to me except in Ireland.

We walked over to Benmullet where we found no mail and nothing of importance but the wild weather made us thankful that we had not kept the sea. Departure was difficult; we might easily have been bottled up in that inlet and why was it called French Port? Spanish traditions are common on the coast, French is not, though Christianity came to Ireland from France. The Irish Bennetts traced their name back to the Benet of French origin. At 4.00 am, we were at sea almost as if we had never left it and that whole incident might have been just another dream. The day passed as we crossed Donegal Bay, out of sight of land, until 4.30 pm when Rathlin O'Birne bore north north east about ten miles. A thunder storm meant a reef and a head wind, followed by a long tiring night of difficult going, trying not to wake the other man while dealing with the conditions and struggling against sleep. We came up to Tory Island in the morning which resembled an Inishboffin. We began to feel a subtle change in climate and topography. Somehow, though beautiful still and as wild as ever, this coast was harder. We heard someone say, "Och aye". For the first time we felt that we were being plundered. Millionaire trouble! A very rich man from America owned the island and this had apparently altered all values so any stranger was assumed to be wealthy and therefore fair game! We collected our minimum necessities and sailed promptly.

Tides ran ever more strongly and at last we rounded Ireland's North Point, as significant as Bloody Foreland had been. For the first time the wind did not head us round this corner and we made Portrush in the night; a tricky entrance with onshore wind and sea. There we had the best sleep for a week but only because the alarm had failed. It did not matter, our tired brains had not correctly sorted the mysteries of the tides at Rathlin Sound. We now found that we had time to shop and feed before tackling our last passage. Gray, singing the sea shanty, "Only one more day", had a store of songs that had cheered us and somehow we had maintained a sense of humour in every crisis. Rathlin Sound presented no difficulty as we timed it correctly and so dodged the dangerous eddies and overfalls rather similar to the Pentland Firth. We were not so lucky off Sanda Island but a grand breeze took us up Kilbrennan Sound in the very early morning. Our time was up, we started packing and shaving by turns to another sea shanty, " For it is time for us to leave her". This was too much, the wind promptly headed and for the last time we reefed down and plugged what seemed a long way to Tarbert. We sailed in as the ferry came out and anchored at 3.30 pm. Arrangements were soon made with Dickies Yard as they knew 'Bluebird' well. We caught the last bus to Glasgow only thirty minutes later. Both of us had engagements in the south next day and by travelling all night we were there on time. In three weeks, 'Bluebird' had sailed 1,000 miles, 400 of them in the last seven days. Gray and Ken had both been magnificent and I was quite proud that 'Bluebird' had completed her toughest circuit in my hands. A friend asked Gray where he had been. "With Robin Balfour on the west coast of Ireland". "Don't they call him twin keel Balfour?" "Yes, and 'Bluebird' has got twin keels". "Isn't he a little mad?" "Yes, but quite divinely mad". Well, well, it is nice to know, I had often wondered! But this seemed to express what I had felt in Ireland, the lessons had affected my thinking and my plans. I knew better than before that the wind is your friend, but how far? It is the sea that is the enemy, but how soon? Even if the men can stand, any yacht has her absolute ceiling, the point at which she cannot be sailed off a lee shore. 'Bluebird', as good as she was (and still is), was so small that this ceiling was low; too low for safety on the west coast of Ireland or the north of Scotland. If my ambitions were to reach out further, I must think again.

'Bluebird' completes a Circumnavigation

'Bluebird' became an important part of my life and in the years between 1926 and 1938, this continued. After that year, I did not sail in her again but she had not passed out of my mind as will appear later. In the memory, a pattern emerges involving the part 'Bluebird' played, changing with my circumstances but always there in the background in good years and bad, forming a gateway to friendships with outstanding men. Experience increased. There were developments with two cruises that merit description. I might well have done many other things in the time devoted to sailing but there are no regrets as I should have missed so much if I had not had this outlet. It was not only sailing on holidays but an escape from pressure and responsibility, relief from overwork, a refuge from tragedy or a joy shared with others close to me. The thoughts on design began to lead into some writing, lectures and a sound reason for taking photography seriously enough to help the memory by keeping a good visual record.

For a time, 'Bluebird' was based at Rockferry and laid up at Bonds Yard. While she was in commission, a very nice Conway Cadet, who could not play games owing to some heart damage, was allowed to spend his time in her. His father owned a Morecambe Bay type yacht and he was knowledgeable and worked on her with real enjoyment. We cruised the whole of the North Wales coast, Anglesey to the Isle of Man, up to the West coast of Scotland and the adjacent coasts of Ireland. Once we entered the midnight race to the Isle of Man, which was organised by the Tranmere Sailing Club, and thought we were the smallest yacht and the smallest crew. Ken and I finished sixth and 'Bluebird' was not disgraced. 'Bluebird' made three train journeys and one passage back to Sheffield by canal, finally being based at West Loch, Tarbet, Argyll and cruised on the West coast of Scotland. Increased work and responsibility, two business trips around the world and almost a year in India, were incidents and progress in my other life affecting sailing plans.

I have been accused, and with reason, of forgetting people, even the names of former girl friends, while able to produce a creditable sketch and the vital statistics of any yacht I have ever seen. Nevertheless, the inevitable happened; girls entered our lives and nature did the rest, not only in yacht materials has there been change! In my young days there would have been a horrified hush if the word 'sex' had been uttered in a polite drawing room. There were no instructions at school with television aids and not because television did not exist, and finally there was no pill. Today one may wonder how the world carried on since the fable of the Garden of Eden but I cannot remember any great difficulty. I, Ken, Dick and Jack all married in time. We all had children. Jack married my sister, which somehow surprised me more than if he had married someone else and I never thought of him as a marrying type anyway. His father had died and as Jack could not use them, I took over all that was left of his father's drawing office and records. However inaccurate, I liked to think of myself as Linton Hope & Company, Naval Architects. I still have many of the old drawings and the much prized register of all Linton Hope's designs including some early work on record breaking power boats of around 1904 and early flying boat hulls in the 1914/18 War.

'Bluebird' was also based in Conway for a time and there ladies entered her spartan accommodation. First my wife for a cruise and then Ken Flather's wife. This was a civilizing experience and gave us a new look. They adapted and accepted, we modified our ideas somewhat, but 'Bluebird' remained without much change. More leisurely and less ambitious plans developed with detailed exploration, such as taking her up the river to Tallycafn. This involved working a high tide over a stretch of river that was part waterfall and part rapid at low water. On the trip back, we drudged back to Conway with the chain on the bottom to give steerage way as we tried to keep in the winding channel. We took the ground frequently and deliberately and occasionally, accidentally but without ill effect.

It seemed not unlikely that the quite usual progress of work, family cares and increased cost of living and decreased energy or enthusiasm, would make the sailing life contract and become of lesser importance, but fate took a hand in my case. Imagine an unseen sniper above the busy crowd, with an armoury of weapons but unknown motivation, capricious, malevolent or just mad. A scattering of bird shot might symbolise an influenza epidemic and buck shot, fever victims or perhaps polio. The bullet from a heavy rifle might wipe out one or two as in a fatal motor accident but the small bore, high power rifle, the precision weapon, releasing a deadly germ on one individual. In those days you had only your own defences if septicaemia developed. Medical help then became almost powerless. In a few days, my wife had gone and I was left with my one year old son for whom I could do little however hard I tried. It is said that not a sparrow falls. I thought long and hard, unable to resolve the conception of religion, faith and random chance in relation to science and medical knowledge. I still do not know that I understand and certainly have no answer.

In 1929, only a year later, Fleming invented penicillin and in the next twenty years, a whole armoury of antibiotics appeared and came into medical practice. Hitherto fatal illnesses are now under quick control, indeed there is the risk of antibiotics being so casually used as to develop tolerance so that they might become ineffective in their turn. Wounds should heal in the body of a healthy subject but much scar tissue may remain. I had help, I had work and travel, many interests, wide reading and a mental and physical escape to the sailing life that was perhaps crucial. It certainly appears that I intensified my interests in many directions.

One such was Alfred who came to me for sailing advice after he had done a single-handed cruise in a hired yacht without previous experience, while home on leave from India. I took him sailing in 'Bluebird'. After a fortnight during which we were never really dry, I realised that he was a man with special qualities. He was unimpressive in physique and appearance, of medium height but light and slight. He was quiet in manner with a deeply buried sense of humour. He had a yogi-like ability to ignore hardship or discomfort, combined with a truly remarkable endurance. This appeared to be as much mental as physical and derived from sheer will power. We had experiences together in various countries as well as at sea. Together we climbed thousands of feet above sea-level in the mountains of New Zealand. He had been high in the Himalayas and loved the solitude of heights as much as that of the sea, where he was an instinctive seaman. He had tried to fly a Moth aircraft back from India, crashed in Persia and walked out alone and twice crossed the Persian Gulf in a Lateen rigged fishing boat. I could tell many tales of Alfred adding up to quite another story. Our friendship grew the stronger with time until he died.

During the years at Tarbet, we saw the declining herring shoals and the transition of the Loch Fyne skiffs from sail to power. Distances on the west coast were given in hours and this was the average time it would take by sea in a skiff with a 15 horse power petrol/paraffin engine. Eventually the boats increased in size, the design adapted to power, the rig first reduced and then disappeared but the Kelvin remained and increased in power. Sometimes spare parts for these engines were used as a form of

savings bank, they were bought in and stocked when fishing was good and sold when times were bad. The way of life in the islands was changing also from the traditional fishing crofter to greater dependence on Government aid. Wrapped bread from Glasgow and tins came in and made a much less healthy diet than the old. The difficulty of marketing produce when the cost of transport to the mainland left no profit, however wonderful the universal service of Macbrayne.

My cousin Beatrix, also cruised with me. She was very young, keen and became a good crew, fitting into 'Bluebird' and learning her ways with an attachment that was to have surprising results. With her, I remember exploring the slate quarries at Easedale, where one old man was still working odd pockets of slate and we collected handfuls of crystals that fell as the rock was split from the pockets in which they formed so many thousands of years ago. Gradually, I came to know the whole area and played the game of swapping anchorages with other people on the coast. At this game, we were years behind the masters, a small band of men who had spent their lives in these waters. There was Botterill of the 'Molly', a G. U. Laws canoe yawl, rather in the Albert Strange manner and through her I met Joe Wells who also sailed with him and other Yorkshiremen who regularly took their holidays climbing, fishing and sailing from the 'Molly'. There was also 'Lynam' (headmaster of a well known school) of the 'Blue Dragon', not the original but the second 'Dragon', a comfortable fishing boat.

In contrast to the west, this coast can show the most idyllic weather and become one of the most beautiful cruising grounds in the whole world. The scenery and the soft colours are superb with the atmosphere that one only finds in northern latitudes. I remember an enchanted evening when a great stag watched us in a wild anchorage from a bluff not forty yards away.

I married Nancy Rundle in 1926 and her first sailing experiences were in such a fortnight. I will always remember a hash of wind in Broadford Bay, and her entering the sole house on one island because, with no other response to her knocking, she had heard noises, only to be bowled over by an enormous ram which charged out of the kitchen. Whether she had destroyed the genetic breeding scheme of years, we never discovered, but friendly relations were restored when the owner returned short of almost all supplies, as the skiff that supplied them had not been out for a month. We sailed one Sunday from a similar island anchorage and, on a commanding rock at the entrance, stood a gaunt wild figure, a magnificent man, his plaid flying and his white beard flowing in the wind. Like a biblical patriarch, his hand raised high, he cried in a great voice, "No good will come to ye who sail on the Sabbath Day".

The day came when I felt the urge to explore further round the coast to complete a circumnavigation. That is a massive word conjuring up thoughts of the world and Columbus or Vasco da Gama but we were thinking only of England! Dick joined me for this venture while he was home on leave from India. He was thin and he had not the same endurance as some of us but he tackled any project and came back for more. Hesitant in speech and manner, with a serious approach that was misleading until you knew him well. We had adventures also in Bombay and together won a tankard, racing 'Tomtits' (a Linton Hope design class of 18 foot open boats) in Madras. He had also learned to fly, he was a Sheffielder and one of six brothers, who is now retired living near to me.

We started from the Clyde. 'Bluebird' had been in Sheffield for a refit and had been sent to Greenock by rail. The start was not auspicious. Busy with preparations and still stowing gear, I ran her on to the tail of the bank with onshore wind and fouling tide. Alfred was with us for a few days and he and I dived in fully clad and, with our shoulders against the hull, we marched her off while Dick sailed her. This grim operation succeeded and having kept a prudent line trailing, we were able to get back aboard. With a yacht as small as 'Bluebird' and only 3 foot draught, this method does work and can be the only way to get out of a messy situation. The next few days would once have been a tremendous adventure but was now pleasant sailing in well-known waters as we worked through the Kyles of Bute and on to Ardishaig through the Crinan Canal, then the tidal boils of the Dorus Mhor to Oban, Loch Aline and Tobermoray. Alfred left us; it was just possible to squeeze a third man into the fo'c'sle but 'Bluebird' was really meant for two. His enthusiasm had brought about a complete clean out and re-stow extending to a 'brighter bilges' campaign. He always maintained that in any yacht, life began and ended in the bilge.

Tobermoray is a gateway to the north. Ardnamurchan -'the great nose' thrusts out and the open Atlantic reaches in through the islands so that there is always the prospect of a stiff passage. This time it was long, hard and wet until we sailed at

Top: My cousin Beatrix Templar enjoyed sailing with me up the west coast of Scotland.

Above: Cape Wrath lighthouse (marked by arrow) from Little 'Bluebird' in a rising gale from the north west.

night into Mallaig, an unattractive place but one of the few rail heads on that coast. We had a day of rest at Totaig, a lovely anchorage inlet from the Kyle of Lochalsh and one week out from Greenock. Dick was ill and rest was indicated. He saw a doctor who said that he might carry on. Skye is magic, whether as scenery with the grandeur of the Cuillins or Dunvegan, the ancient home of the McLeods, with the legend of the fairy flag. The next day started badly. The ferry crashed our dinghy but the elastic construction saved her and we got compensation for a broken scull and minor damage. Our luck changed. We had a fair wind and a glorious rushing sail up the magnificent coast with the last rail head astern and even the Clyde Cruising Club directions had ceased to serve. We turned inland at Rudhriegh Lighthouse and anchored in a bay behind Fura Island. We were well sheltered in that wind but it was a wild place with nothing alive in sight except the terns flying about in pairs with slender drooping wings, their little shrilling cries, plaintive in the dusk. Some swell came in and there was a background noise of surf breaking on the rocks.

The Wrath To Come

Next day, with more wind, we took in a good reef but set a reduced spinnaker and rushed away in a trim that made 50 miles, not too difficult a day to Kinlochbervie, where 'Bluebird's draught enabled us to use a land locked pool instead of a rough and deep anchorage outside. Another desolate impression was enhanced rather than reduced by the little scattered dwellings where small patches of wall enclosed oats and potatoes, all eloquent of a grim struggle against relentless skies and a long dark winter. We bought the last scrap of bacon and a few eggs but that night in the snug cabin, warmed as well as lighted by a gimballed Aladdin lamp, we agreed that there was a fascination we could not explain. With no radio, we had of course no other forecasts and when snugly anchored in a small port, it was often difficult to assess what the state of wind and sea would be out of the next exposed headland. I said, "Today Dick, it is the Wrath to come". A few hours later, I might have wished I had not said that; and so we put to sea in the early morning and found that it was long and short tacks to make our course towards Cape Wrath and that we needed a reef. Some hours went by, we made steady progress but I noticed that the barometer was falling steadily. The sky looked like wind and the wind was indeed increasing and so was the sea.

Let us jump forward some hours and I can describe a very different situation. We had achieved our offing off Cape Wrath, the wind had increased to gale. I had taken in a third reef, the sea was increasing and had come through thousands of miles of open ocean. The barometer was still dropping and there were all the indications that we were in for a very severe gale if not storm from a general northwesterly direction. We were still making progress to windward, the bi-ped rig was doing its stuff, morale must have been good as I have a photograph taken at the time and one can just see the top of Cape Wrath Lighthouse with buoys on the sea and dim as this may be as a photograph, it earns its place in the archives. I suppose that one can say, "Anything can happen once or there is a first time for everything". But what about this one? At that moment, Dick collapsed with the onset of a bout of malaria and a temperature that would have been 105°. This altered the whole picture, not only was I single-handed but I had the responsibility of a helpless man on my hands.

Still making to windward with anxious care, I was glued to the helm. We were approaching a situation well-known from previous experience. Under these conditions, 'Bluebird' did her best, almost hove to, but with a man at the helm dodging the seas as much a possible. Two men sitting to windward in the cockpit, kept a lot of water out with their backs and shoulders and when well-heeled, what came over their heads and shoulders, didn't fall into the cockpit. The other essential way of dealing with such a situation was that the second man went below and pumped. Our massive bronze Beck pump which had been designed as a trench pump for the 1914/18 War shifted about a bucketful with four strokes; the valves were lead balls, rubber-covered in a cage almost unjammable and accessible by two wing nuts. It had a long handle and it demanded the determined attention of a man with some strength but it would keep 'Bluebird' afloat in almost any circumstances. It had already saved our lives in the past, it could do so now and would no doubt do so in the future but it needed the second man. When single-handed, you could steer or you could pump; when you didn't steer, 'Bluebird' shipped more water and it can be readily imagined that somewhere ahead in this situation lay the spectre of exhaustion. A modern yacht would have a wonderful double diaphragm pump mounted in the cockpit where it could be worked by the man at the helm. Also 'Bluebird' had no centre well to collect the water so it was necessary to direct the flexible inlet to the most effective point in the bilge. Here I must confess one of 'Bluebird's' less amiable habits in weather such as this.

The bilge water would slosh up her side almost to deck level so that the berth was saturated and there wasn't a dry stitch in the ship. The engine was quite useless, of insufficient power and impossible to start, unlike a modern diesel which starts reliably except in very cold weather and is of sufficient power.

The situation was serious and I did some serious thinking on my course of action; there was no hope of rescue. In those days we had no radio, there were no fast lifeboats, there were no inshore lifeboats and of course no helicopter rescues so common and effective today. If you got into trouble in those days, believe me it was real and you were on your own. You got yourself out of it or else! The list is almost endless; there were no self-inflating life rafts, no inflatable dinghies and no sea-activated lights. Yes, we did carry half a dozen flares but I have never fired one in anger in the whole of my career. Outboard engines would not be applicable with 'Little Bluebird' but in those days they were few and very dim. An uncle of mine had an "Ole Man Evinrude" and I remember it took about half a day to start it. My original objective would have been Tongue, now some twenty miles ahead but before this could be reached, we should have to round two important headlands, The Stack and Fair Aired Head where no doubt the already tremendous sea would have been even more dangerous where it encountered swift tides. The big question was how much more would wind and sea increase? It was still just manageable but it might so easily reach the point where 'Bluebird' was completely unmanageable, might indeed be overwhelmed by breaking seas and would drift helplessly in upon an almost unbroken range of deadly cliffs. Had Dick been sound, I am almost certain that I should have gone for this option and we should probably have made it but now not only were the odds vastly increased against me but I had the feeling that somehow I must get Dick out of this.

I had, as was customary in those days, no detailed charts but I had of course, studied the general chart with anxious care and I now remembered noticing to the east of Cape Wrath, an inlet called Ballingall Bay. My picture of this was that it was wide open to the north west, a small shallow bay, probably with a sand beach as there was a valley with a river. The river would of course be unattainable with a tidal entrance and no doubt a sand bar and this would have the sea breaking solidly across it. But it was sand not cliffs and when it came to saving life, 'Bluebird' could take the beach and if lucky, running up on a great sea at high tide, might even avoid destruction. But even if I lost

'Bluebird', life could be saved and I could get the helpless Dick ashore. I decided to try this and bore away somewhat to swoop and swerve towards this new objective. As we approached, we also neared the coast to starboard. This was indeed formidable; cliffs with great seas tearing at their base. The thought crossed my mind, "If anything breaks now, in little more than a few minutes, we shall be cast up to destruction", with only the incredible chance of being thrown up into a cleft or crevice from which we could get ashore above the waves but even then with the problem of scaling the cliffs before reaching safety.

At last the entrance to the bay was developing as I had imagined and a little further and it would be a case of choosing my spot; but then near the entrance to the bay on our port hand, there were some scattered rocks. A wild hope leapt up in my mind; was it possible? Working my way across to port, I approached those rocks. Was it just possible? Try it and see - in any case it might be the best place to take the beach. And so, doing my best to choose a spot, I rounded up into the wind, downward of the rocks, lowered the sail and anchored to leeward of the rocks. I let out plenty of chain (thank God I had such an ample length of chain), then I lowered a weight down the chain and finally raked my bi-ped mast as designed for these conditions, (you raked the mast aft to about 60°, took the weight on a pole to the crosstrees and the effect was quite dramatic; the yacht lay streamed true to the wind, did not sheer about and the bow was raised slightly against the oncoming seas). I was able to relax somewhat, get a hot drink and some food, watching uneasily though there was little I could have done had it gone wrong. I was to find that at high water the seas came over the rocks, we had minimal shelter, motion was severe and our hold was marginal. At low water I had to take in a lot of chain as, although far better shelter, the stern would have been in the breakers on the beach. With night, the gale developed as I had feared, (I don't know whether we should have survived our other option) and this continued through the next day and the next night.

On the second day, conditions were improving. If the wind had veered sharply one way, we should have improved our shelter; if the wind had backed heavily, we should have lost shelter though I might then have been able to move into better shelter across the bay but the wind didn't shift much. On this day at low tide, Dick was considerably recovered (he had ample supplies of quinine which, if my memory serves, was at that date the only remedy against malaria). Naturally, pretty fed up with two days of this, we decided that we might make it ashore. We launched our little dinghy and made it - a wet job. We then walked up to a farmhouse where Dick was hospitably received, given a cup of tea and a scone and rested. I walked out along the wild northern cliffs to that strange haunted place, the cave of Smoo. We could not stay ashore long because of the tide and on the return, we carried the dinghy well up to windward behind the rocks, launched her, wet to the waist and head to wind, drifted back to make 'Bluebird' safely.

The next morning we were up early and what a welcome change - there was now the 'after the gale' feeling, still plenty of wind but conditions obviously improving. We got in our chain, made sail, still reefed and put to sea along on long and short legs to windward until we had an offing for the Stack and then at last we could bear away. There was still a great sea and I wrote in my log book at the time, "The sea is so large that 'Bluebird' is almost bewildered in the hollows thereof". But 'Bluebird' was good at this. With her twin rudders, control was excellent and she was fast. A long day passed as we swooped along the north coast of Scotland, offshore until we finally made Thurso Bay and the security of Thurso. What a transformation! For the first time in four days, there was peace. We were still, we could adopt civilised patterns of sleep, food, relaxation, human contact, help from ashore to dry out our sodden bedding and a general feeling of thankfulness. The Pentland Firth might lie ahead; what of it? Just another challenge - 'Bluebird' had survived the Wrath.

Continuing the circumnavigation from Thursco back to the Humber, the Pentland Firth could be an even more formidable obstacle than Cape Wrath. The sailing directions read like a nightmare: quote, "The velocity and turbulence of the sea in the Firth is greater than any other part of the British Isles so that in a strong gale with an opposing stream, the sea is, in places, impassable and even though the wind has subsided it continues to break with violence for some days". This is quite true but it doesn't mean that the terror is constant. Under the right conditions, there is little to fear; I have taken the Firth under sail in yachts three times without undue difficulty. I have also seen it from a battle cruiser when a considerable reduction in speed had to be made as escorting destroyers could not live. In only moderate gale conditions, they were lifting a quarter of their length into the air and pitching their stemheads under. Ken joined us and we walked out to the headland. The scene was quite terrifying and we needed no persuasion to wait another

day. We then made the passage and although conditions had improved, it was a wet and giddy episode as, with two reefs down, we sported with 'the merry men of Mey', one of the more notorious tide rips. At last we gybed round Duncansby Head, the north east point of Scotland. As we entered the North Sea, as at a signal, the sun shone, the wind fell and the sea decreased. Half and hour later we were enjoying a light-hearted sail; reefs were shaken out, the big foresail came up from below and we were able to have a good meal.

The past week had been a struggle against the forces, from the cold wastes of the north and west in which, as we said, "One leap from the relentless jaws", we had dodged at the right moments and escaped. In that relaxed moment, I ignored the 400 miles still to go. In two successive nights, we beat into Lybster and Gardenstown. These entries under sail could be done in 'Bluebird' with a confident crew and they provided one of our most satisfying thrills in their achievement but, they had their dangers. When we saw the entrance to Gardenstown at low water, we should not have attempted it had we known. Provisioning here was a joy. We gave commands and a posse of boys scampered off at our bidding and returned successively with all our requirements, wetting their wee breeks as they waded out to us as the rising tide was spreading its film over the harbour and waking to life the small crabs and little fishes. Fraserburgh erupted with more than 100 drifters and a brief entry made us wish that we had remained at sea. The oily fishy mixture in the harbour and the smell were both revolting. A long stretch without incident brought us to Montrose but I was almost single-handed again; Dick had another bout of malaria and Ken, some severe internal spasms, while I was tired. Fifteen hours sleep was the answer and I could look out on the crew without seeing doom on the face of a Flather or reflecting on the sad wreckage malaria made of Dick. A thirty hour passage took us across the mouth of the Firth of Forth and down through the Farne Islands to Priors Haven at the mouth of the Tyne. We were back in England.

Dick departed. Ken and I sailed to make another night passage to Scarborough. There we secured to a motor yacht. A comfortable lady looked out and looked us over, "Ee dear", with motherly concern, "yer all wet. Yer look fair flummoxed, coom on up and have a good breakfast. I likes me yachtin' in ploosh". We were back in our native Yorkshire. We rounded Flamborough Head to Bridlington. A steady stream of holidaymakers and day-trippers walked up and down the pier. Numerous comments floated down and I particularly remember one of them, "Sithee, it's a yacht. I'm tellin' thee it's a yacht, there's yachtsmen. Yer can tell 'em they've got their boots on". Bridlington was of course a friendly haven, almost a home port with its welcoming Yacht Club and Ronnie Gresham's wife whom we always called Auntie Mabel, who dried us, washed us, fed us and looked after us. The passage to Spurn was fast. There we crossed the track of 'Bluebird's' outward passage in 1924. We had sailed, omitting some rocks and islands, round England, Scotland, Wales and Ireland. The night rushing up the Humber was long and tiring, losing our tide at Hessle. We took the ground and had a brief sleep before turning up to Brough, when we floated in in the morning. We had sailed over 1,000 miles on this venture at a speed of about 4 knots. There was much satisfaction, 'Bluebird' had almost reached the limits, she had also justified her original conception and I had gained enough experience to exploit the possibilities, well knowing now that a ship will usually stand more than the men.

Chapter Four

Experience of Other Yachts, Other Places

The wish for a new yacht was not a sudden decision. It would have been relatively simple to set out what I thought I needed and then look for a suitable second-hand yacht or commission a new design to be built in the conventional way. For a considerable time in parallel with the cruises in 'Little Bluebird', I had been designing, making models and testing them. This was a much more sophisticated approach than previous efforts had been. Meanwhile and in the last twelve years, all my circumstances had changed, not only in age but in experience and ideas. I had a family and my son would soon be at the starting sailing age. My work and responsibilities had expanded. I had more resources but there were more calls upon them. I felt that I had insufficient experience of other yachts of the size that I was now considering. It seemed wise to remedy this deficiency even before I set out my requirements. So for the summer of 1938, with no 'Bluebird' sailing except the last delivery trip with Alfred, I sought other experience.

Trade Wind

I sailed across the North Sea in 'Trade Wind', a sturdy and heavily built 6 ton cutter to a Harrison Butler design with an 8 horse power Britt engine. This yacht might well have been regarded as the conventional equivalent of the one I should have built instead of 'Bluebird' had funds and knowledge permitted at that time. The passage was an easy one with no hard weather and though I liked 'Trade Wind' and had a great respect for her qualities, she had established two things: I ought now to leapfrog this size and go bigger and I thought that her performance did not show enough over 'Bluebird'. In this game, negative knowledge proving what you do not want may be important.

Cariad

I then went up to the Orkneys and joined Frank Carr in 'Cariad', his Bristol Channel pilot cutter. She was a good example of the type. He had bought her and fitted her out to sail the world but never got away. This explained an enormous water tank which did not improve arrangements below. She had a Kelvin paraffin engine with a wing propeller and her gear was virtually unchanged from the original service. Of course to jump from 3 tons to 30 tons displacement (she might have been as much as

50 tons) must have made it difficult for me to assess her qualities fairly. We were a light crew; Frank Carr, a great seaman, had even handled this considerable vessel single-handed and he gloried in 1.75 miles of heavy hemp rope in her running rigging, halliards with multiple blocks, tackle on tackle. These pilot cutters were well known as the only working craft to have a roller reefing boom. The boom on 'Cariad' was 36 feet long, 9 inches diameter and must have weighed more than 1 ton. When this gybed under 2,000 square feet of sail, it imposed enormous stresses on the sheets (again multi blocks), restrained by a massive iron fitting at the outer end of the boom. I found that at some time this had been broken and a 'bodged up' repair was now dangerously cracked. On my return, I designed an entirely new fitting from good quality steel, feeling if I neglected this I might have a life on my conscience.

Christopher Ellis, then a schoolboy, completed the crew. He later became well known for his exploits in 'Theodora', a later, faster and better designed pilot cutter. I was appaled at the sheer labour in this vessel. It took two of us, under Frank's direction, about an hour and a half to get ready for sea and set the mainsail, hoisting the weight of a great gaff and sweating it up with a second purchase. When all this work had been done the feeling of solidity was splendid but the men were panting and the sailing performance was not outstanding. At 6 knots, you seemed to be punching a lot of ocean about, 8 knots would be about the limit with even more commotion. Early one morning in a wind force 4 and some swell, I was alone on watch and put her about. She missed stays. Up came Frank and I found that under those conditions you must first harden in the mainsheet then sail her off until she was tramping fully before sailing her up as the helm went down and finally leaving the foresail aback until she had paid off on the new tack.

We sailed north to the Shetlands, part of the business of this cruise being to meet the old men who still had memories of fishing craft no longer in use and collect models of them for the National Maritime Museum at Greenwich. Frank was at pains to record details before they were all lost and it was fascinating work recorded in his book "Vanishing Craft". Our mission completed and after a call at Symbister House in Yell, we rounded Shetland and sailed south. Crossing the Pentland Firth at night, we came again to Thurso where I left 'Cariad'. I had learned much and I was clear that she was altogether too big and too heavy to work and there was no reward from all those

Left: 'Cariad' - Frank Carr's Bristol Channel pilot cutter.

Right: 'Stavanger' - a Colin Archer type Norweigian pilot boat yacht.

tons of displacement. I did not like inside ballast and this experience had only confirmed that gained from the memories of 'Cerise'. I had now bracketed the size of the target - to use a gunnery term.

Spanish Cruise Avoiding Spain

The next opportunity was entirely due to the Royal Cruising Club. I had been elected to membership (apparently they must have heard about my exploits in 'Bluebird' and invited me to join and 'arranged' the proposer and seconders) and I thought this was wonderful. In those days a sizeable proportion of the most distinguished cruising men were to be found in the Royal Cruising Club. Meeting some of them was a terrific stimulus and this became, as it were, one of the avenues of the sea up which I travelled, making friends on the way. Fate now gave me a lucky break. A casual conversation with Lord Stanley of Alderley developed a strange compact. He was limited by time and wished to cruise to Portugal, an area he had not visited previously, whilst I, also limited in time, sought experience. So would I take his yacht 'Merlin" to some destination from which he could sail her back to England. With 'Merlin" would be his trusted Parsons, a paid hand from Brixham who had been with him for some years and Alfred would come with me, quite happy to have no destination. I had an admiration mingled with amazement for the faith and trust with which Stanley turned his yacht over to me, giving me an entirely free hand and knowing that I had not commanded a yacht of this size and type before.

Alfred and I joined one night at Dover. Stanley was still aboard and we sailed at once. We bashed off to windward, down the channel until we fetched up the Isle of Wight and the race of St Catherine's. The engine was used when it served, until it failed. We then sailed in to land Stanley at Bournemouth Pier, after 36 hours on passage. There had been talk of the far north. The east had been possible but discarded and we were now bound south and west. With no engine we sailed into Poole by day, making an entry that was excellent practice and gave us confidence in handling a strange yacht. 'Merlin' was an honest to God cruiser, designed by Captain O M Watts and built with the best materials by Phillips of Dartmouth. She was 36 foot, 6 inches overall. 29 feet x 2 inches water line, 9 feet 6 inches beam and 6 feet draft. She had a well rounded bow with a very short bowsprit, a long keel and a short tucked up counter. Her displacement would be about 10 tons and she had a Bermudian Cutter rig with working sail area of about 600 square feet. The accommodation was conventional, with Parsons in the fo'c'sle, Alfred and I were in two berths in the saloon and another berth was possible. She had a diesel engine, rare in those days and almost unknown in a yacht of this size. This example was a massive R N single cylinder job about 9 horse power. I could hardly have found a conventional yacht closer to my ideas at that time.

We started work early and devoted the whole day to a thorough make and mend. We inspected and repaired gear, we repaired a sticking valve on the engine. We shopped, sorted, stowed and filled tanks. We went through every locker in the ship to discover what we had, where it lived and what we lacked. When we sank exhausted before a plate of fish and chips at 21.00, we felt that the day had not been wasted, that we were ready to start on a cruise and that we had emerged from the first part of the process known as 'getting to know your ship'. At 05.00, we sailed her out to a light northerly breeze. The day was fine with bands of mist. The land breeze failed and we had to start the engine off Swanage and use it considerably during a day of light westerly winds to which we remained close hauled on the starboard tack. We were bound for Guernsey and the landfall was satisfactory but it seemed unlikely that we could carry our tide there with headwinds. In that case, Alderney was attractive as we had not been there before. We anchored at 19.00 after carefully avoiding the submerged breakwater which really could be a danger to strangers.

It was 05.15 before we were under way next day and soon making short work of the Swinge Channel with a fair tide, though we again had a head wind. The weather was fairly thick while wind and tide put us to leeward for the Little Russel, but instead of accepting our position, we spent forty minutes in proving that we were only wasting time. So we took the Great Russel after all; indecision rarely pays and a late start never does whatever its cause. We were now late on our tide and tempted therefore by the short cut between Herm and Jethou. This was entirely successful and we came to anchor in St Peter Port at 11.00, intending to sail again on the west- going tide at 16.00. In spite of certain deficiencies in our appearance, we were received ashore, given an excellent lunch by General Broadbent, an uncle then Governor, and driven back to our ship. There we found Parsons emerging badly shaken from an interview with a reporter. In the resulting laughter, we went off on the wrong tack at 16.30. It took us 19 hours to make Roscoff after another passage in light headwinds and it was Roscoff only because a

Left: 'Merlin' - 45ft cutter, O.M. Watts design.

Below: 'Dunlin' - a sailing canoe designed for Ken Flather for use on Lake Windermere with twin angle dagger boards.

tendency to fog and a foul tide made L'Abervrach seem quite a long way on. It was now calm and we entered under power. I discovered that the handle saying "Ahead neutral astern", was more comforting in theory than at close quarters. There is however an admirable adjunct to a Diesel motor, aptly called the, 'stop lever'. When you pull this up sharply, the engine stops. It is absolutely dependable, a great virtue, though once done it cannot be undone. In spite of this, it became a favourite method of control. We made fast to the outer pier at 11.30.

After a day's rest, we sailed at 02.15 and I took her out by the small channel to eastward round the Rannic beacon. This seemed the easier exit to me as it is short, the tide sets fair through it and the marks are close while the tide sets right across the longer and more orthodox approach. We called out times and courses until we had fetched up and cleared the outlying marks and could set watches for the remainder of the night. During the morning, we set all our light sails to the first fair wind of the trip and enjoyed a delightful sail along a grand coast. There was some jubilation when we passed through the Chenal du Four and hauled our sheets again for the Goulet de Brest. At least we had cleared the channel and surely we thought, a greater freedom on course might give us better luck with our winds. We had heard naval guns all day and some of the targets were towed in past us. We could not tell whether they had been trying to hit them or miss them! We anchored in the Port de Commerce at Brest at 21.00. We were tired and did not go ashore until the morning. It was a hectic business shopping against time and provisioning the ship on ample lines. We bought charts against the most distant possibility and wrestled successfully with the problem of Diesel oil in small quantities. We staggered back to the ship in a converging stream of packages, hot and bad tempered but we sailed at noon clearing up the shore mess of bits of paper and string and having lunch at the same time.

We had a fair wind and we had caught our tide. The wind freshened and we soon passed through the Toulinquet passage. We set the reaching staysail. The ship liked it. The log spinner began to skitter on the surface as it came down the face of a sea. 'Merlin' was making seven knots and had nearly reached her maximum speed. We had not expected to pass the Raz de Sein on the same tide but now we should make it easily. The general plan had been to cruise to Belle Ile calling at any convenient port as inclination or conditions warranted. From Belle Ile, we had felt that we could start a longer passage.

Portugal or Spain? This had been the jest of each landfall and betrayed our thoughts. Time was short but this fair wind went to our heads rapidly. It was Alfred who first said, "Why not start now?" The logic was obvious and the policy was settled. Within twenty minutes I had completed the business of courses and distances across the Bay of Biscay to Cap Finistere and we had meanwhile whizzed through the Raz de Sein. We tackled the deck and prepared for a long passage by unshackling the chain, stowing anchors and securely lashing all the gear. There was already a tacit understanding that for obvious reasons we should not enter a Spanish port unless there were some real necessity. Spain was Spain and in Spain they had a war. Parsons was not going to be mixed up with that war of theirs if he could help it and this provided some light jests and also a promise that I would not leave him alone with the ship should we finish after all in those parts. My course was set for a landfall on Cap Ortegal and not a course to clear Finistere as it should have been had we meant 'Portugal or bust'. To the extent of some few miles Westing I was temporising with fate and keeping an alternative at hand. The wind was north, north west, force 4. The course on the steering compass was south west by south half south. The night came down. I shall not forget my watch that night.

The unexpectedness of the departure had added a certain thrill to the usual solitude and clarity of mind. A gentle ambition was being achieved as I made a good 6 knots and every mile a new mile south under sail. The compass swinging before my eyes became as dim as the course in my mind. What did it matter? The thing was to keep the mast swinging across the Milky Way. That was important. Important also to keep the wind splitting past my right ear to keep the bubbles hissing happily into the long phosphorescent wake making rhythmic curves across the swell. The ship and I seemed one sentient thing alone and questing on. Eventually I handed over to Alfred and made mysterious marks on the chart reflecting sleepily that it was perhaps as well that no sextant had been left aboard for me to use and with which I should probably have shaken my confidence. I fell into the deep berth and slept magnificently. The enchanted hour of the night had gone. The log has a large bracket covering the entire day. Against it reads: "Light, variable headwinds all day". We used a little engine. We pitched heartily at times. We made some progress and saw many tunny-men; in those days they were under sail. Day watches assumed an irregular and convenient pattern. We moved on a watch each night and fell easily into a sea routine, delightful and quite restful in good weather when compared with coastal cruising.

It was a soft grey day with some light rain and the wind became a dead muzzler on our course. We made the best of it and on the whole deviated to the eastward of our desired track. During the morning there was a panic party. We found that the engine had used lubricating oil at an abnormal rate since Poole and we could find no cause. I had bought a reserve tin but Parsons now found that the normal reserve tank was empty. This was merely a nuisance. Then the galley fresh water pump sucked dry. Thank heaven I had myself seen a four gallon reserve filled. Mentally I worked out daily rations while we struggled to open up the tank and dip it. A hammer was required and I know we all felt that the other fellow was pretty clumsy with it. Alfred remarked that this was called, "Getting to know your ship". I snarled at him. At last the plug came out. We dipped. The tank was, as it should have been, more than half full. It was the pump which had failed. So that was that! But I got a two-foot rule and calculated the capacity of every tank before I felt better. We felt that we had earned our lunch. We drank beer with it but Alfred produced from some secret store a carton of milk purchased in Poole eight days before. This he had nurtured through stages of nauseating ripeness to the consistency of junket. It was quite good. Alfred had his ideas on food. While not exactly vegetarian, some of his dishes were unconventional. My principle was the same in any ship, "If you cannot eat my food, I can eat yours", and I enjoyed most of his concoctions. But not Parsons. As he received an enormous plateful, I detected a certain look on his homely countenance as he retired to the fo'c'sle. A few moments later, a splash overside was followed by the sound of a tin opener and later on, an empty bully beef can was left out where we could not fail to notice it. The hint was taken.

Meanwhile the sky had been getting thicker and thicker and by evening began to look unpleasant. The wireless gave news of a complex depression from the Bay of Biscay to Iceland. Though not covering our area, we calculated from our barometer readings that we should be south of the real trouble. Night came early and pitch black and with it the wind veering sharply round to the north west. It started to blow and at 23.00 we turned out all hands to reef and made her snug for the night. Down staysail, hove to, then we took three half rolls in the mainsail. The gear worked well, the top of a sea came aboard and I scooped a fish up with my hand and landed him but the poor little Garfish got stepped on in the night avoiding the pan in the end. Fish stories are no good anyway; Stanley caught three like this on the way home. For a

time it blew harder but the wind soon began to ease again. It was a good watch and I got a new feeling of respect for the ship as she dealt competently with the only breeze of wind we had met so far. We were already on the best of terms with Parsons but that night as he dealt with the job required in an entirely matter of fact way as if he had sailed with us for years before turning in again, we developed a new regard for him. The landfall came at dawn with the wind backing again to the south west and still pretty hearty. The glass rose and the sky improved rapidly. No need to ask, "Spain or Portugal?" as we slowly closed the land which we had sighted at a great distance. The navigation proved accurate and the time had come for a new decision.

We had some 200 miles of Spanish coast on either hand and we had said that we would avoid Spain. The nearest useful Portuguese port was some 280 miles and was then to windward. Lisbon, whence we could have shipped home, was 460 miles, France was 230 miles away and then lay to leeward. A series of calms or light head winds would make us overdue anyway owing to the lubricating oil problem and I wondered whether I should be popular with Stanley if I committed him, as I should have done, by plumping for Lisbon. We would then have to contend with the Portuguese trades and fail to get home within his time limit. Reluctantly I bore away for France. It was the logical and correct decision but I felt so blue about it that even compliments on the landfall hardly cheered me. A grand run followed and the sunshine soon dried us out, but there was a bad relapse when the wind finished up once again as light ahead, the changes leading up to this had involved a good deal of sail drill but we had made good progress. 17.00, found us wallowing about off Cap Penas where the swell piled up and became confused although we were still far out from the land. There was no escape from this as we had now closed the engine down for good with enough oil in the crankcase to form a last reserve. We had reached a latitude where the sun had power. It was grand to feel it bite but the resulting exposure gave opportunity to an invasion of stinging flies which came aboard in great numbers. The watches were slow and painful with little progress.

The dawn was magnificent as the sun rose flaming into a cloudless sky with heat increasing every moment. The land showed pink and the hills rose in serried ranks with scattered bands of mist across them. The coastline and nearer hills were dwarfed by the distant peaks rising to 9,000 feet and still showing russet streaked snow in the northern gullies. It was a shame that it was closed to us. The waste and futility of war seemed emphasized by our detachment. Into this dawn and these thoughts came Parsons with a grin and some new yarn. It had become customary to exchange such pleasantries in the hours between morning tea and breakfast and I need hardly say how much we valued this unfailing cheerfulness, added as it was to a willing competence. At eleven we spoke to a small power tunny boat and displayed our ensign and an empty oil can. After a heated debate amongst themselves they rounded up nearby. We launched the dinghy and Alfred and I sculled across to them, dodging the numerous tunny lines. There were fourteen men aboard; a pretty tough looking bunch speaking nothing but Spanish. They thought we needed water and it was not easy to conclude a deal in Oleo. They were obviously suspicious but prepared to be friendly, trying us repeatedly with various forms of salute to which I returned what might be called an impartially non-intervention grin. A quart of Oleo and a tunny in exchange for coffee resulted and the atmosphere became more jocular. They started a conversation with noises illustrating war, shooting and other forms of violence above and below the belt. The effect was good as we could not discover their parts in the act nor determine whether they were in the past or the present or whether it was intended as a forecast of our future in Spain. We shook hands all round and returned to 'Merlin'. We never did know whether they were for or against Franco - the whole incident became known as 'Oleo without Imbroglio'.

The day was sweltering hot and glassy calm. A confused swell set in and the motion became maddening. The ship pitched herself into a static coma. The Stem head, at times level with the sea, at times appealing to high heaven. Doors and lockers burst their bonds and an inferno of unpredictable crashes started below. The boom battled against sheet and guy while the sheet blocks beat a devil's tattoo on the deck. The log line drooped inert, the helm had kick but no feel and our course would have disgraced a wounded jellyfish. The magnificent coast made us the more puny and insignificant. Finally Parsons burst out, "She surely do bloody well misrepresent herself". From the worst of this, we were saved by that quart of Oleo. The engine was used throughout with care. There was a set of conditions when sail alone gave us 1/2 knots at 51/2 points off the wind. Power alone would have given about the same on our course but power and sail at 41/2 points off the wind gave us 31/2 knots and it was thus justified. At eleven that night, we were approaching Santander and I decided that we might as well remain hove-to,

as by doing so we should lose little distance and in the morning we should see whether the sky looked more like wind or whether we could repeat the episode of 'Oleo without Imbroglio'. If neither transpired, we might enter Santander and take whatever was coming to us rather than wallow indefinitely.

I took the dawn watch and sat on the foredeck in a soft warm air from the land just sufficient to keep the sails asleep. The jib was aback, the staysail lowered and the bow rose and fell on a more regular swell. As the light came, the stars paled and the shore lights faded. The coast began to come into focus like a puzzle. Suddenly the key piece dropped into place; in the centre, the Royal Palace, standing as a tragic symbol of other days in Spain. A breeze came and though it was ahead, the sky looked less calm. We saw two launches working pots and letting the jib draw as we approached them. Again we were lucky and collected another quart of oil. This time we were within easy visibility of the shore and it was obvious that the crew wished us to be gone, not caring even to await the money we tossed back to them with their empty can. "Via!" They said urgently and we went. "Engleesh good! Roosian no good!" Thus giving us a poor picture of conditions ashore. We sailed 50 miles to make 37 on our course but it was a pleasant contrast with the day before. We sailed over a big regular swell, past Bilbao and on to Cap Machicaco in the evening. At dusk we were not far from ill-fated Guernica which the Germans had wiped out as an exercise in pattern bombing. Light head winds continued through the night.

Parsons turned me out at dawn; I looked out and found that he was heading in past Cap Higuier for Irun, St Jean de Luz being hidden in the haze. "Nearly in", he said with some relief. "Into Spain!" I said, and his face changed. We crawled slowly into St Jean de Luz at 08.00. Alfred's sailing directions were to "keep blue tent open of fat lady". I wonder what he would have said if told that her bearing was 151° true. But in spite of that, we entered and anchored in the outer harbour but the rolling was intolerable so we entered the inner harbour at high water slack and took a mooring indicated by the pilot as he went out. We had been all round the bay, a nice little sail of about 550 miles and we called this, "A Spanish Cruise avoiding Spain". From England, we had sailed about 1,000 miles in a fortnight. We were on time and after fixing up Parsons with facilities ashore and recourse to an English speaking friend, we returned by train. Stanley went out and after adventures in Pasajes and San Sebastian, he returned to Dartmouth via Concarneau, making good 542 miles in eleven days, the cruise being described in his book "Sea Peace". The whole cruise had been successful in spite of the apparent lack of plan. I wonder now whether I should have risked everything and taken 'Merlin' to Lisbon. What would have happened? You cannot go back and I shall never know.

This had been my longest passage, our furthest south, a first experience with a paid hand and a diesel engine. The paid hand was a very good one but at that age and stage, I preferred an all amateur party. You could not fault 'Merlin'. The only possible criticism was that the engine was rather heavy for her and I believe the design had been influenced by this. So far she was the other man's boat that I had liked best. This private verdict has been endorsed by the years. As I write, 'Merlin' is in the Pacific on her way to New Zealand, in the hands of Dr Ronnie Andrews. In spite of trouble with the oil leak and not too easy starting, I was very impressed with the engine. This was the sort of engine I thought for a cruising ship though it imposed size and weight problems.

Rose of York
Still trying to extend my experience of different yachts, I managed a cruise to Brittany in a new and very nice yacht designed by Jack Giles and Partners at Lymington. She was called 'Rose of York'. This yacht, about the size of 'Merlin', was extremely attractive. A little faster and with the indefinable responsive feel at the helm sometimes achieved by the best yacht designers. She was probably a little lighter in displacement than 'Merlin' as she did not have to carry a heavy diesel engine. I think I should have been happy with this design for my next yacht had I not already decided that I must have a yacht somewhat longer overall.

The Lateen Rig
I had of course another life and this had provided opportunities for business journeys and world travel. Even on the sailing side I had been able to find surprises and adventures. I took a chance and went off down the Nile for 300 miles in a small lateen rigged boat, about 22 feet long and half decked. I saw the life of Egypt apparently unchanged from Biblical times; temples the tourist never sees and, though it is hard to believe, found regions where the pestilential touts and beggars did not make life a misery and baksheesh was not demanded. The lateen rig served well in this setting. True it was dependent upon a small boy with prehensile toes, who swarmed up the slender yard to furl sail. Windward qualities were slight but the seasonal wind and the river current

dealt with that problem. There was too much dependence upon the will of Allah, suddenly overtaken by a sand storm and high wind, the crew with one accord fell upon their knees, heads down to the bottom boards and their dirty cotton clothes flapping around them as they prayed. Meanwhile, Allah had to do his best with an unbeliever at the helm. It will never be known whether Allah or the unbeliever saved the vessel as the crew could not possibly retain any compass bearing on Mecca and their cries may have gone out on the wrong wavelength or the wrong beam. In truth the flexibility of the yard which might have smashed, allowed a bend which spilled enough wind to avoid capsizing. I well remember the awesome colour of the sky and the choking sensation. Luckily the storm soon passed.

The East and the Antipodes
I sailed in India, I sailed in Australia, here handling a lovely Shepherd yacht of about 50 foot and a beautiful little Herreshoff design about 30 foot. In New Zealand some racing types and then China and Hong Kong; the fascinating junks in all shapes and sizes. The wonderful battened lugs with the multiple sheet so ably adapted for the first transatlantic Challenge Race by Colonel (Blondie) Hasler, (later for 'Joker' an all Chinese craft). The Yuloh sculling system used may well be more efficient than oars but I have never seen a practical comparison or mathematical analysis that gives a dependable answer. Junks make one think about their lines and construction as well as the rig but what about the huge rudders providing lateral resistance as well as control, capable of being lifted and with holes in them! I love the tale of the western designer who after a long search found an old Chinaman, far gone on opium, who was reputed to be the master in knowledge and design of junks. After days of preparation he at last found a lucid moment and asked, "Tell me honourable and ancient one, skilled and wise in the way of vessels, why are there holes in the rudders of your junks?" After a long and inscrutable silence, the reply came, "Heaven born, they are to let the water through". I compared this with the half round groove in the thick after edge of the best sailing tunny-men of Brittany and wondered, could there be any connection!

In Hong Kong, I met another amateur designer known as 'Cock of the Dock'. He had evolved his own theory and method for producing balanced yacht designs. The result had a rather thick keel but was otherwise normal to the eye. I sailed a long race in his yacht: She was balanced, she could sail and perform well. Taking another opportunity where it offered I went off from

Rockhampton with my wife to an island in the Barrier Reef. The yacht was a 30 foot converted ship's boat. The work was crude but effective with a gaff yawl rig and an old American car engine. We went down the river in the afternoon and into the dusk. The flying foxes came out and so did the mosquitoes. The very sunset was dimmed by bands of mosquitoes, their milliards throwing a shadow over the sun itself as it touched the horizon over marshes where, on other occasions, I had shot black duck; people have doubted this tale but it is true. Anchoring in the night, we had a meal of enormous prawns, three were a large plateful, thick slabs of bread and butter and strong billy tea. This produced nightmares in the greediest member of the crew, a tough Australian. The boat swung in on the tide and took the ground. Heeling at low water, she slid the greedy one off the upper berth. He woke in panic yelling, "Ere, let me out". He clawed his way on deck and was starting to climb the mast when we restrained him. In the morning he was clutching his ample stomach, "Gee I feel crook".

The sail out to the island was uneventful and the weather glorious. For three days we experienced freedom. The island was about a mile long and half a mile wide, with twin hummocks and it was uninhabited. There were wonderful beaches in a bay in which we anchored and some coral reefs. There were mosquitoes and, until we came, they presumably fed on rabbits as there was nothing else but a large population of spiders to help to keep a balance. And what did we do? We sailed, bathed and swam, exploring the reefs and taking all the sun we could stand. After an evening meal, we talked or sang on the beach by a driftwood fire which was intended to discourage the mosquitoes. When tired enough, it was simple to lie down in the sand and sleep, waking up with the sun in the morning to another glorious day. A few oysters could be knocked off the rocks at low tide, we shot a rabbit or two to provide the day's food, otherwise today was like yesterday. It was idyllic but strictly limited in interest, three days had been intended and three days were enough. We sailed back again, reporting to the lighthouse so that we should not be posted missing. When we regained Rockhampton, that little, one street, tin-roofed town was quite the 'bright lights' but, a snake in the gutter, rats in the bathroom and cockroaches nearly as big as the rats (that is an exaggeration though not as much as you may think) were a reminder that civilisation also has its drawbacks.

A different sort of seafaring was a trip up the Barrier Reef from Brisbane to Cairns in an antique tin kettle about 400 tons, which did a sort of unscheduled parcels delivery up the islands. Some stores might be dropped here, a goat there, some shell might be picked up and one or two casual passengers. The accommodation was in the stern where a saloon contained a shaped table with a fixed bench all round it. Behind the bench were several pilot berths. If shut in, these were completely stifling and if open, completely public. Three Australians returning to the north by the cheapest route, came aboard very high and proceeded to get quite drunk. They remained under the weather with brief, more lucid intervals, until they left the ship. The essential convenience was a little house on deck aft with a good sea view. The Master, wearing distinctly informal clothes, had a battered trilby hat which was his badge of office and retained for meals and all purposes; we don't know whether he slept in it. His false teeth fitted him badly and if stirred to utterance, he said, "My word", and avoided trouble. If at all excited, this became, "My bloody oath" and his teeth invariably fell out! Communication was thus limited but he did know his navigation up that dangerous coast and from him I learned the problems and pilotage very necessary for survival in coral areas.

Lymington Gauntlets

I then had a very serious look at the Lymington Gauntlets and had a short sail in one of them. The standard Gauntlet about 37 feet and very similar to 'Merlin' also had a short bowsprit. There was a larger version about 44 foot which I then thought beyond my means but this type would have been my choice. I examined other yachts, new and secondhand but came back to Gauntlet. I had reached the point of decision and also a point of no return. It was so clear, if I were sensible and could find the money, a Gauntlet would have served well but my own design had become a challenge that I could not resist. Of course I convinced myself by a process of supposedly logical reasoning that I was doing the right thing. The die was cast; I had decided to build my own twin keel design once again.

'DUNLIN': A Sailing Canoe

I suppose the idea had always been stowed away in the back of the mind and had never left me since, the rather abortive attempt at a sailing canoe in 1915. Why not build one and find out now what it should have been, a new challenge. I designed one; I could not build it myself as I was too occupied with marriage, business and a world voyage. I must have leaned very heavily on Ken Flather but he built it and made a splendid job of it. Very lightweight skantlings as appropriate for a canoe of this type and the construction known as Riband Carvell. It came out in 1935 and was used on Lake Windermere. Before I give a verdict on it, I must say more about its design and construction. I could not of course refrain from some experiments and so I had twin angled plates instead of a centre plate, this was not an original idea as I had heard of a class of racing yachts in the great lakes of America and Canada which had employed this idea, and though I had no details, apparently it was a success. After all, it was analogous with twin keels, why should it not be equally successful. These plates were not flat plates or flat boards, they were slightly symmetrical foils and they were angled towards the bow at 2° each. The sketch shows both the construction and the location of the plates. The other experiment was due to Professor Lumstrom, a Swede who had produced a controversial but interesting rig which wound round an unstayed mast and, with double sails, opened up to increase the area when running. This had always attracted me but I had always felt that it had lacked a foresail which would surely have made it more efficient. And so in 'Dunlin', we tried this experiment also. We had the conventional Lumstrom mast and sail, a little further aft than usual and then we had a similar mast angled from the bows towards the main mast, with a single sail as a foresail. I think there is a very easy summary to this story. Ample materials of allsorts were readily available and 'Dunlin' was an almost miraculous success. She sailed so well, handled so well and on Windermere gave enormous pleasure for a number of years. Lightly constructed as she was, she literally began to fall to pieces and fell apart in about 1960. The experiment had been interesting, constructive and completely successful. I had learned a great deal from this.

'Curlew of Walney'

My friend and collaborator, whom I could almost call a disciple, with his extensive experience of 'Bluebird' in the 1920's, had determined to build himself a 'Bluebird' but this project, which should have started about 1933, was delayed because he was moving from Sheffield and going to live at Ulverston in Lancashire. He was married and producing a young family; a son Mark and a daughter Valerie. He was starting and working hard to build up a small foundry business of his own at Barrow-in-Furness. So pennies were not plentiful and with all this the project did not get started before 1939 when of course, the Second World War, put a stop to everything and the years after the war were so difficult, that it was 1952/3 before the project came to the surface again. He designed his 'Bluebird' and whilst he collaborated, it was clearly his design not mine. One thing I do remember however, was the stern. Ken found, and he would not be the first designer to do so, that the stern is more difficult than the bow; after all the bow does come to a point but to get a stern which matches the bow, looks nice from all angles, and functions correctly maybe far more difficult and so I did redesign the stern of 'Curlew'. He had nobody to help him; she was built in a barn close to his house and he was lucky to find, and engage, a retired yacht builder who was splendid in his skills but had one defect. He was apt to lift his elbow too frequently with a glass in his hand and bouts of this exercise delayed the proceedings more than somewhat. So that it was 1955 before 'Curlew' was finished. Ken's objectives in the design were quite clear, he wanted a 'Bluebird', a little larger 'Bluebird', but not so large that it lost transport ability and not so large that it was beyond his means; otherwise it would be very similar but eliminating all the defects that he had noticed. When I set out to write this chapter, I had a stroke of good fortune as I was able to get in touch with Mark Flather, Ken's son, then in Sheffield, and he came and spent an evening with me, when we had a delightful time exchanging reminiscences and checking our memories. This was an enormous help with dates and details and he was able to produce for me a photograph and a design which I can now reproduce and they show the vital statistics of 'Curlew'. Incidentally, and it has nothing to do with this tale, I knew Mark's great grandfather, then a very old man in his last years at Bannercross Hall. Mark is now approaching 60 years, he has two married daughters and a pack of grandchildren. If, as is right and proper, they are brought to see me they will be the sixth generation of Flathers I have known. You can't keep them down can you.

Construction was similar to 'Bluebird', double diagonal planking, a flush deck, rudders as with 'Bluebird' with skegs ahead of them. The keels were cast iron this time, they had lead bulbs and Ken's design, according to Mark's memory was for asymmetrical foils. According to my memory, it was symetrical foils, but we both agreed that they were parallel to the centre line. The engine was a Stuart Turner 8 horse power; a well regarded, sturdy, marine engine twin cylinder two stroke and also a variable pitch and feathering propeller. The bow and stern frames were cunning little phosphor bronze castings produced in his own foundry. The rig was Bermudan sloop and the dinghy, knocked up rather hastily and not beautiful, was from the now available marine plywood.

Chapter Five

First Bluebird of Thorne

Design and Building

Having assessed the theory, gained experience of sailing some fifteen different types of craft and decided after all to do it my own way again, a veritable frenzy of design and preparation followed and the result of all this became 'Bluebird of Thorne'.

My first contact with my builder Dunstons of Thorne had been many years before in the dinghy days when Mrs Richard Dunston, then living in the Lock House by the canal, took in two, cold bedraggled men, dried them out and gave them breakfast. That was myself and Ken. The arrangement with Richard Dunston to build 'Bluebird of Thorne' would have made lawyers shudder and businessmen turn grey. In a simple letter, Dunstons undertook to build the bare hull to my drawings and specifications and, subject to my supervision, for a lump sum. Everything beyond the bare hull was a magnificent blank but with the intention that between us we should complete the yacht; they had never built a yacht before, nor had I, or at least not one like this. I was building in steel because it was easier to design in that material to take the stresses of the keels in this much larger hull and also because if things went badly wrong, it would be more practicable to take an oxyacetylene

torch and cut bits out prior to welding up again with modifications. It also happened that Dunstons were twenty miles away from my work which made supervision possible and I think Dunstons were pleased and proud of the first 'Bluebird of Thorne'. I doubt if they made a penny out of her. I never regretted the decision. I had a sound yacht, rugged and splendid value, which served me well for twenty two years until I sold her in 1961. She is still sound and good after over fifty years, thus confounding some of the critics about building in steel.

In the final decisions, size had been the most important and the most difficult. I had started to design a 12 ton cutter and I talk always in actual displacement as a limiting factor. The 12 ton cutter became a 16 ton yawl and 48 foot, to house a Diesel engine, adequate fuel and water capacity, a 9 foot dinghy and a cruising load of up to 3 tons. It also gave me full head room without a coach roof. But the mainsail had become too large for me and my intended crew so I had the yawl rig which I never regretted. I now consider that the size was correct and it has stood through another vessel, while several of my experienced friends, after making voyages in similar yachts, have finished up with similar dimensions. The engine decision had been made after careful reasoning. I wanted not less than one real horse power at the propeller per ton of displacement. Effective under starting and simple maintenance, the propeller must feather so that the yacht could sail. I haunted lorry parks on frozen winter

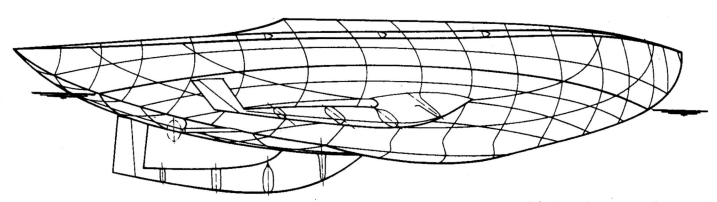

John Lewis's isometric drawing of the first 'Bluebird of Thorne' 1939.

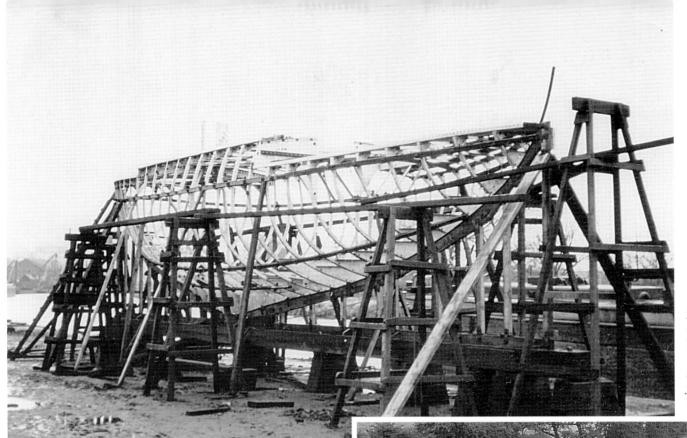

Left: The frame structure - first 'Bluebird of Thorne'.

Below:- The complete frame, first 'Bluebird of Thorne'.

mornings to watch and enquire as the not so common heavy diesel lorries of 1937 had their struggles. There was fortunately a clear verdict: Gardner for starting and also for reliability and economy. The fact that this series of engines had originally been designed for and from marine engines was decisive. This led me to Gardners of Patricroft, Manchester, and my friend Houghton steered me through all difficulties. How nice it is that after more than fifty years, that I can still say I would lean over backwards to have a Gardner diesel in any yacht of mine.

The Trial Cruise

There is a special mixture of thought and feeling when a new yacht starts out on her first passage. There is relief in escaping and the hope that all the months of work will have been worthwhile. There is the excitement in discovering if the design conception has been correct. The handling of a new vessel has to be learned and this may be very different from the last. There is trepidation with the unfinished state, the list of things still to be done and some doubts as to whether everything will work at all or as intended. Finally, and in my case, invariably on such occasions you are bound to be tired, if not exhausted. All this applies even when the yacht has been bought or produced in a conventional way. How much more so when it has been literally a personal creation.

'Bluebird' sailed out of the Humber on one bright morning, heeling to her brand new sails as we headed north at the number 2 Binks Buoy. Fifteen years earlier, 'Little Bluebird', as she had now become, the first twin keel yacht, had left the Humber heading south. It was a glorious day and we did not waste it, throwing ourselves on the gear, setting and trying new sails, adjusting, testing, whipping and splicing, while 'Bluebird' looked after herself and displayed perfect manners from the outset. Behind us lay the muddy waters of the Humber and the smell which had hovered over us during our stay in Grimsby. Gone were the efforts of the past six months culminating in the last ten days when we had worked all day and half the night before we slept in the carpenter's loft with the rats scampering around us. It had been good fun in parts and would never be regretted because we did know something about this ship. "Scene in Indian Bazaar", Alfred had said one sweltering afternoon over the writhing bodies of eleven men all trying, like ourselves, to work in the saloon. Behind us lay the compass adjusting, the stowing of stores and our only spasm of anguish over Diesel engines in sickness and in health. Ours was not to give us a moment's anxiety henceforward.

I hoped that a passage to North Wales would not be too strenuous but would give a chance to find out what this 'Bluebird' could do, while I learned to handle her, but I had charts aboard for Denmark, Norway and Ireland. You never know! Christian came by right of suffering the previous year. Alfred was there to see what I had produced and compare it with his 'Little Bluebird'. Lance had been a helper in the design stage, his experience was of small craft but he was an engineer and a metallurgist and had applied this specialised knowledge. From pure enthusiasm he had done checks on my design with stress studies and calculations on the keel and rudder structures, mast and rigging. This had not shown up anything ugly but had been an invaluable safeguard. We sailed at midnight carrying mainsail and staysail only. This was sheer prudence that first night for we had not steered her running in a seaway and did not want to have more than one man on watch. The breeze freshened and we made up to 6 knots very comfortably. The steering bothered us until we found that the trick was to avoid moving the tiller, after that it was pretty simple. A rather cheerless morning turned into a fine grey day with the wind falling away. It had given us a famous shove but we had to start the engine in the afternoon to take us into Boulmer Haven. The name describes the place which appeals to me strongly. I can hear now the booming of the sea on the reefs that run up to a mile off shore. It is a curious haven, it looks so dangerous and exposed at high water, when there is no apparent shelter, yet it is so completely snug when the falling tide uncovers a ring of reefs all round the little lagoon of clean sand. It is so admirable for 'Bluebird'. She dried out and sat upright in the midst of the cobbles that alone use the place. Any deep-keel yacht would avoid it like the plague. Plague it was for us: Lance learned that his small boy had diphtheria. Was he carrying any infection? For a few days he took his simple meal from a selected mug.

Next day on passage up to the Farne Islands, we deliberately plugged into wind and sea under power until in a tide rip we were taking heavy water over the foredeck. Christian, determined as ever to miss nothing, took a dollop of cold North Sea straight in the face. This produced the characteristic scream that she reserves for such occasions, admitting that it is only when someone else is there that she screams and then not for anything deadly serious. In exactly the same way, the Skipper may swear profusely when trivial incidents are annoying but she says that he never does so when something really serious happens. After this test, we knew how far we could maintain steerage-way and control and the performance we could expect in an emergency from the engine alone. It had not faltered and I was quite pleased with the result. We were thankful when we had made sail and the pitching which had been quite excessive, became almost unnoticeable. I had a watch below, the others reporting a magnificent sail past Berwick and up to St Abbs, where she was going like a train on a long port tack away from the land with all working sail and number two jib. I think it was that night we felt the touch of a frozen north. It seemed to be getting colder, greyer and more inhospitable with every mile we made. We all found the night trying as it continued with more or less head wind and sea, until we made Aberdeen for breakfast. Next day was a rather nasty-looking morning with cold rain.

In the evening, we took a tram to go uptown from the docks. At our enquiry for bath and meal, the conductor recommended us to apply to the Missions for Seamen, "But they'll not take ye", he said with a dour look at Christian. Bypassing this suggestion, we fetched up at the Station Hotel where our needs were attended to but when the bill came, I emptied my pockets and put the contents on the table: a knife, some marlin, a shackle pin, a screwdriver and other bits and pieces. The Manager was alerted and the staff were closing in preparing for the worst, when having staged this deliberately, I produced a £10 note. Their faces were a study and it must be admitted that from the conductor's reaction, we were not a very smart outfit. The grey mariners had a good evening in the granite city.

Cold head winds with patches of fog were our lot all the way up the coast and across the Moray Firth, but as we approached Duncansby Head, there were realities to be faced. These were no conditions in which to find ourselves at the eastern entrance to the Pentland Firth and tide and time would not serve. We found a gap in the fog and crawled into Lybster, which I should not have risked had I not been there before. Once inside it was ideal; quiet, sheltered and quite clean. Taking the ground every tide, gave us a feeling of superiority as the fishing boats lay over on their bilges and 'Bluebird' remained serenely upright. Alfred had worried us that day by crawling away into the stern, with a blinding headache, to be alone. Unfortunately he had not told us and we thought he had gone overboard, actually putting the ship about to start a search before he was found. The day was promising but Alfred had a high temperature. We could rule out sunstroke; frostbite was suspected as the weather was so bitterly cold, so we gave the doctor a free run to see whether he would diagnose

First 'Bluebird of Thorne' in Aberdeen harbour.

diphtheria. No cause was found for his condition and it is all too probable that this was perhaps the first onset of the brain tumour from which he died some years later. Lance heard here that his boy was on the mend. Meanwhile, the day passed by with useful jobs. The doctor's wife showed us with pride that she could grow almost all the plants and vegetables she had been accustomed to in the south of England and was scathing about her highland neighbours, "They won't even try and they won't believe it when they see it. It had never been done in Caithness so they must be right". Alfred seemed better and yearned for warmer climes. In vain we told him that the cold winds had swept as far as Italy; he followed them. That twenty-four hours delay had allowed a north westerly gale to become well established in the Pentland area. We sat tight, having no real choice in the matter if we wished to be prudent. Pentland would be unhealthy, imagination was not necessary as I had actually seen what the swell could do when it tripped on the tide and burst into a chaos of broken water. The barometer fell 0.4 inch in twelve hours. We began to want to get round that corner. Northerly gale warning for all Scottish coasts. "How far is it to the Caledonian Canal. They say that it is closed for repairs!" At 21.00 the forecast was the same. Is the radio a good thing? This was getting serious.

After five days in Lybster, it was still cold, still blowing but looking brighter. We are getting nervous. Something must be done. We sailed at 06.30 before we could hear the weather forecast. Outside we found a really noble swell with a top on it and quite enough wind. We logged force 7 in the squalls. 'Bluebird' climbed comfortably over this under mainsail and staysail with the engine turning over about 600 revolutions with half throttle. What a blessing a really solid, slow-running engine is. Without fuss or bother, we made really effective and pleasant progress to windward in this trim but we could not carry the correct tide for the Pentland, so we went into Wick and secured to a massive Swedish fishing boat. We received a cheerful blonde welcome and after listening to the Swedish forecast, they said, "No weather Pentland!" whenever they saw us on deck. If that massive Swede, two Greenland trawlers and a coaster could not take it, we felt it was not our turn to play, though Wick was inferior to Lybster. At the start of the cruise, 'Bluebird' had felt enormous. Already she seemed more our size but the Swede made us look like eggshell china. We held another council and decided, "Unless we make Pentland tomorrow, we must run back to the Caledonian Canal". It was open after all! The Swedes said, "Hungry and expensive time".

On Monday morning the world had changed and it did not need the abdominal rumblings or the smoke rings from the wide exhaust of a 100 horse power, single-cylinder Bolinder to tell us that our luck had changed. The whole harbour prepared for sea and we made our crash start at 10.15, a little later than I cared on the tide. By using the engine, we got off Duncansby by 11.00 and were off St Johns an hour later with the ebb slackening. This gave us a perfectly smooth passage (by the inner sound), but off Dunnett Head, it was by a small margin that we beat the first of the flood. We had made the corner but we must now force a passage to the west coast. A lazy swell came in from the north and light winds from north to north-west filled all our working sail. We used the engine as necessary to maintain speed and to catch our tide at Cape Wrath. The day was crystal clear, too clear to mean good weather but it was magnificent. The whole wild and majestic coast of Sutherland was visible. We could see from Cape Wrath to Dunnett Head, some fifty miles away. The background of the Western mountains rose slowly higher as the Orkney Islands sank into the sea. The sun dipped at 22.30 and it was still quite light when we rounded Cape Wrath at midnight, just saving our tide and we were able to read a paper easily. Another vital corner lay astern but within an hour of our alteration of course, the wind came up from southward. Dead ahead! It veered a little during the day and we had a lovely sail beating down inside Skye through Rona Sound and on to the comparative civilisation of Kyle Akin. There we nosed on to the sand alongside the jetty to ensure a quiet night. This breakthrough had brought us 190 miles by the log in thirty-four hours. It had put us in waters where yachts were seen and where Christian and I could carry on by ourselves if need be, or where another crew could join us. It allowed Lance to catch the early train the next day and land him back at work on time.

We were too busy to miss the crew and a gale forecast did not tempt us out. The evening brought news of a new crew and we enjoyed the beauty and warm friendliness of a coast so different from the east. By this time, Christian and I knew that we could handle the ship, though we should probably have finished up on the Clyde if we had not had help. Derek joined us that afternoon, it would have been pretty grim without him in the weather that followed. It was now Friday and it did not look the best day in the whole cruise. We sailed her out of the little pool to show Derek how she handled but there was so little wind that we motored to Kyle Rhea to use the whole of the fair tide from the narrows. The clouds were low on the hills and it rained gently until we cleared

Left: Robin Balfour in Naval uniform, his brother
Francis Balfour in the army 1939.

Below: The sinking of the aircraft carrier 'Ark Royal'
near Gibraltar.

the Sound of Sleat. The wind then came in from the north-west, the sky cleared and the sun came out. We set the Genoa (for the first time for ten days) and began to enjoy ourselves. It was simply heavenly to romp along under the nice conditions, working up to the best sailing speed of the trip. Off Ardnamurchan, the swell piled up, as it always does, and she danced through it at over 8 knots with a rainbow in the bow wave and steering beautifully. She must have made a lovely picture and we wished we could have captured it for the memory. The Genoa had to come in when we turned into the Sound of Mull but we ran on, ignoring the foul tide. We reached Loch Aline just as the ebb was making in the entrance, but beat in to this snug and beautiful anchorage as a fitting end to such a glorious day.

On Saturday, just beating the onset of the next gale, we made Oban, where we picked up Pringle and spent another day in one of our old anchorages beyond Kerrera Sound. Christian sailed the dinghy for the first time, trying out the lungstrom rig. It was a great success. Here I developed a not very serious hope that we might get a slant of wind that would take us quickly to the west of Ireland but this was abandoned at dawn with the next south-westerly gale coming up, a seasick crew and especially filthy seaway, so we turned back to Portrush. Our next port was Larne, which we entered in the early morning hours of Wednesday and the log that day reads, "An utterly beastly day, high winds, rain, low scud clouds, rotten forecast, evening fog". On Friday we battered our way to Donaghadee Island. Saturday was our last official day of holiday. I sailed, announcing to the crew that I would take her to the Clyde or to North Wales, whichever the wind best served. Christian maintained that it would be a head wind both ways and the forecast was so uncertain that she could well have been right. But we had a good passage and closed Anglesey in the evening. As we roared along the coast from Lynes Point, an object rushed by in the night. Only later did we find that this was the mark buoy for the wreck of the submarine 'Thetis', which had been lost with all hands, save one or two, while on initial trials, owing, as I remember it, to a tragic chain reaction commencing with a simple test-cock which was blocked up with paint. The weather news surpassed itself with storms, flood, cloud burst and havoc by land and sea. Yachting abandoned, they announced. It was not easy to take 'Bluebird' into the Menai Straits by night and I was relieved when we anchored safely at Beaumaris.

On her first passage, 'Bluebird' had been tested up to a point and so had we. In three weeks she had travelled from her builders on the other side of England and in that period there had been eight gale warnings for our area and more than our share of head winds. This 'Bluebird' had never frightened us or worried us, however weak the watch or the crew. There were no serious defects, no alterations were demanded, she promised well. We felt quite a sense of achievement in spite of, "No weather Pentland!"

The balance was so perfect that it was positively uncanny; she would sail herself under almost any conditions and her behaviour could perhaps be best illustrated by two incidents. When a crew member strange to her took the helm, he would tend to treat her like other yachts he had known, expecting to waggle the tiller back and forth to some degree. After watching him for a while, I would be impelled to intervene and say, "Put the helm amidships, take your hands off it, leave her alone, she will do the job better than you can". The other feature was that in any condition of wind, sea, angle of heel, wind direction and set of sails, she would as it were, find her groove, settle into it and maintain it regardless. From this all you had to do to get the best results was to see that the trim was adjusted so that her groove was in conformity with your desired course. This may sound like a dream of heavenly bliss but alas it was confounded by a less desirable feature. With two large and heavy rudders, the long tiller had been so connected that it moved about half the angle of the rudders. This avoided the undesirable sweeping of the whole cockpit by the tiller but it had produced a completely dead and unresponsive lack of feel. I later reduced the size of the rudders and reduced their weight and this caused some improvement without altering the characteristics. The yacht herself was amazingly safe and seaworthy and her balance characteristics contributed to the fact that I was able to have single-handed watches in almost all weather by day or by night, even with unskilled crews, surely a tremendous plus factor. I must, however, mention another feature which is controversial. In extreme conditions such as running before a really dangerous sea, if a sea picked her up, carried her and threw her down at an angle of perhaps 15° from her previous course, she would not respond and try to regain her previous course; she would just carry on in the direction in which she had been placed. Once aware of this, the man at the helm naturally corrected for it as swiftly and even violently as he could but I think this feature was definitely more minus than plus. I had gained enormous knowledge and experience, I had a yacht which was and remains extremely safe and manageable and already I was beginning to form opinions on what I should try to achieve if I ever designed and built another 'Bluebird'.

The war was imminent; not long after the end of this cruise 'Bluebird' was laid up with Morris & Leavett at Gallows Point, Beaumaris, hauled out in the open and there she remained for six years.

When I took the decision to build, I had anticipated war and it had affected my reasoning, "I may as well put my shirt on this yacht", I thought. "If there is a war and I do not survive, it will not matter. One cannot see defeat but in that case it would not matter either. If it is victory and I live and life goes on ostensibly as before, everything will probably cost double and it would then be impossible to build". This was good stuff, I turned out to be far-sighted and correct but I had overlooked one important factor. "Bluebird' might well be requisitioned or smashed up or lost. While in Naval Service, I happened for a time, after Dunkirk, to be in the Small Vessels Pool and I heard that 'Bluebird' had been twice inspected and considered for requisitioning. The first time she was turned down because she was considered too slow and underpowered with a 6 knot maximum speed. On the second occasion, the twin keels frightened them off and so by the pure accident of her peculiar design, 'Bluebird' had been preserved.

Chapter Six

A Cruise Round Ireland

RCC award the Romola Cup 1946

The war was over. It was 1946 and I was no longer a 'temporary' gentleman. A lot may happen in six years but that is almost a book which I have written up elsewhere and I need only say that, imagining myself in a reasonably small craft at sea, I found myself in large craft attached to the Fleet Air Arm and then very little at sea. I had not seen my family for four years. All were alive and well but I had to get them together and start up a home again. Jack Hope, my brother-in-law, had been killed in the air over France. My business was difficult and there was a vast amount of work required. I was also threatened with Public Office, deferred from before the war. All in all, 1946 was a year of great strain and one which I would not like to repeat. Somehow in the middle of all this, 'Bluebird' was put together and launched from Gallows Point. Her simple and rugged construction had already paid dividends and she was unharmed. Morris & Leavett had done well and 'Bluebird' was one of the first yachts out that Spring.

Going foreign would have been difficult so why not the Ireland I loved so well? Away we went once again, making for the southwest corner of Ireland. Ken came almost as a matter of course. For Christian and myself it was the first holiday together for seven years; I had married Christian Hill in 1933 and this was her first real sailing experience. Henry, an enthusiast with ocean racing experience, who had recently been navigating on an aircraft carrier in his temporary Naval career, accompanied us. We said that he was only there out of curiosity to discover whether 'Bluebird' compared with the ocean racers he had known and whether she sailed forward or only sideways. There had been debate to discover whether we went round Ireland clockwise or anti-clockwise. Previous experience had indicated that Ireland was a square sort of island with a head wind built in at every corner. "In that case", we said with a certain amount of logic but some probability, "It will be the same either way". Sure enough, approaching the south east corner at the Tuskar Lightship, the usual depression came in with a southwesterly wind increasing, cold, heavy rain, bad visibility and falling barometer.

We laid our course for the Coningbeg Lightship and drove her hard to make Waterford as soon as possible. It was really one of the grandest sails of the cruise, though we did not appreciate it fully at the time as conditions were rather beastly and on that first passage there was some seasickness in the ship. It was a rough ride. Under staysail, mainsail and mizzen, she put her rail under and worked up $7^1/4$ knots for two consecutive hours at five to six points off the wind. No Coningbeg and sail had to come off her. We handed the mizzen, reefed the staysail and ran for Waterford, thankful that it was a reasonably safe coast to fetch up under those conditions, but now so trimmed that we could beat out if necessary. We averaged our course by gybing periodically as the sea was too awkward for a dead run. Time passed. The visibility was worse, we sighted nothing. Henry and I agreed that this sort of thing was an excellent passage when it was over but we should be delighted when and if we made a correct landfall. It was about four hours since we had dropped the Tuskar and we could not help wondering whether we had altered course correctly. Our D.R. placed us plumb on the Hook Head light. A few minutes later it loomed enormous in the murk, right on the bow and only half a mile away. With such visibility, the failure to sight Coningbeg was not surprising.

We ran up river against the ebb to Ballyhack and there anchored. On another occasion, with more local knowledge, we should take 'Bluebird' into the little harbour of Passage East. We were glad to be in shelter. There was a gale that night and one of our neighbours dragged half a mile downstream, but we were secured. When the gale was over, we sailed to Youghal, a new port and a nice one, and entered under sail with a band playing on one hand and a Corncrake sounding off on the other. This quite tiny place had provided 148 men for the British Forces and 46 had been lost. It was Admiral Cunningham's home which might explain these amazing figures, but Ireland had provided immense numbers to fight in our war. In contrast, and in my sphere, when a Naval aircraft came down in Eire, the instructions were the same as for enemy territory - "Destroy everything at once", as it was said that information on any secret equipment would be in German hands within a week.

A more amusing tale, but I cannot vouch for the truth of this one, was told of Donegal. When, on my lawful occasions with the Fleet Air Arm, I flew into Londonderry, it was possible to cross the border in civilian clothes and have a pleasant evening in a different atmosphere with a very warm welcome and unrationed meal at Buncrana on Lough Swilly. A naval companion and I did this two or three times. It was said that a party of Fleet Air Arm

Officers on one occasion found another party in progress and it transpired that they were officers from a German submarine sheltering in the Lough and enjoying the same amenities. From experience in 'Little Bluebird', I knew that Lough Swilly could have been a magnificent hideout for an 'Unterzeeboat'.

The butcher's shops had a fearful fascination for Christian, with the knowledge that one could walk in and buy a whole sheep at will. We devised a joint of our own, which was practically square and just filled our pressure cooker. Under Christian's manipulations, what became known as a 'Foregripe' of mutton, gave us at least three meals for all hands. The afternoon passage was as perfect as the morning. We set everything we had, including the mizzen staysail, took photographs and revelled in the conditions which were to be all too rare. Approaching Kinsale, we tested her with the genoa close hauled in a freshening wind making 7 knots and watching the mast for any deflection. The beat into Kinsale was practically a repetition of the entry into Youghal but was, if anything, more intricate. We discovered the best rig for this kind of nonsense to be the big number one jib and no staysail. With this, we had an effective area, a head sail which set magnificently on the wind and only one pair of sheets to handle when short tacking in a narrow channel. The day ended with a laugh on Henry. He was piloting us to a berth with great accuracy. I knew the harbour, and without a word to Henry, I gently edged her on to the mud. His dismay was comical; court marshal might have been threatened.

Kinsale is delightful and we loved once again the picturesque charm and repose. We were told that, in the past, the fishing boats had been so numerous that you could have walked across the harbour on their decks, but time had passed by. Tourism, new residents from England, an air service to London and the deep sea fishing launches, all lay far in the future. I was offered a lovely house on the harbour for less than £1,000; today that house might well be £100,000. But nothing is a bargain if you cannot use it and still less if the money is not available. From this point onwards, we were generally the first English yacht since the war in most of the small places we entered. The Blue Ensign seemed to cause a good many questions. It apparently gave the impression that we were a Naval outfit proceeding incognito. We tested this by entering alternate ports without wearing our ensign. There were fewer questions without it. We never found any reason for this rather curious attitude but nothing marred the friendly and helpful welcome we received everywhere and I made friends in the ports I had known previously. Leaving Kinsale we worked along the south coast and at one point found ourselves almost becalmed in Stags Sound. There was a strong tide and sudden fog shut down the visibility to 50 yards. A fishing boat crept past heading home. I set course deliberately for the nearest and clearest large rock and Ken went forward as lookout but not knowing my intentions. A startled yell came from him as a mass of rock loomed up all too close. He came aft, a shaken man, only to be told that this was exactly what I wanted. We heard him muttering, "I wish we were back where we knew where we were and then we should know where we are".

I could now set another course for Kedge Island which we must fetch up on the starboard bow as sawtooth reefs lay between it and the mainland. After this landfall, the fog lifted and we made Baltimore without difficulty and there we picked up mail. I discovered that Mark had embarkation leave and hoped to be able to join us in a few days. The morning was occupied by a series of telephone messages passed by the kindness of Father McCarthy at the school, through the Police Barracks and so to an expectant world. We found here, as elsewhere in Eire, that any post office would have a personal interest in our welfare and take endless trouble to obtain relay messages from other places so that we never failed to collect news from home, though we might be far from the mail address we had given.

We had a fascinating day, sailing in varying winds, mostly ahead, through Gascanane Sound and across the mouth of Roaring Water Bay and among the islands and rocks. In the afternoon, we had a sudden shift of wind; it banged out of the northwest and blew fresh. We were carrying the big number one jib but as there was no sea and not far to go, we carried on and drove her in a magnificent beat for the remaining distance into Crookhaven. We hired a boat here to save launching and hauling up our dinghy, with the advantage that the shore crew acted as runners to put us in touch with all we might need without delay. Crabs came in from one quarter, a hen made a welcome change in our diet, a bottle of Irish whisky replenished our diminishing store and gems of picturesque description entertained us the while, but our guide's vagaries caused many delays and he got drunk in the process. That night the wind screamed through the harbour and the squalls bounced off the rocky hillside. The till in the pub was stiff with notes of foreign currency, principally U.S. dollars. The sons and daughters of Ireland, spread about the world, sent funds home to the old people. These contributions added up to millions and without them, Ireland's balance of payments might have gone bust. Here as elsewhere, we found that any enterprise which seemed to have life or success in it was usually headed up by a Scotsman, an Englishman, a Cornishman or even a Frenchman. We wondered why this was so when the sons of Ireland were doing so well in foreign lands and yet there appeared to be such apathy at home.

There was a strong westerly wind. The next passage was significant as we must reach Bantry to change crews as planned, and who knew what the morrow might bring; so we went about the business of reefing down and preparing for sea in rather more serious mood than usual. Henry was obviously revelling in the prospect but as he cleared the deck and lashed everything more securely, he said, "This little ship is going to take an awful beating". We sailed under reefed main and reefed staysail, giving us an area of some 450 square feet against our working rig of 850 feet. It was exactly the right canvas for the conditions and she made a lovely job of it, beating out round the Mizzen in a man-sized sea, 5 points off the wind at some 5 knots. We took some water on the foredeck but I wish one of the seven big trawlers, which passed us as they ran in, could have taken a photograph. At last we could check sheets and make 8 knots past Dunmanus Head to Castletown Berehaven. There had been no "beating", "no drop she would take aboard her that would wash a fly away". At that moment, a crest struck and we had the cockpit half full. Of course this caught Christian; the unexpected splashes always came her way: - another scream!

Walking up the hill road out of town in the evening after market day, we encountered a string of ass carts and on each of them, one or two recumbent figures, drunk or asleep, while the patient moke plodded them home. This time we ran up to Glengarriff and Bantry to meet Mark and have an 'interlude', as Christian called the rather rare times when we had one or two days at leisure in one place. Ken left us but did not return home without further adventure. Somehow a passport had not caught up with him which had not mattered at all to us but when he tried to board the boat at Dublin, he was stopped and a typical Irish situation developed. "Because you haven't entered Ireland officially, you are not here, so how can you leave?" "But I am here", said Ken. "How do we know?" said officialdom. "What can I do?" Asked Ken. Then the Irish answer, "If I were you, I should go the Yacht Club, ask if anyone is sailing to England and go with them. Then we shall never know that you were here!"

This utterly logical remedy could only have been produced in Ireland, and so it was. Ken volunteered to crew a small yacht, and after an interesting passage and finding himself overdue for a family party, he was rowed ashore one early morning in Anglesey. The English bureaucracy was efficient and less logical. They traced him, arrested him and threatened him with dire penalty or durance vile for illegal entry and possible drug smuggling offences. He escaped with a stern warning. I found the mistaken British efficiency as compared with the Irish illogical inefficiency, quite delicious.

Digby joined with a calor gas cylinder and a ham. He lived at Ballylickey but his burdens had both taken a deal of organising. I had encountered Digby when he bought 'Trade Wind' from the friend with whom I had crossed the North Sea in her years before. We met up with the jovial and hospitable Paddy O'Keefe, the King of Bantry. "If you want anyting, sure and the world is yours". He was as good as his word, anything we could not get, he produced at once. He owned 'Sheila II', one of the best of the Albert Strange canoe yawls and in later times, this same 'Sheila II' was sailed single-handed to New Zealand and I encountered her again in the Swan River in Western Australia. Mark, on unexpected leave from the Navy, joined us with Edward, a friend of Digby's who was making gliders. Their bus from Cork pranced into the square with a panache more like a four in hand coach. The driver and all passengers were very merry from libations taken at every stop on the way.

I had expected that the long beat out from Bantry to Dursey might take two days but a rare calm and the motor saved a day, though fog made Dursey Sound difficult to find. Once entered however, it was so narrow that the fog hardly mattered. Once again and now with wind, we sped across to Derrynane. Christian, catching a remark not intended for her, heard Edward say to Digby with genuine astonishment, "But she sails". The critics must have been working on him. We emerged suddenly from fog into sparkling sunshine and by contrast the wonderful display was of dazzling and unforgettable beauty not lessened by the relief of the navigator; thus, Christian was introduced to my favourite place in the whole of the wild west and she was not disappointed.

After another short interlude, we sailed this time to Dingle under easier conditions to sound our way up a channel and anchor in the largest fleet of fishing vessels we had yet seen. We had the choice of taking the ground by a quay or anchoring and here we dried out so that Digby and Edward could inspect 'Bluebird' and see the keels. We were now five aboard which was unusual for us but easily accommodated. We were approaching the halfway point and I could begin to compare this cruise with the one in 'Little Bluebird'. Ireland was still Ireland but there had been no repetition of the rather odd or psychic incidents. We were far more comfortable, drier, better housed and well fed. Perhaps like the mediaeval religious fanatics, scourging and suffering is necessary to make you dream dreams and see visions. The size and power of this 'Bluebird' made seas seem smaller, the wind less strong and passages more certain, while the engine, more necessary perhaps in a larger yacht, was a tremendous asset. With the wireless we received weather forecasts but it became evident that out in the west we were in the area from which the forecast came. Time after time we were already experiencing the weather predicted in England, so we still had to interpret our meteorology in the light of our own experience and the general inference. The wind force was usually greater than predicted but perhaps the exposed coast and the effect of sea and swell contributed to this impression.

I now wished to make a direct passage to Galway whence Mark could return and this would put a rather uninteresting and potentially dangerous stretch of coast behind us. Beyond Basket Sound, with a light wind, we encountered a growing swell. Somehow this is always ominous. Around midnight the gale arrived with a bang from north west. The log entry is expressive: "Reefed staysail on deck then reset. Handed mizzen and jib. Hove to and reefed main. Smashing into increasing sea". With this powerful 'Bluebird', there was no thought of seeking shelter in Shannon as I had done before. Later in the night with a now serious gale we hove to again and took the second reef in the main. It was the first time we had done this and it took us down to trysail area. It was not easy to do but it was satisfactory to find that she hove to perfectly while the work was done. We could still make 4 knots on our course. The sea was impressive in the morning light and we could feel how 'Bluebird' was picked up, shaken and thrown to leeward bodily by the power of these seas. The 'Green Terror' indicated that no small vessel under sail could bear to windward on this coast when conditions were bad enough and that if driven on the shore, Mutton Island (how unimaginative the names of these islands), was the only hope and that if a vessel missed the rocks and gained the partial shelter of the island lives might be saved though the loss of the ship would still be certain.

We could see this Mutton Island and there was no margin so we set the reefed mizzen and drove her harder and closer to the wind to work out an offing in case the wind might head us. Had it not been for Mark, we should have gone to Aran or Cashla on the principle that every time you run up a deep bay on the West of Ireland, it is long odds on that you will have a long beat out again. Galway it had to be and when we reached the smoother water in the lee of the Aran Isles, we squared away, shaking out reefs in staysail and mizzen but leaving both reefs in the main as it was still likely to blow hard. We anchored under Mutton Island (another of this name) while we checked up in the port entrance and made sure that the dock gates were open. The anchorage was poor and might become untenable with a shift of wind to southward, so we got our anchor and started in under power refusing the attentions of the Pilot Launch. We had to beat off a gang of five men who appeared likely to claim salvage. The situation was ugly for a few moments.

We were secured in the Commercial Dock at 14.45. Everything below was clean and warm and dry. Nothing had smashed or carried away. We celebrated with a drink and enjoyed the relaxed pause while food was being prepared, we ate largely and caught up on our sleep. It had been quite a passage and had tested the gear in many ways. The performance had been satisfactory and we had gained some useful hints for detail improvements. We only found out afterwards that a broadcast had given a full gale warning for the whole area. This time the interlude lasted for three days. Christian's regular participation in sailing had really started when 'Bluebird of Thorne' was completed. Believe it or not, her early experience had started with the old type of luxury yachting. As a girl she had been a guest on a large steam yacht and gone day sailing from that base in racing yachts, all maintained by paid hands. This impression had been tempered fortunately by her own deeply implanted sense of values. When we married, Christian told me that in sailing, as in other pursuits, she had always felt deprived as she had no brothers and that had given her few opportunities to try such sports. From this though she was ready and willing to pitch in quite undeterred by the spartan way associated with me and the 'Bluebirds'.

Seasickness was unfortunately quite serious at times and a handicap to be overcome. Before long she became competent to the point where she was much better than she herself realised; good at the helm and particularly enjoying handling 'Bluebird' in rough weather. She was useful on deck and below but learned by observation and example rather than by study and theory. I was known to call this, "suck it and see" method but it worked and was only shaken when something happened suddenly beyond previous experience. Long after this trip was over, Christian confessed that she just about reached the breaking point at Galway and had determined to go home with Mark. She had been cold, wet and seasick and depressed by the exposure and the wildness of the sea, though never frightened, too much and too often. But then, and this was typical of her, she had reasoned with herself, "If I go home now, I shall hate myself afterwards and find I have shut myself out of an important part of life. It is not worth it, I had better stick it". And so she did with the happy result that before the cruise was over, she had turned a vital corner in experience and never felt like this again though she always preferred cruising to the long voyages in open water and never failed to find a thrill in the discovering of new places, new coasts, people and ports.

This was a period rather like that at Bantry, except for the weather. Thursday was thoroughly beastly and we sat tight and enjoyed the fleshpots with baths and a meal ashore, particularly as Mark was able to stay with us until early Friday morning when I saw him start a journey which ended in Malta. Friday was equally beastly but we were happy enough and the space and headroom below decks were a joy when cooped up and confined by teeming rain. We watched the salmon running in the river Corrib; one could lean upon the bridge parapet and count hundreds. It was laughable to see a fisherman solemnly casting back and forth over those unresponsive fish, all plainly visible. We did not see one caught on rod or line but they came in by the dozen to the nets each tide. We even had one leaping alongside us in the dock; in the evening a cast from the bridge with a plain lead and a hook would be almost certain to snag one of the close packed salmon in the river. Poaching, as elsewhere, in Ireland was rampant.

I was fascinated by the Galway hookers and managed to obtain some photographs and notes on these unique and rapidly disappearing local craft. On another visit with more time, it would have been good fun to take 'Bluebird' up the canal and river to spend a day or two in Lough Corrib, her shallow-draught and handiness would have made this quite possible. Each tide, we looked out and debated a getaway but it was still blowing hard and still a head wind for us. We were paying the penalty of our run up the deep bay on Mark's account. At this stage, Digby began to prowl around the ship, making notes on the gear and saying, "Will my ship have this?" On the fourth day we left the dock under power at 06.00 with mainsail and staysail set. Outside there was quite enough wind for this canvas so we stopped the engine and settled down to a long plug to windward. Long and short legs developed, the day improved and by 17.00 we had reached Golam Head and had increased to full sail with number one jib.

For the next $3^1/_2$ hours, we had a magnificent sail with intricate pilotage through a maze of rocks until we anchored abreast the little harbour of Roundstone. Again the pleasant drink, the glow of satisfaction and the interchange of yarns with the tendency for me to say, "In 'Little Bluebird'" and the crew to chorus, "We understand". Here I extended my notes on hookers with information on Pookhauns and Gloacherns, the former a small hooker type with gaffcutter rig, the latter similar but with lug and single head sail. We had reached a part where sail was king. The motor was unknown and boats were essential among the islands, both for livelihood and ordinary communications. To sail in, as we had done, was a passport; to see the boat handling was a treat. Even the local trading craft had no engine and sailed, while we were there, with a cargo of kelp, destined ultimately for iodine extraction by I.C.I. Only one Irish yacht had been into this perfect place three years before. Memory produced no other precedent and nowhere in the whole of the cruise had we found such an atmosphere of friendliness. We seemed to be accepted partners in the activities of the place. One good lady greeted Christian, "Your yacht looked so beautiful sailing in from the sunset that it made me cry and I have brought you some butter as a gift". The proud designer who was standing within earshot, was much affected by the unexpected tribute. Not so his wife who seemed preoccupied: "could it have been butter?" England was still rationed.

The fog had gone but it was blowing force 6 - 7 with a swell on the rocks that commanded respect. I had vivid memories of the sea off Slyne Head; had I not been virtually dismasted there in 'Little Bluebird'? Local opinion said the sea was very 'dashturbed'. How right they were! So we enjoyed a delightful day ashore. Edward and Digby disappeared into the hinterland with borrowed tackle and returned exhausted in the evening with eighteen first class trout. Christian and I had a magnificent walk; surprising things we found, not least what looked like a gold mine as well as the sadness and ruins, an ever present reminder of a reduced population. There was no wireless set functioning in this place, it was remote and beautiful. When we sailed again, care was needed through the rocks and then making more sail, we crashed past Wild Bellows and on towards Slyne Head in a confused and steep swell, so enormous that no adjective seemed adequate. I was glad to pass that evil place unscathed and we carried on past Inishboffin wondering whether the Genial Giant had delivered his coal. We just had to go into French Port. I was remembered and greeted once again by the man in the Bauneen coat.

The next passage was memorable and in some ways a record. We made 8 knots with steering perfect in a big sea on the beam. The sun upset a bitter wind and we congregated in the cockpit to prepare and deal with an enormous crab supper. The coast simply reeled past and an occasional sea-top slopped into the cockpit looking for Christian. We carried on until we could run up Lough Swilly to Buncrana. After search ashore, an obliging Customs Official confessed that he had never cleared a yacht. Another corner had been rounded and Ireland's north point was at hand. For days we had been tantalised by reports of lovely weather in England and we now badly needed a smashing breeze and we had no wind. It was a very pleasant contrast but it meant using the engine to make Larne where Digby was to leave us. We were nearly home. The anticyclone reached out to us and as we closed Anglesey, Christian began to say, "Back to Belsen", as the rigours of the west were forgotten and the cares of the housewife in a severely rationed land, loomed ever closer. We returned after another 1,000 miles. On the whole it had been a summer of southwest gales and never ceasing strong southwest winds but I could only say how much easier it had been this time. 'Bluebird' was awarded the Romola Cup by the Royal Cruising Club. She had made her mark.

First 'Bluebird of Thorne'.

Chapter Seven

Fifteen Years of Family Cruising

In the years following the Irish cruise (1947-50), a new pattern developed and I now see how this was influenced by my circumstances. I had acquired increased work and responsibility involving business journeys overseas. These were shorter than in the 1920's because air travel had improved rapidly and become effective so that, rather to my sorrow, it was no longer practicable to go out by ship and wander from country to country on business. However determined I might be to maintain my sailing, time was short, the other pressures were great and I suppose I already had rather less energy. Christian had the cares of home and three children, widely different in age and temperament. With children, it appeared that I worked hard for ten years between designs, though these gaps in age had actually been caused by accidents of fate, wars and illnesses.

Costs were rising and so, with much more income, we were still no better off in terms of spending and living than we had been in the 1930's, ten years before. The maintenance of a yacht like 'Bluebird' was favourable as she was so simple and rugged, but it could have been far less had I not lived so far away inland that I had neither time nor opportunity to do my own work. In spite of this, I always checked all vital matters, particularly rigging and I did my own engine maintenance. This introduces another factor. Some people in my circumstances might well have spent a lot of their available time happily messing about with a yacht and doing their own work, but if so they could only have done local sailing or far less ambitious cruises. I can see now that such a course would have been very pleasant and easier for all concerned but it was not for me. I preferred to use my time sailing, indeed I chafed and felt frustrated by the limitations. I did consider sharing the yacht to do longer cruises by the one out, the other home method, like the Spanish cruise in 'Merlin' but I did not search very hard or I was not lucky enough to have a friend to whom I could entrust 'Bluebird' and whose circumstances fitted in. A partial solution was found later when I laid up abroad for three winters.

My increased commitments had another effect; time after time we would scramble off on a cruise, tired and in spite of all efforts, hardly prepared in the manner I now consider prudent. At the end of a cruise we would dash back, balancing time and weather against distance and on return to England, race back to home and work without a chance to clear up and put 'Bluebird' to bed properly. I also found that short weekends became less and less worth the effort involved. We did many of these to North Wales, but gradually it became a long weekend less often, while holidays such as Easter and Whitsuntide were turned into a week for fitting out and passage making. What a handicap we suffered in the English climate, it is so wasteful of time and effort to lay up after five months in commission. When everything is in good order and working well, it seems criminal to pick it to pieces and put it all away. In the Spring, all this work must be done again and then it involved a real struggle to repair the ravages of winter and the mere process of the lay up. Sometimes, when fitting out early, we had snow or ice on the decks while we worked. Sometimes the weather was so bad that the painting was not up to programme. It did occur to me that this whole performance was a curious form of endeavour and I wondered why I did it; but everytime there was a family discussion on holidays, the final vote always came down for a cruise in preference to other and more conventional exercises, so the family backed me up.

In other lands, the climate does not compel the full lay up process and if the utilisation is greater, not only is there more reward but the maintenance actually seems to be less. So utilisation is another key. If this was limited in my case, how could I justify the effort and expense? A partial answer to this was what we called, 'Boy and Girl Weeks', so that holidays for the whole family could be offset against the cost and this formed part of the pattern. In those days, we laid up at Gallows Point, Beaumaris, with Morris & Levitt. I heard them referred to as "muck it and leave it" but this was quite unjust. They did well for me and for 'Bluebird' becoming friends to the family. I remember and think kindly of all the exchanges conducted with them and their soft Welsh voices and accents. The Easter week was usually fitting out and a sail to see that all was well. Perhaps we should then have one or two long weekends before Whitsuntide. These Beaumaris weekends had their moments. Driving down on a Friday night, there might be a pause for fish and chips at Rhyl and we often arrived around midnight. We then had to find the dinghy, which had been left ready for us and carry the gear down from the car in the dark. Often it would be blowing a gale and I was in doubt whether to risk a rough ride out in the dark with strong tides to an exposed mooring or to be prudent and sleep in the car until dawn. We always went out and we always made it, but sometimes it involved two or three trips and it could be touch and go.

A sail to Lynus Point usually improved the weather. Looking back to the mountains of Wales, the clouds could be seen massing and discharging rain while we might be in bright sunshine. When it blew too hard, we could have a racing sail in the Straits as a good exercise and once I remember we gybed round the stern of the Conway. We noticed a rather unusual enthusiasm, everybody seemed to be waving and cheering at us. No doubt we thought they are admiring 'Bluebird' and the way we handle her in wind force 8, but a glance astern showed that our dinghy was being towed upside down, porpoise-ing in an enterprising fashion, it had been flipped over by the wind as we gybed. We even did one or two races though without special preparation; but our blunt cruising instrument won no prizes. We were always short handed and in cruising trim and though in a good wind we could occasionally do well running and reaching, we would be left behind if beating to windward in light weather. I made friends with Peter Brett, another amateur, and admired his attractive designs. I had short experiences in other yachts including a converted 8 metre racing yacht which I considered a disastrous form for cruising requirements. An encounter with 'Bluebird' by a man named Rayner was to lead to the success story of the 'Westerly' twin keel yachts he produced in years to come. On one occasion in a pub which we rarely frequented, we heard 'Bluebird' discussed: "Do you know anything about that big blue yacht at Gallows Point? asked one. "No, but I have seen the owner. He looks like a broken down bruiser", was the reply. I was not allowed to forget this; the family thought it very good value.

When Whitsuntide came, I would take 'Bluebird' down to Falmouth with a crew of two men. From Falmouth we would go away on a cruise in the Biscay area, returning to Falmouth after three weeks or so. In the school holidays, Christian would go down by car with the young and their friends and use 'Bluebird' as a seaside bungalow for three or four weeks until I could rejoin them. There would be from two to five children aboard, they had beaches available, they could learn to swim, there was the dinghy for learning to row and they could learn to sail; picnics and excursions, a lovely life, a gorgeous holiday and extremely good for them and Christian, handling them with practiced ease and understanding, always maintained that they behaved better in

'Bluebird' with the hint of sea routine and authority, than they would have done at home. Of course there were incidents and of course there were accidents, luckily nothing deadly with which Christian could not cope. Some incidents were amusing, some trivial. I remember one such example: one day when I happened to be aboard, which was rare, Frances came to her mother in the morning in a rare state of distress and Christian receiving her as always with sympathy and understanding, set about finding the cause. Eventually it transpired that Frances, put to bed early, had been in a berth from which before she went to sleep she could hear us talking in the saloon and eventually she told her mother, "Last night Father said he was going to do a wicked, cruel, murderous thing". Christian of course said, "No Frances, you must have been wrong, you know your father would never do anything like that". With tears coursing down her face, Frances told her mother, "Father said he was going to kill two chicks with one brick!"

Christian became an absolute genius for dealing with the young in 'Bluebird', keeping them occupied, happy and under firm control and of course well fed to avoid mutiny. It is true that most young, given leadership, do react and will accept discipline and do their share on an adventure far better than in the home. While the threat, "No nonsense or you go home at once", was usually sufficient to quell a riot but, and it is a big but, we realised how boring sailing can be to the young. For years after the adults tended to expect it, children are far happier messing about on the beach, paddling about in dinghies, learning to swim and sail, having picnic parties, expeditions in search of blackberries and mushrooms and of course in and out of the sea all the time. We evolved a theory that boys and girls should not be taken to sea unless, or until they burst into tears of rage and disappointment when Dad and 'Bluebird' went off without them. The age at which this happened in our experience was not before they were thirteen or fourteen. Daughter Frances started cruising at eleven but only because a death in the family had altered plans and alternative arrangements could not be made. Luckily she was stoic in everything, including seasickness and her imagination was seized by going foreign. A great gift for languages received a useful stimulus from finding French a live language in which she could go ashore, have fun and do shopping by herself.

As they developed, my three all continued to come for holidays at their own option. Mark, when he had no more exciting preoccupation but without the driving urge to own his own

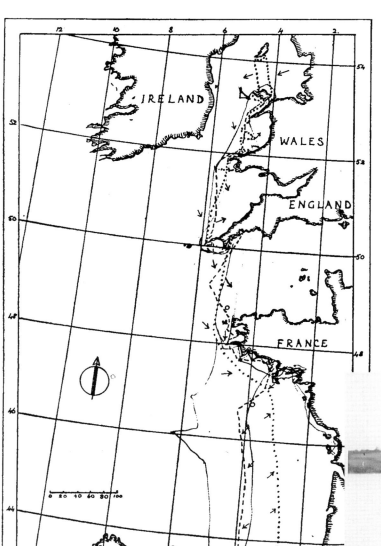

BLUE BIRD OF THORNE. 1948.

Left: Family cruises down the Bay of Biscay.
Below: Boy and Girl weeks' holidays.

yacht or equip himself to take 'Bluebird' away on his own, which I should have encouraged. He was the best of the three as a crew as he was not seasick. He was a really good all round hand and good company. David, a 'boffin' by temperament and slightly seasick, was fascinated by the theory and navigation problems but with his mind revolving happily on some higher thought he was apt to leave a line on the loose or put a sheet the wrong way round the winch. He was particularly conscientious at the helm for maintaining compass course. Frances, stoic as I have said, was good at the helm, interesting and fun to travel with, enjoying the coast and shore going, more than passage making. Boy and Girl weeks were twice organised with 'Bluebird' taking the ground inside the shingle bar of St Just in Roseland off Falmouth harbour. This was perhaps the most successful venue and covered two years. The family made many friends locally and Christian found that an English family who had lived there for ten years were still regarded as 'resident visitors' in distinction to the native born and to the annual horde of summer holidaymakers.

Another good place was Fowey. There 'Bluebird' went up the river and secured to the trees with two anchors out astern in a charming inlet. This involved a dinghy trip across the river to land or shop but friends had a launch and this for picnics, bathing and mackerel fishing, was a great help. The Kelvin engine was so old that the timing gears were open and oiling was made by libations from a large can. Could it have been 1908 vintage? A happy pursuit was wading up the estuary at low tide and spearing little flat fish and it was by no means certain that all children would return with their feet intact. Chichester Harbour was not as good as the anchorage inside East Head, it was too exposed and Christian had an anxious time in a gale when it was impossible to go ashore. She would have been in real trouble if the anchors had not held. Beaumaris itself served one year but on the mud to avoid the exposed anchorage, it was the mud itself that imposed the vital limits. At one time or another, all the tribe had their sea-boots pulled off and went into the mud on their faces.

The last and very successful meet was in Oulton Broad. The young were then not quite so young and the more sophisticated shore pursuits obtainable there were popular. At the end of a boy and girl week, I would return, give them a sail if possible and Christian would then take them home to get ready for school while I, with two men, made the passage back to Beaumaris. This became known as "The Trade Trip" and was

seldom without its difficulties over that rather storm swept course which averaged 275 miles sailed to Anglesey. Holyhead and Fishguard were the only refuges in bad weather that did not give away a lot of distance; I think there were ten "Trade Trips" in all and these never seemed to be without difficulty or incident. More than once it was so rough in the Bristol Channel that even in 'Bluebird' the watch could not safely leave the helm at night for long enough to call his relief. There was the time when Mark, still young and inexperienced, turned me out because a fishing boat was chasing him. When my brain cleared I realised that in light, baffling winds, it was Mark who had become mesmerised and was sailing slowly round and round a trawler. We have to learn!

Storm in the Irish Sea
One "Trade Trip" I will never forget was in the middle of September one year when Mark, Ronnie Gresham and I arrived from the North after an all night train journey. We had breakfast and I put Christian and the boys ashore to start for home by road. Ronnie Gresham had become one of my regular crews. We had sailed together often and were to do so many a time again. A tough Yorkshireman, he was shrewd, capable and hard working with a timber business he had built up himself, but above all he was a dedicated seaman. Long ago he had studied at nights and got an extra Yacht Master's Ticket. His experience of a wide range of yachts was vast, both passage making and racing. In the war he had ended up in command of a Frigate and he could produce a wealth of informative yarns with salty humour and real effect. I would have trusted my ship to him anywhere and we understood each other with such confidence that discussion was hardly necessary when decisions had to be made. His peculiarity, if it be one, was a preference for passage making; the longer the better, and once committed he would drive a ship hard against all odds until the destination was achieved but he tended to lose interest if pottering or detail pilotage and cruising ensued. It was as if he said to himself. "This is not the real thing, anybody could do this. Let's get to sea and get on with it". One of his characteristic sayings when bad weather threatened, "You get what you bloody well get!"

'Bluebird' was at sea within two hours. This was partly due to our practice in making the change over from seaside houseboat to sea-going cruiser and partly to the inherent simplicity of 'Bluebird' herself. The start this time was no exception to the usual form. We plugged to windward to Lands End with a struggle to save our tide. It was our practice to go inside or outside the Longships, according to wind and sea conditions. It was outside this time and the Longships were abeam at 15.00.

Meanwhile Christian's land passage was in trouble. Her motor was one that I had picked up in 1946, just after the war when cars were like hen's teeth and we had to have one for duties in a public office. This example was unbelievably awful. The under body appeared to be made out of beaten-out oil drums. Scrawled over its intimacies was the ominous message, "Not fit for export". Its cylinders had to be re-ground at only 12,000 miles, but now the steering broke. After hours of crawling and struggles with disinterested garages, a temporary patch-up job was in progress but there was no hope of reaching home that night and some accommodation had to be found for herself and two boys.

The weather information indicated a serious depression away to the north-east with gale in Rockall. We judged it too far away to be an immediate threat. The local forecast was wind, south-west, fresh to strong, visibility moderate and our barometer was quite high at thirty minutes. We had actually wind force 4 and conditions were quite pleasant with bright sunshine. The sea was rough and we squared away on a northerly course to clear the Smalls. A big ketch, we judged about 40-50 tons, had left Falmouth ten minutes astern of us. So far she had almost duplicated our tactics though we had gained on her, possibly because she had a reef in her mainsail and had stood wide out to avoid the race at the Lizard. We little thought that we should remain in company with her for nearly 200 miles. With the ever present fear of the wind coming ahead by veering north-west, we were anxious to make all speed and set genoa and mizzen staysail until we snugged down for the night at dusk, with the wind south-west, force 5, we reduced to main mizzen and no. two jib. The staysail was lifting behind the main and was hardly effective anyway. I was inclined to reef the main but we did not do so and it did not prove necessary until the morning. The night watches passed with the wind slowly increasing, fine rain commencing at midnight and progress excellent at 7 knots or more.

At 06.00 next morning we in 'Bluebird' had the Smalls abeam to starboard, estimated two miles. In the early evening we had worked out a lead on the big ketch. During the night she passed us in Mark's watch when we lost distance owing to trawlers and shipping. She showed a masthead light throughout and so presumably she had her engine running. She was now four points on our port bow and about two miles distant. The forecast was now - Fresh to strong south-west, gale - Rockall, Shannon, West Sole and (the first hint of trouble for us) a secondary depression west of Ireland deepening and moving north-east. We gybed and altered course to north-east by north for Bardsey Island with the wind on the starboard quarter.

Ashore Christian was now setting out again but had a ghastly steering wobble and could only proceed at less than 20 mph. Well meaning folk stopped her repeatedly, if they could do so, to tell her what she knew only too well - that her wheels were wobbling.

In 'Bluebird' we hove to while we reefed the mainsail. It was well that we had all the reeving and lashing lines we required ready to hand throughout the passage. We then handed the mizzen and continued on, north-east by north. The forecast then gave us gale, Irish Sea, south wind increasing steadily to gale, severe at times. We were not surprised and merely remarked that we had bought this one though I do not see how we could have foreseen this nor what course we might have taken had we done so. If we had known it at the time this was a point of no return. Had we then sought shelter in Fishguard we might have got in before the gale became serious and it would have been prudent to do so but it is unlikely that we should have moved out again for four days. By 13.00 we were running under reefed main alone, the barometer was 29.7 and we logged a wind force 7 to 8. We made all reasonable preparation and decided to continue as long as it remained prudent. Our progress was so rapid that we thought we might make Holyhead before darkness and before the gale developed its full strength. I think Ronnie thought this a reasonable bet but I thought it a poor chance. We sighted Bardsey Island bearing east approximately ten miles.

The situation was getting out of hand because the sea suddenly became vicious as the tide had turned and gathered strength against the increasing gale. We had run too long and I paid the penalty as I was at the helm. 'Bluebird', my utterly dependable and docile 'Bluebird', was picked up by a sea and thrown bodily off course. I fought to get her back and it happened again, this time throwing her the other way. She gybed, the boom guy was useless in these conditions and she was in such an attitude with the stem down and laid far over that the mainsheet came across a few inches forward of any previous limit and caught me across the shoulder. I was smashed down on my back across the coamings, twisting to try to get out from under the main sheet. A moment later and I was head down in the sea and saved from going overboard by one leg crooked round a stanchion at the knee. I was conscious and angry with myself. I was not frightened but I knew that I was badly hurt, with no power in my legs and no hope of getting back again

The crash brought the others up and together they got me inboard. Ronnie took the ship, an obvious necessity, and Mark somehow got me below and into my berth. I then sent Mark up to Ronnie with orders to heave to, though as soon as Mark was available he knew very well what to do. The jib and staysail went below. The storm jib was set and hoisted on the forestay, the mizzen - reefed and set and a moment chosen when they could then bring the boat round and heave to without the mainsail. Heavy warps were prepared and made ready to stream if required. The heavy weather boards had been rigged some time before. For 18.00 the log reads - Wind south, force 8+. Visibility less than one mile. Sea dangerous. Abandon Holyhead. The forecast was more definite. A dangerous secondary depression had developed unexpectedly and was crossing the Irish Sea. 'Bluebird' could have continued to run under the storm jib and with warps astern if necessary, but to approach a lee shore with that visibility would have been lunacy. The relative peace and relief when hove to after such a struggle is always surprising and has to be experienced.

At 20.00 the log entry was - Hove to, wind to port, lying west by south to west south west. Drift estimated 2 knots north west. Log handed at 02.9. 'Bluebird' behaving well, rain squalls well over force 8. I was flat on my back, wedged with cushions. I had made Mark get me a pint of hot drink, stiff with sugar as a precaution against shock. I was warming up and beginning to feel a little less battered. The others had fed and could rest. We had nearly made the passage at a speed of 7 knots, failing by two or three hours and half a tide. With Mark's help I made cautious experiments and found that I was not paralysed. A light was lashed up and we set the watches; Ronnie to take the first, I the middle and Mark the dawn. I should have considered a watch quite unnecessary if we had not been so close to the Stacks and in the steamer track. With the strong tides, a shift of wind could quickly have put us in jeopardy and all the shipping in the Irish Sea appears to pass within ten miles of that corner.

Meanwhile Christian had reached home exhausted and with much to do. She was telephoned at about this time and informed by a well-wisher that the wireless had announced, "Gale Storm, wind force 9 to 10, North Irish Sea". She did not appreciate this, particularly as she knew 'Bluebird' was likely to be in or near that area.

On watch it was not necessary to do more than look round every ten minutes or so and watch the course as the wind did tend to veer to south by west and south south west with heavy rain squalls. In between the visibility was fairly good and we had the South Stack and later the Skerries lights in view The wireless reported winds force 9 and 10 not far to the north of us and shipping was a worry. Two or three steamers, sighting us, came out of their course to have a look and, though their intentions were kind, they made us nervous. Then a big vessel, probably about 10,000 tons, lay to windward of us and remained there. That frightened me. If we made any signal he would assume that we were in distress. If he closed us there would be two or three crashes and 'Bluebird' smashed or sunk while we went up scrambling nets to the ship. It did not occur to me, crippled as I was, that I could never have made it. My only thought was to save the ship and I had complete confidence that we should take her in ourselves. I told the others to get the largest jug we had and, propped in the hatch, we would go through the motions of pouring it into mugs and drinking. As the ship's searchlight was trained on us I hoped that would convince them that we were alright. To complete the act we let draw and crawled across the stern of the steamer. That did the trick and she resumed her course for Liverpool. We never got her name; I could not thank them, but had things been otherwise they might have saved our lives.

At 06.00 on Thursday the log read, "Bar 29.4, wind force 8 south west". We had breakfast and then wore ship and let draw, making $2^{1}/_{2}$ knots east. It was wet and we were shipping breaking crests. Ronnie said, "Can we get anywhere like this"? I said, "I am doubtful, if you and Mark can set the trysail, let's have a bash". We logged the wind south by west, force 7 or over. Trisail set; course south-east by south. Sky better - gleam of sun. I was unable to continue at the helm and Ronnie took charge. The next forty-five minutes were simply magnificent. Laid right down to her effective limit, she balanced perfectly, required no helm and smoked along at about 7 knots. Contrary to my expectation we did not take heavy water aboard. A continuous drift like smoke came over the weather bow and the lee bow wave was a continuous curtain of fine mist rising high and far to leeward. A big steamer approached and behind her I sighted Holyhead Island. The bearing was almost too good to be true as we had it to leeward. Bearings in the night had been difficult but had indicated that we should pick it up on the bow on this course. Obviously the south-going tide had set us back since then.

It might be well to emphasise at this point that it was spring tides and this was one of the biggest tides of the year. Already this had had considerable influence and had affected the sea, undoubtedly making it more vicious. It was the big factor in our next decision; dare we run round the Stacks at the full strength of the tide? Could we make Holyhead, if we did so, without being swept down to Carmel Point and the Skerries? To do this we should have to go through the worst of the tide race at the North and South Stacks where the tide might be running up to 5 knots over an uneven bottom. We handed the mizzen and kept the trisail sheets well in so that we could ignore a gybe. The die was cast; we ran and at first it seemed easy. We then found the tide was setting us north-west so that we had to steer east to keep the South Stack on a constant bearing. This brought the sea on the quarter and increased the task for the helmsman. The South Stack approached. At just the wrong time the wind increased and remained hard, probably funnelling somewhat round the highland of the mountain. Mark started the engine in case we should need it if and when we had to beat to windward in Holyhead Bay.

We entered the race and the sea went mad but I hoped that when it had burst itself, though it might still be vicious, it might lose its main weight and power. This did happen to some extent but it had regenerated before we reached the North Stack and the race there was worse. Meanwhile 'Bluebird' was magnificent and was being beautifully handled. It was even exhilarating. I hoped for a slight lee from the North Stack to the end of the breakwater but we now saw some shocking seas ahead, whether caused by shallow water or an eddy tide, I do not know. The remaining mile or two was awe inspiring. Great seas crested up and broke almost bodily. Once or twice 'Bluebird' was picked up by such a sea, put her nose down at an angle that made you think, and then with a roar, went off like a surf boat for 60 or 100 yards at a time, the white breaking foam abreast of and higher than the cockpit with the quarter deck flooded. Yet we never really pooped and she never tried to broach to, thanks to Ronnie's skill and 'Bluebird's' steady good manners. At the height of such surf

shoots, we heard a roaring vibration and, though it was no time to crawl around to look below the floors, it appeared that the propeller, which was set in normal ahead position and running free, was running at something like 12 - 15 knots. We even argued that at times the propeller stopped, reversed and ran at high speed in the opposite direction, but we did not prove this.

I think we all felt the exaltation of spirit produced at such moments and though there was danger we were all confident in the ship. One last swoop and we were literally flung past the end of the breakwater and in a moment more we had smooth water. In came our sheets, up went our scrap of mizzen, in went the clutch and we drove her to make the anchorage. We need not have worried; such was the relief of smooth water that she would certainly have made it easily under sail alone, just possibly under power alone, but with both she went like a scalded cat up the other side of that long breakwater with two long legs and two short ones. One last battle with the canvas and the anchor went down in the lee of the Island in 6 fathoms not far from the old lifeboat shed. It was 12 noon, Thursday, 14 September, $52\frac{1}{2}$ hours from Falmouth - an average of almost 5 knots in spite of nearly 12 hours hove to and some 12 miles lost distance. The tide was slackening. Two steamers crawled into shelter. The stretch of water between Carmel Point and the Skerries was a continuous white surf. The barometer was still 29.4 and the forecast very bad. Wind force 10 from north-west imminent. We were glad to be in and wondered where the big ketch was at that moment. We went below, peeled off our outer layers of garments and tackled a good meal with the satisfaction of a job well done.

With hindsight we should have hove to earlier with more sea room and less shipping although, had we done so, in all probability we should not have made harbour for another 18 hours and on the Saturday there was an even harder blow reported 90 m.p.h. We had been quite right in our original assessment that the deep low up towards Ireland was too far away to give us more than good strong winds which would be favourable once we had battled our way round Land's End. Why then the storm in which we were enveloped in the Irish Sea? As sometimes happens with a low in the Atlantic covering a wide area, a secondary depression developed to the south-east of its centre and this secondary came roaring round the southern edge of the main depression, deepening and gathering strength as it progressed, so that it had almost maximum effect in the Irish Sea area. It was deflecting wind force 10 as announced on the warning issued in the middle of programmes on the radio and television. To complete this part of the story, as the centre of this secondary moved through, the forecast for Saturday night when we had reached Holyhead was for north-westerly winds again force 10. A final incongruous detail; for hours after we came in I could feel the tug of the chinstrap of the sou'wester that was no longer there. I had been very lucky to have Ronnie and Mark with me for this somewhat exacting trip and I had been more fortunate than I realised at the time.

While it is not strictly part of the yachting scene I have decided to relate the medical and other circumstances surrounding and subsequent to my accident, as I think there are lessons to be learned. I have already indicated the yachting lessons don't run too long, heave to in time, make sure that you have some attachment to the yacht. Know how to get a man back on board when overside and helpless. Know how to reject ship assistance when it is essential to do so.

I have also recounted how Christian struggled slowly northwards in a car with damaged steering at less than 20 miles an hour and a crew of tired children until she arrived home almost exhausted. She had heard on the car radio on the way, the warnings of storm force 10 in the Irish Sea but she told me afterwards that she was astonished by the number of people who rang her up. Is there something slightly macabre in human nature that takes almost a pleasure in announcing bad tidings? The general tone was, "Are you back home with the boys? Isn't this the weekend when Robin is bringing 'Bluebird' back to North Wales? Have you heard that there is storm force 10 in the Irish Sea?" Christian, as ever, was completely stalwart and her answer might be, "Yes, but 'Bluebird' is strong and seaworthy; Robin has a good crew with Ronnie and Mark and I am sure they will bring her into port safely". Ronnie Gresham's wife, whom we called Auntie Mabel, had the same situation to deal with and her reply was on the lines, "Ronnie has had so many gales and storms that I know he will know how to cope with this one". My mother, romantic as ever, was heard to remark, "How Robin must be enjoying himself with all this jolly wind". My father's reaction, equally predictable by me and those who knew him well, "Where is Robin, I must get a message to him, there's an urgent meeting on Monday and it is essential that he attends". When people spoke of storm and tempest it meant nothing to him and so on Saturday he rang up Morris and Levitt at Beaumaris and spoke to Levitt, "Where is 'Bluebird', can I get a

message to her and to Robin? Levitt in his soft Welsh voice said there was a severe storm in the area. "I think 'Bluebird' will be hove to and might be anywhere in the Irish Sea, I doubt if she will be able to get into any port today but hold on and I will ring a friend in the Coastguards at Holyhead". This he did and the Coastguard's reply was much the same as he had given my father, but then, "Wait, I see something, I will get my glasses. There is something coming round the breakwater; it's a blue yacht, my God, I think it's capsizing, I can see its red keel in the air". Levitt in a calm voice, "Don't worry, it's 'Bluebird', she has two keels, what you see is only one of them, she will beat up the harbour into shelter". Of course he was right. Reporting this to my father, the latter said, "I knew it must be possible", and Levitt offered to drive over to Holyhead to see that I got the message correctly. From our angle, safely at anchor in a safe port, smooth water and lovely weather ashore, it was pure heaven to relax, let the stress and strain of the last three days drain away and, in my case, to virtually pass out in an at least motionless berth. An hour later, a hail from the beach and a figure waving a paper. Ronnie and Mark launched the dinghy, went ashore, exchanged news with Levitt and collected my father's message. This was the famous message, "An important meeting has been called by the High Speed Steel Association for 11.00 am on Monday to discuss prices, essential you attend". I put this out of my mind feeling that if I could not attend I could arrange for one of our directors to take my place.

A car was sent over with a driver on Sunday morning. Getting out of 'Bluebird' into the dinghy, ashore onto the beach and up to the car, was not fun even with help. The journey in the car was not too bad but, again, at home, what heaven to stretch out in my own bed and pass out again for some 18 hours. Monday morning I struggled up, I was assisted into my clothes. I remember the visit to the loo as being the greatest agony I had yet encountered and I still don't understand why I had not felt so much pain; I think it must have been partly shock and partly the emergency and determination to bring 'Bluebird' in.

I drove my own car to the famous meeting, yes it was important, yes we agreed an increase in price for all the high speed steels. I then drove to my doctor. One look and a few words and he reached for the telephone to the top Orthopaedic Surgeon in the area. He told me afterwards that virtually the whole of my back was swollen and bruised and now beginning to develop all the colours of the rainbow. Again I struggled into the car, drove myself to the orthopaedic surgeon, struggled in, hoisted myself on to the x-ray table and there relaxed talking to the surgeon and telling him what had happened while waiting for the development of the x-ray plates. When the nurse came back there must have been some Calvinistic signal which I did not see; his face changed and turning to me he said, "Lie still and a few moments later two men came in and lifted me carefully from the x-ray table to the examination couch. I remember vividly what followed. After a full examination and armed with the tale that I had recounted, the surgeon was considering long and deeply until I asked him, "What now?" He then said, "You have five lateral processes broken on the right hand side of your back in the lumbar region. It is an injury I more often see in such a case as a miner trapped after a roof fall in a mine. I have seen two or three processes broken, I don't ever remember seeing five processes broken but had you come to me as normal within hours of the accident, you would have been encased in plaster from neck to knee and so remained for weeks and after that there would have been months of therapy and treatment to try and get you going again but now when I think what you have done in the last three days since the accident I cannot believe that putting you into plaster will do you any good". "So what will I do", I asked. He said, "Well, were you a miner, by the time your Union and Union's solicitor had fought your case for compensation for disability to a conclusion, you would be completely convinced that you were so disabled and you would probably never work again". "But surely that is not my case?" I said, "what do I do? Shall I be able to lift heavy weights, pull ropes and start a heavy diesel engine?" He said, "Be very careful but gradually explore and experiment with what movement you can do, aiming always to extend this without doing any damage, until you regain normality and total movement. Meanwhile I will arrange for you to be driven home and you start by doing nothing for at least 48 hours".

Eight weeks later I started shooting again, four months later I went deer stalking, a year later I was starting the diesel engine in my yacht. I saw my surgeon at a fortnight, a month, 6 months and a year. For some years afterwards I would occasionally, by some incautious movement or stretch, pull something and have a fortnight of pain and difficulty until it settled down again. The five broken processes of bone never of course reattached themselves but there must have been an effective reattachment by the development of muscle and gristle and when I had these periods of difficulty I picture it as tearing loose a little bit of

gristle. Meanwhile my spine, which had a lateral curvature of six inches, gradually came straight again and the only long term effect was that my right leg ended up effectively half an inch shorter than the left leg. My tailor dealt with the trousers and I dealt with the limp by building up the right heel of my shoes. In conclusion, how lucky I had been when one thinks that people can have trouble for years from a simple thing such as swinging a heavy suitcase on to a rack in a railway carriage and suffering a displaced disc.

Many times in a life during which I had tried most things, I had had previous smashes, small and large. Once again I had been lucky and I healed up more or less unimpaired if not quite as good as new and I have started engines and handled anchors ever since. I think the fact that I had carried on at sea rather amazed the medical profession. I suppose the sense of emergency, the feeling of command and perhaps even a measure of shock, all had something to do with it. I do not believe that I can have been conscious of the pain that I should have been expected to suffer. The lessons were short. Do not run too long. In such conditions a back-up on watch would be wise and finally in those days we did not have a safety harness. This showed the necessity for them. They came in later.

Biscay

During these years we cruised in the Bay of Biscay area for four consecutive seasons and with two other years a total of six seasons with the first 'Bluebird of Thorne'. In these cruises, there were few ports and anchorages we did not visit on the north coast of Spain and the French Biscay coast but especially in Brittany, including the north west corner round to the English Channel and the port of L'Abervrach.

There were customarily four of us in the crew, occasionally five with overlaps. Christian and Mark most frequently and many others, some friends of Mark, some those who had graduated up from 'Boy and Girl' weeks. One or two became regulars and two eventually came with me on ocean voyages. My cousin James, then an architectural student, had once started out on a yacht voyage to Australia; this was an example of how things should not be done. The yacht gave trouble at all times. The Skipper inspired no confidence and quarrels broke out, the funds ran out and a 'situation' developed before the yacht had left Europe. We said that James did all things slowly and with deliberation. We even said that he slept slowly and therefore had to put in a lot of time, and work hard to get his rest. He walked slowly ashore but he was a good crew and he was kind and considerate, a good cook with an impregnable stomach, but more important was of the right temperament and he had a sense of humour. We all liked him with us and he wore well. James was a man you could probably live with on a desert island; a long yacht voyage may be similar and no less of a test. Christian swore that she had to hurry past when James was at the helm or he would say, "Do you mind taking her for a moment?" And if she did so, within five minutes a faint zizzing noise would be heard. James would be fast asleep and Christian would find that she was on watch.

Dennis had trained in H.M.S. Conway and followed the sea but swallowing the anchor when still young. He was in the motor trade but spent his spare time yacht racing from Bridlington. His experience of yacht cruising started in 'Bluebird' but he had bubbling enthusiasm and he taught as he learned so that we all gained when he was there. He invented the cry, "Thank you, thank you Skipper for bringing us to this lovely place". This started at exceptional and gorgeous spots but was apt to become a satirical chorus by the whole crew if we fetched up in a disagreeable anchorage. We used to evade the rigours of a rationed Britain by stocking up with merchant seaman's rations for a voyage, sanctioned by Customs. Merchant seamen did very well in our view and it was not unknown for some of these stores to be found in the bilges on return and become a God-send for Christian coping with the hungry boys and girls.

The first year in post-war France was a revelation. Severe as rationing was in Britain, France was really in trouble. Even bread was rationed and to transients like ourselves, meat, butter, eggs and many other stores were unobtainable, or only in small amounts after so much time and trouble that we abandoned the attempt. But there was Black Market Camembert and we used this as a substitute for everything. In ripening stages, these cheeses permeated the ship and in the end we all smelt of cheese and were heartily sick of it. Our usual departure was from Falmouth and more than once it was blowing a south westerly gale. When we assembled the impatient young would urge me to sail and probably thought me pretty stuffy when I refused until the barometer started to rise and the wind to veer towards the north west. Then, well reefed down, we would soon be reeling off the miles and reeling in another sense in the sea left over from the gale. "From Ushant to Scilly is 35 leagues". How well we knew that stretch and commonly, though not invariably, set a course well clear of Ushant and its fierce tides and steamer traffic so that we might or might not sight the powerful light at extreme range. "Life begins at Ushant", became a ship's chorus. With that we often made the Armen buoy at the end of Chausse de Sein. Though we must have taken the Raz de Sein at least six times bound north or south.

Audierne might be our first French port and when rationing had ceased, our first good meal ashore with special appreciation by Christian who might have been seasick in a hard passage of 175 miles. "I have eaten too much, I have drunk too much and it is simply lovely", was one of her comments as we returned to 'Bluebird' after such a night ashore. We exploited 'Bluebird's' powers by taking the ground innumerable times as intended but just occasionally by accident. The planned approach was a great convenience offering many places that a deeper draught single keel yacht would have shunned. A refinement in such ports was to look for the local crabbers fitted with legs. They would be tucked up in a safe corner on a clean bottom. We went and sat alongside them without legs and at the invariable and well meant warning, we made the crew learn by heart if they had no French, "Nous avons deux quilles. Nous prenons le sable tout droit. Les bequilles nous ne sont pas necessaire". 'Bluebird' herself adventured up almost all the navigable rivers as far as the first fixed bridge or other obstruction. Sometimes, as in the Charente, we could sail up against the ebb even with a head wind, again by exploiting 'Bluebird's' peculiarities. If the banks were clean mud or sand, we could sail until we touched, then spin into the wind reducing our draught, shoot up, often with a favourable eddy, before falling and gathering way on the other tack to cross the stronger stream and repeat the process at the other bank.

At Roche Bernard with the great viaduct destroyed in the war, there was a bridge of boats closing the river to us. We anchored below and had an especially good evening ashore. Returning late and in the dark we found our dinghy poised above a slope of glistening mud, steep, deep and stretching more than 50 yards. "A lifeboat launch", I cried. We piled in and with all set I took a run, started the dinghy and fell aboard over the stern as she gathered way faster and faster, maintaining, thank goodness, a straight course and into the river where she took quite a lot of water over the bows, but we floated in the rushing tide. I realised afterwards that this episode could have gone wrong in a big way. Try anything once! I sailed into and out of port wherever possible though sometimes I had the engine running ready for emergencies, particularly with an unknown place. This was perhaps more necessary for 'Bluebird' as there was no start at the touch of a button. The diesel was hand starting and though practiced, it took me about two minutes and that can be a long time in an emergency. It was usually my job though I taught the others and Mark was reliable. Others might fail as it required a nice mixture of strength, knack and confidence. On one occasion, with no engine, we sailed into Presque Isle de Quiberon. A ferry casting off, forced me to turn to starboard and run fast down a lane between fishing vessels and moorings. A launch with several trippers aboard emerged from behind a fishing boat to cut straight across our bows; they had not seen us. At my stentorian yell, the Patron reacted instantly and correctly gunning his motor, he turned away on to our course as I gave what ground I could and we finished almost alongside at the same spot. We had escaped running him down by about 10 foot and the possibilities with those trippers, most of whom probably could not swim, needed no imagination.

During our years in the Bay, it was sad to see the magnificent fleet of sailing tunnymen in decline. Some tried insulated holds and ice instead of the traditional method of hanging the tunny from racks on deck under an awning. How often the catch must have gone bad as light winds and calms delayed their return to port. About thirty tunnymen were being laid up each year, many were very old and the young men were not anxious to crew them. A great number ended their days at Ile de Groix, where some were broken up. Then the discovery was made that sardines could be kept alive in tanks and used as tunny bait if the water flow were great enough to aerate and maintain temperature. Only powerful pumps in a power vessel could do this and so the dual purpose vessel evolved which could be a trawler in winter and a tunnyman in the summer season. The old sailing craft were an inspiration, evolved with real differences from British fishing boats. In Nelson's time, our faster Frigates were those captured from the French and I believe most of the French types would have easily beaten their English equivalents. The gear was attractive in its functional efficiency, down to the little seat built into the end of the counter. What better fitment could be devised for a crew of fifteen men. The lovely and varied coloured sails would be seen in the Bay no more and the rivalry between builders and owners, a thing of the past.

On one of the passages to Spain, we had hard weather and, beating to windward, we made slow progress thinking wistfully of another passage during which our mizzen staysail had been set for 36 hours on end. For the whole of one long day, we were in company with a tunnyman. He was well reefed and so were we, but he was 60 tons and he would be drier and more comfortable, but to our surprise we held him in speed. In the evening it blew hard and he shortened down further and hove to. If he found that necessary, it was time for us to tuck our head under our wing and we followed suit. A quarter of a mile apart, we lay to into the night. Our lights visible until our faster drift took us out of sight. We remained hove to all the next day; that was the year we had deck leaks as the canvas was due to be renewed next winter and deck leaks are the difference between comfort and misery - and we were miserable!

Christian had now developed a greater confidence and more skills. She took off my shoulders the whole weight of the domestic side in cruising and provisioning. It was perhaps surprising that she really liked steering best when the weather was quite bad in a hard wind, but perhaps it was because 'Bluebird' then came to life and there was far more feel in the tiller, though it never demanded much physical effort. One of her special skills was in judging exactly when a meal would be required and she would prepare with no fuss at great speed something suitable which would be ready the instant we were clear after entering port or some manoeuvre at sea. But the real gift was that all my crews of any age, enjoyed a cruise the better when she was aboard. She seemed to act as a catalyst, bridging ages and temperaments. She distrusted the bachelor parties and laid down stringent orders, "How clean is my galley", we called this and James, Dennis and Ronnie were perhaps the only three who passed with flying colours. But it was Christian who headed up my only mutiny. We fetched up in St Jean de Luz after a direct passage from Falmouth which had taken so long that it worried me about the planning of the whole cruise. I liked St Jean de Luz but I had been there twice before and I was anxious to go on to Spain. Incautiously announcing this soon after arrival, I was greeted by an ominous silence. A little later Christian announced, "I have all the passports, you can sail if you like, the rest of us are staying here". So we had an 'interlude' for three days and very good value it was.

In France, we had frequently been greeted as liberators. Often firmly kissed by ample ladies who claimed that they had been in the resistance movement and that their first love was England. But on St Jean de Luz, we met the Mony Freres and their charming families. They were ardent admirers of Great Britain and they recalled with pride that Churchill had spent some time in these parts. During the war, the area had become a rest and recuperation centre for the Germans; they did not want trouble here. It was fairly remote from the fighting but it was also the Spanish border and British airmen were escaping and incredibly crossing France and reaching the border of Spain. So there were two opposing forces. The 'peace and quiet' contingent and the 'root them out at all costs' Gestapo element. The population reacted in a Gallic fashion that baffled the Germans better than studied offence. Outwardly everything was calm and friendly but incidents, apparently accidental, usually harmless and almost always amusing, happened constantly; the Germans seldom saw the joke. A campaign in the curfew in which someone on a bicycle would disappear down an alleyway, drawing off the patrols to enable those who wished to stroll unmolested to see their friends, worked up to such a pitch that the Germans banned all bicycles. German thoroughness and a triumph of logic - not a bit of it, within 24 hours, every miniature wheel or roller skate had been fashioned into scooters on which the population continued as before. One of the Mony wives was Spanish and she gave us a fascinating insight on the similarities and the differences on the two sides of the border with Basque variations. She recounted with pride how, when refused official permission to visit her relatives in Spain, she spent a long time studying the bridge post and its organisation. She then made up a costume, impersonated a well known German officer and crossed the bridge twice with impunity by sheer effrontery.

The corner of the Bay of Biscay is relatively windless though subject to swell and this has influenced the design of the local craft. They have great flaring bows, powerful engines and are like overgrown launches but with a pointed cruiser stern, adapted we were told, to running the river entrances and bars such as that of Arcachon where the rollers can so easily produce a dangerous breaking sea. We sailed to San Sebastian and secured in the little port to meet a new fate. It is true that the situation politically was tricky and there had been notice that vessels might not call even for fuel or water without special permits and visas and even then they would be required to pay in gold or in Swiss francs, but we said hopefully, "Surely they cannot mean little things like us?" An hour later after considerable altercation and language difficulty, I was marched away up the quay to Durance Vile. One sort of police with a pistol at the ready and the other sort with a rifle in my kidneys and as I went, a well known voice floated up; if Christian wishes to make her point she can be heard, "What do we do now he has gone?" I had apparently been written off. My fate was not too bad, as after three hours interrogation and explanation, there was a long, clammy pause. I found out later that there was some contact with the French Navy on smuggling matters and they had telephoned to St Jean de Luz. Our friends had not only confirmed our story but had given us a good character though I suspected that this might well have been on the lines, "Oh that lot. They are so mad they practically must be harmless". So 'Bluebird' and her crew were given a 'laisser passer' within the confines of the port for 48 hours. Later on they even promised to telephone Santander and arrange for a similar dispensation for us. Before I returned to 'Bluebird', I thought it well to contact the British Vice Consul. I was courteously and correctly received as he balanced the desire to be as helpful as possible with a caution, doubtless bred of other experiences.

But far better was in store. There are ways of doing things. His aide de camp was a charming girl, half English, half Spanish. She met me outside the great man's office and she had apparently heard the whole conversation. She knew exactly what to do. "Let me see", she mused thinking aloud. "You will want to go somewhere, you cannot very well go to the hotel - too expensive for you. A good restaurant might do, but no, they will not let you in unless you are dressed up". Then her face lit up, "I know, go to Derteanos, they will do you well and cheap. Go and have a look at it while you are here". As I said farewell on the steps, "Psst!" With a cautious glance around, "Do you want some black market Pesetas? Of course you do. Come back in an hour's time, go up that alley and turn right and wait for me by the little door". I went back to 'Bluebird' to find a much relieved crew. Christian was at pains to explain that they had only been discussing how to rescue me but she was not mollified when I revealed that I had a girl in this port; if not in every port. We did however take the Spanish girl's advice and one evening discovered, Derteanos. The set up was not attractive and when we entered I said to the crew, "This looks to me like what I think a Spanish brothel might look like". There was a sleazy bar and a dirty red curtain at the end. "Can we get a meal?" We asked. "Yes", they replied pointing to the curtain. We went through, up a dark and dirty staircase and then sure enough a little restaurant where we had a delicious meal.

Spain produced a very different atmosphere and though we were happy there, we were aware of this and did not like it so well. There were the two types of police and we did see men and women arrested and dragged off screaming and protesting. There was a great contrast between rich and poor; there was religious intolerance with an anodyne of frequent fiestas; few tourists in those days. Skirts for Christian, no trousers; long pants for the boys. You could enter no reputable hotel without a tie, jacket and leather shoes. Mark and I were in trouble one day as we strolled unthinking through the market in shorts and all the women drew their shawls across their faces, muttered and gathered together as if to mount an attack at this affront. Bull fights? Of course all our crews were intrigued and most went once; I more than once. To me the sheer showmanship, the techniques, the music and the reaction of the crowd were more important than the death of the beast. But the crews sorted themselves into the English reactions, mostly that which provokes Spaniards to say, "But you are cruel to your children", and true it is that we have our RSPCA in contrast to the NSPCC.

We soon realised that yachting on the Spanish coast is sparse, the pastime of the few, more like our Cowes of 1900 with paid crews a matter of course and the social side perhaps more important that sailing. One day, a titled Spaniard we had met, descended on us unexpectedly and also unexpectedly his wife was with him. Mark, in shorts, picked up my muttered cue and seizing a rag started to clean the winches. "El Marino?" Our guests enquired glancing his way. "Si, si", said Christian and our stock, which had wobbled, rose to a safer level. The reason for the wife's presence, transpired when she confided to Christian, "I am Cuban, don't expect me to be confined like the Spanish women and I am not going to have a child a year for twelve years until I am dead or worn out". I must say that extremely, magnificent and handsome lady was herself a recommendation for a more liberal attitude.

On to Santander with the path made smooth and back to St Jean de Luz where we heard the tale and thanked the Naval Commander. We thought it prudent to formally re-enter and clear France. We had found this a pretty casual performance anyway. A notice on the Customs shed at Benodet, "back tomorrow', might mean an absence for three or four days, but now the Customs were on strike and the police were in sympathy. Christian and I were invited to their sanctum and found them in the best of spirits, celebrating 'La Greve'. We were invited to join them with a glass or two during which we introduced our ideas which started quite an argument. The result would have done credit to Ireland: "No we cannot do anything for you because we are on strike but we would hate you to be embarrassed elsewhere. You see that row of stamps over there on the desk, the third one from the left is quite a good one. Stick it on your passports with the date". And so we cleared ourselves. But before departing, they threw open a large store cupboard, "You wouldn't be wanting anything out of here", they asked. "Contraband you know, seized from smugglers". Indeed some of the items were attractive. "A contribution? Oh no, of course not but anything placed in that little box over there would be very welcome for the strike fund". I would go back to St Jean de Luz anytime, it is one of my favourite places.

We were cunning in working night and day winds when returning northwards from La Rochelle to Ushant against prevailing north westerlies. We sought shelter from an occasional summer gale; we explored the Morbihan and saw the cruising luggers at their work. It was astounding to see them beating to windward and going backwards and sideways at 6 knots on the tide. With their simple rig, they could handle anything from gale to calm at minimum cost, while their tides did most of the work. We smelt our little ports in Isle d'Oleron and around the Pertuis de Breton, Antioch, Maumusson and the canals of the River Seudre, the moat at Le Chateau in which we bathed until we found the water red; it was slaughtering day in the local abattoir. The Fier d'Ars and a meal of oysters at 100° in the shade with no 'R' in the month and one of the crew laid low with mild heat stroke. Rocks and foul anchors, pilotage with the hair standing on end and 'Bluebird' taking it all in her stride. The whole of these experiences must have added up to another 12,500 miles and I suppose we had acquired an increasing competence.

We moved to anchor in the Bay and did our tour. I collected our Pesetas and then we were leaning on a bridge and as if by magnetic attraction, three other figures came and leaned alongside. They were Nordic types, Norwegians - Christaan Nielsen and his brother, with Lilleruth Kittleson. They were in the great Colin Archer yacht, 'Stavangar'. Then and there we started a friendship that continued until Nielsen lost his life in a yacht near Gibraltar, and then with Lilleruth, who had become Mrs Nielsen and her delightful small boy, Yeppa. A great ship and a great seaman. "There I was in Newfoundland. News come,

I must go quick to Norway, so I find Atlantic track with strong wind and I sail. When it blew force 8, 'Stavangar' took one reef in mainsail and she go good". If my memory serves, on that occasion he made Norway in 18 days.

On passage up the bay, another danger threatened. All cruising books talk about the risk of constipation at sea, I have never discovered why, as in 50 years with about 100 crews, I have known this happen about three times, while the opposite effect is far more prevalent. But this time, James was the exception and the day came when a worried Skipper faced a worried James over the breakfast table. I produced a 'Very Pistol' cartridge, sliced the business end, decanted the powder charge into a little dish, poured a little milk over it and proffered it to James saying, "Cigarette lighter please, we don't want a premature discharge".

Like the jug waved at the would-be rescuer, you need not really drink. It is the power of an idea that counts.

The Chenal du Four now had no terrors, we knew the tides, we knew the eddies and we could sneak through as it were by the 'escallier de service'. If I have emphasised other aspects of life in 'Bluebird' rather than the perils of the sea, it had been quite deliberate. Life is a series of checks and balances, a yacht can be anything from a houseboat to a non-stop, single-handed world voyager, but in any case it is a getaway to travel and experience of places and people in a way it would be difficult to match. Christian might say to me when exasperated by my tendency to press on, "Why don't you sail straight out into the Atlantic and then come back again. If that is your idea of a holiday, you do it but I am not coming with you".

Chapter Eight

Nine Years of Baltic Cruising

It was time to make a change. I felt that the possibilities of the Biscay area had been exploited and, though Christian's leaning was ever to the south and sunshine, I started looking north. I was hard pressed in my business life and found that it demanded increasing time and energy to prepare for a cruise and to see that 'Bluebird' was ready and seaworthy. The western coast of Spain and Portugal were possible but more difficult to organise from Biscay. The Mediterranean was costly and far and I had not enough time to justify it. It also did not appeal to me at that time and I had the quite irrational feeling, "I can always do this when I am older". We again discussed other holidays but the family agreed that we were prepared to use our precious time in cruising though we might well be missing other travel we should have enjoyed; you cannot have everything in this life. It was a little different in my case as I did so much business travel and that now entailed rushing about by air so that hotels and conventional tourist resorts were almost like business to me and not a holiday.

Scandinavia and the Baltic generally was the obvious place and, in spite of Christian's misgivings, we did our reading and prepared ourselves for a new venture in 1951. We little knew that this area was to open our best and richest experiences in the first 'Bluebird of Thorne' or that we should cruise that area for nine years, broken by more Biscay cruises and a year in which I did not fit out for other reasons.

You can creep up to the Baltic from the Channel with no long passages but we had other plans. At Whitsuntide, we left Beaumaris not knowing that we had laid up there for the last time. Dennis and Lance, two of the trusties, were with me when we sailed north and in seven days, made the 300 miles to Inverness by traversing Crinan and then the Caledonian Canals. This had involved a night off the Isle of Man, when we had to change to storm staysail and trysail. We then beat to windward under this rig; it was a beastly, cold and testing passage for 18 hours until we could anchor at the head of Luce Bay inside the Mull of Galloway. We were as close to the weather shore as water would allow but a northerly gale howled over the low neck of land from Stranraer and we were pitching with spray spattering the decks. We remained there for two days and it was so cold that we spent some of the time in our sleeping bags reading, and when we next required the engine, we failed to start it and had to light a little bonfire under the induction system before we succeeded. This was the only time in twenty-one years that we were reduced to this extremity with the excellent Gardner.

We anchored off the entrance to the Caledonian Canal at midnight after another testing passage. The sight early next morning was magnificent. It was freezing and the light, northerly breeze cut through our clothes. Masses of snow still lay on Ben Nevis and the clarity of the colour in the sunshine was remarkable. A cuckoo was calling close by and golden eagles were in sight overhead. We entered the locks. Lance on the foredeck rhapsodising about the eagles, took his mind off the job and in a moment, 'Bluebird' sheared into the side of the lock fetching up with a nasty crunch but our steel stem gouged out a chunk of stone and suffered no harm. A nice little terrier bitch came and made friends as we mounted the locks. It so happened that we had recently had a family discussion and as a joke had written a specification of the dog we wanted for a house dog and for my daughter. I realised that this terrier, part Cairn, part Skye and part West Highland, an exceptionally well-bred mongrel, corresponded exactly to what we had written. I followed her home through a village, spoke to the owner and commissioned a bitch from her next litter. This curious way of selecting a dog was never regretted and provided a family friend and companion for thirteen years.

In July, we made a good, fast passage of 400 miles from Inverness to Kristiansand. We now had a hot moulded, ply dinghy. The 'Fairy Duckling' had replaced the much heavier clinker dinghy that was old and battered. We had a small outboard for the first time but still sailed the dinghy and I made up a Balfour Lungstrom rig which we thought had considerable merit. We entered the inner leads very much on our toes on this first trial and, using the excellent Norwegian charts, we came to Grimstad.

The first impression of this coast was good. It was comfortably hot and the lovely fruits and berries were appreciated. In the marketplace an attractive clinker-built launch was displayed for sale. Christian began to approve in spite of her misgivings. We met up with the Nielsens in 'Stavangar' and renewed our acquaintance with this magnificent outfit. With further experience in the leads and amongst the islands, we evolved a

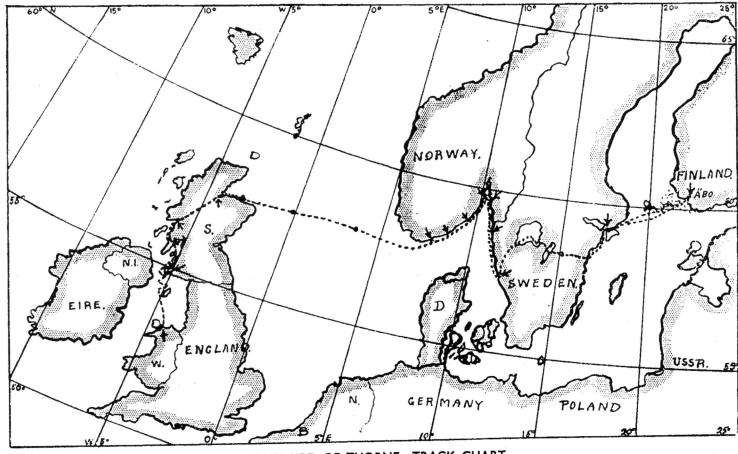

BLUE BIRD OF THORNE—TRACK CHART

pilotage system which became a standard. One man handled 'Bluebird', another on duty had a plotting board with the detailed chart and it was his task to mark the ship's position constantly with a coloured pin. Sometimes another pin would be left on the last fix position and yet another on the next danger or objective ahead. When we tried sailing at night, we found it exciting. In the main channels, the lights were excellent with coloured sectors but under sail and without a searchlight it was arduous and all too easy to find a rock about to tangle with the crosstrees. So we only practiced this to complete a passage or of necessity. We were to find later that in midsummer on the northern coasts, it was so light that the navigation lights did not come on at all.

We worked up to Tonsberg, then the great whaling centre with rows of fast whale catchers fitting out for the next voyage to the Antarctic. To save time, we went from Tonsberg up to Oslo by train and returned by ferry after spending two days in a little hotel, twenty minutes out of the town. "Have strong breakfast", we were advised and it was just as well since the next solid meal was at 16.30. The Viking ships, the 'Kon Tiki' raft and the 'Fram', kept me occupied but whatever the pursuits, this interlude was good value for all. We then crossed to Sweden and worked down through Marstrand to Goteborg with all reasonable despatch, encountering more traffic as we neared the city. We were rarely out of earshot of the 'boomp, boomp' of the big slow-running semi-diesel two strokes. Some of the

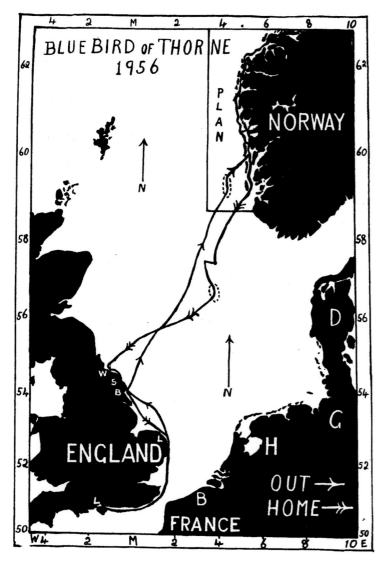

A Norwegian cruise.

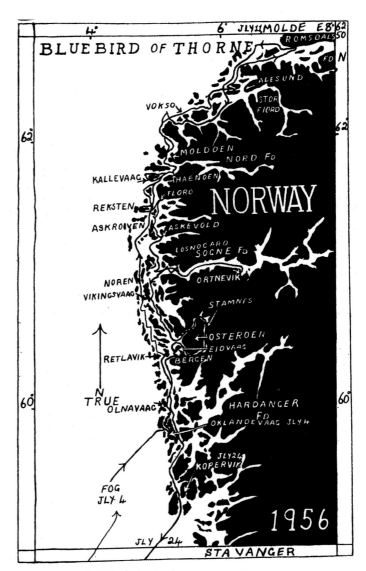

Detailed chart of Norway cruise.

old Bolinders were as large as 120 horse power from a single cylinder and both cylinder and exhaust pipe about 16 inches in diameter and these great machines only ran at about 150 rpm. All had the variable pitch reversing propeller with no clutch. I argued the merits and demerits of this constantly and studied the way in which they were handled.

The Gota Canal was a joy but we did not get full value and had to spoil it by pressing on too fast. I should like to spend a week at least in this system and sailing in the big lakes 400 foot above sea level where it would be quite easy to be seasick under these unique conditions in fresh water. We had been appalled by the current in the Gota River just below the Trollhatten Locks; perhaps there was a spate but at 6 knots, our effective maximum, we only just made it round one or two critical bends. These big locks are so deep that they have a system of inset pins and if prepared for this technique, with two lines ready bow and stern, ascent is easier than with the more usual long lines to the summit.

When we entered the small canal system, life was real and life was earnest with locks, more locks and bridges; hard work for all hands, but the lovely stretches where the canal dives into a narrow cut through the forest, are almost beyond description. The trees appear to meet overhead, the rocks are close at hand producing an almost tunnel effect and everywhere the birds, particularly the attractive Crested Grebes with their skittering offspring. We crossed the watershed and started on our way down to the inland sea. "Sagte Fahrt, Sonnen, 4 knopp til Sluicen", became familiar watchwords. In the ports, so many seamen spoke English that there was no difficulty but here inland, Christian found shopping a trial until she went ashore to the villages armed with a pack of 'Happy Family' cards. Mr Bun, the baker was understood instantly. Once, when Christian badly needed a 'hair do', which to her was a sacrosanct necessity, she went to find a suitable establishment. She had some difficulty with this, partly language and partly because she did not know what to ask for in Swedish terms. She finally returned triumphant announcing that she had had a very successful 'dam frisering'!

The landmarks after traversing Lake Vettern were confusing as there were a number of prominent buildings not marked on the chart. Perhaps they explained the rumours we had heard about guided missiles as Karlsborg has a military establishment and when we walked ashore, we found camouflage and barbed wire areas in the woods. A delightful contrast to these reminders of war was provided by numerous glowworms or fireflies in the evening dusk. The days wore on, the weather was perfect. We passed the steelworks at Motala and I, as another steelmaker, felt a little jealous of people who could have their works in such delightful surroundings. At Boronshult, we were held up for an hour or more by the Gota Canal trip steamer and an auxiliary ketch trader which came up to the locks before they would let us down. His bowsprit waved up and down 20 inches (measured) at each stroke of the great single-cylinder diesel engine. Leaving Lake Boren, we just managed to pip a schooner which was coming down and beat him for entry into the lock and road bridge. Later, however, in a broader place in the canal, he hooted us down and made us slow and let him pass. The thud of his diesel, made 'Bluebird' shudder as he went by.

Everything looked so prosperous in Sweden. We never saw an unpainted or shabby house. The farms looked well kept; the crops were lush, the sleek, brown cows in the best of condition and one could picture the enormous barns simply bulging with the fruits of the earth. Thankfully we reached the last flight of ten locks and entered Lake Roxen. Here we were able to sail again and although it looked as if it might be a little tricky, we determined to tackle this stretch to reach Norsholm that night. We succeeded in doing this though we found it difficult enough in the dark. This part of the canal is not normally navigated at night. At Soderkoping we were not very clever and went aground in a brisk wind. After a brief struggle, we secured to better advantage and went ashore. A certain amount of organising took place here, including a telephone call to our agents in Stockhom. Feeling rather full and sleepy, we tottered down the last stretch to Mem where we secured in the Basin, deciding to have an early night as we found ourselves irritable, a sure sign of fatigue in a normally sweet-tempered ship. The plan was to press on to Stockholm and we were glad to leave the locks behind us. The weather was lovely but some intricate pilotage lay ahead in which we scored our one and only rock for this cruise. "If every dog may have his bite, 'Bluebird' must be allowed one rock in such a cruise".

Light variable winds persisted. Most of them were useful to us but some were ahead. It was in such perfect weather that we realised how much we liked this sailing, how interesting the pilotage was, how perfect the scenery and how delightful to have no tide. At the same time, however, we had to admit that we were missing the cruising ground by pushing on so remorselessly to keep to our programme. It would have been so much better if it had not mattered how far we sailed in a day or whether we reached a given point or not. Once again we were jealous of those who had more time. We also had to admit that in a way we were misusing 'Bluebird'. The winds were not strong enough for her to sail to proper advantage under these conditions. Everywhere about us little skerry cruisers with their light displacement, efficient hulls and tall, narrow rigs were scudding about and sailed tight on the wind in a strength of breeze which would hardly serve us. We worked through Oxelsund, where we were spoken to by a Customs launch. Next day we worked up to Sodertalje and entered Lake Maleren. In the afternoon, we anchored off at Stadstaholm Island and went ashore to bathe and sunbathe with the temperature over 80°. Christian was roused to fury when I called this a typical interlude. "How dare you call it that when we only paused for three hours for the first time in days".

So we entered Stockholm, sailing in slowly by the back door with the weekend throng of craft in that boat-conscious and yacht-owning place. Very impressive with every last one of them calling a greeting and giving us a wave. We were told that there were 40,000 small craft and what a fascinating playground is spread out for them. We secured, by permission, to a Yacht Club buoy and enjoyed the bright lights of Stockholm where everything is so clean that you could eat your dinner off the town hall steps. Already the days were shortening, the nights drawing in and we realised that in longitude 20 east, we were so far from Greenwich that our sun was 80 minutes earlier. Sweden kept British Summer Time but it was light very early in the morning and dark quite early in the evening. It was best to organise the days with an early start and anchor early in the evening but somehow this always seemed difficult to do and we were apt to run too late into the evenings, often losing the breeze and arriving tired and late for supper.

Welkomm to Finland

The passage to Finland was no problem now we were practiced in the pilotage, but open water felt strange, even stranger the thought that this is frozen solid in the depths of winter and sometimes a way can be cleared over the ice for lorries to ply between Sweden and Finland. We had decided to go to Abo or Turku as we were short of time and reports of the Russian occupation of the Porkala Peninsular, with convoys to Helsinki, were disconcerting. We made a final approach by night through a congested port. There were many ships and nearly every funnel bore the Hammer and Sickle, while most of them had an ice-breaking bow form. We felt that we were poking the fringes of the Iron Curtain as we crept gingerly into a berth behind a square-rigged ship. We had reached the furthest objective of this cruise.

Difficulties beset us next day. We were told that we should have cleared at Degerby and the exchange was ruinous at 660 kroner to the pound when we had hoped for 830. Costs were higher even than in Sweden. The language was impossible and it took us 2½ hours to telephone our friends in Helsinki. We made no progress with a meal in a restaurant until I achieved an enormous involuntary sneeze; for some reason smiles broke out on dead pan faces and people began to help. When we returned to 'Bluebird', our friends had arrived and as we came up behind them, we heard them say, "Surely they cannot have come from England in that little yacht". We were glad to see them and all difficulties evaporated. 'Bluebird' was left on a mooring at the Yacht Club to be cared for by helpful members. We departed by road to spend the night at a delightful country house three hours away and one hour from Helsinki. During the night, in the peace of that lovely land, I thought I heard guns. When I mentioned this to our host at breakfast, the reaction was swift but surprising, "You were quite right, it is the Russians, they have exercises. Look you can see them". He handed me a pair of binoculars and there across the lake, little figures in uniform were scurrying about among the trees.

In Helsinki we saw the tragic reminder of a heroic resistance in the war cemetery and as we walked out our host pointed behind us, "That man is the leader of the Communist Party". Equally sad the political division and economically, Finland was still paying a heavy price by building ships and supplying goods to Russia. We became aware of another division. We noticed that our hostess spoke differently to the children; it was not baby talk and it transpired that our host was a Swedish/Finn and his wife a Finnish/Finn. Each spoke to the children in his or her native language. One of the little girls, charming and about four years old, had the dark eyes with the covering at the inner corners and the tilt which, with the shape of face and high cheek bones suggested the type that roamed the north of the world unbroken by sea in the Ice Age and established in many lands, here represented by the Lapps. The elder daughter was a beautiful Nordic type. Mark dropped a social brick in the Yacht Club in referring to this subject and was told quite sharply that he was in the Swedish section of the sailing community.

Memories of Helsinki stem from three visits. The second time we sailed there in 'Bluebird' was after the Russians had relinquished occupation of Porkala and with convoys no longer necessary we could enter freely. On that second occasion after wonderful experiences in the Archipelago and sailing by inner leads literally through the forest (the wealth and the green gold of Finland), we approached Helsinki on a glorious day. Frances was tempted to bathe and I let her do so on a bowline as we drifted slowly along. It was great fun until a sudden squall, when Frances at 5 knots, had difficulty in stopping herself revolving and porpoising and was retrieved gasping. I re-learned the rule, never to let anyone overboard when underway.

I also visited Helsinki on business and on a Trade Mission, contributing a different sort of experience. We were lucky to have many friends speaking English or French since the Finnish language, as Christian and I discovered when we had the loan of a house in Helsinki for three days, was completely impossible. We had never been so defeated in any country before. Communication really was by signs and pictures. The words are of inordinate length and there is an extensive and fantastic alphabet. In the peculiarities of this language, I once appeared in their press as, 'Lordi, Lordi'!

In Finland there are hundreds of miles of channels in the densest Archipelago in the world. Pilotage is exacting and quite serious for, once off the marked route, a rock may lie anywhere and the islands are so alike that once an error is made, you can be lost. We said that it would be sad if we wandered away, struck a rock and were marooned on one of a thousand islands, existing on berries, squirrels and snakes until the winter freeze-up when we could sledge our way out. An exaggeration of course. Even here there was the unexpected welcome in the solitudes of rock and pine. We passed a rare yacht with friendly waves as it proceeded in the opposite direction. An hour or so later, we secured to anchor and tree in a little bay just off the channel. Half and hour later the same yacht appeared and followed us. "Is this yacht 'Bluebird?" "Yes". "Is it from England?" "Yes". "Is your name Balfour?" "Yes". "Welkomm to Finland". This was fame. We spent a delightful evening together. They had of course read articles of mine in yachting publications and were fascinated by 'Bluebird'. Fortunate in our friends and contacts, we had no difficulty in rating Finland and its people, very high in our Scandinavian assessment. It might struggle perhaps to equal Norway and it was handicapped in its struggle to recuperate from war.

We returned from Turku that first year with a gale blowing but knowing the channels with sheltered water, we could proceed. On our second day of return, we took a minor channel on the Finnish charts marked at 2 metres; this was very close work for our draught and it was very narrow also. We left the Archipelago, working through the outer islands in a strong breeze. We could just lay our course to Soderarm in Sweden and I went below and turned in, feeling really thankful to have a good rest with clear water ahead and no less than 150 miles of sailing in the Finnish Archipelago achieved without a false move or ugly moment. However fascinating, the pilotage becomes somewhat exacting when you are sailing long hours; one does get used to the sheltered water sailing. The crew accused me of becoming more alarmed about the return crossing of the Aland Sea than I had been about taking the boat across the Bay of Biscay to Spain. In spite of this, I slept solidly for about three hours until Soderarm was on the bow and not so far away, while they had had a grand sail with quite rough water at times. With the aid of smoother water and a little pinching and scraping, we were able to hold the same tack until we were quite near Furusund, when, with the wind falling lighter, we handed sail, started the engine and picked up a Yacht Club buoy at 22.30. I confessed to feeling pretty thankful that we had Stockholm under our wing and that the gale had not prevented our return.

After a quiet, calm night, we were under way at 10.00 after clearing Customs most efficiently and quickly. It was a nice, fine day but the weather had not settled down to the hot, bright weather we had previously experienced in these parts. There was a brisk breeze which was mostly ahead. It was colder and we all felt that the short summer was already reaching its close. A sweater was welcome by day and at night it was no longer a case of lying under one blanket and we all crawled gratefully into sleeping bags. We worked on with periods of sail and periods of power until at 18.00, we secured to a buoy at the yacht yard on Lidino, where we intended to leave 'Bluebird' for the winter. The cruise was over. It had been a complete success at the time and in retrospect. It left us with memories that are unforgettable and the desire to cruise in those waters again, but preferably with more time and in a more leisurely manner. Mixing business with pleasure, had worked perfectly smoothly; I think this was largely because all the people in the northern countries understand boats and the sea so well that due allowances were made. This was in marked contrast with Spain. The outstanding feature of the whole cruise was variety, we had absolutely everything: a rough, open sea crossing, pilotage, sheltered water, deserted islands, charming, little, unspoilt places, big cities, the hospitality of friendly people, experience of the countries ashore and away from the ship - one could continue almost indefinitely, but all this built up to something that we had never done before and was infinitely worthwhile.

We had one day of really devastating toil at the end of which we felt that we could leave 'Bluebird' in good hands. The next day was a mad dash round Stockholm and in the morning we boarded the aircraft for England. The nuclear-powered ice breaker, which can keep this sea open in winter, was still to come and so was the Hydrofoil service to the Aland Islands. This was the first time I had laid 'Bluebird' up overseas and I had some misgivings. At a dinner of the Royal Cruising Club in December, the Commodore told Christian that, although it had not been announced yet, 'Bluebird' had won the Claymore Cup for the cruise to Finland. Christian's instant reply is reputed to have made history. "Oh no Roger, we can't have won the Cup, we enjoyed ourselves".

The winter lay-up at Lidino near Stockholm, was a great success. Owing to the snow and ice, yachts were all under cover and the gear was in stores. At that time, a Swedish craftsman was paid about 50% more an hour than in Great Britain but whether working better or with better direction, the total cost was smaller and there was one bonus: when we went out next year, not only was the work well done and ready on time, but the whole yacht and all her gear was spotlessly clean. How often I had begged and prayed for this in England, offering to pay extra. It had never been so thoroughly done. Air travel had arrived, primitive though the aircraft were compared to the standards twenty years later, but even with this relatively dim equipment, it offered a magic carpet, facilitating a lay-up in Sweden and speedy travel. We found it pleasant to take a week's holiday when we flew out to fit out, putting up for a night or so in some lodging or a small hotel before living aboard and I found that this compared well with two or three weekends of exhausting motoring and the work-up that had been the English equivalent. We had only one

moment of fright when under way for the first time, the engine stalled. Accustomed to feathering propellers, but not the type on 'Bluebird', they had overhauled it unasked and reassembled it accidentally one tooth in advance. It was only necessary to change the marks on the control and we found that our performance was slightly improved as a result.

Sweden, in marked contrast with Denmark, Norway and Finland, had not suffered the ravages of war. Everything was new, clean, painted and prosperous. The standard of living was the highest in Europe and it had happened that the war, whatever their feelings and sympathies, had been profitable and advantageous in neutrality. All this did not seem to have reacted so favourably on human happiness; in some quarters there was an almost apologetic reaction, however unnecessary. We saw the holiday crowds disembarking from a ship at Gotland and on a Public Holiday, we all remarked that there was little joy on the faces of this holiday crowd. How extraordinary that, with a high standard of living and little poverty, Sweden has one of the highest suicide rates in the world. The country has its own characteristics and it would be hard to say whether we preferred the west or the east coast after quite extensive experience, though the south was relatively dull from the cruising point of view and the Skaargard round Stockholm was physically the most extensive playground. We had our friends there on an outer island and so learned something of that way of life. It could be embarrassing when you were a guest for the whole of a long day that no reference was ever made to the useful little out-house. We never found it and we never saw our host slip away. Handicapped by language, our enquiries for a comfort station did not register; somewhere in the forest there was a little house but we never found it!

It is understandable with the long winter that the short summer should be exploited to the full. For nearly three months, schools, shopping and business are at a minimum and families are out in the open. Father may perhaps commute to a short week's work; there was a good service of fast launches and slower ferries but now the Hydrofoil craft have cut the time in half for return to Stockholm. During the summer, we found that the weather averaged better than England; you could have a good year or a bad one. It could be hot or cool and we had one year with relatively a lot more rain, but this was balanced by a superlative year, always dry and with temperatures up to 90°. On a very remote island, we asked our friends what they did over long periods, and the reply was, "When the sun shines, we swim and we lie in the sun. When it is wet we fish".

On the west coast, the rocks are pink; a perfect colour for the sunbathers. How delightful to lie on a sun-warmed rock with the warmth of the sunshine in one's face. The sunbathers are camouflaged against the perfect colour and how beautiful the tan of the lovely blonde girls, after long, long hours of mild sun, so like the burning glare of the sub-tropics. Nearly always we found a good sailing breeze and this explained a few coasting vessels still trading under sail. There might be an occasional gale, it might be severe but it did not matter as much with so much sheltered water. We visited the main yachting centres on both coasts, preferring perhaps Marstrand, but we were happier cruising in less smart surroundings. The Swedes had a sort of yachting uniform which was smart and also practical. Typically, this was a blue or grey suit, the trousers somewhat like ski wear and the blouse jacket somewhat like a battledress but smarter and tucked into the waist with flap pockets and a smart forage cap to match, all in a serviceable material like a tightly woven whipcord. Christian caused a sensation at Marstrand on Regatta Day; we were returning rather late and in a hurry from our shopping at lunchtime, walking down the main street with our packages. Opposite was the terrace of the main hotel crowded with the yachting throng. Christian gave a loud scream and cast her load from her. There in the dust, five little flat fish gave their last despairing gasps - they had come to life in her arms! This performance raised a positive cheer, even from the reserved Swedish temperament.

At Rosenlunde, not far away, was the home of Madame and Bjorn Prytz, who had been Swedish Ambassador to Great Britain. We could visit and secure 'Bluebird' to their buoy or to their jetty. Ashore, near the water's edge, there was a little guest house and there you could repair for a shower, a simple meal or sleep. Next day a card or a chit to the house and, if at home and if convenient to your hosts, you might be invited to a meal, you might be visited, or otherwise remain on your own resources. What delightful hospitality and how beautiful a place. There we experienced the traditional Swedish customs and the rather formal protocol with toasts and a formal speech of thanks to the hostess from the senior guest at each meal. In contrast, the life in the open was as free as air. In deference to the guests, there was a cabin for ladies on one arm of the little bay and one for men on the opposite

headland but no bathing dresses were worn in the water. There was sailing, water-skiing and walks in the wooded countryside by lakes and by arms of the sea.

On one cruise, we entered Karlskona by a channel that might be termed the back door and after a night at anchor, we sailed slowly away through the front door. A fast Naval vessel came up at 20 knots; a very personable young Lieutenant spoke through a loud-hailer, "We will now take you out of here", he announced. Unwittingly, we were sitting in the middle of their torpedo test range! We handed sail, a towrope was passed and off we went at 12 knots; never had 'Bluebird' done that speed before and, fascinated, I studied the resulting wave formation. It seemed familiar and I realised that I had seen its exact counterpart when towing the test model in a tank twenty years before. The torpedo boat slowed down and we cast off. Again the hail, "Give my love to merry old England", was the parting cry but the aura of mutual happiness was rather spoilt as they managed to get the warp round their propeller and remained stationary while we stole silently away under sail.

Whether on business or pleasure bent, 'Bluebird' was a passport to all communities at any level and the crossing of the North Sea ranked to a Baltic yachtsman almost like an Atlantic passage to an Englishman. We crossed that so many times and usually by the longer routes, only once returning from Ymuiden. We had our experiences and the outward passages averaged with more fair winds and the homeward with more head winds, but there are no rules and we had everything one time or another. On one occasion at Whitsuntide, we had intended to make Cuxhaven from the Solent. Another time, we sailed from Lymington to Bridlington at an average of six knots.

I now marvel somewhat at the light-hearted ways in which we tackled our cruising. Usually Christian and I, with one or two unskilled young, might depart from Lowestoft or Bridlington, bound for Bergen or Kristiansand. Christian might have, as on one occasion, a leg like a football after a nasty fall and operating rather in defiance of doctor's orders. Almost always I was the only man aboard who could do everything or navigate or direct. We kept single-handed watches under almost all conditions however unskilled the crew; this was only possible because of, and it was a tribute to, 'Bluebird's' safe and vice-free habits. I was on call day and night but I was excused cooking and washing up unless, as could happen, all others were seasick and in those days

I was not immune from this ill myself. Avomine, now fully tested and launched, was the ship's handout to those in doubt and it was helpful. The crew always said that when washing up was mentioned, the Skipper disappeared into the chartroom. Christian said she could always tell when conditions were serious as I was then apt to be found standing in the saloon, one arm crooked round the stanchion that acted as table support and fuel filler pipe, swaying to and fro, while I concentrated on navigational problems. Such was the scene when we should have sighted the Naze some time before. Christian had convinced herself that we had missed Norway and were bound for Spitzbergen and the polar bears. She then sighted a lighthouse, it was Torungen and there was great rejoicing. That was the only time I had not attended to compass swinging myself. It had been done at Lowestoft in my absence and we had an error of 8° on north east. I had anxious moments in serious weather when lying in by berth resting; I had to steal myself not to turn out or when to do so and with what excuse. The young and the unskilled had to learn and I had to force myself to leave the responsibility with them as much as possible. But I must correctly assess each man and his capability and temperament. One over-confident would not call me when he should have done or would not admit ignorance or error and so might become dangerous. Another man might be careless or slap-happy but the other type was doubtful of himself that, without support or encouragement, he could crack up or fail. Most of them made the grade, most of them came back again and there were new ones as earlier crew married or became involved in other pursuits. A new phase began when the first married ones began to come back again. The nicest and most understanding wives would approve and allow them to go cruising occasionally; few of the young wives could come as they were mostly tied up with young children. I was conscious that I was not universally popular in every home but later on the wives themselves came and all were my friends and I do not remember that 'Bluebird' has caused any broken homes.

'Bluebird' still had no electrics but a more sophisticated battery radio gave us Console. Mark was the patient exponent of this method and we came back across the North Sea using this guidance as a test. It was good but for some reason we never discovered we were constantly about 5 miles south of our other methods as confirmed by landfall. We still had no echo sounder and 'Bluebird' lagged in the application of new equipment, though plastics, headed by the bucket, had begun to come aboard.

The North Sea area that most frightened me was that between the West Danish and the North German coast with the islands and sands on the one hand and Horns Riff on the other. There is menace in a severe north westerly gale; I do not believe that a small yacht can escape and she would be lucky indeed to get into shelter with the tides, the channels and the seas breaking on the sands around that Bight. For some years after the war, there was not even the hope of shelter in Heligoland, so shattered was its harbour. Friends of mine have met disaster in this area and I have passed through it six times, encountering only a dangerous but short-lived thunderstorm. On another occasion, we ran into the Elbe under conditions that would have been quite impossibly dangerous in storm and bad enough in strong winds through a gale. On yet another passage, we came out of the Elbe, reefed down with wind force 6, and we had to beat to windward for 52 hours from Cuxhaven to the entrance to Terschelling and Harlingen, whence we entered the Isselmeer. It was lucky that we took no chances, the characteristics of a vital light on Ameland had been changed unknown to us and had I been careless, this could have been fatal.

On one cruise, we visited seven countries and this coincided with much hard weather. We were reefed down for fourteen days out of twenty-one. We had fourteen nights at sea and much distance was to windward. By the time we were back to our base in England, we had begun to wonder why we sailed at all. That cruise might illustrate our finances. We ran these rather on the Communist system, "From each according to his means, to each according to his needs". Into the kitty, usually a jam jar, went what was contributed and from the kitty, all needs were met. It only remained to put in a note book, what each had put in and how long each was aboard. At the end of the cruise, I converted everything to English currency, reduced the total to an average cost per man/week; this, compared with contributions and having regard to means, gave a plus or minus to or from the ship and many a crew was surprised to receive a cheque they had not expected at the end of the holiday.

The Kiel Canal is pleasant and efficient. It is convenient to use an agent and the United Baltic Corporation are splendid, with the attraction of payment in sterling in London. We explored Danish waters more thoroughly than on our previous passages and laid 'Bluebird' up at Vordingborg; there, in a little yard of Rasmussen og Egholm, we found the Danish equivalent of Morris & Levitt. 'Bluebird' just went up on their small slip during the winter, leaving their other way available for their normal fishing boats. The only yacht of her size or from overseas, they looked up on her as their own property and took enormous pride and pleasure in her welfare. For two winters, we were there and enjoyed both laying up and fitting out. We made a circle of friends, a local doctor was our interpreter and we were invited to some of their functions. Christian christened some of the fleet dinghies the school had built.

As in Sweden, everything was spotless and it was typical of these people that when disaster of the type, "anything can happen once", had occurred, they tackled it without reference to me. A diesel tanker, delivering fuel too fast and failing to shut off, flooded a Dorade ventilator and from this, some fuel got back through a breather pipe into the main drinking water tank. They wrote to the fuel company, got the best advice, stripped the tank manholes, cleaned the whole system and flushed it repeatedly until the water was tasteless. If they had not told us, we should never have known that this had happened.

I suppose it is a matter of taste, but we rated the shallower waters round Denmark and the more frequent artificial harbours, rather lower than the areas in Norway, Sweden and Finland, that we liked so well. The war had left strong feelings here. The resentment of the occupation was intense and we were told of instances where Germans had come, bringing their wives to show them where they had been billeted in the war, demanding entrance with complete absence of tact. As the years went on, the resurgence of Germany brought further outrage as larger, smarter and more expensive German yachts began to appear, some with paid crews and often demanding facilities at yacht clubs and joining races uninvited. To the Danes, this rather said, "We were the masters then, we have the money now".

The cruise in 1960, illustrates how plans are changed by circumstances and events beyond foresight or command. We fitted out at Vordingborg and had a pleasant local cruise with the family at Whitsuntide, intending to return to England later, but from that point, events took charge. My mother died and that altered the date of the cruise and complicated crew arrangements. Christian was ill and it was uncertain whether she would be fit enough to start. Christian's nephew John dropped out at the last moment as his father had died suddenly and without prior illness. Rather shattered by all this, I attempted a more leisurely cruise of lesser scope but exploring more thoroughly the Swedish west coast and returning by our well loved Norwegian east coast, thence through Lim fiord and some of the Great Belt, both of which would be new to us.

The start was interesting piloting by the Storstrom Channel and a sail past Copenhagen to Skobshoved. Unlike most Baltic cruising, this artificial port, close to Copenhagen, is crowded and dues are charged, while local residents have to wait for or inherit a berth. We entered Helsingor to avoid bad weather and, of course, explored the castle. The weather was poor that year and after uncertain weather in several ports, we just beat a severe gale into Varberg after a day's delay. We sailed at 05.00 hours in company with a motor sailor, with whom we had made friends. He passed slowly ahead of us in the early stages but as the wind built up, we set all canvas, gradually overhauled him and finally left him astern. Again the wind built up much as it had done two days before until it was force 6 in the squalls and we made our best speed. We entered the rocks, thankfully putting them between us and the growing sea and rushed up the channels towards Gothenburg. Our friend was bound for Langedrag. We carried on and it was a case of, "Gothenburg was a nice place, wasn't it?" as we crossed the entrance to the port so quickly that we hardly realised it was behind us. A busy time plotting, gybing, navigating through the channels to Marstrand, which we entered by the back door, securing to a fishing boat at 14.15. It had been a really wonderful day's run at nearly 7 knots average, but what a pity that it was not fine. We had covered such a wonderful coastline; much of it had been anxious work and we could not see the scenery.

Marstrand we found in an atmosphere of fevered preparation. Next week was not only regatta week - the big event on the Swedish west coast, but it was also a Centenary. Five hundred boats were expected, Royalty to attend, the American Transatlantic Race was due to finish at any time and several large square-rigged sailing ships were coming in. Eagerly all the festivities were explained to us. We were pressed to stay and take part in them but we decided that cruising types like ourselves would be out of place in the gay throng of racing craft and we slipped quietly away next morning, 15 July, to Rosenlunde, to go alongside the little quay belonging to our good friends, whom we had not visited for some years. To our great joy, they were at home and we again experienced the delightful reception we had so well remembered. Tearing ourselves away with regret from our kind friends we headed north in very heavy rain again, this time there was very little wind but what there was was ahead. In these circumstances, one has the choice with 'Bluebird', either you must use the engine, in which case you may as well use the inner channels and have the fun of intricate pilotage and also smooth water, or make one's way out to sea, clear of the rocks, where one can sail, but if visibility is bad, it is not always easy to find one's mark for entering again up the coast. That afternoon, we followed the inner channels and went through what I might call the 'cod area'. Racks with drying cod were spread over the rocks on either hand. We passed masses of fishing craft and fishing villages; a pity again that the rain blotted out the scenery. On the whole of that coast, the most important thing in the world was cod. I once asked a family what they would give their guests on a special occasion such as Christmas. Without hesitation the answer was, "cod". We passed innumerable craft heading south under sail to the Marstrang Regatta and we plugged slowly along to the North. Again the day finished unpleasantly with pouring rain and a rising wind. We entered Fiskebakskil and casting around, secured to a fishing boat at a small pier. Next morning there was some sunshine. We walked ashore and took photographs of Professor Lungstrom's craft and rig; this being his home port. Again we had a day with enough, and at times more than enough, wind but again it was a fair wind and so we went through the inner leads in preference to the rough sea round Soteskar, but as we were sailing through passages not much wider than 'Bluebird's' length, we kept a reef in the mainsail in the interests of safety, as there were moments when we were sailing 6 knots down a narrow channel in which it would have been quite impossible to turn and we might have met an obstruction at short notice. As there was some sunshine, we could see the scenery; the pilotage was amusing; at every turn there were naked bodies spread out in the sunshine on the pink granite rocks. The day was good fun but it ended in disaster. About ten miles before our intended anchorage, Christian who was steering with her mind on the pilotage, was caught by a squall which bounced off a high cliff on a nearby island. 'Bluebird' gybed suddenly and unexpectedly and Christian was flung violently onto the coaming. She was in great pain and in the midst of our concern, I forgot the pilotage for a vital moment. This you can never do in these waters. It might have been fatal, and to be quite certain of our position, I retraced our steps until I picked up the last marks before proceeding to the nearest anchorage I could find, where we could straighten ourselves out

and attend to Christian properly. Again it was a wild night of thunder, heavy rain and much wind with some violent squalls, all of which we were able to observe, as Christian was in pain and had little sleep and I was trying to do what I could for her.

In the morning, Monday, 18 July, we made our diagnosis of a broken or cracked rib and decided to make for Stromstad, which seemed a good centre for medical attention, if it was needed and also within touch of the point at which we could arrange a crew change from Oslo in Norway. Worried as we were about Christian, it was not a good day. We sailed under number one jib in light winds but again the day turned into prolonged thunder, very heavy rain and later on more wind. At one moment, we were surrounded by rocks. The fresh wind was constantly changing direction, all marks were blotted out and the visibility was about 100 yards and consulting the chart was difficult in streaming oilskins. I simply hated this anxious situation. Eventually we made Stromstad as planned and secured in the harbour, only to find that it was very crowded. Twenty-one fishing boats came in and it was obvious that we were not too popular and would have to tend warps and make ourselves as inconspicuous as possible. There was a bad sky and a bad forecast in the evening, with the night following the usual pattern. Half the fishing fleet went out but some returned as it was blowing too hard to fish. I do not think we should have sailed in any case on Tuesday, 19 July, but with the help of a friendly Swede, whose daughter acted as interpreter, we were able to fix an appointment with a doctor, avoid hospital, X-ray and complications, get Christian's injury confirmed as a broken rib, get her strapped up and she of course, full of courage, decided to carry on. Obviously this was not going to be fun for her and she would not be able to take any active part in the ship's affairs but, as she said, she could not possibly face the idea of travelling back to England in that condition and, quite indomitable, refused to consider leaving the ship to stay ashore.

We continued to juggle with the numerous heavy fishing boats, their entry and departure and tend warps more or less day and night, so it was with a good deal of thankfulness that on Wednesday, 20 July, we sailed at 04.15. It was a soft morning, not surprisingly there was some rain. At 10.15 we entered Evjesund. This had been our planned crew change point from which we hoped to visit Oslo without the labour of taking 'Bluebird' up the Fjord. It was a charming place and within an hour we had made contact with friends to whom we had an introduction. They smoothed our path, their daughter drove us to Oslo and back, they helped us with our affairs and could not have been more kind. We were on time for crew change and up to programme.

Christian stayed quietly in the ship, in contact with our friends. We drove up to Oslo to meet Frances and Brian Leach who came in from the airport and finally returned to 'Bluebird' with our good friend, engineer Erik Asker who had not seen 'Bluebird'. In our Norwegian trips and in England, we met many Norwegians who became firm friends and some of them exchanged visits with us in England. They ranged from a talented lady pewtersmith and her small boy. She was the Lilleruth Kittleson who became Mrs Neilsen of 'Stavangar', already referred to. There was also one of the largest ship owners in Norway; he had a beautiful modern yacht, but for sheer enthusiasm I would give the palm to the engineer, Erik Asker. It mattered not whether he was talking business, engineering, design, yachts, elk-hunting, war or his beloved little car, the enthusiasm came through with a kind of puckish thought and theory. There was great personal charm and standards that made tremendous demands on his own stamina. He was a man who could go out alone in the Norwegian winter with his dog to hunt elk, virtually without food or shelter for three or four days and nights. That such a man should become a leader in the resistance movement when Norway was overrun and occupied by the Germans, was natural and perhaps inevitable. There was danger to himself but the strain on his family, the danger to them and his knowledge of this, must have demanded a devotion and self-discipline that few can imagine. We in England, never conquered or occupied for so many hundreds of years since 1066 and all that, have to encounter some exceptionally vivid experience to understand the feelings engendered. When Erik Asker came to know us well and talk freely, we had such a moment.

Imagine one evening in 'Bluebird', in the calm majestic beauty of the Norwegian coast, talking until the short night was dawn. I remember so well that some inner torture of the soul was being re-lived and Erik Asker finished a recital of experiences in the resistance, "I did my duty to my country. I did all I could to satisfy my own conscience" during this time knowing the risks that I ran, yet I sent many men to danger and some to capture or death. Through them, I did great damage to an enemy and caused the death of a great number of Germans. How often I wished that others might have had the responsibility or that I might have

strangled a particularly brutal character with my own hands". We realised that after all the years some tears were running down his stricken face.

But what of this same character, feeling that after the war when all was over, he must play his part by deliberately employing known quislings in an equally heroic effort to regain normality and help rehabilitation. Not surprisingly these efforts were not universally understood and seldom successful. And what a bad driver he was! His car was a personal friend and as he drove he talked to her, encouraging response under rather tough treatment. On snow and ice, he might say, "Careful now Tulla, it is pretty but you must not dance too much".

A council of war rather changed our plans. James and Rosemary had intended to leave us here but sportingly offered to stay for another week as, with Christian out of action, it was obvious that we should be short-handed and Christian needed care. This meant that we should be six on board and I had never done this in 'Bluebird' before. It was however a great success; of course 'Bluebird' is amply spacious for this number, provided they fit in well and I realised that Christian and I had perhaps become a little selfish in refusing to cruise with more than four people aboard. Rosemary followed Susan to become the second wife of the young men to join 'Bluebird' and in due course she became a regular crew.

This was a nice day! We sailed partly outside, partly inside the leads and came to anchor in one of the most idyllic spots we had ever found. This leisurely cruising gave us a chance for exploration ashore and land exercise on most days. Some of us climbed the hills and roamed round the island. From the top we had a wonderful view of the Skerries and the channels stretching out in every direction. A similar and very enjoyable day of sail followed. We fetched up that evening at the island of Boroen and this, in its quite different way, was voted the best spot yet. A long walk ashore in the evening yielded as many berries as we cared to pick. This was more like bathing weather. So far we had not been tempted but alas, whenever we had felt like a bathe, the sea was full of an abnormal number of jellyfish. Some of them a really nasty sort and we were warned that it was bad to tangle with them.

Two of us took 'Bluebird' down to Arendal before breakfast. We secured to the town quay, and there we did much shopping which had become necessary, buying a Norwegian jersey for Frances, which gave her great pride and pleasure. After lunch, we sailed gently down to Hvalo and sailed in but found the best berth was occupied so that there was inadequate room for us. We then met the yacht 'Vulcan' and her owner, Sigval Bergesen, who asked us to follow him to a good spot he knew. This we did and finished up at Malo Island off Grimstad - a really delightful anchorage. He was sailing with his wife and four daughters and we exchanged visits and had a good evening. He told us a delightful fairy story of the island of Hesneso and we went out fishing in the dinghies until dark.

In the morning, two of us took 'Bluebird' into Kristiansand before breakfast. Here we left a message at the Post Office for 'Stavanger' and then sailed at noon. It suddenly blew up to force 6 and, feeling leisurely we said, "Let us do what we never do when we are cruising. We will simply have a sail". So we did, actually retracing our steps and finishing up at Rando. We could not have done better. We fetched up at a little private 'brigga' and were made welcome by the owner with his fishing boat. This was very old with a very old engine but by dint of hard work and with great pride, he earned a good living from it. He had a spotless and delightful house nearby where we were made welcome. We walked round the island and we learned from him much of the life of a little place like this. Everybody was complaining about the season. A girl in Kristiansand had told us that they had had only three days without rain in seven weeks. Stockholm had recorded the heaviest rainfall since 1926 and there had been terrible floods in Poland. We were prepared to start our passage across to Tyboron if the forecast was right, but our good fisherman friend told us that it was bad and he had heard on his fishing forecast from other boats that "there was big wind west of Hantsholm". So as time was not critical, we went on down the Norwegian coast, working down into the rather wilder scenery and finished the day at the island of Skjerno. From a little foot bridge, we watched thousands of jellyfish drifting past below and among them were some real giants. We saw one which must have been 3 foot in diameter and the sun glinting on its streamers, gave them an estimated length of 18 foot. This again was an absolutely 'picked' spot and Frances and I did a long walk to the other side of the island. Christian was nearly mended; for a day or two now, laughter had become the most painful exercise and two days later she was prepared to go to sea from Mandahl.

We went out at 05.45 on Saturday, in fog and light airs. We found, as we had found before, a surprising nasty sea off the entrance to Mandahl and only cleared this when we had made an offing from the coast. The wind came in ahead and slowly rose. We were unable to lay our course and we were being headed off to the east, but the wind went slowly round and pushed us further until we were able to go about and make fine progress on the correct course for Hantsholm. Heavy, thundery rain developed and we only sighted Hantsholm at two miles distance. From there the passage was trying; we made our way down the coast, progress was fast but the weather was very unpleasant and threatening. So heavy was the rain and so bad was the visibility that the powerful lights of Tyboron and its neighbour up the coast were both invisible at two miles.

At midnight we were approaching Tyboron. I almost despaired of taking 'Bluebird' in and prepared to stand off the coast and heave to until the morning. There were fishing vessels about but, apart from the danger of 'following father', we rapidly lost them in the gloom. I had indeed reached the ultimate moment of doubt when I dare not close any more; I was turning slowly in circles before standing out. Then the rain lifted a fraction, I thought I saw what might be the first of a pair of leading lights. Closing a little cautiously, we confirmed them and so we were able to creep in and rather thankfully berthed in the inner harbour after a twenty hour passage. It was now blowing quite hard; the crew of a neighbouring fishing boat rushed to help us with our warps but, as they had been celebrating Saturday night, some of them fell on their faces and the rest were not frightfully helpful. However, with the utmost goodwill, this was all sorted out and no damage was done.

I approached Lim Fjord with a very open mind. Three times I had not taken it, either preferring to go round the Skaw or to visit some other coast. English friends had told us it was delightful, but many Danish friends on the other hand had told us it was nothing very exciting; everybody seemed to run aground sooner or later. We therefore started out with pretty anxious care through the tricky first canal and emerged unscathed into the open water. It was a dull, grey, humid morning. There was not much wind but rain soon developed. We worked along, unable to see very much of the scenery through the pleasant fiords, finishing up the day at Nykobing. Here we made friends with a North Sea fisherman whose home port was inside Jutland and who was proceeding to his fishing grounds but was held up here because one of his crew was ill. From him we learned a lot about the economics of Danish fishing and he very frankly told us how it all worked out as far as he was concerned, with the cost of his boat, the fuel, the maintenance of his engine, the cost of his gear, his average returns and finally the discouraging fact that he usually landed his catch in England because as he said, "The English will buy fish three weeks old and pay a good price for it, whereas in Denmark, anything that is more than a few days old goes to the fish factory". We also heard that Denmark, so short of North Sea ports, was going to revive the port of Hantsholm which had been partly completed and destroyed by the sea and that the new port would be ready in 1965. This was under the shadow of the Fort where the Germans had mounted their siege guns, so powerful that they could reach Norway.

After two days in Lim Fjord, James and Rose left us early one morning, at Logstor, to start a complicated journey that ended in Morocco. Their extra time with us had been a great success and had bridged the gap until Christian, if not fit for all duties, was able to get about again. It was not a good first day for her to do more about the ship as within an hour of sailing, we were hard aground on the leeward side of the channel with a wind force 6 and one of the channel buoys almost touching us; we had joined the select company of those who go aground in Lim Fiord! All can imagine the fun and games that followed. We were honestly surprised and rather proud of ourselves, when slightly battered and exhausted, we found ourselves afloat an hour and a half later by our own exertions, but thanks also to a sixty fathom nylon warp which I had carried for some time for such an emergency. Everything went wrong. We got heavy weed on the propeller, the engine began to overheat, a hard head wind made progress very difficult and we thought very little of this part of the proceedings where narrow and intricate channels, miles from land with shoals on every hand, precluded visit to villages which looked delightful but were impossible of access. However, we stuck to it rather setting our teeth in a spirit of grim determination and eventually made Aslborg, passing both bridges and coming to a berth at a wharf beyond. There, Brian and I finished a rather black day by going overboard in dirty water to make quite sure that our propeller was intact after these adventures. Next day brought fog and anxiety. We made our return to Vordingborg in three days of unpleasant and uncertain weather. If this year sounds like a tale of discouragement, I think the weather that year was bad everywhere and we had rescued what we could to make quite a good cruise in spite if it. Our opinion of sailing in

these waters was unchanged and we had again confirmed our love of the Norwegian coast from Mandahl to Oslo Fjord and the opinion that it was one of the choicest areas we had known.

So near the Midnight Sun
I have said little about the west coast of Norway because it is a separate area, geologically different and it formed different impressions and memories, conveniently grouped together, even if they were not consecutive in one year.

A contrast in departures might be a prelude to the sterner stuff. Lymington to Dover: entered in a gale from the north east which persisted during a battle to Ramsgate and still continuing when a dreadful passage was made across the entrance to the Thames estuary, ending at night in Lowestoft with a very anxious Skipper neatly balanced in mind, between the risks of entering and the nastiness of trying to proceed with passage. Once in Lowestoft, as the weather continued adversely, the passage had to be abandoned as time was short. I hate to be beaten and it would make the plans for the main cruise much more difficult and restrict our limits. At this glum moment, Christian was no help; "I know exactly what is wrong with him", she announced brightly to the young crew as they awaited my decision, "he's getting old. About twenty years ago there would have been no argument, we should now be hove to somewhere in the middle of that beastly North Sea". This hurt a bit as it had the horrible impact of truth. No further comment!

In contrast to this failure was an earlier trip from Lymington to Bridlington in sixty hours, averaging 6 knots on the distance sailed. "I don't think we shall ever beat that one", I said. When we departed from Bridlington in June, I had the trusty James, Paul, a young man on his first cruise and Christian. She had all but broken her leg in a fall a week earlier; it was swollen to a shocking size. The doctor had issued dire warnings and it was further immobilised by enormous protective waddings, so we were not a strong crew. The forecast was bad so I played the cautious trick with a large reef in the main but carrying the largest headsails. The wind did rise to force 6/7, with rain, but it was fast if uncomfortable. There was seasickness; only James was quite impregnable, but progress was maintained at 8 knots and after the second night out it was never darker than twilight. It began to look like a fast passage but we ran into very thick fog and, nearing Norway, there was steamer traffic and many fishermen. Our position was unknown as the murk had precluded sights and, in prudence, I had to heave to and so remain for 16 hours. This was most frustrating and cold and clammy. If the fog lifted slightly, we should draw and sail a little only to slow down again. It was not until 17.00 on the fourth day that we glimpsed the mountains of Norway.

As we closed, it was difficult to identify the coast and then ensued one of the most dramatic landfalls I ever remember. With a mass of rocks and islands before us, which were virtually unidentifiable, we at last sighted a lighthouse and within half an hour we could undoubtedly have fixed ourselves by this, but ahead there was a haze and astern - although the day was now fine and sunny with a smooth sea - there was a black mass of fog rapidly rolling up on us. Could we identify the coast in time or should we have to clear out to sea with a not very good forecast and possibly face another twenty-four hours before making a proper landfall? Obviously it was going to be touch and go. At that point we sighted ahead two fishing boats. They also had seen the fog and were heading for home, but signalling to one of them, they waited for us and when we came alongside, I was able, by showing him our charts, to identify our position. Even as we did so the fog enveloped us and a new situation developed.

It was almost as black as night; the visibility was not more than 40 yards and our supporting fisherman had no compass in his boat but I could see from the position that, with his local knowledge, it was a safe approach to one or two islands which were steep and had no outlying rocks. We therefore led with our compass with his launch keeping us company and sure enough we eventually sighted the rock only 40 yards away. Brought up from childhood in those parts, he could almost recognise every patch of lichen and, from then on, it was easy. Skirting round the island into the leads, we entered waters so narrow that even in the fog we could see both sides and so with the help of this good and delightful fisherman, we made a passage through the leads for two miles to the village of Oklandsvagen on Bomlo Island and there secured against a little jetty in admirable security and delightful surroundings. No landfall could have been more delightful, more picturesque or more dramatic and the contrast to clearing out to sea and heaving-to for an unknown period in increasing winds and bad weather, was most attractive. We were thankful to have made port and felt that we had done it with good luck in the nick of time but without taking an unseamanlike risk.

We were in Norway. We were on our intended cruising ground and the passage of nearly 400 miles had taken 84 hours, including the time hove-to in the fog. The weather forecast was wind force 8 south west, rain and fog. We were very thankful to be in shelter. As usual on arrival after such a passage, we savoured the pleasure of a long, unbroken sleep, a relaxed day and quiet satisfaction and reflection. I thought once again how a cruise benefits from a passage at the outset. Ship and crew pull together and everything seems the easier after such a start. Christian's leg was recovering; we were unkind and said that she had ensured rest for the leg by taking a lot of horizontal exercise due to seasickness. This was untrue as well as unfair; even at the worst of the passage, she had always taken her watch. Away we went to the north. How far dare we penetrate? There is more than 1,000 miles of this coast and it is said that the outline of the coastline and the islands would stretch half way round the world. It was cruel that we could see so little of it and gain impressions only with our time so limited.

From the open sea, the outer rocks and Skerries give way to little islands; wind and sea-swept, harsh, barren and uninhabited but from there partial shelter and inside the larger islands, a little more shelter until trees appear and some with a fishing village where the coastal fringe is deep. Still larger islands, more wooded and more inhabited with deeply indented coastlines behind them rising high and rugged, perhaps to 40,000 feet or more, with the fantastic fjords. The leads are well marked and there is a virtual highway for ships; this is admirably done and at this time of year, it is so light at night that the sector lights in the channel do not come on at all. Communications on this coast were then so predominantly by sea that the Government maintained the mail and passenger steamers. There was a doctor service, electricity and telephones everywhere, however remote the hamlet, this made the easier by the abundant water power. The power lines could be a navigational hazard as they cross and re-cross the channels. There are three usual heights, the main leads will pass most ships, the minor leads would pass 'Bluebird' with her 55 foot from the waterline, but the inner leads may have lower heights and these were our danger. The charts show the major lines and a board on each shore gives the height, but these are weathered and difficult to read or hidden by trees and you may be approaching at speed in a strong wind with little room for manoeuvre but that was not the cause of our undoing. One night at minimal light on the very border of our chart, we approached an attractive inlet. We could see a jetty and boats with masts and from experience this all indicated a good spot to secure for the night. Crawling in very slowly under power, I posted a look-out on the foredeck thinking of the possible unmarked rock. Suddenly there was a sizzling noise and looking up I saw our mast head in contact with a power line which had been invisible against the dark background of the trees. It sounded like a welding plant in action. The startled crew on the foredeck scattered in a rain of molten metal. By automatic reaction, my foot had kicked the clutch out and my hand went to the big brass wheel controlling the propeller by which alone I could reverse. They say your past life flashes past your eyes in a moment but in that instance, my thought was technical: how many volts passes through me when I touch that wheel? There was no shock, the current must have earthed through the rigging and the steel hull to the water. The elasticity of the wires was sufficient to bring us to a halt and we drew astern but not before three of our rigging wires had been melted through and the masts scarred. We anchored elsewhere. There were no repercussions though several of the scattered houses were in darkness and we were a badly shaken crew. We were able to effect temporary repairs ourselves from our own resources. Christian and I have automatically ducked ever since when passing under overhead wires!

It was easy as we progressed along that coast to plan alternative routes south that would enable us to see as much fresh territory as possible. The outlying headland of Stadlanet, reminiscent of Ardnamurchan, must be rounded fully exposed to the open sea and this one had off-lying rocks. It could be a cause of delay, whether bound north or south, in bad weather. The coast gradually became wilder as we went north, the villages smaller and simpler. Any one of the little towns at the head of a fiord, might have been the setting for an Ibsen play. The introspective melancholy of this place could be appreciated the better on the spot and with the imagination of the long dark winters in the isolation of former years. Alas we had no time to reach Narvik and the Lofoten Islands. Just north of Romsdal fiord, we had to turn south but we had taken our photographs at midnight with a pink flush on the snow of the high mountains inland and our name for this cruise became, 'So near the Midnight Sun'.

We liked Losnagard, near the entrance to Sogne fjord. Here there was a natural gathering place geographically and a huge stone slab whereby reputed 'things' had been held and kings had been crowned. Sogne fjord itself was our largest and deepest penetration. It was so awesome that we felt humbled. These deep fjords can be a waste of time for a sailing yacht. The wind must blow up or down; if it is fair, well and good, if

not it can be a very long and tedious beat out while stronger wind or a cross wind overhead can produce dangerous vertical squalls. This said, the geology is fascinating. There, plainly seen are the glacial remains, perhaps with a sharp vee notch where rivers have later cut their way. The depth of water reflects the theory that much higher mountains existed before the sea rising perhaps after an Ice Age broke into these valleys. This explains the shallower soundings at the entrance to the fiords and inevitably there was a ford over the main river at the head of the fiord, where now there is a bridge if a road exists. In some cases, a road or track up a valley gives access to the highland plateau, the siting of the villages resulting from farming or fishing or a natural centre of communications.

In one of the outer islands, we secured one night in a sheltered creek, to which we were directed, as the boat that moored there was away on a trip. In the night, we heard nothing, but the following morning we found that we had been moved, silently and carefully, and we had been secured again in an equally good berth. The fishing boat had returned from a six week voyage and found us sitting on their doorstep. They had been to the west coast of Scotland, fishing for basking sharks and they returned loaded to the gunwales with reeking casks and drums of sharks livers, valuable for oil. They had struck a rock, had beached themselves and made temporary repairs. After all this, and on their return, they had been so kind to us. French fishermen would have cast us adrift, the Scots would have roused us to do it ourselves and we feared that English fishermen might have been very rude!

At every village there would be a reception committee and when this drifted away, the young would remain. Rows of boys and girls, almost like peas in a pod, fair haired and blue eyed, well made and so well mannered. We could go away for an hour or a day and nothing would be touched and the ship carefully moved if another vessel came in. Another of our more inland explorations was around the island of Osteroen and here the scenery, so grand in scale and continually changing, became too much for Christian and she came to me almost in distress, "Can't we stop", she said, "I simply cannot take any more of this". We all knew what she meant and we fetched up as soon as possible. This is not always easy. A shelf must be found and even then it is likely to be steep and poor holding ground where a river had pushed a stony delta out from its mouth. In some cases there are rings in the rocks ashore, with an anchor used only as a means of holding off. When we were there, some firms in Bergen would trade by sea, fitting out a fishing vessel as a travelling showroom and sending it up the coast with salesmen twice a year. This method has now been abandoned I believe as it was costly and time consuming, while the road communications have been much improved. Our Gardner diesel engine was a type almost unknown here and aroused great interest. Typical was one comment after inspection and demonstration, "Oh how it does run so softly". We had to buy diesel used by buses, not the universal Solar Olje used by the local semi-diesel.

To avoid the harbour scrum in Bergen, we found a berth in Eidsvaag. This was quite convenient and we could go into the city by bus where we had friends who could collect us by car and this enabled us to do shore excursions and see more of the country away from the coasts. Here of course sailing was fully understood and, on business or pleasure, 'Bluebird' was an asset and an introduction. Eidsvaag, our friends told us, had been the assembly point for the fleet which sailed to invade Scotland but the Norsemen had been defeated at the Battle of Largs. Our friends said rather sadly, "We remember this because it was defeat; the Scots remember because it was victory but the English do not remember it at all". With crew change due, we entered Bergen for a temporary call and secured just ahead of the SS 'Leda'. Christian and James walked into the customs shed with their baggage. Their passports had not been stamped but there was no difficulty here. When asked how they had arrived, we requested the officer to come with us. After a few paces from the shed door, I could point down the quay where 'Bluebird' was visible. "They came from England in that and I am the Master". The passports were made good at once.

Ronnie and Dennis had arrived by the same ship and we have never had a neater crew change; Christian and James departed and had a passage only notable because of the predominance of a rampant posse of blue-rinsed American widows, with a courier in charge of them. Our time was short but in three days running down the coast to Kopervik we were able to show the new crew the sort of cruising we had been doing. In the course of this, we did two hours between lighthouses down Bomlo fjiord, where low land did not obstruct the wind and recorded 9.3 knots for this period. It was the record speed for this 'Bluebird'.

We tackled the return passage home sailing from Kopervik with a stiff north west wind and a poor forecast. Before long, it was a hard wind and there was a gale forecast. There was no thought of return to the Norwegian coast and we worked out that the centre of the depression should pass north of us if we could make enough distance on a south, south west course before the gale arrived, and in that case, we might expect a useful shove when the wind veered through west to north west. To achieve this we had serious business to do. We drove 'Bluebird' very hard, first to make a good offing and then the best course we could make west of south. We shifted and reefed sail as necessary until on the second night out at 04.00, I was awake in my berth wondering how long we could continue when there was a bang. We had shipped a big sea and it had carried away the staysail sheet. There was no damage as Ronnie, the good seaman, had secured the weather sheet as a precaution, but it was a warning that it was time to heave to. The wind was force 8 and there was an awesome sea. Later in the morning the sky cleared, the sun came out and we sat in the cockpit doing a sail repair. I was thankful we had made good our intention and there was at least 150 miles of clear water in a circle round our position. Dennis made a memorable statement, "Thank you, thank you Skipper, for bringing me to this beautiful place. All my life I have waited this moment. Here I am in good, strong 'Bluebird', hove to in a gale in the open sea. It is a marvellous experience. Thank you, thank you Skipper". For Paul it was all new and for me a good example of a gale. For Ronnie, an accustomed experience. It will be appreciated that morale was good and a gale in open water no longer held any terrors.

By 19.00, we could let draw and make some progress and soon we were increasing sail with the wind north westerly. The strategy had worked out; we now made good progress until we found ourselves in the middle of a fleet of herring drifters, about thirty strong, not so far from the English coast. It was quite difficult to work through them and their nets in the night. In the early morning of the fourth day out, we made our landfall by sighting the glow of the slag tip from the blast furnaces at Dorman Longs, near Middlesbrough. This was quite satisfactory but we decided to enter Whitby as we had picked up something on our propeller. At low tide, we dried out and found a fragment of rotten net; a legacy from the fishing fleet. The barometer was falling steadily and there was another gale warning to the west of us, with a deepening depression due Newcastle by midnight. There was an exceptionally severe gale in the English Channel that day but we were determined to make some progress and worked a tide to Scarborough. It was only 18 miles but by the time we arrived, it was unpleasant and we were glad to be able to enter. Soon after that, the seas were breaking over the pier to the harbour but we dined ashore in peace. It was a full gale and almost storm by 20.00 and the forecast now gave gales up to force 9, covering a tremendous area. We remained at Scarborough and gusts up to 57 miles per hour were reported from Flamborough Head. Dennis had to depart, though he found the thought of work unattractive. Paul had a telegram - he had achieved an Honours degree and, as his intention was school teaching, there was jubilation. Gale forecast remained but we sailed and battled round to Bridlington. This was Ronnie's home port so baths and home comforts made a welcome change; his wife, known to all of us as Auntie Edith, took us home for a memorable meal. We had sailed from this port less than a month before.

We were on the move again that night, when the tide served, reefed down in poor conditions but likely to improve, in our judgement. Off the Humber it was sheer dirt, the tides ran strong and the sea was chocolate coloured. There were horrible holes and lumps, while a lot of shipping complicates courses at night. When we had sorted this out, I took a long watch down to the Dowsing Light vessel and we put 50 miles into six hours, broad on the wind. Cromer came up. We were still on the wind but we had smooth water to the Cockle Gat. There, we had a steep tidal sea, the wind right on the nose and it let loose with the next gale forecast and heavy rain, but we had a fair tide for five hours and forced the ship to the limit. With the engine turning over slowly, we battled on, making Lowestoft. We approached in a violent squall, all shelter lost and the reefed mainsail blew out. I could have run back to Yarmouth, but with only 200 yards to go, I opened up the faithful Gardner and in the idiom of steam, sat on the safety valve. We made it, just, but only just, and in the scud, we saw a yacht entering ahead of us; we thought it a 10 tonner under storm canvas. When we had secured, we found that it had been so dwarfed by the sea, that it was in fact a 30 ton motor sailor and she had been swept into collision with one of the piers, receiving considerable damage. The seas by then were breaking right across the entrance and over the piers and it would have been quite impossible to enter. Time was up, we had to abandon the passage to the Solent after three gales in ten days.

After the boys' and girls' holiday in Oulton Broad, we sailed 'Bluebird' back to Lymington and then to the Cruising Club Meet in Beaulieu River. Remembering my previous remarks, I added up the two passages from Bridlington and this time it was only 50 hours. It had been a big year with about 2,250 miles and 'Bluebird' had returned from nine years in Scandinavia.

Chapter Nine

Design and Building the
Second Bluebird of Thorne

'Bluebird of Thorne' was twenty-two years old when she returned to Lymington in 1961, after three more years in Scandinavia and with the war years lost. We had cruised in her for sixteen years and covered about 40,000 miles. When I built her, I said that she must last my life-time as I then thought she might be impossible to sell as, even in 1939, she could well have been considered a strange amateur design, but ideas had changed. She had been successful and she was, and still is, a good cruising yacht within the limitations of her design concept and her time. It is impossible to own such a yacht without saying, "If I did this again', or "I wonder if I could improve that". Almost without realising it, I built up the concept of a new 'Bluebird' with notes and sketch designs that had changed from time to time. I had a list of all the modifications that I should do to prepare her for the Atlantic voyage that I had never had time to undertake. Other influences were at work quite outside my own changing ideas, requirements and experience. I was twenty years older and my family had changed and developed over that period. The explosion in yachting that took place in the 1950's was continuing and there had been tremendous development in materials and equipment, more so in ten years than in the previous thirty to the start of the Second World War.

It is instructive to examine a few of these changes because their influence on design was powerful. Perhaps the most important was the advent of synthetic materials. Sails were now terylene, but to my disappointment, no-one had developed a welded seam without stitching that was so clearly demanded by this material. Hemp, cotton, sisal and coir cordage were gone for ever, replaced by terylene, nylon, ulstron and polypropylene. Hardly an item of yacht furnishing remained unchanged by this revolution. Glass reinforced plastic (GPR) was fast taking over for yacht hulls and, already established in the smaller sizes, was extending its range steadily upward but in 1960 might be considered as bounded by 40 foot in length. Masts had become predominantly sea water resisting, light alloy, preferably anodised and sound deadened. These special light alloys could also produce a hull and had attractions but needed effective welding techniques which were then still being developed.

Another revolution was the availability of smaller and lighter diesel engines in the lower powers. These had appeared and were fast taking over in the cruising field from the petrol and petrol/paraffin engines. These in turn began to make possible an entirely new approach to a better and more attractive type of vessel than that known as the motor sailer concept of the previous thirty years. With the diesel came a standard of safety and reliability that had never previously been attained in marine engines. Stainless steel had arrived for wire rope, though better in the fixed rigging applications than flexible. It was also applied increasingly to stanchions and much other equipment. Stainless steel is inevitably expensive but its use in wire had been much boosted by a change in the galvanising applied to the ordinary plough steel wire as compared with the dip methods of the 1930's. That wonderful metal Superston Bronze, originally developed by Stones of Deptford as a propeller material, had caused the development of a whole new family of winches, rigging screws and fittings, and increasing demand had made quantity production possible so that in some cases there was an actual reduction in price.

The growth of ocean racing, had 'improved the breed' and this rendered an immense service to the cruising man. I must emphasise that the best ocean racer is not necessarily the best cruiser, nor is it necessary for the cruising man to have stainless steel sheet winches, almost jewelled in every bearing and costing hundreds of pounds. Their purpose is to save a few seconds in the racing game. Miniaturisation and electronics and a wonderful range of instruments developed. For the cruising man, the echo sounders, the radio and RDF (radio direction finder) and the extensive battery of instruments, now considered essential for every racing yacht, was in the future and still remains unnecessary for the cruising man. Inflatable, synthetic rubber dinghies and life-rafts were arriving and with them came a much more effective range of outboard motors. The small cruiser yacht at last had an answer to the dinghy problem which for so long had been, "Must have it, cannot tow it, where to stow it and too small anyway". Finally came the blocks in stainless steel and tufnol, replacing an essential part of yacht's gear that had remained virtually unchanged for hundreds of years. Light weight anchors headed by the CQR (a new type of anchor), removed what was the limitation of a yacht's size in Claude Worth's day. Self-stowing with the addition of hydraulic or electric winches completed the process in larger vessels. GRP sheathing externally had conquered the Teredo worm. Steel corrosion was better understood, paints and varnishes had changed and were a different and improved breed with one pot and two pot synthetic types.

Electric equipment, refrigerators, deep freeze cabinets and charging plants, once no part of a serious yacht, were now considered essential in the larger and more luxurious types and invariably in full powered yachts. A vast increase in the range of dried, processed and canned foods made stores easier and more attractive. Radar was to come for larger yachts though a bitter jest at Lloyds had some reality, "How much extra premium should be charged when a vessel is fitted with radar?" The development of wind vane steering gears was starting but had not yet received the impetus of long distance, single handed racing. Powered systems of self-steering, compact enough for yachts, were still confined to the larger power vessel.

Meanwhile the whole approach to yachting had changed. Increasing affluence and more leisure on the one hand, congestion on the roads and in other pursuits on the other hand, had made yachting, once the rich man's sport, now accessible to all in defiance of rising costs, with capable but smaller yachts increasingly mass produced. Some of the rising costs were in elaboration of equipment which was fashionable but not really necessary. Alongside this was an entirely new approach to what an ordinary man could attempt and the voyages that could be achieved in smaller yachts. This in turn fired the imagination and attracted more exponents. Bompard crossed the Atlantic on a rubber raft; single handed Atlantic races became a regular feature. Single handed world voyages and even a non-stop round the world race were to come in the later 1960's.

Yachtsmen are a conservative breed and technical advance is not achieved without mistakes. Many developments were accompanied by unhappy use of new materials, incorrectly applied in design, method and execution. One essential fact emerged; the enormous displacement of the old time yachts was shown to be not only unnecessary but a fallacy and a handicap. Though I had started a serious approach to twin keel yachts in 1922, I was quite astounded by the proliferation of small twin and bilge keel types. "None more surprised than the striker". Mostly utilitarian and some shocking examples of design, they increased until at the Earls Court Boat Show in one year, there were more than twenty examples. A questionnaire, designed to obtain the most popular type of yacht for charter, produced an astounding number of replies favouring the twin keel type. While this development had taken 25 years to get under way, it was now a feature of the yachting scene.

Meanwhile, catamarans and trimarans were starting a swift development. Damaged in the early days, perhaps by the rather fanatical approach of their protagonists, these types have a part to play, though even today the exact field and application is not well defined, but a breakthrough in speed under sail and some astonishing voyages are already to their credit. How incredible such a passage of the Atlantic under sail would have been twenty years before, but Eric Taberly and a light alloy engineering phenomenon, looking like a flying bedstead, demonstrated this and went on to beat the largest and fastest schooner from San Francisco to Honolulu. One earlier account of a passage in a Catamaran of light plywood construction referred to life below decks, "Speed was reckoned in units of fear, existing in an atmosphere like the inside of a violin played by a mad violinist". In contrast to this, Lewis circumnavigated the world in a catamaran with his wife, two small children and another woman for part of the time as described in his book 'Daughters of the Wind'.

It was of continual astonishment to me that in this climate so few designs appeared with separate keel and rudder structures. For more than twenty years, model yacht designers had proved that they could make satisfactory and relatively faster racing yachts, fully balanced and completely controllable in this form with no helm aboard, but in full scale yachts, No! Not until the late 1960's was there a breakthrough here. This was sudden and it is now almost unfashionable to have a yacht with the older configuration, though many of these new types demand much of the helmsman and some have been known to broach-to out of control. Much of this was due to undesirable influence from racing and rating rules and the necessity in winning races to carry on until the bounds of seamanship had been left behind, but it was being established that a cruising yacht could be and should be faster and this was an advantage which had not been considered desirable or possible twenty or thirty years ago.

When I approached a new design more seriously in 1960, I started with all this in mind and 'Tahiti John' had been a considerable influence. I first knew him when he was already experienced with Pacific voyages in his little 'Stoetebeker'. He came to England and built the first 'Kochab', designed by Arthur Robb. I urged him then to have a longer yacht than the

40 foot limit he had adopted; I now know that Arthur Robb similarly advised him and had tried to get him to agree to 45 feet. This was about the size of 'Beyond', the light alloy Giles designed yacht in which Tom and Ann Worth made a brilliant voyage round the world. At that time, John refused to go beyond 40 foot, mainly from the fear that he would then become too dependent on crew. In 'Kochab' he sailed 80,000 miles and made magnificent passages. On one occasion on arrival in New Zealand from England, he went out and won an ocean race, merely cleaning her bottom and shipping a stronger crew. I knew 'Kochab' and admired her greatly. When he was home again he sailed with me in 'Bluebird of Thorne' in Scandinavia and the North Sea. This experience had effects on both of us though I gained immeasurably the more from his experience. Slight, tough and wiry, 'Tahiti' John spoke little but he brought with him the atmosphere of the long voyages. He taught me the art of coming off watch and, if no urgent task of food or navigation intruded, he would be in his berth and asleep in a few moments. He also had a fatalism borne of so much seafaring that did not detract in the least from his alertness. "Do not worry, it may never happen. Do what is necessary and never get into a flap". He did not say this but it expresses his attitude.

We had many discussions and I absorbed some gems from his rare utterances: "In voyaging, you suffer more from too little wind than too much. You must carry plenty of light sails and as large as possible. A slow, heavy yacht has heavy gear, it knocks itself to pieces, is hard to work and heavy sails are far more difficult to repair. The slow yacht has a big wetted surface to get foul and ends up hardly able to move. She needs more crew, more worry and more food. Why not have a fast one". "What happens when it blows?" I might ask. "Don't worry about that, if you have sea room you will not be carrying any sail". Marrying this to my own experience, a clear definition emerged. The fastest yacht I could devise without losing essential balance and sea-keeping qualities of the old 'Bluebird' that overall had no vices. Design a small working rig that can be reduced right down to bare poles without losing balance and combine this with the largest light weather sails. John had started out in 'Kochab' with ample diesel power but had bad luck with the engine and eventually replaced it with a powerful American petrol motor but this was not always in working order and he seemed pretty indifferent about it. My conception became: an underpowered auxiliary is useless therefore have enough power but keep it simple. You must be able to hand start it and maintain it.

At the end of our time together in 'Bluebird', John said to me, "You were quite right, your 48 foot 'Bluebird' is no harder to handle than the 40 foot 'Kochab'". A year or two later when he had sold 'Kochab', he replaced her with an ocean racing yacht, 51 foot overall. The choice was dictated by chance and a good bargain but also by speed as he saved a year against building afresh. This new 'Kochab' has served him well and I think he is satisfied. I believe he would make a success of a voyage in any yacht. Others of my friends graduated from single masted yachts of under 40 foot to two masted yachts, around 50 foot. With all this experience, I was in no doubt about the size and I was clear, "You can voyage the world successfully in any size up to 40 foot if you must, but have 40 to 50 foot if you can."

Another influence confirmed this. Tom Worth and I got together because he had sold 'Beyond' and had the idea of a 'Package Yacht' in which he could do the voyages he had done in 'Beyond' but which could be picked up by a ship's derrick and taken across any area in the world he wished to avoid. He had checked the size and weight limitations for this purpose and decided that twin keels were essential as this would avoid a cradle. We decided to develop this idea together, hoping that the same design might serve both of us and so reduce design and construction costs. He had received an encouraging response from Arthur Robb and this chance brought the three of us into discussions, and so I met Arthur Robb myself for the first time. Arthur was born in New Zealand and had earned his MBE designing small craft for the Navy during the second world war. My relationship with him was interesting and quite complicated; my first contact with him was through Tom Worth, son of the famous Claude Worth, whose exploits and designs became quite famous. I discussed many ideas with Tom and had an interview with him and Arthur Robb to see whether the ideas would marry and produce something that would satisfy both of us. Alas, this fell flat on its face as the requirements could only be met by a yacht which was too heavy in displacement and too low in performance to satisfy either of us. I had, however, been so impressed by Arthur Robb that I now approached him on my own with my design of a new 'Bluebird of Thorne'. I always remember his analysis which ran on these lines: "As a professional designer, I should not normally consider collaboration with you in the development of an improved twin keel. There are however, special circumstances:

1.   I have been engaged in the design and testing of a design for the America Cup; this has been cancelled for financial

reasons but the time devoted to it has damaged my other work and I have a big gap in my programme.

2.   You have proof that the idea does work.

3.   You have given me a design which I find attractive.

4.   I think a professional designer must occasionally do some innovative work to continue to be creative and avoid falling into the rut of repetition."

It was agreed that our association would be expressed publicly as "in collaboration". There was a significant moment when I went into his office one day and found him in a high state of excitement, "Come and look at this", he said. There on the drawing board were the lines of a light yacht and a tracing of the lines of another yacht. He placed the tracing of one on top of the other and announced, "See this, the underwater body lines are identical; there is no place in 48 inches that is 1/8 inch apart." Impressed but mystified, I asked, "But what are these designs?" He replied, "One is your design, the other is the underwater body lines of 'Uomie', a design of mine which was the RORC class champion a few years ago. I consider it one of my best designs, it is fast in light winds, medium winds and heavy winds, it is fast on the wind reaching and running and the owner says that it handles so beautifully that when he wants to take his grandchildren for a sail on a Sunday afternoon, he takes them out by himself in 'Uomie' rather than in any other craft". More discussion followed, his line, "How on earth did you achieve this similarity?" I was able to reply, "I have never seen 'Uomie's' lines (in fact they had not then been published), I have never seen 'Uomie' and the lines are solely and entirely my idea of what my yacht should be". If there had been any doubt or hesitation in his mind, it was completely removed by this extraordinary coincidence. His further reaction was simply, "I need not worry anymore, all we have to do now is to design, test and develop and application of your twin keels to this plan instead of 'Uomie's' single keel, and if the tank tests are satisfactory, we shall be home and dry"; and so it proved. He said later that he had been hoping for a 10% improvement on my previous 'Bluebird' and we were both delighted to find that it was more like 15%. When it came to the building of 'Bluebird', again with Dunstons of Thorne, but this time with Michael Dunston in charge as his father Richard Dunston had retired, Arthur Robb was, alas, gravely ill and so it came to pass that instead of his participation in the building process and help with any possible difficulties or modifications, I took charge of this myself. There were a few anxious faces at times, one or two difficult decisions and an occasional glint of humour as when the yard foreman said that he had spent the weekend on top of the church tower at Thorne, long sighting the lines of 'Bluebird' in the yard to get the angles of the keels exactly right. Arthur Robb was well enough to attend one trial sail in the Humber and expressed himself as well satisfied with the handling of the yacht.

We now move, alas, into a sad and inexplicable period; Arthur Robb had been so interested and impressed with the whole venture that he had intended to design a twin keel yacht for himself in which he could live, use as a drawing office and from which he could carry on his yacht design activities. He had also intended to produce a fast twin keel design for ocean racing, as we found that the 'Bluebird of Thorne' design with no thought of ocean racing or any look at the rules and regulations, measured so well to RORC's requirements that Arthur asked me to let him produce a skipper and crew and ocean race her for a year. This I was unable to do as it was in straight opposition to my plans for voyages. He had produced one twin keel design for a Scandinavian owner, a splendid yacht which I later encountered in the Mediterranean and found myself impressed while her owner was delighted with her, but Arthur's second wife took a complete 'scunner' on the whole twin keel activity; I don't think she objected so much to me personally, perhaps she thought that this venture had been the main cause of his illness, but whatever her reasoning I found that she was hell bent on preventing him from doing any further twin keel work to the point of being rude and offensive to callers and literally refusing them entry if she found that they were enquiring about a twin keel design.

There had been the moment when Arthur said, "You know you must place your work on twin keels on record, there might be a risk that somebody will come along and try to upstage you and claim the credit", and it was this that prompted me to prepare a paper on the design of twin keel yachts to read to the Royal Institution of Naval Architects, and this was actually done in 1967. I found out that his wife, hearing about this, had gone to the Secretary of the RNIA, protested that the whole of the work was Arthur Robb's, that I had had nothing to do with it and demand that the paper be withdrawn and that I should not be allowed to deliver it. Her whole attitude was so unreasonable and incorrect that she was turned down flat. When Arthur Robb died, she endeavoured to sell his yacht business without success. I think she had a quite exaggerated opinion of its value and her

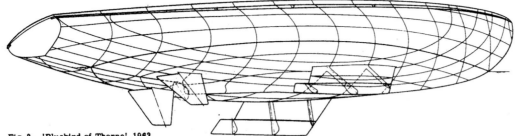

Design drawings of the second 'Bluebird of Thorne'.

Fig. 3. 'Bluebird of Thorne', 1963

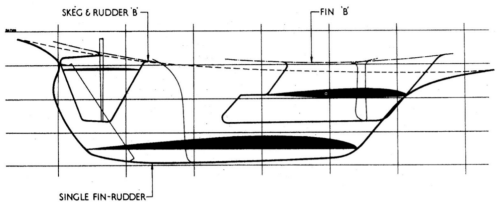

SKEG & RUDDER 'B'

FIN 'B'

SINGLE FIN-RUDDER

Fig. 4. Sketch comparison

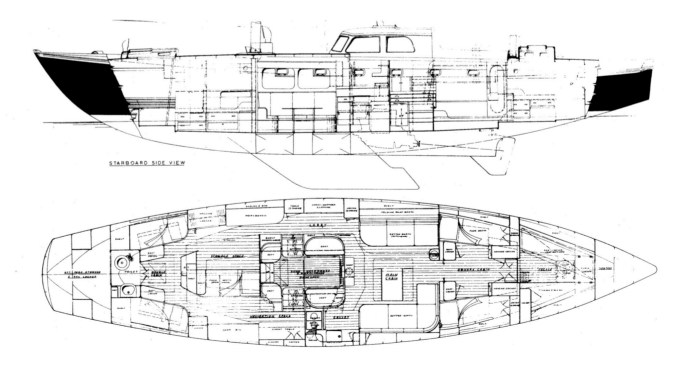

STARBOARD SIDE VIEW

demands were unreasonable. But I now became involved as people came to me to consult me about twin keel designs or with the intention of building a 'Bluebird', and she and her lawyers maintained the attitude that I had no rights in the design and that the copyright was entirely his property. After the failure to sell the business, his designs eventually went to the Mystic Maritime Museum in America but for three or four years, the lawyers made money and kept the whole ownership and copyright issue unresolved. Mrs Robb herself died in rather extraordinary and not very pleasant circumstances and happily as I happened to know personally one of the Governors of the Mystic Maritime Museum one simple letter from Mystic to me settled the whole question to my satisfaction and thankfully we could tell her lawyers to take a running jump. The demand for 'Bluebird' was then such that I prepared a package, design, specification, photographs and information, which I sold to suitable interested enquirers. It was not exactly a money making venture, but I earned a few pennies and gained a lot of interest from the contacts involved. I cannot say how many 'Bluebird's' were built, or modifications or derivatives; an intelligent guess might be that there are some fifteen or so somewhere in the world and there were alas, two total failures - the thing which always frightened Arthur Robb with his own designs. One character in Sidney, Australia, had the idea of building 'Bluebird' in numbers with ferro-cement hull construction. This was without any reference to me or without any permission whatsoever. He got his sums all wrong, the first one was so overweight that she was quite useless and his idea fell flat on its face but I always wondered whether he went about blaming me for a bad design rather than admitting his own mistake. I had a nice illustration of this point from New Zealand; Laurence Giles, a friend of mine, perhaps even England's foremost yacht designer, told me this story. A character in New Zealand, without reference, had taken one of his designs from a yachting magazine, enlarged and built it himself, only to find when launched that it floated 8 inches deep at the bows. Horrified, he wrote a letter to Laurence Giles accusing him of publishing a dangerously inaccurate design. Laurence's reply was to send him an invoice for the fee he should have paid for permission to build and a correct set of plans. Another near disaster was a character in South Africa who, again without reference to me, was building a 'Bluebird'. Luckily one of my friends who knew 'Bluebird' saw this and realised that he was putting the keel foils inside out. He persuaded him to approach me and we were able to avoid another costly disaster. Inevitably, demand for 'Bluebird' designs tapered off over the years. Where I was once receiving

one a month, it is quite astonishing to find that nearly 30 years later, I am still receiving one or two a year, and reviewing this, I think my all time record was an American citizen in the US Armed Forces who wrote on these lines, "I am in the American Forces, I am at present stationed in the Aleutian Islands. I shall be retiring in two years time, I intend to go sailing about the world and I am convinced that your 'Bluebird' would be the best yacht for my purpose and I intend to build one. I have lots of help available from my comrades in the services, but my only ready materials in the Aleutian Islands are driftwood and an unlimited number of empty beer cans and the like. Can you tell me whether it would be possible to build a 'Bluebird' in these circumstances?" After a hearty laugh I said to myself, "Well it all depends on the driftwood!"

The Package Yacht idea died after the first discussions and rough sketches. To contain all Tom's requirements and keep within the shipping limits would involve a chubby and low performance type. This confirmed my previous belief that a larger and longer yacht was essential. My own design rough out had brought a conviction that 13 tons actual displacement in cruising trim was the indicated minimum for world voyaging. The development of this had involved decisions on water capacity, stores, crew, dinghy, engine and fuel. Without realising it, I was very near the point of decision and another session with 'Tahiti' John was remembered. He had said, "You have done all you can with this 'Bluebird', you and 'Bluebird' have twenty years behind you and both of you will get older. I don't think you will be satisfied unless you go ahead with a new yacht and make a voyage". It was only afterwards that I realised he had focused my thoughts and that I had then made my decision.

There was much to be done. I was quite determined to sell this 'Bluebird' before I embarked on another one. The burden and the distraction of the old yacht and whether to fit her out or not, while involved in the new venture, would be intolerable in both effort and time. I took advice on values and decided a fair figure and from that I deducted the cost of a winter's lay up and a Spring fit out. I then imagined myself as a new owner deciding what I should spend if I bought her; I deducted that figure but added it back again if I could save a broker's commission. 'Bluebird' was quite well known, her type was now acceptable but there was still prejudice against older steel hulls (though my experience and her condition discounted that factor). 'Bluebird' would however appeal only to a small and limited market.

How could I reach a large enough number of potential buyers to find at least two serious prospects quickly enough? I wrote a description in verse, took a large space in a yachting publication and went ahead with a good photograph. This idea worked, I sold 'Bluebird' after a sailing trial and a survey, which was completely reassuring, advising only two small matters for attention and all of this was done in a month. How satisfactory that she also remained in the Cruising Club and her new owner and his family became friends and let me use her again for Meets of the RCC. 'Bluebird' served them well for a range of requirements not dissimilar from my last ten years in her. I had realised a £1,000 more than her cost twenty-two years before but what had happened during this period to the value of the money in your pocket considering the replacement cost would be at least three times as much.

I went to Arthur Robb after I had produced my design in rough form and I did not reveal at that stage how much work I had done or how far I had taken the calculations. Long discussions followed covering every aspect of design, materials, construction, rig, power and equipment. This was fascinating 'cut and thrust' work with two minds bent to one end and very much on the same wavelength. It was enjoyable in the highest sense and could not fail to produce an interesting specification. But what about the all important question of balance for the design of this, the second 'Bluebird of Thorne'?

You may remember that by what skills I then had, and what I feel was a 'hell of a lot of luck', we had achieved something very near perfection with 'Little Bluebird'. With the first 'Bluebird of Thorne' and a good deal more knowledge and designing skill, I had paid almost exaggerated attention to the question of balance and the resultant entirely fortuitous coincidence with Admiral Turner's theory, had produced a result which was theoretically perfect and authenticated in practice but I am bound to say that it was dull. Through the years, cruising in that 'Bluebird', I had often wondered whether the secret might not be to discover just the exact degree of slight imbalance to impart a more attractive and responsive feel.

With this new design, there was an entirely different set of problems; once we had discovered that the hull lines were identical with those of 'Uomie', there was a different set of questions. 'Uomie' had been widely acclaimed as beautiful to handle under all conditions. We now had to discover whether the new design would retain these characteristics with twin keels and twin rudders as against 'Uomie's' normal format. Arthur Robb was confident that she would do so, I was I think, a little less confident but extremely hopeful. We both knew that either model sailing tests or interpretation of the tank tests would confirm this balance or show up anything that had gone adrift, and so it proved. Everything came up satisfactorily and this 'Bluebird' was quite delightful to handle, the balance was beautiful, she was well-mannered and, at the helm, there was that indefinable sense of response and feel that was almost like a living thing. On one occasion, I found Arthur muttering, "Can't understand it, all the bulkheads come right , the weights check, the mast position seems good enough at this stage; I don't find anything that wants altering. Might perhaps move the rudder stocks slightly aft". This was a rewarding moment but if I smiled it could only be inwardly as it endorsed the work that I had done and had produced the check that I had intended. At a later stage in his meticulous work, Arthur was worried. "The vertical CG (central gravity) is higher than normal". Luckily I was ready for this one, "Suppose that you could increase the displacement by another 10 hundredweights and put this into the ballast, then drop the CG of the keels by increasing draft 1 to 2 inches, which will be necessary to accommodate the extra ballast", I said. This produced an instant reaction and relief. "I will have to work it out but don't worry it will come alright now".

Though it was not important at that stage, we foresaw a difficulty in the future arising from my strictly amateur status and his professional reputation. We agreed that the design could be described as 'Arthur Robb and Lord Riverdale in collaboration'. In convenient alliteration, I called this "A Riverdale and Robb job". The material discussion had quickly boiled down to steel hull with light alloy upper works. This was strongly weighted by my previous experience and the desire to build with Dunstons to permit my supervision. Very willing collaboration was already ensured with Michael Dunston, as it had been with his father twenty-three years before. GRP was a serious contender and we only eliminated this because both of us were worried about the flexibility inherent in this material when applied to a yacht of this size. I am sure it would have been adopted at 40 foot. The cost in GRP would have been too high in this size in a one-off job; had it been 1970 and not 1960, the sandwich method would have been available and could have been chosen but it was not then fully developed. Had I been constructing a racing yacht, we might have adopted cold, moulded ply with all laminated frames and backbone, but with twin keels and rudders, there would have been more weight and complications, also involving cost. We both liked light alloy but at that time it seemed unreasonably costly and references we knew had revealed some problems in the riveted construction. Once again in 1970, Argon Arc welding and more developed techniques could have swung the decision.

We proceeded to discuss the tank testing and this is no place to discuss the wizardry and skill of the boffins, the complications involved and the analysis of the findings but it is proper to pay tribute to the complete acceptance by Crago, Flewitt and the team at Cowes of yet another amateur's ideas. I shall never forget the thrill of those occasions when I was able to sit in the chariot and, on runs down the long tank , study the behaviour and the wave formations of the models so closely, with the eyes only a foot or so away. I like to think that I gained a new understanding in this process and we were lucky. Tempted by this, we could not resist a measure of research, not strictly necessary to the project and it was tricky to decide how far to take this process as it involved delay as well as extra cost. I realised that the knowledge Arthur had gained from the 12 metre tank testing was of great benefit and had developed expertise in the tank test teams also. There was a practical assurance value in the comparison between the new design and that of the 1939 'Bluebird', which I knew so well in full scale performance, and also with 'Uomie' in single keel form. We had to stop.

Meanwhile I had authorised a start and Dunstons were cutting and bending metal. I had a photograph of the hot bending of the first frames to prove it. Fortunately they could go quite a long way before the final decisions on the keels, rudders and their positioning was announced after completion of the testing and the anxious discussions derived from study of the tank reports. It was satisfying to see the lines full size on the loft floor, and another tribute to Arthur Robb's work, there was virtually no adjustment to make from the applied offsets. Then disaster struck; Arthur, who stressed himself highly, was gravely ill and at a bad moment for this project. Everything was in his head, his office could not produce the drawings, Dunstons could not proceed, nothing could be done but the delay was frustrating and costly by its effect on the programme of work in a shipyard.

There could have been only one answer. I should have had to go back to the drawing board and work it up myself. I was relieved that this did not happen and overjoyed in every way when Arthur recovered. In time, the drawings came through and work could go ahead but the delay and Arthur's illness did result in a change of tactics which, though it threw more weight on my shoulders,

may have been beneficial overall. I took over all supervision (full supervision by Arthur was not in the scheme anyway) and I assumed all responsibility for modifications which became necessary or were dictated by events in the building processes. Had there once been an idea that going to Arthur Robb would mean less work for me, forget it. I had already found that in a different way coordinating progress between myself, Arthur, the tank team and Dunstons was in some measure more difficult than the 'do it yourself' process with the former 'Bluebird', and now I was virtually back in the same role for the latter half of the building programme. Delay breeds delay; components were not delivered on time, we ran into winter and the weather affected work so that we ended up nine months behind the original schedule when 'Bluebird' left Thorne. Though this long period was a strain, it was also one of deep satisfaction. I was doing something challenging and creative which was an enthusiasm so that it was an intense experience and a pleasure. This can be illustrated by examples: One day, I found at Thorne that a drawing had been misread due to Dunston's team being unfamiliar with the rigging of yachts. A vital stage had been taken without provision of attachments for the mizzen shrouds. A solution had to be found and it was found on the spot and without delay. It was effective, practical and as cheap as the original and it has never given the slightest trouble. Remote supervision from a distance with insistence on the details of design would in numerous instances have caused intolerable delay, extra work and consequent cost.

This introduces another study. Building a yacht in a commercial yard must have drawbacks. I simply took the line that any gaps in Dunston's knowledge must be made good by me but I was not always there. On the other hand there were great advantages; the whole approach to values, sturdy, practical strength and workable solutions was, in my view, better than in a yacht yard. For a conventional racing yacht, the answer would be no, for my purposes I probably got a better job and better value. Another example was the working out of the auxiliary drives from the engine. This involved the engine makers, the yard, several component suppliers and I had to tie these up and take the decisions with much aid from the builder's experience. This rather important engineering assembly has also been a great success.

The steering had to be modified from the drawings to provide clearances. Accustomed to tiller steering in my former yachts, I had approached wheel steering with suspicion and could not

Above: Second 'Bluebird of Thorne' partly plated.
Right: Hundested adjustable pitch and feathering propeller.

tolerate the idea of low geared steering. I had experienced this and found it horrible with a badly balanced yacht running hard with a big sea on the quarter. Arthur had assured me that once I tried a wheel, I should never go back and he could quote other owners as evidence. The design had provided a large wheel and three turns from hard a-port to hard a-starboard. I took a big risk here and to mate in with other modifications, I geared up to 1³/₄ turns of the 29 inch wheel. Nobody could approve this but I drew heavily on experience of the former 'Bluebird's', believing that their intrinsic balance and steering habits would make this possible. It has worked and provides a positive feel and control, truly remarkable for any wheel system, but I would not dare to apply this to most other yachts.

In all this, a partnership developed with the excellent team in the yard. Good humour and cooperation never failed and gradually a mutual confidence built up. It was splendid to find ideas coming up to be examined; the craftsmen doing a job ought to, and can, make things better as he goes but equally decisions were required and if good ideas had to be turned down for some reason, a tactful explanation had to be supplied. To maintain my own sense of craftsmanship, I could not resist a few pieces of loving care. I made the steering wheel myself, devising my own joints and incorporating a complete light alloy reinforcement; the result I think is unique. There were other examples that were luck or inspiration and one or two failures. I had the idea that the two stanchions in the sunk deckhouse, which were quite essential as hand holds, should be Narwhal tusks and whilst I had experienced a delay of a month in getting one stainless bolt that was not standard, I had a matched pair of Narwhal tusks in my hands in a week. They had probably come to England in an Arctic whaler at least one hundred years ago.

Launching this 'Bluebird' was not a ceremony, just an incident in the building process but involved an anxious moment with a 20 ton mobile crane. The overload alarm bell rang insistently as the reach out over the canal reduced the lifting capacity, but all went well. This vital crane was another piece of equipment that had not existed twenty years before. I managed a photographic record of every single stage in the building. If Christian still thought I was killing myself, she stopped saying anything about it and all the family backed me up though I was aware of a good deal of doubt and disapproval buried in the background. A wonderful tribute was organised by my brother who teamed up the whole family down to the most remote nephew and the result of this was a little plate in 'Bluebird's' deckhouse announcing

that the masts were presented by 37 members of the family. My daughter performed the naming ceremony at a later but far from complete stage. She looked lovely and that was the verdict of the party on my daughter; I was thinking the same about 'Bluebird'. The thought crossed my mind that, if my regime has been to work hard for 15 years and then build a yacht, then my grandson, present on this occasion at the age of 2¹/₂ years, will have to launch the next one. But if I do build another yacht, it will not be provided by 15 years hard work but, in our modern society and overtaxed system, it might well be an offset against a more imminent estate duty.

The engine of this 'Bluebird' after 20 years was lighter, faster and more powerful, but still a Gardner and I had the help from Houghton, whose father had advised me with the former installation. I savoured an amusing moment when watching with the Gardner Board at their works, I told them I had originally chosen the engine 23 years ago because of its starting qualities, and continued, "Your claims were quite correct and the decision was justified as I have started that engine by hand myself for 22 years". The faces of the Gardner team were quite a study - pride, horror, incomprehension and plain disbelief, were all registered.

Taking a yacht from Thorne is not a matter of gaily hoisting sail on a fine day or proceeding out of harbour to a blue, sparkling sea. First you must escape by finally fixing a day, finished or unfinished, then move down the canal below a fixed railway bridge to a wharf, where a crane used to remove the sailing gear from the old Humber keels and sloops as they came in from the rivers and before they went up to the towns. Masts and leeboards were lifted out and racked until they returned. For the first time the masts and rigging went up, a brief struggle, but thank goodness everything came together as planned and another departure could be made down the canal to Keadby. There the whole of the gear had been brought by road to be taken aboard and stowed; yet another departure looking out into the Trent and Humber with their muddy waters and strong tides to Grimsby. This under the Yard's pilot as there had been no trials and I had not yet accepted the vessel. Grimsby dock was not a beautiful setting for the first night aboard.

We went out next day for compass swinging and this was quick and effective as trawlers demand and get a first class service. To my great joy, Arthur Robb was able to come down on Trials Day. Under power, everything went as expected though we had a small back pressure problem with the exhaust system which I

Left: The Launch.

Below: Christening by my daughter Frances.

solved by an unorthodox modification. The great thrill was the first time under sail, who was the more anxious, Arthur or I? A nice point. The performance was brisk, balance impeccable, the wind was kind, and finally I took her on a continuous tight series of figure of eight turns without touching the sheets. She performed this severe manoeuvre without difficulty and better than the old 'Bluebird'.

The day had been short and the trials sketchy but we were jubilant and not dismayed. The new 'Bluebird of Thorne' was in commission. The collaboration with Arthur had been successful and 'Bluebird' was a far better vessel than either of us could have produced alone. As far as Dunstons were concerned, they were proud of 'Bluebird' and I was satisfied. An unusual and difficult experience had left us all with more understanding and still good friends.

The first passage from the Humber to the Solent, that track well worn by two previous 'Bluebirds', taught us much and confirmed our satisfaction. We did up to 8 knots on the wind, touched 9 knots under sail and 150 miles in 24 hours. The speed through the water on this passage was 6.6 knots and an indication of head winds given by sailing 100 miles more than the direct distance. The four crew members, who knew the former 'Bluebird of Thorne', all agreed that she was faster and more comfortable and that she was pitching less. There had been no test running in a big sea or at high speed, but control with the high geared steering was satisfactory so far. A measured mile trial under power at full cruising setting (not full power), was effected under ideal conditions and at cruising displacement gave 8.1 knots. This worked back through the curves from the test tank, indicated a propulsive co-efficient of 55% which the boffins considered very satisfactory.

'Bluebird' attended the Royal Cruising Club Meet in September 1963. Daughter Frances was my hostess and during a beautiful sunny morning, a great number of visitors appeared and revolved rapidly round the Narwhal tusks in the deckhouse. The parties inspecting the Stately Homes of England were taken round by Frances and a beautiful friend of hers from Austria. This may have had some effect but the general verdict was satisfactory. Margaret Bennett (my long time secretary), who had fetched daughter Frances and driven her down from school, was sunning herself in the corner of the cockpit and was approached by a well known senior member of the Cruising Club who might possibly have fortified himself thus early in the day. Gazing intently into her eyes at short range, he said, "I am having awful trouble with my futtock shrouds". The Skipper passing by will never forget the horrified expression on Margaret's face as she contemplated an imminent fate worse than death.

Chapter Ten

Now We Know

The First Atlantic Passage

As the summer months of 1963 slid past I realized that unless I escaped from England before the autumn was too far spent, the dreadful alternative of laying up and waiting for another year would be the only course. I forced myself to make a programme. If 'Bluebird' is finished, if nothing serious is wrong, if I can get away, then we shall sail at the end of September. First stop Gibraltar, an Atlantic passage and Christmas at English Harbour, Antigua. It seemed impossibly unreal. Could I get away? I was not retired, but the idea of a long vacation for the first time in forty years was discussed with my colleagues. I shall be eternally grateful to them; they backed me with cheerful understanding. It has been said that the hardest thing about a voyage is the decision to go in the first place, closely followed by a necessity to set a date for departure; the end of September was the deadline. Less than a month for trials, passage South RCC Meet, working up and all preparations for departure. The task seemed quite impossible. Christian said, "You should have done this ten years ago. The old 'Bluebird' was proved and tested, you had merely to turn up a page in a notebook to know what was required in preparation for an Atlantic crossing. Now you have nearly killed yourself with overwork, you are ten years older and you are probably crazy to start out with a completely untried vessel".

I ought to have added to the preliminaries, "If I have a crew". I am not a single-hander and 'Bluebird' was not designed for this role. The crew problem was not as difficult as it might have been. For twenty years Ronnie Gresham had said he would join me if I ever made such a voyage. He now did so without hesitation and after several conferences, took charge of the whole navigational side as, 'Vasco' the navigator; I don't know how I could have coped with that additional load. My task in producing 'Bluebird' was difficult enough, it followed that I had to make the care and running of all machinery and electrics my own 'part of ship'. George Allen and Donald Tew, both Cadet members of the RCC, signed on with the blessing of their families. George, after similar conferences, took charge of stores and stowing and Donald dealt with the bosun's requirements. I had many volunteers for the passage to Gibraltar, most of my old 'Bluebird' crews who had not time to do a voyage were anxious to sail in the new ship. I was so worn out that I doubted myself. 'Vasco' was recovering from pneumonia and for these reasons I was glad to take Dennis Hatfield and Brian Leach, two of my trusties on the first passage, though a crew of four total was the objective for the main voyage.

'Bluebird' was slipped at Lymington at the end of September for the last coat of antifouling. I was in Sheffield clearing up affairs. To my horror, a telephone call advised me that a dangerously corrosive condition of the underwater body had been revealed. An urgent conference was held; the people whose paint recommendation had been followed, failed to produce any report or recommendation; the whole voyage was in jeopardy. Thank heaven we had not sailed without discovering this trouble. I had to authorise an immediate paint-stripping job and a treatment to the recommendation of a well known firm of paint manufacturers. We were lucky with the weather and the job was completed in 10 days. It was a hellish time, we were living on board but feeding ashore. There were horrible grinding noises and dirt everywhere. All this made endless lists of work and the receipt and stowing of stores even more difficult than it would have been otherwise. I don't know how we survived. My brother-in-law, Claude Muncaster and others, visiting at this time, all had the same impression which he recorded and produced later, "In my opinion, Robin was so completely mentally and physically exhausted that I do not know how he carried on and I doubted if he would be fit to sail". However we sailed 10 October; it was late enough in the autumn to face what might well have been the third and greatest difficulty of the voyage - getting out of the English Channel. We were lucky. Winds up to force 10 were sweeping the northern half of the country but a blessed little high over northern France held the gales at bay while we sneaked out round Ushant in thick fog with little wind. It was not funny; a radar reflector, some help from Consol and determination, did the trick. I believe some of the crew felt that the Skipper had rather too much nerve during this episode, when there were so many unseen steamers in the fog.

The crossing of the Bay was easy, though it might have been the fourth difficulty; seldom were there less than four vessels in sight in the shipping lane. A whaling fleet bound for the Antarctic passed us and one of the catchers spoke to us. Approaching Finisterre, a notoriously windy spot, we had a good force 6; this was literally the first time that 'Bluebird' had ever been running in a seaway at speed. We hung on to the big genoa and drove her up to 10 knots to see what happened. We found that she was quick and sensitive, her steering and handling on this vital point of sailing were satisfactory, she was dry and lively and had a feeling of great power. On our way down the Portuguese coast, we had light winds and calms. There were many patches of fog and usually a large swell. We encountered numerous fishing boats and from some of them we obtained sardines in exchange for coffee. At night we saw phosphorescent displays made by the shoals of fish darting away from our bows. With a fair wind from the Berlengas and on past Lisbon, we were able to try our twin running sails for the first time. They promised well.

We made good time and Gibraltar seemed relatively near at hand when we rounded Cape St Vincent with a fair wind, but after a few miles the wind came in right ahead and slowly increased. After two days beating on regular tacks, we hove-to and changed from 'A' mainsail to 'B' mainsail for the first time. We also took this opportunity to have a brief rest and a good meal. We were delighted to find that this 'Bluebird' would heave-to quietly and exactly like the old one; a very vital quality for cruising had been proved. By now it was obvious that we were facing a real Levanter. Cadiz Bay was tempting, but it was rejected: "With a ship like this and a strong crew, of course we can make it!" We at least had the prospect of a favourable current as we reached the Straits, but this meant a horrible sea and that night we logged force 8. In our watch, George and I decided that we must slow down. We put her about, leaving the staysail aback to avoid disturbing the watch below. There was little difference in speed; still sailing 7 knots, she was taking such a hammering that we had to hand the working jib. By breakfast the wind had eased to force 5, the sun was shining, porpoises were playing at the bows and life was pleasant again as we entered Gibraltar. My last visit had been in the first 'Ark Royal', the aircraft carrier, in 1940.

Gibraltar treated us well. Dennis flew home and Brian followed him at the end of the week. We laid out a programme for six days, generally working on the ship pretty hard but taking some time off for relaxation and excursions. We found an extremely good and reasonable restaurant - 'The Bayuca', where we dined most nights (onion soup and half a partridge). One day we made an expedition to Torremolinos to see something of the developments on the Spanish coast and to endeavour to trace an aunt of mine, (we failed). After 5 days we felt ready for sea. The Levanter had caused damp and humid

Vasco the navigator - a lifetime friend.

conditions but now it was declining. Our job list was looking much better, membership of the RNSA (Royal Naval Sailing Association) made us free of the Naval Harbour without dues. The usual route from Gibraltar is via the Canaries, however we decided to sail to Madeira; some of us had visited both groups of islands and preferred Madeira. Sailing from St Vincent to Gibraltar and out to Madeira, entailed much extra distance but, "what is an extra 200 miles in a real voyage".

It would have been too bad to beat out of Gibraltar against the current and against a westerly wind but we sneaked out on the very last of the Levanter. On the first night there was quite a fracas with miles of lighted tunny nets and their guardian fishing boats. The wind came in ahead but we could lay our course. In the morning we found one of our head sails, which had been lashed to the rail, disfigured with fuel oil which had splashed up from the sea during the night. The wind increased and forced us off course to the north; once again we changed down to 'B' mainsail. This time we said, "We are long-distance cruising, we have a basic crew of four, we are not going to become exhausted". We hove-to with wind force 7-8, dodging along under 'B' mainsail so that we did not lose too much distance.

We could have let draw in the early morning but there was a foul sea so we remained hove-to until breakfast. Off we went with the wind well forward of the beam, easy canvas and magnificent sailing which continued to Funchal, Madeira. We had covered 150 miles in the last 24 hours. 'Vasco' had satisfied himself that he could take sights under difficult conditions and our landfall on Porto Santo light had been exactly as predicted for time and bearing. We thought 5 days was good for this passage, experience was growing and confidence in 'Bluebird' was increasing. We were still working up a new ship and again made a programme for 6 days in port. A very obliging agent saved us a lot of time and bother, taking care of the ship's business and many odd jobs ashore. The President of the Yacht Club introduced himself, made us free use of all their facilities and looked after us personally. After a morning's work, we used to walk along to their delightful premises and have a lazy afternoon sunbathing.

What ever has been done previously, there is apt to be an atmosphere of nightmare on sailing day. All members of the crew remember something that they must do ashore, stores arrive at the last moment, the unexpected happens, laundry is missing and clearance takes longer. An hour from noon, it seemed impossible that we should depart that day. A harassed Skipper and crew let go at 1500 to make all sail in the harbour - this was the start of the real venture. We were off across the Atlantic but nobody would have thought so. We were all quite matter of fact and much too absorbed with detailed matters to feel a sense of occasion. Three thousand miles to go and we were on the wind with 'B' mainsail set, a lumpy sea and only just able to make our desired course. Hopes were high that we should soon find the northeast trades, but before long we had a southwest wind. According to the Pilot Chart, there was no such thing in these parts but 'Vasco', whose remarks were pungent, uttered his famous dictum which was oft repeated throughout the cruise; "It is a load of - - - -, you get what you get", and we did! On the starboard tack, we were forced within sight of the western-most Canaries and on towards Africa. I began to think, "Always beware of the Bay of Benin whence few come out though many go in". Eventually the wind died completely and it was a relief as we had felt it was wrong to stand off north of west on the port tack. We now used power, still seeking the northeast trades. At last a faint breath came in from the right direction; we stopped the engine and coaxed the ship along, but it was three or four days before we could feel sure that we had the trades at last. The sky assumed its characteristic look, the sea its lovely blue, while the temperature was perfect. We had flying fish on deck and all the things that we had read about came true, except that the trades we had expected to be force 3-5 remained force 2-4.

The time had come to rig our running sails; we did so and they worked well. Rolling was not a problem with this ship, she gave us the feeling that she was trying not to roll. After some experiment, we made her steer herself. The gear, while an adaptation of a well known principle is, I think, unique in detail and a happy accident of the ship's characteristics and our high-geared steering. This was christened the 'RCC Gear' which was short for 'Riverdale Constant Catenary', though there was fierce argument on the precise meaning and application of the word 'Catenary'. We were practically self-steering for a fortnight, but we did not break our watches. I felt it better to keep our routine, though the time on watch could be occupied in other ways. I started writing an information book for the ship, Donald wrote a monumental journal and George a circular letter. There was still working up to do, occasionally conditions were awkward and one steered a little. 'Vasco' navigated with fanatical zeal, so much so

Second 'Bluebird of Thorne'.

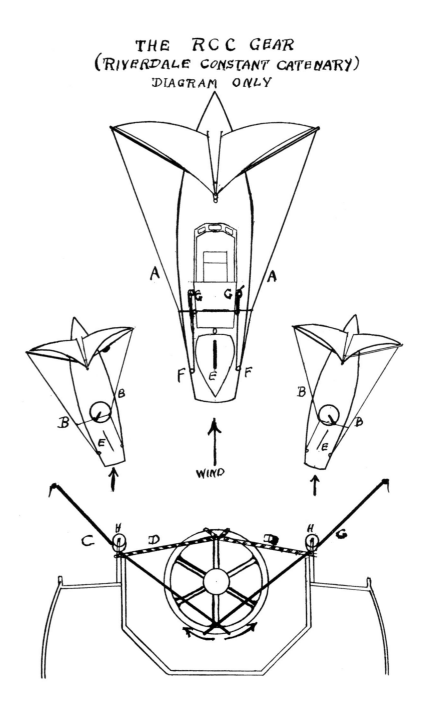

The Skipper invented a self-steering gear for twin running sails which was very successful in the north east trade winds.

that the rest of us found it difficult to practise our sights and get access to the chart room!

I found I was thoroughly enjoying myself. It was delightful to brown up after carefully acquiring tolerance by wearing pyjamas in the midday sun and thereafter to wear few clothes. It was delightful to turn in without bedding, wonderful to turn out in the morning to the hot sun, the colour, and a feeling of well being. Not for many years had I felt such peace of mind combined with a sense of physical fitness. Together they induced a tranquillity of spirit, the cares of the land had evaporated. The watchkeeping routine worked smoothly and I found myself looking forward to the changes this system provided: one day cook without watchkeeping, another day a long night in, another day my favourite early morning watch and so forth. The routine did not grow boring, I had remembered and understood Admiral Goldsmith whom I had heard say in his later years, "If God is good, may I be granted one more passage in the northeast trades".

Progress was broken by one ghastly night of tropical storm, with thunder, lightning, heavy rain and wind squalls of quite savage force from all directions except west. Hoping that this was temporary, we could only keep the wind on the back of our necks. Dawn was welcomed and it was a relief when the weather gradually re-established itself next day. We were now picking up a stronger trade, our day's runs lengthened out: disappointed at our speed, we said, "It is better to enjoy ourselves than be uncomfortable". We were aiming at a happy mean between dawdling and driving and our running sails had been designed for wind force 5-6. The ocean currents did not help as we had hoped (possibly because of the weak trades). Again we had a perfect landfall and in the early morning, George and I, anxious not to be in too soon, sailed slowly along the coast of Barbados under the large genoa and mizzen. We had handed the twin running sails and did not bother to hoist the mainsail. We beat up into Carlisle Bay and shared the feeling that we would not have cared if the passage had lasted for another ten days. It was a delightful ending to a wonderful passage when we anchored alongside 'Kochab' and 'Tahiti'. John turned out to welcome us and give us breakfast. This made it perfect. We had much news to exchange and he could give us helpful information on our needs ashore. The passage had been twenty-three days and to our surprise was the fastest so far recorded this season. We had thought it slow and we knew that given a good trade, this 'Bluebird' could have made the passage in under twenty days.

Caribbean

We enjoyed our time in Barbados; we had good friends ashore who enabled us to tour the island. We had much discussion with John whose advice had influenced me in the design conception of this new 'Bluebird'. We had much to do and we laid in a stock of the best rum we ever found at a very modest price. We were anxious to start our cruising in the islands. 'Vasco' had to return home. For these and other reasons we decided to cruise fairly fast to English Harbour, Antigua, whence he could connect with a Geest Line banana boat. There must be special moments in the memories of a voyage. One of these was the early morning sail as we closed St Lucia. It was an absolutely perfect example of trade wind sailing, the sky with beautiful clouds and wonderful sea colour with sparkling white crests. We were running at 9 knots; native boats, incredibly frail, were beating out to their fishing grounds with the crew baling and standing with a trapeze line to keep their tattered canvas or shaky masts and rigging up to the strong wind. Flying fish were bursting under our bows and the first of the really picturesque Caribbean islands was growing up and taking form and detail before us. We could not have picked a more beautiful scene for our first experience as we sailed up to Castries. This was what we came for. A cruising heaven; if it was not perfect, I for one will not complain, rather make it a dream memory. The smells, the heat, the light, the colour, the lovely islands and the trade wind.

The next sail was also memorable, in close company with Grant MacMurray, owner of 'My Destiny', his beautiful 65 foot Alden schooner. We found to our delight that we could outsail her on all points but most decisively on the wind. We managed to put George on board to take some photographs. This was hazardous in the swell with both ships under sail at 6 knots, but it was accomplished and the result was some beautiful photography. We beat up to Fort de France, Martinique, with its delightful old French atmosphere. We were extending our experience and when we reached Iles des Saintes, they were voted without compare, the finest and most beautiful of any of the islands we had yet seen. Here, Captain Brown, an RCC member, made contact with us. With a friend and a native boy, he had cruised down from Antigua in a small catamaran. After some repairs, they set off for the rough passage to Guadeloupe, making a tentative rendezvous with us at Deshayes Bay. When we came in at dusk, we found them on the beach, glad to see us, as the catamaran was breaking up under them and they could not face the 40 mile open water beat to windward necessary to return

Above: Nelson's dockyard, English Harbour, Antigua.

them to English Harbour. They sailed with us, leaving their catamaran to be collected later.

When we sailed at midnight, we carried all the sail that was prudent and had a rough ride but 'Bluebird' showed what she could do and even if there was a slight element of 'one-up-manship', it was nice to have Bruno Brown to take us into English Harbour for the first time. We were able to sail in and to anchor in time for breakfast. We had attained the objective that we had always set for the first half of the voyage and it was one of the great moments we shall remember. We felt at home at once with a warm welcome from the Nicholson family: My son Mark had served with the Nicholson's son in the Navy and I had met the whole family on their yacht at Fishguard before they made their first passage to the West Indies. They had now established a successful yacht charter business based in English Harbour. We had the freedom of 'Freelance' and all we had imagined, unlike so much tourist literature, did not lead to disillusionment. English Harbour was to be our base for longer than we then knew.

'Vasco' left us to join his banana boat for the passage home. This left George, Donald and myself and we decided to cruise in the Leeward Islands before Christmas. We visited Nevis, St Kitts and Barts, also calling at St Johns to do our Christmas shopping on our return to English Harbour. This was an enjoyable and successful small circuit and added much to our knowledge of the islands. Impressions were crowding in our minds; in these waters there is so much history and so much atmosphere from the past that it was easy to imagine how these islands had once been considered one of the prizes of the world, more desirable even than Quebec and Canada. Wars and conquests, piracy and prosperity based on slavery had all left their mark. Maritime nations had battled for supremacy with changing fortunes and the present illogical pattern is the result. The islands had attained a high state of development and a way of life. Nelson found his bride in Nevis, Napoleon's wife came from Martinique.

It can be imagined how reluctant I was to leave 'Bluebird' at this point, but I had to return home to do some work and for other reasons. It was strange to fly into London in eight hours by jet aircraft in comparison with eight weeks Columbus style. It was forbidding to step out (wearing my pyjamas under thin suiting) into a freezing fog at London Airport. The tasks awaiting me were devastating. I had intended to spend a month at home before flying out to rejoin 'Bluebird' at English Harbour. In the meantime, George's father and mother were flying out to have a fortnight's holiday and cruising in 'Bluebird' and this with a programme of work and maintenance, would occupy the time until my return. We had then intended to go up on Grant's slip at Martinique. I was feeling fit and bursted into everything under a full head of steam, but after a week, my right arm felt stiff if I raised it over my head. After a fortnight, there was a pain under my shoulder blade and I could not easily raise my arm above shoulder height. This would not do; doctor, specialist, nursing home and operating theatre followed within 48 hours, under the general theory that I had somehow taken a knock and damaged muscle had balled up. When I regained consciousness, I sensed a more serious atmosphere and it was soon confirmed that the operation had taken four hours. A tumour the size of a pear had been removed. It had been thought advisable to treat it as cancerous, remove all tissue in contact, two sections of ribs and to inspect the lung pleura just in case. The pathologist's report was awaited with interest.

Nothing like this had ever happened to me before and when a healthy man finds his physical integrity threatened, there can be many reactions. In my case, I realised that this was quite different from a smash-up like my damaged back. I had no experience of this sort to guide me and I felt helpless and in poor shape. I was more scared of possible handicap from the big hole in my back than the pathologist's report. I was thankful that I had achieved the cruise and the Atlantic passage. If in doubt do something; I sent for Margaret Bennett and sent a cable to George. From that moment came a determination to resume the voyage as soon as possible. The pathologist's report came in. Apparently this tumour was rare and exceptionally interesting. They had really enjoyed a sort of forensic investigation. And the verdict; well it could be cancer and again it might not be; it could recur but again it might not do so. My reaction was quite definite; rejoin my ship and complete the voyage, what was there to lose. I bent all my determination to recovery. As soon as I could stand, I started exercising, as soon as I was allowed out for a walk, I walked two miles. In a month the surgeon was giving me an Oscar, "I don't know if it is because you were so fit or because you don't smoke, but I haven't had anyone of any age who has healed up better". "When can I rejoin 'Bluebird'?" I was back aboard six weeks from the operation and George and Donald were glad to see me back. My extended absence had been too long, the resumption of the voyage and some decisive leadership was indicated. I think they were rather appalled when they realised my state; I was not in good shape, but they could not have been kinder and more tactful, unobtrusively making things easy for me for the next three weeks until I began to pull round. I had nearly overplayed my resources. With me I took out a young man, John Caulfield, feeling that it was a shame that only three of us were enjoying this lovely cruising ground and that it would be helpful as none of my family were free to join. We had proved that four was the best complement for longer periods in this ship.

Slipping at Grenada and my state of health gave us the opportunity to cruise in a leisurely way, and this was good value. None of us would have missed Bequia and the Grenadines, while I rated Grenada high in my impressions of the Windward Islands. We had our first introduction to coral navigation and Tobago Cays will always conjure up one of the most lovely pictures of tropical island and reef. Slipping was successful and it was a great relief to find that the repaint treatment had proved to be satisfactory and that the previous trouble had not developed under tropical conditions. On this stretch of the cruise, we had made friendly contact with many of the yachts in the charter business. We were invited to join some of their parties and many of their charterers visited 'Bluebird'. We cruised in company with Fred and Joan Georgeson in 'Alano', RCC.

We now had a speed recorder, as Philip Allen had given me 'Corista's' log. 'Bluebird' was not at her best with a foul bottom, but it gave us great pleasure to see the pointer hard up against the 10 knot limit on several occasions when we had a strong trade wind on the passages between the islands. A tour of Grenada was good value and we sat down in the cabin afterwards and wrote the names of plants, spices, vegetables and fruits we could remember to a total of thirty-seven. If I were crossing the Atlantic again, I think I should make my landfall at Grenada and then work north up the islands, though I do not regret our wanderings, as we saw more than we should have done otherwise, visited more places, encountered more yachts and learned more about the life of the whole area. By the end of our time we spoke of the few islands we had not visited rather than the great number we had seen.

Cruising here is too good to be true, it could almost become boring if too long continued. With the knowledge and experience of one or two cruises, it would be possible to sail up and down these islands without a chart, without a compass and without a log. There is no fog or bad visibility except in rain squalls; almost always the next island can be seen. Once an anchorage has been visited, there is no trouble in future. Currents and tides are slight and, with some limitations, the colour of the water is the criterion over coral. Our big genoa never left the deck, we went into port and lashed it along the rail, we sailed and up it went. The engine was useful for arriving at a convenient time by getting through calms in the lee of the islands and sometimes for entering or leaving port - it was rarely a necessity. Using the engine as little as possible, we developed the habit of running it for one hour at each departure to raise anchor and leave harbour. We thus kept our batteries fully charged.

A very grave menace I have not seen written up elsewhere are fishing floats. These are lengths of bamboo, anything up to 10 feet long and up to 6 inches in diameter. They are heavy, strong, waterlogged and difficult to see. They are scattered freely in the approaches to many of the anchorages, particularly Deshayes Bay, The Saintes and English Harbour. Entering under power in dusk or at night, it would be easy to smash up your propeller and stern gear with dire results in an area where spares and repairs may take months. One of the biggest hazards to a charter boat is to go unserviceable for any reason in the middle of the charter season, extending to the end of March. Few yachts of our size were not in the charter business, and this gave us a certain distinction, but through friendship with the Nicholsons we were one of the family. We could pass messages through the radio when the Nicholsons at English Harbour called up the charter yachts between 0900 and 0930 every day. This was known as 'Children's Hour' and the messages ranged from routine information to dire crisis and pure farce. It is easy to see why and how many yachts starting a voyage round the world remain in the West Indies to earn an agreeable living in the charter fleet.

We intended to make a direct passage from Grenada to Antigua. This would be out of sight of the island most of the way, but would not suffer from calms in the lee of the islands. If we encountered the same winds as had served us when cruising down to Grenada, we might exceed 200 miles in the day on this passage and we started out with this intention. It was also a test to determine whether I was now fit enough to stand such a passage with full watchkeeping and all duties. Alas for our hopes, we were nearly hard on the wind for 24 hours; another example of 'Vasco's', "you get what you get". We carried the big genoa, we drove her hard and we averaged 7 knots, but our hope of a record day's run had gone. The wind then headed us and blew one force harder so that we could not lay our course to English Harbour. This gave us an opportunity to try something new. We ran the engine at modest revolutions, pinned in the sheets and sailing closer to the wind than we could have done otherwise, we made Antigua in another twenty-three hours, averaging 6 knots. The whole passage of 300 miles was achieved in forty-seven hours at an average speed of $6^{1}/_{2}$ knots. To prove that conditions can be exceptional even in the trades and outside the hurricane season, we had winds from the north of up to 40 knots for two days, due apparently to a deep disturbance near Bermuda. I was delighted the passage had been a work out, I had not regained full stamina but I had stood up to a tough passage with watchkeeping and all duties.

The second half of the voyage commenced at this point and an assessment of plans revealed that we were six weeks behind the original programme owing to my operation and to the delay in slipping. I was recovering well and enjoying myself, but I had not yet regained full energy and stamina. We had sailed 7,000 miles and we had charts, crew and tentative arrangements for the second half of the voyage, which would be another 7,000 miles. 'Bluebird' was in good order, there were not many items on the job list and most of them were not urgent. Maintenance had been fairly well achieved and we could return to England without slipping again and without the need for any major refit or work other than that which we could do ourselves while cruising. We all had the feeling that we had stayed rather too long in the Windward Islands and it was time to press on. We departed with light hearts and keen expectations.

We now concluded that we must save time on the passages between English Harbour and Florida and that this could be done whilst still visiting a representative selection of the islands and territories between. It would, however, mean hard driving and I think this was the main motive in asking Jill Baty to join for the stretch. She was well known to some of us; she had crossed the Atlantic with Humphrey Barton in 'Rose Rambler', but owing to a change of plans, she was available and seeking a berth to the Americas. The weather had settled back to normal. We made a night passage to St Martin, which was easy. We liked St Martin and managed to tour the French side of the island as well as the Dutch. This unique two-nation ownership of the island seems to work extraordinarily well. In the Free Port, all currencies were taken and dealt with without the slightest hesitation, the atmosphere was friendly and we enjoyed the visit. One disappointment was alcohol; we had relied upon the Free Port to replenish our stocks advantageously. It was a Free Port, but not curiously enough for anything containing alcohol.

We sailed in the evening and made another night passage to the Virgin Islands. At dawn next day, I really felt the reawakening sense of exploration and discovery; we were moving into an entirely different group of islands. We had resumed the voyage and we were on our way. It was at this point that we had a salutary warning; I would not say that we had been careless or that we did not know where we were, nevertheless, a black object out to starboard proved to be a wreck on Herman's Reef. At the same moment, the bottom showed beneath us, though in this extraordinary clarity, it was at 8 fathoms, startling enough nonetheless, after the deep blue of almost bottomless depths. The islands were spread out before us. Our log had been under-reading owing to weed and the current had pushed us somewhat to the north. There was no danger, but how easily the voyage could have ended on that same Herman's Reef; other yachts have done so.

After this experience, we skirted the well-named 'Invisibles' with anxious care and entered Gorda Sound, a relatively narrow entrance between broad fringing reefs. It was our first with a man up the crosstrees (via a rope ladder that we had constructed and lashed up the rigging for this purpose), watching the colour of the water, quite fascinating and something entirely new to us. Gorda Sound was charming and delightful with the choice of many anchorages; we visited one, made friends with a vessel already there and exchanged visits. We moved to another which we preferred and there met 'Tontine', a large schooner. One of her crew was known to us. We bathed, the reefs were fascinating and our first impression of the Virgin Islands was good. "Virgin

and arid", we wrote, as they were brown and far more barren of vegetation than most of the Windward Islands, and certainly less populated and with little tourist development.

Next day, we had a magnificent sail in company with 'Tontine', anchoring near her at 'The Baths', why so named I do not know. Here is a collection of granite boulders, some as large as a good sized house. They are in geological terms 'erratics' as the nearest comparable rock is some 2,000 miles away. My own theory, and I stick to it, is that they could only have arrived here carried by ice in some far-off age and dropped when the parent berg grounded on these reefs and islands. Under the guidance of 'Tontine's' skipper and with his help, we went in by dinghy, anchored off and swam ashore through the surf. The scramble through the rocks was quite sufficiently arduous for me and too arduous for some of his charter party. Swimming them out through the surf, getting them into the dinghy and back on board, was an undertaking not without its moments. We then sailed again in company for Marina Cay. We had the legs of 'Tontine', but so manoeuvred as to follow her in. We picked up a buoy under sail and made our number with the hospitable Bathams, whose foresight, enterprise and hard work had made a little paradise out of this island which was once a wilderness. A very delightful two days followed - some of the best snorkelling on the reefs, sunfish sailing for some of us and other explorations. Humphrey Barton was chartering 'Rose Rambler' from this base but he was away in Anegada (where some sort of rocket range was being constructed).

We called at Beef Island where there was a slip and we were able to collect excellent water, though we had to ferry it off in drums. In the next few days we visited Norman Island (the site of the film 'Treasure Island'), Roadtown twice and Peter Island. There was great excitement at Roadtown as the Royal Yacht 'Britannia', with the Queen Mother aboard, was due. So horrific had been our first-hand description of the treatment of yachts by the authorities at St Thomas in the American Virgin Islands, that we decided not to visit these islands at all, coupling this with our desire to save time. Our last night at Peter Island was cheered by a hospitable reception from the Chubbs in their yacht 'Antilles'. After many years' experience in the Bahamas, they found that the climate in the winter was better than in the Virgin Islands. This was their first year with a property at Peter Island, they were delighted with it and made us welcome to their domain. Here we cut coconut fronds and wove palm hats - a trick we had learned from one of 'Tontine's' charterers. We also had a deep-diving excursion to recover 'something' dropped overboard in 30 feet of water, locating it by glass bottomed float, loaned from 'Antilles', lowering our anchor weight close to it so that Donald could pull himself down to the bottom on the rope; a successful 'bikini hunt'.

We sailed from our anchorage and a brisk trade took us through the American Virgin Islands. They looked attractive and we half regretted our decision not to visit them. There was unwanted steamer traffic and we were passed by four American warships. This was to be our longest passage for some time. We settled happily to sea routine and with five on board, watchkeeping was almost too easy, but this gave us an opportunity to practise celestial navigation. We had all done some preparation on this; George and Donald were both determined to become proficient. In a day or two, we were able to record that all three of us were getting our position lines in agreement and within a mile or two; this was very satisfactory. We felt that the standard 'Vasco' had set could be maintained and we could now tackle the longer passages with confidence and any one of us could fix the ship or check the others. For an American yacht proceeding from the Bahamas to the Virgin Islands, this stretch of water is a nightmare with the prospect of an unremitting beat to windward against the trades for 500 miles; the only alternative being an occasional 'norther' which would mean unpleasant weather and probably a very strong wind. We therefore had the statistical probability of a fast passage with a good fresh trade. We had light winds astern, we had light winds on either quarter, we had light winds on either beam, we had some flat calm. The wind blew the wrong way out of Windward passage and finally we had a firm headwind as we approached Great Inagua. All day we beat up to and along the reefs of its southern shore, approaching Mathew Town in the last light. The wind headed again and the anchorage, which like so many in these parts is an open one depending on the lee from the prevailing trade wind, was quite untenable with a high sea rolling in and a surf on the shore very visible through the glasses.

We had been on passage longer than had been expected and while this did not matter in the least we were anxious to put in somewhere. It seemed a shame to go on through the islands without doing so, we were compelled to forego Inagua with its wild horse, pink flamingos and parrots (tourist literature). Why not visit Hogsty Reef, only 45 miles away? All night we beat to windward and the next day, feeling this a test for our navigation, we closed in on the nearest example in the Atlantic to a Pacific-type coral atoll. Nothing in sight, then from the crosstrees, a merchant ship. Donald claimed she was a wreck whilst the rest of us howled him down, but he was right. Soon we could see the changing colour of the water and we entered the lagoon. There was plenty of water over the coral heads, but threading our way through the dark patches that might have meant danger, we came to anchor in 2^1/$_2$ fathoms on coral sand abreast the island. Down went the anchor, our heavy weight on the chain; we made sure that we were holding securely, cleared up the deck and then looked round us. The colours were marvellous with the encircling ring of reefs and the white seas smashing over them and the deep blue water beyond. Our little island a couple of cables away was about 100 yards long by 40 yards wide, only about 15 feet above sea level, with one stunted palm tree and a little struggling green vegetation on its crest, a conical erection and one post with a light on it; there was nothing more. The only other land was a little hummock of bare sand. A light aircraft appeared and circled the wreck, then it was our turn. This could have been the setting for a yarn by Hammond Innes; the wreck containing missiles for Jamaica captured by counter-revolutionaries and we involved by accident and enlisted to take off the marooned Trusties against the machinations of the bad men. We recorded this as the wildest and strangest anchorage we had ever known, and after a night's uneasy rest, we sailed away.

The wind had veered and, as had become our almost invariable practice, up went the biggest genoa – 600 square feet in use except for flat calm or vicious squalls. We had come to use it without the staysail, which contributed little additional drive and entailed more chafe and another pair of sheets to handle. Up went the mizzen staysail, another 400 square feet and with mounting seas we surged on our way. Hogsty Reef sank out of sight so quickly it might never have existed.

That was a magnificent sail. At 9 knots we were soon closing the Mira Por Vos passage, neck and neck it seemed with the liner 'France', carrying, though we did not know it, General de Gaulle who had been visiting Martinique and the French West Indian possessions. I wondered if that strange man had nostalgic memories of the days culminating at the battle of the Saintes when, had victory gone otherwise, the control of the West Indies might have been retained by France. Strange to think that in those days, France had thought the Caribbean Islands so valuable that she was willing to concede the whole of her possession in Quebec and Canada to Great Britain if we would accept her dominance in the West Indies. Through this passage, we came on the wind, there was less sea, our speed hardly dropped but the light failed and we crept in to an anchorage in the lee of Crooked Island, circling carefully in an endeavour to ensure that there were no coral heads before we came to anchor.

Next day was equally memorable as we made our record speed on passage. There was a really large swell on the beam, the sea running true to a good force 6 wind, which was abaft the beam, making the apparent wind just forward of the beam. Carrying everything we had, we logged 10$\frac{1}{2}$ knots for a period; it was magnificent. After a time we lowered the mizzen to tame her down slightly and with reduced speed, came to Rum Cay. Here we had a problem and another warning, the charts were singularly uninformative; the latest correction was by a merchant ship in 1927. None of the authorities gave helpful indications, there were no easily identifiable marks or bearings and as the water shoaled, the bottom clearly visible, we handed the genoa. Then it happened! The wire threw a turn off the winch and jammed. It was blowing fresh, the reef was under us and growing shallower - a moment of crisis. George rushed for the big wire cutters, the Skipper left the helm and forgetting all about operations, threw himself upon the halyard and held it by main force until the foul turn was cleared. We smelt our way in through the reefs and anchored. The only attraction here would be to mount horses and ride round the island, but it was not ten days from Peter Island and we were anxious to reach relative civilization, so we sailed in the morning to make another fast passage to Great Exuma.

We had a fresh and rather shattering experience of the pilotage in these parts. The great swell of the day before was still running, smashing high in white foam on every reef. We roared up the 'tongue of the ocean' until the depth decreased in half a mile from 1,000 fathoms to 10 fathoms. We were confronted by a string of cays indistinguishable from each other, the passages between them a mass of foam. The pilot book and the chart in obvious disagreement as to which passage between which cay led to Georgetown; I almost decided to stand off. Eventually we were able to reconcile the marks, or hope that we had done so. We found a passage where the swell was not breaking clean across, it was narrow enough and it looked very shallow inside. With my heart in my mouth, we entered the gap. There was a horrid moment when the ship checked and hung as the swell sucked back on the shallow bottom and I thought that it might break, but we were through. Our troubles were not over; several uncharted miles of shallow water lay between us and the hurricane harbour at Stocking Island. Patience and a man in the crosstrees aided by the echo-sounder took our tortuous course to this refuge and at last we were completely protected. It was the first absolutely secure refuge we had seen for long enough. It was a treat to relax, listening still to the thunder of the surf which shook the island.

Georgetown was an anticlimax. As we rowed in next morning, we said, "At last we have managed to avoid arriving at a weekend". We had several needs, but when we landed we found to our horror that it was Easter Monday, a simple fact that we had quite ignored so none of our needs could be satisfied except a thirst and a rather expensive meal. The tourist influence was apparent and the prices were in American dollars and rampant. After two days here, which we enjoyed with various simple excursions, we prepared for a new type of pilotage on the Banks. Thank heavens we had here obtained an up to date copy of the 'Yachtsman's Guide to the Bahamas'. This is absolutely essential as the charts, as we have said, are almost useless for detail work. The American charts which one might suppose would be helpful, as it is so near to the States and so many of their vessels navigate these islands, are slightly less informative than the Admiralty charts and many bear a notation on the bottom, "Taken from information contained in British Chart". All other marks much be regarded as unreliable, as I have described at Rum Cay. Sea marks can so easily be mistaken for a dead and topless palm tree or a private flagpole.

We sailed up the string of islands, having determined to enter the gap at Galliot's Cut, the first that promised navigable water inside and over the Banks to give us a reasonable chance of keeping 'Bluebird' off the bottom. The Guide in effect said, "4 feet 6 inches draft is desirable, 7 feet is the giddy limit". In our present trim, we were about 5 feet 7 inches upright and 6 feet 8 inches when well heeled under sail. Once inside, we settled down seriously to learn new rules and new tricks. We must get used to sailing constantly with only a few feet beneath us, we must work the tides though only 2 or 3 feet, with so little depth of water, they can be deadly important. Generally the tide runs in or out of the gaps in the islands leading to the tongue of the ocean and runs on to the Bank, but in what direction or at what speed or with what timing, nobody seemed to know. A constant watch from the crosstrees on the colour of the water is essential, but a change in the light or the colour of the bottom can utterly defeat this. Passages must be timed to leave with the light behind one in the morning and preferably at high tide, proceed during the day's run on a course devoid of major hazards and arrange if possible to approach an anchorage in the afternoon with the light behind one and the tide rising. We visited Farmers Cay and Staniel Cay; already we had smelt the bottom with our keels more than once but not on coral and we had kept moving.

This place gave us the feeling of the Bahamas outer islands. The weather was cool, the winds were more variable, there was more overcast sky. We contrasted this unfavourably with our memories of the more tropical regions but on the other hand, what heaven this would be to Americans escaping from the rugged climate of their mainland winter. Here we collected a haul of conch. In those days the Bahamas were full of conch though sadly today they are very much depleted and quite scarce. We all went round with great enthusiasm collecting the great shells until 'Bluebird's' cockpit was filled high. Skips, George and Donald valiantly banged them out of their shells while Jilly tried every conceivable way of cooking them. We cooked them and ate them with varying reactions; an awful lot of work for an awful lot of chew! We crossed the island through appalling, scratchy scrub and over old broken reef, jagged and razor sharp; a rugged expedition from which we carried scars for many days. We explored caves from the dinghy with a snorkel and flippers - some of the most dramatic views and underwater colours we had yet seen. We could have continued a similar course up the islands of the Exuma Cays, many of them might have been different or more attractive, some less but we only had time to visit Normans Cay. As we approached Nassau, which is the hub of the universe in these parts, we were meeting an increasing number of other yachts.

The passage across the Banks was thrilling and heart-stopping. A dogleg course over 45 miles, all shallow but crossing a neck between two areas known as the Yellow Bank and the White Bank, both very shallow and studded with coral heads. With a brisk wind, we were sailing at 7 knots or more, the light was not too good. Our Brookes & Gatehouse echo-sounder was voted the finest instrument for giving one heart failure that had ever been invented as we roared along in 12 to 15 feet of water with the reading bouncing spasmodically to 10 feet or less as we crossed coral heads, sometimes coinciding with warning signals from the man at the crosstrees and sometimes not, until we switched it off to let our nerves snap back. We survived and I suppose that one gets very used to this. Even the entrance to Nassau has coral heads, and one is told to look here for a white ring caused by the fish who shelter beneath them nibbling at the weeds around them, the bottom otherwise being too dark generally to distinguish these coral heads easily. We went into the main marina; this was the fabulous Nassau, the bright lights, civilisation, tourist centre, millionaire's playground, and for us, a pause in the programme, yet something so different from our way of life that we were not sure how we should like it. There was something intolerant and oppressive in the feeling here that did not appeal to us. Tourism pouring in money on one hand and an undercurrent of resentment and strife. A feeling that law and crime and concession or trade, were subject to a rather sensitive domination by the 'bay street boys' (a sort of rather evil local Mafia) and dictated by standards of greed with a record of smuggling rackets in the days of American drink prohibition. Of course the dollar was triumphant and costs were on the scale of the States and frightening for our currency restricted state.

This Vast America

When we sailed, we had changed our minds. Originally we had intended to cross Great Bahama Bank to Cat Cay or Bimini, but serious study of the implications showed that they were horrid. Much of the passage must be done at night or we must anchor on the Banks. We were bound to reach the worst part of the shoal water in the wrong light, the tides did not fit and I shuddered at the thought of being caught on the Bank if it should blow up hard from the north. "It can be done", we said, "we are not frightened". But why push our luck too far? Decision was indicated and I said, "We go round the outside in deep water. Let us make sure that we do sail to America". A good, fast passage took us past the Berry Islands. One evening we saw the trail of a space rocket from Cape Kennedy. 'Bluebird', under the usual full sail to the big genoa but now on the wind, was steering herself at 7 knots, the wheel free. The lights, the fantastic and fabulous lights from Fort Lauderdale to Miami were growing as the light faded and closed in. Eventually we went under power for the last few miles inshore to dodge the Gulf Stream and entered Miami by night, securing to a sailing schooner inside. It was quite a moment; this was America. We reminded ourselves that this was not necessarily the real America, indeed Americans had been at pains to assure us of this and we had mentally prepared ourselves by saying, "Whatever happens and however it strikes us, remember we gotta have fun".

In an endeavour to insure ourselves against the dire possibilities and formalities of Health, Customs, Immigration and police, we had visited the American Consul at Nassau and asked advice. Nobody could have been more charming, greeting me as "cher collegue" (I have a Consular appointment), he provided the whole crew with every possible form of visa, all done in an hour at no charge whatsoever and with wry humour, assured us that which ever way his colleagues wished to play it we could produce the necessary answer, and so it proved. We have indeed a suspicion that the path had been further smoothed, but the whole of our entry to America in all forms was effected with the greatest goodwill and amity and no difficulty whatsoever. What a relief!

By midday we had secured at the municipal marina, right in front of the skyscraper blocks of downtown Miami. Miami was Blackpool, Brighton, Torquay, Bournemouth, all rolled into one and then some. Here was America retired or at play at all levels and their levels are almost entirely those of the price bracket. The pace was frantic and the difficulty of tending 'Bluebird', trying to see as much as possible, sorting out the really interesting from the ballyhoo, 'genuine injuns in genuine Adobe huts', coping with astonishing hospitality and trying in vain to keep within our budget. We picked up the atmosphere of the luxury yacht, many of them with professional skippers, moving up the waterway in the spring for the summer season in Maine, moving back down the waterway in the fall to, for example, Pier 66 at Fort Lauderdale, where the owners could fly down and live on board for a milder winter climate. As we arrived, these craft were all moving away north up the coast with the spring and out to Bermuda where the winter gales were over. We had varied luck with the weather on this coast, much of it was delightful, some of it was very hot, a little was disappointing - cool or overcast or rain. The wind always worked round clockwise, the southern sectors giving the better weather.

We rode the Gulf Stream outside and entered Fort Lauderdale by night. We took the Inland Waterway for experience to West Palm Beach and up to Fort Pierce. In the marina at West Palm Beach were four yachts designed by Arthur Robb. Each place had its different atmosphere; yacht clubs were not yacht clubs in our sense, they were merely rather more exclusive marinas with a distinction by price and open to anybody virtually who could

sign their name in a book. We went off in each place for a day returning from these forays usually triumphant but exhausted with an order for some Brass Rubbings from some museum, art gallery or cultural society. In each port, the Press assailed us, sometimes direct, sometimes at the instance of a social hostess who could use us to get her press notice. The gem from this collection was, "A real live English Lord. His twinkling blue eyes matching his T shirt and with hardly a trace of a British accent". We endeavoured to do our maintenance, but under the pressure of life, this fell behind. George frequently, and Donald occasionally, were assumed to be my sons; I felt this shed a pleasant and rather flattering light on our relationship.

We left the Inland Waterway at Fort Pierce. Here we had grounded on a muddy sandbank, unmarked, and right in front of the Yacht Club Marina. Someone remarked, "We used to have buoys (pronounced 'bu-oys') but took 'em away last week as the depth was the same right across". An American Coastguard launch pulled us over the bank; it was well that my Samson Post and stem-head gear were designed on rugged lines. They had need of it. I had signed an exemption chit from damage; the launch gave it the works and about 1,400 horse power. We went over the bank and everything stood. We were then inspected and given an approval sticker as being okay by their standards. Rather shattered by all this, we went out of the inlet where an ebb tide met the incoming sea and wind between training walls. Forgetting to close our ports, we not only took heavy water on deck but had a little flood below; these inlets could be murder under really bad conditions.

Once again we rode the Gulf Stream, astonished to find from our sights that we had made good fifty-six miles more than our log distance in 24 hours. The usual experience of good winds, head-winds, light winds and no wind, but we were thankful to approach Charleston under easy conditions, as we had been warned that the swell could build up in a most unpleasant way on the shoaling water of this immense bay. Better, we thought to miss Jacksonville; with the Press-formented racial tensions, our presence might have been misunderstood. We entered Charleston by night. This was a rather trying experience as it is fourteen miles from the entrance buoy to the marina, with no less than four sets of leading lights on four courses. We fetched up at dawn. The atmosphere here was utterly different and we liked it. We could not, we said, have picked a better place as a contrast from Florida and for our last port in the States. There was the atmosphere of age and some history, tempering the new, the pace was more leisurely than the Northern States but the frenzied holiday atmosphere was missing. This was where the first shots had been fired in the Civil War. There were old cannon and fortresses jealously guarded. Here was the setting of the 'Gone with the Wind' story. We were invited to a plantation of cotton and, though this has been preserved by an infusion of wealth from industry, it was exactly as it had been in the days before the Civil War. The house of the period, charming, the trees dripping with Spanish moss, the swamps and creeks filled with alligators. A long row of kennels with hunters for the quail shooting and the slave quarters, echoing ghostly and with all the implements of the past including chairs. Gracious living, interesting company and charming hospitality; our host excusing himself after dinner - to drive home the coloured help. What could have emphasised one contrast more effectively.

In Charleston we gravitated into close friendship with Jan, a Dutchman, and I think this was because we were Europeans. He was a Professor at the University of Charleston and somehow I found myself giving a series of talks to senior students. One of my subjects was 'European Economics after the Second World War'; on such occasions, one must hope that the audience know less about it than you do. This was a wonderful experience and an opportunity to meet American youth and get close to them in discussion. You never know what will happen next.

It was time to leave Charleston and our reluctance was reinforced by the realisation that the next passage was the start of the long haul back to England.

Chapter Eleven

Hurricane off Bermuda

I regarded the 850 miles to Bermuda as more serious, than warranted by distance, as we should cross the Gulf stream which could have its own hazards of sea and squall. We should have Cape Fear and Cape Hatteras in play and their reputation is fearsome. We did not sail on Monday owing to a gale warning. Two yachts were in difficulties and were brought in by the Coastguard Service. A small craft warning was still in force when we sailed at 09.00 on Tuesday, 28 April. In the outer channel we were passed by a British warship, HMS 'Ursa' and after an uncertain day, the night was sufficiently dirty. Fleet exercises were in progress and the night watches were made more anxious and difficult by warships manoeuvring at high speed all round us, sometimes without lights or shooting off incomprehensible pyrotechnics.

In Charleston they had said, "We always get a gale at the end of April". We could only hope that this was the end of it. I drove 'Bluebird' hard and used some engine, feeling uneasy, until we could clear the Gulf Stream. Although winds and weather were uncertain and difficult we made good progress, substantially on course, until 08.00 on Saturday 2 May. We were four days out, leaving the Gulf Stream and over halfway to Bermuda with 570 miles astern. Unknown to us, a yacht called 'Doubloon' skippered by her owner Joe Byars, was sailing from St Augustine, Florida, bound north. Utterly remote from our concerns, events were to involve both of us in a strange dance of destiny. Our wind came in force 5, east. A dead head wind. This was not good and if it persisted we should need ten days. Meanwhile press on beating hard into a rising sea with no advantage on either tack. By noon on Sunday, 3 May, the wind still east had become force 6. We had sailed 130 miles in the previous 24 hours and our position by observation was 32° 38 minutes north, 68° 24 minutes west. We were reduced to mainsail and staysail. The barometer was quite high at 1017 millibars. By 18.00 the wind was rising over force 7 and, with the sea then running, effective progress was so reduced that I decided to heave to on the starboard tack under staysail and mizzen. The barometer was dropping slightly and it was obvious that there was an important centre of low pressure somewhere to the south east of our position. Our wind, east, force 7/8, 'Bluebird' was riding easily and relatively comfortably.

'Doubloon' at that time was south east of us and had a west force 8/9, soon rising to force 10 and gusting hurricane force, her barometer was falling fast and was now 996. She was in the strength of the Gulf stream and ran under bare poles into the night and was pooped lightly several times, and twice heavily, causing her to be smashed down on her beam ends. Eventually she lay ahull about 70° to the wind until 01.00 Monday, 4 May when she was rolled 360°, losing both masts and virtually everything above deck and a man (recovered miraculously 20 minutes later). A few hours later she was smashed down again on her beam ends but recovered and at about 09.00 she was once more rolled 360° and she and her crew sustained further damage but she remained afloat; her massive bronze centre-plate was afterwards found to have been bent 30°. The seas had risen to an estimated 18 - 25 feet and were steep, vicious and breaking heavily with the wind at hurricane force opposing the Gulf stream current. 'Doubloon' lay helpless little more than afloat but destined to survive.

At this time, Monday 4 May, 'Bluebird's' noon position by DR (dead reckoning) was 33° 04 minutes north, 68° 18 minutes west, with the bar steady at 1013; the wind still east, force 8 or more. At 18.00 we were able to round up and become hove to on the port tack to regain the Rhumb line for Bermuda. The seas were logged 15 foot. Under these conditions the yacht would almost, but not quite, come about if the staysail was let draw. She could have been brought round by using the engine but the flogging sails and shipping seas might have caused damage. It was easier to unleash the helm, steer off, which she would do, jibe and come up onto the port tack with the staysail already aback.

At 10.25 on Wednesday 5 May, conditions were similar but the wind went down to force 7. I was anxious to make progress towards Bermuda and we set 'B' mainsail, sailing under this and the staysail. At this point the younger members of the crew were all moving into new realms of experience in this or any other yacht; we had tried photographs to record the scene but it now became impossible to risk cameras in the spume.

With 'Doubloon', the worst was over. It was still blowing very hard and the sea was such that no attempt was made to do more than make existence tolerable.

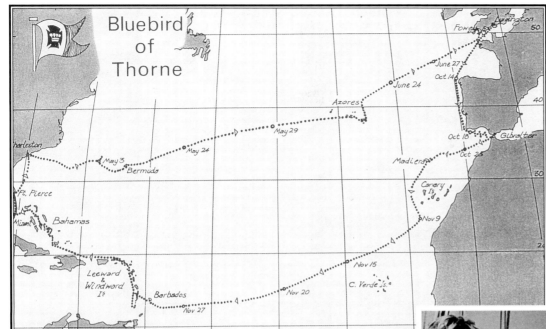

Left: Track Chart.

Below: The Skipper, George Allen and Donnld Tew, part of the hurricane crew.

Away to the east of us and equally unknown to us, Roy flew into Bermuda at noon on Wednesday, 5 May, from England. When the big Boeing landed, he described the scene: wind force 9 with horizontal driving rain, horizontal trees, horizontal waves driving over the lower land areas. He was kindly received by the Yacht Club. He might well have wondered where 'Bluebird' was and how she was faring. He could not tell but our bar was at last dropping at 1008 and by 22.00 the wind was logged east, north east, force 9 and more in the squalls. The sea was logged 20 foot. We were on a course 130° MAG and 4-4½ knots. Shipping but little water in spite of the build up of sea, I was baffled by the weather. I did not believe it was all over but only a slight lull and why so little change in the barometer? Sure enough at 16.00 the wind was again force 8 and rising rapidly with squalls of increasing frequency and severity. 'B' main was handed, the mizzen was set and 'Bluebird' hove to again on the port tack.

These conditions persisted all night until 06.00 on Wednesday, 6 May when the wind had backed to north east by north, bar 1006 falling. At this time the mizzen boom failed. A quarter sheet was rigged and there was no serious consequence as 'Bluebird's' mizzen, being all in board, could be effectively controlled and she remained hove to as before. The failure was due to the glue which had disintegrated under tropical conditions in the lamination joints. 'Bluebird' remained hove to, still under staysail and mizzen, all that night, riding well in wind force 8/9, the barometer almost steady. I still could not understand the weather system, we could feel relatively comfortable and there was nothing to worry us unduly at that time. At breakfast on the morning of Wednesday, 6 May, we agreed in discussion, that we should not get out of this system until the bar made a decisive move and as it was so high, it might well get worse before it got better. How right we were. The motion was severe, the crash and thud of breaking crests punctuated the argument. The Skipper wrote notes on handling and behaviour and a letter. Donald plotted up the DR and he and Jill tried to play cards wedged in a berth. George read. All operations were difficult.

Noon, Wednesday 6 May. The DR position 31° 53, north 67° 56 west, bar 1005 falling, seas increasing, perhaps 25 foot now. Wind increasing. What about the other and unknown protagonists? With 'Doubloon' it was over and at this time her weary and battered crew got in the mess of spas and rigging, which had formed a sort of sea anchor. At 16.00, a freighter offered rescue but stout-hearted Joe Byars refused and requested a tow. This agreed they proceeded until a coastguard cutter, summoned by radio, took over the tow and continued towards Charleston.

In Bermuda, Roy, thinking that we were now nine days out from Charleston (it was eight in fact) and alarmed by the continued appalling weather, made his way to the US Coastguard Service at Kinley Field. An interesting discussion developed. The Coastguards explained that they had suffered much from two situations. When a yacht and her crew were lost, the Press line was, "We spend all this money on the Coastguard and they cannot even save lives from a yacht in distress". When a search was mounted and proved unnecessary the line became. "Why do the Coastguards waste so much money on these futile and unnecessary operations." So they had developed protective rules for small craft situations: ("The information must be authentic. A situation of real danger must exist on their own assessment. A search must be requested by a responsible source. The decision to mount a search and its scope must be taken at a high level.")

Following this line, Roy could give them all information about 'Bluebird' and her crew. Was he requesting a search? No, he agreed with the Coastguards that 'Bluebird' would probably arrive within three days. Did he know when 'Bluebird' had sailed from Charleston? Positively no, probably 27 April but he would cable and check this. Meanwhile the Coastguards showed him the plot, confirmed severe weather in the area and promised to keep an informal plot of 'Bluebird's' probable position and would adjust this when he had a reply to his cable. Roy returned to the Yacht Club and sent the cable to Charleston; that was to trigger another dramatic development.

Back to 'Bluebird'. Before dark, still on Wednesday 6 May, the weather had become decisively worse. The wind logged force 10, sea still increasing and breaking more heavily. The yacht was heeled 20/25° under wind pressure alone, apart from the effects of sea and wind, less than 20 square feet of sail per ton of displacement. It was time to make the next move: rehearsal and all hands on deck. Unleash the helm, staysail first and then as quickly as possible to mizzen. 'Bluebird' remained under control while this was done and then lay ahull. It was at this point that I also moved out and beyond previous experience. I had no knowledge of the behaviour of this new 'Bluebird' under bare poles in these conditions. I was very thankful that the Gulf stream had been left behind, ocean currents would be slight with negligible effect on the sea. Even more important and a Godsend was ample sea room in all directions.

'Bluebird' remained hove to. This was almost miraculous as she was now heeling about 15° to the wind under bare poles and booms, furled sails and rigging which might implement 5 square foot per ton of displacement. Her head lay about 60/65° from the wind direction; she was fore-reaching, perhaps $1/2$ knot and drifting about 85° or nearly at right angles to her heading or 150° from the wind. The rate of drift remained about $1/2$ knot, there was a good visible slick to windward, offering, I hoped, some protection from breaking crests. As darkness came, it was a fearsome outlook and it is difficult to describe the sea or the scene. At midnight we logged force 11 and I think it reveals the atmosphere in the ship that this was the result of an all hands discussion. Two wished to log force 12 and two, force 11. "It must be hurricane force now", was one camp. "We can't measure, it varies so much in squalls and we have no comparison from experience", was the other. "Be conservative and log force 11" was the result. We could not see so we did not attempt to log the height of the sea.

So 'Bluebird' entered Thursday, 7 May. At 03.00 the bar was 996, nothing untoward had occurred though the sea had increased further and was more confused as the wind backed and 'Bluebird' was struck more frequently and more heavily by breaking crests. Now came the first knock down, smash! 'Bluebird' received a blow like a large steam hammer and appeared to be thrown sideways at great speed, heeling over as she went until the masts were 90°/110° from upright. Would she go on down or roll? There was barely time to think as she recovered. By chance we were all on the leeward side, Jill in the fore-cabin, Donald aft and George and I huddled together in the lee corner of the saloon as we discussed the situation before he went to his berth and I took over the watch, which, however ineffective, I had insisted we must maintain. No one was hurt, no dangerously heavy objects were carried away, the mess however was considerable and we afterwards discovered that the acceleration had thrown objects from their storage into impossible positions, for example, a heavy spanner that had been on a shelf in the port companionway had gone upward a foot aft; 3 ft right across the deckhouse down into the chart room and wedged itself behind lockers below the chart table. Astonishing! Inspection on deck revealed no damage. We cleared up the mess and re-stowed. I told the crew and I think I believed myself that

this was a freak wave and I should take no action. I remained on watch, the others retired to their berths to rest. Just after breakfast, at about 09.00 on Thursday 7 May, 'Bluebird' received the second smash.

I happened to be on the lee side of the saloon and looking up through a port. I saw a rising sea away above my angle of vision though as she was heeled that must have been 75° from horizontal. A moment later that wave fell on 'Bluebird' bodily over her whole length, tons of solid water. Everything went dark and again we went down and over perhaps not quite as far this time and more slowly as we were virtually under water. Again 'Bluebird' recovered but more slowly this time and the water, clearing as she rose, became light. This time there was a new noise, an internal noise of squirting water. I rushed to the deckhouse, all intact but a coaming along the bottom edge of one of the deckhouse windows had burst. Hydraulic pressure acting on only an eighth of an inch, had extruded the hard rubber sealing of the decklight round the bottom of the armoured glass and this had burst the woodwork. I couldn't and I cannot calculate the pressure that must have been developed, in spite of weatherboard protection. Luckily it was not serious and only two or three bucketfuls had entered while submerged. We took a piece of timber, cut it to length and shored the burst coaming from across the deckhouse making all tight with two wedges. Again the crew had suffered no hurt but I had been thinking.

Twice was enough, I would not risk a third smash, we must run off and stream warps. I did not like this; it would save us from these smashing blows but it posed new dangers. We might be pooped so heavily as to be damaged. We might broach and in that case we might be rolled completely. 'Bluebird' must be steered and with skill. The man at the helm would be at risk and might be torn away and lost if anything went wrong. In any case it involved fatigue, exposure to the elements and mental stress. I explained all this to the crew and told them to prepare the warps. I did not tell them the real disquiet in my mind. Until this moment, although outside previous experience, I had some more in reserve; this was my last card, after this I had nothing; if it went wrong, even short of disaster, we could only lie ahull again and pray. I knew how important the morale of the crew could be and I did all I could to maintain this by keeping the objective in mind and frequently calculating and discussing ETA (estimated time of arrival) Bermuda. I also maintained ship routines with stand-by watches, regular meal times, inspections on deck, battery charging and other chores.

On two days in the worst conditions, I had the charcoal stove lit. It was not cold but it was comforting to take off heavier clothes and feel warm and dry when the air seemed to be half water, as indeed it was within a few feet of the sea surface, apart from heavy rain. I wrote my notes and a letter to save time when we reached Bermuda. There was a card game at times, rest aplenty and what sleep we could manage. When lying ahull before the big smash, we had wedged ourselves in a row on the saloon floor and read aloud sections from books dealing with heavy weather. This was instructive and one comment raised a laugh, "I bet he wrote that ashore with his feet up and a glass of whisky in his hand". The nearest comparison we could find was from Albert Edward Robinson in 'The Great South Sea' relating to lovely great 'Vanua' of 70 ft and 70 tons in a 40 ft sea. Given this interpolation, his experience and his handling of 'Vanua' agreed with our experience and our methods. The main and most important lesson learned was that any general advice, no matter how great the experience of the author, may be misleading.

The type of yacht, the equipment, the exact sea conditions, the pure chance of tidal seas and the experience, strength and morale of Skipper and crew can alone dictate the strategy. This was afterwards reinforced by an exchange of information with Joe Byers of 'Doubloon'. I do not and would not criticise his handling though it was in contrast with ours and had different results. The yacht was different in type but above all he had the Gulf stream seas. Although his length was 40 ft against 'Bluebird's' 50 ft he almost certainly had the more dangerous condition. Under similar conditions I should again handle 'Bluebird' in the same way but it would demand as good a crew and plenty of sea room and I would reserve the right to change the strategy for any reason if the judgement demanded it at the time.

The crew were good, there was no break in morale, Jill, intrepid and with her ocean racing experience, determined to show that she could turn up a good meal under the worst conditions. Maybe something simpler might have served better as the effort was exhausting to her and the clearing up afterwards, which we did, was equally exacting but not for worlds would I interfere. Donald, tough and unimaginative, would not easily encounter fear. His main task was to keep a detailed plot. I was able to put drift angles and speeds from former experience and with regular

logged records this was so successful that after five days and nights observation, there were only twelve miles between our DR and our true position when we could at last take sights and get a fix. George, a more complex subject, so much more imaginative and sensitive that he had in fact more stress. Also he must have feared that he might fail through seasickness from which he had suffered. He did not go down, finding perhaps as I had done years before, that fright or exaltation of spirit can overcome that bogey. But George it was after the first smash who said, "Skipper, would survival be as important now as ETA Bermuda?" "Yes George", I replied, "I have been working out what to do if we sustained damage. It might then be better to make for the Azores but not on any account back towards the Gulf stream".

No fear. Anxiety when I went beyond all previous experience, a feeling I did not like when we ran after the second smash but one new phase of thought on these lines, "If this is it I don't mind and more than before I can feel I have had a good innings". This was rapidly followed by the thought, "I may now have less resources so that makes it more important to fight beyond all reason to get these youngsters home". When the situation became serious and I had decided to change sail or attitude and in the ultimate to run, I summoned all hands, told them the decision and why, not hiding the risk that running would be dangerous if it did not work and this time I had no further card to play. It would mean steering the ship, the man at the wheel would be at risk and we should all have more effort, more exposure and more fatigue but I would take her first until we saw how it went. I then had them all tog up and assemble in the deckhouse. A detailed plan of operations was discussed, duties allotted to each, and every possible preparation made before we started. I should take the helm, Donald the toughest deck jobs, George back-up or help when aft. Jill, though tough, not having the strength of a man, with me to carry messages as the situation developed or in case of change or danger and to help if anyone got into trouble. Action is helpful at such a time and in the violent motion a job that would normally occupy ten minutes becomes an arduous task for an hour.

Out came a 60 fathom second anchor warp. It would be streamed from the bollards aft on each quarter in a bight and around the bight we rolled and bound our tropical awnings, first twisting them tight, then the mooring lines to make a second bight of warps with a drag of 45 fathoms. I decided that she would be fast enough under bare poles and I had great faith in her control and behaviour down wind. Tog up, assemble in the deckhouse and rehearse operations. All ready, but wait. Before we went off I had five big sail bags packed in the cockpit in front of the companion and its heavy weatherboards, they must be securely lashed, they would reduce the area of the cockpit, protect the companionway and cushion shock if we were pooped. I might have added that they would be a softer fetch up for the helmsman if he were torn from the wheel and thrown down by a great sea from aft.

Action. Ready. The wheel went over, she hung on and then began paying off. All well, warps out and we were away. Good, nice steerage about 4.5 knots. I ordered the others below; Donald to stand by inside the companionway; I had my harness clipped on each side of the cockpit and a line round me and the mizzen mast. We now logged the sea 30/35 ft, the wind still force 11 and the bar rising. I found that there was no undue difficulty in control. The seas were taken up to 20° on each quarter and there was no attempt to break unless she swung to 30° as she yawed or the confused seas changed direction. Donald recorded that she was rolling at times 35° either way in five second periods. I was hardly conscious of the movement as I concentrated on the task. But the seas! I had never seen the like. Jilly recorded the experience afterwards:

"When the hurricane was in progress, I had gone forward with my harness attached to the fore and aft line to tie down a sail that had escaped its bondage, I was suddenly lifted high on a wall of wind and water and smashed back down into the deck. When I had recovered sufficiently to turn my head, the whole of the stern aft of the yacht had disappeared beneath a great breaking sea. Fortunately although shaken somewhat, I was not bruised owing to the amount of clothes I wore under my foul weather gear; we had all been feeling the cold in the high latitudes. During the peak of the storm it was impossible to tell day from night or sea from sky and the noise was like 10,000 banshees in the rigging."

"After we had been capsized for the second time, the Skipper decided that we must now run with bare poles, streaming warps with drags on them astern, this was beyond all his previous experience, it would be our last resource and it might not work. Typically he had foreseen this as a possibility and under his directions we had prepared the warps and drags. These were now completed and with some difficulty and danger, we got them streamed, sterned and secured. The Skipper now took the helm

and slowly 'Bluebird' paid off until she was before the wind and gathered way. There was nothing more that we could do so we went below to rest as best we could leaving Donald lashed inside the companionway to keep watch and see whether the Skipper needed help".

"Before the companionway was finally closed and bolted, I peeped out through the slit; there was a magnificent sight which remains implanted in my mind. Behind the sail bags in the cockpit, the Skipper was seated behind the steering wheel. The stern, grey seas crested up high towards the sky, his sou'wester firmly lashed to chin, his grey ventile sea jacket, both hands on the wheel, his feet and legs against the sail bags. He was lashed to the mizzen mast with bands round his chest. He was also lashed with strong ropes to secure stanchions at each side of the cockpit so that if we were pooped solidly, he could not be torn away and thrown overboard. But I shall never forget the expression on the Skipper's face and at the time I felt a mixture of surprise and almost shock. He had a complete serenity which, if it had not been somewhat serious, could have ben called a look of happiness. Thinking this over afterwards, I came to realise that he had made a complete contract with life, nothing mattered anymore, there was nothing left except a determination to win through this ultimate test. Braced behind the steering wheel of this yacht that he had designed and created, he was starting a spell that was to last for seven hours through the height of the hurricane. He was steering for our lives".

The surface of the sea was invisible with the spume and spindrift, all distinction between air and water is lost. The predominant colour white, as streaks of foam covered the surface. When heaved high on a crest, there was the sensation of looking down onto a valley, quarter of a mile across and quite deep, all indistinct and in violent movement. Then the bow went down and down. The feel of the helm changed under my hands as the speed increased and with a roar an enormous sea broke over astern. It seemed inevitable that I should feel the smashing weight of water, tons of it, pouring over the stern but incredibly only the blow as from a bucketful or two was thrown at me from behind and between the shoulder blades. The shriek of the wind, the notes from the rigging, higher still in the squalls and deeper notes in the lull. If you turned into the wind it would be difficult to breathe as I found when I glanced aft to assess a sea and look at the warps; they were doing their job. When high behind, I could see them tearing their way through the seas, the awning on the bight causing its own little bow wave. We did not charge down the seas, never I think above 5^1/$_2$ knots, with steerage-way down to 2^1/$_2$.

After an hour, while we might be pooped at any time, I relaxed slightly and the next three hours passed so that I was hardly conscious of effort and experienced indeed an exaltation of spirit in which I could appreciate the magnificence of man whilst 50 ft and 15 tons of 'Bluebird' were almost literally tossed to and fro like a toy boat in breakers on the beach. Surely it was less savage, perhaps the worst was over. After seven hours, I handed over to Donald and went below. I then realised that this long period of intense effort had taken its toll; I was almost exhausted. By 17.00 it was better, we logged force 10 and the rising barometer indicated that the centre had passed and lay about north, north-west close to the west of our position as indicated by wind changes. By evening this was confirmed, the wind falling but the sea remained so unmanageable that I decided to continue as we were until dawn. Somehow, Jilly had managed to get some food into us at intervals and this undoubtedly contributed to our condition and survival by staving off the exhaustion that would otherwise have been inevitable.

Meanwhile in Charleston, the might of the American Press were assembled at the marina. Alerted by the coastguards at Cape Morgan, they awaited the arrival of the battered 'Doubloon' and her battered but indomitable skipper and crew. 'Doubloon', completely repaired and made good, took part in the Bermuda Race only six weeks later. What better tribute to her sound construction and the determination of Joe Byars. Roy's cable arrived and they must have fallen upon it like a pack of wolves. This was almost too good to be true. Not only 'Doubloon' but the possibility of a greater disaster, they might have thought. Back went the reply to Roy in Bermuda. Back he went to Kinley Field and the friendly and helpful coastguards. They decided to wait another 24 hours and if there was then no news, to alert shipping in the area to keep a look out for 'Bluebird' and report. If that brought nothing and we had not arrived in another 24 hours, it would be time to consider mounting a search. But the cables also flashed to England and that evening and through the night of Thursday, 7 May and the early hours of Friday, 8 May, when our ordeal was in fact already over, the English daily papers and a local paper went into banner headlines.

They telephoned Bermuda and were told the truth. Weather severe, yacht's position unknown, considered likely to arrive within 48 hours, if not perhaps a search. Despite this the headlines were more dramatic on the lines of, 'Lord Riverdale's yacht 'Bluebird' lost in Atlantic storm.'

Then the telephone calls. Christian was away but later gave a stout-hearted reply. Then the suggestion, "Did you know that there was a woman aboard?" Christian equally indomitable replied, "Yes of course, she's a friend of mine". Mark escaped this pestering as he was away at L'Monde. My cousin Gerald, at the firm, knowing nothing of the sea, was appalled and at a loss in his replies. Ronnie Gresham (one of my regular crew members), "They will be alright; a good skipper and a good crew". Second son David took his telephone off the hook and daughter Frances escaped as she was away in Germany. Donald's mother, herself a redoubtable member of the Royal Cruising Club was, like Christian, completely unshakeable and her reply was, "I expect them to sail in in a day or two". The press treatment of George's mother I found horrifying when I heard about it later. She happened to be alone in her house when they rang her up in the middle of the night, "Have you a son called George? Is he your only son? Is he sailing with Lord Riverdale in a yacht called 'Bluebird'? Did you know that the yacht was reported lost in an Atlantic storm?" She virtually passed out unable to reply. Jilly had no relatives whom the press could contact. Margaret Bennett was telephoned at 2.00 am, "Where can we get a photograph of 'Bluebird' and Lord Riverdale? Reply, "At the works". "Can you get it?" "What do you think when Lord Riverdale may be drowning in the Atlantic?" Then they sent a car for her and insisted that she went down to the works in the middle of the night to get the photographs. From this and other contacts I later discovered that they were preparing my obituary.

After a night's rest, conditions next morning were sufficiently normal to allow us to make sail and proceed on our course to Bermuda. We were able to fix our position with proper sights. We found that our careful DR over some three days had placed us only twelve miles away from our exact position. A grand sailing day, great speed and the expectation of landfall and reaching port. Noon position by observation 31° 53 minutes north, 66° 23 minutes west. Wind north west, west force 4, bar 1015. I well remember the little stormy petrels, I had seen them in the storm and thought they cannot feed in this. Now they must have been hungry and collecting behind us like gulls behind a plough, they crisscrossed our wake eagerly collecting the minute fragments of plankton thrown up by the passage of our keels.

Landfall as dusk was closing in. Hove to for an hour or so before tackling the channel and the coral reefs at dawn and threading our way to harbour by the ship channel in the lagoon. As we entered port, a launch met us. Not customs this time but the Press in great excitement. Only then did the horrors hit us. An English daily paper had authorised its agent to charter a plane and search for us; I refused to burst into song. We berthed at the Yacht Club at 10.30 am on Saturday, 9 May and there was Roy, glad to see us. Then a telephone call by Press request to London lasting thirty minutes, "Crew all well, ship undamaged, not really overdue, only one day beyond slow passage estimate". Realising that the bubble had burst, there were the provocative questions, "I suppose you would have abandoned ship if a rescue had been possible?' "Certainly not, a rescue in these conditions would have been more dangerous than our situation". Finally in desperation I said, "Of course it was serious weather and something might have gone wrong but what can I say to make you believe that there was no emergency or panic. We read books, we wrote letters, we played cards!" That did it, I ended up with the serious request, "Will you at once contact all you have spoken to and inform them of arrival, all well and undamaged in eleven days. Please publish this and make clear there was no call for help and NO search". I regret to say that not all were contacted and the closure was a small paragraph, not prominent and on the lines, "Lord Riverdale's yacht, 'Bluebird of Thorne', has been reported and has arrived Bermuda, the search has been called off". We were no longer news and so ended the crisis that never was but there are thoughts from this. I then considered and still find it quite illogical that when we were reported lost, my firm's shares plummeted on the Stock Exchange only to bounce up equally sharply when our arrival was reported. I find it a strange thought that in monetary value I was then apparently worth more than has ever been the case before or since.

I found it difficult then and I find it difficult now to deal with the serious aspects of such an experience without over-playing the danger on the one hand or making it sound quite trivial on the other. After my return to Sheffield, I summoned the local press for an interview. I told them that if they had believed my wife and the American coastguard, they could have scored a unique scoop by reporting that we were expected to sail in after a day or two, in contrast to the total loss reported by the press in general. I then said, "Fair is fair. If you show me the obituary you wrote I will give you an exclusive account of what really happened". To my astonishment this was treated as a sort of insult. Did they think I was attacking that 'sacred cow' the freedom of the press? Whatever the reasoning, I was bad news and more or less written off for some time to come.

Back in Bermuda, we went about our normal duties. Repairs to the wood around the deckhouse window coaming. Hospitality and friends. I must mention 'Shorty' Trimmingham, a well-known Bermudian yachtsman whose house became our haven of rest while we were in Bermuda. Excursions and relaxation. Jilly noticed something odd which she reported to me afterwards. On the one hand we could hardly stand up straight and walk when we first landed and on the other hand, people told her that when we were sitting in the Yacht Club for example, our limbs might be shaking gently and not of our own volition. I had been rather exhausted when we sailed from Charleston, I realised that I was now in far better shape and had suffered no ill effects from a severe passage; on the contrary, I even felt I had recovered my full strength for the first time since my operation in January. We had a de-briefing session with the Coastguards which was interesting. Their plot had been very accurate and we gave them our information; they confirmed wind 65 knots, gusting 75 knots, seas 30 ft and agreed that we might have had more severe conditions in our position. Their barometric trace was interesting, totally different from our record. They also confirmed that the hurricane had re-curved and so may virtually have passed over us twice. This explained the abnormal length of time during which we had been in danger and also the abnormality of the seas we had encountered. From them we learned more about 'Doubloon' and the slow build-up of the weather system was explained. Usually a cyclonic storm moves fast but this was the exception out of place, out of season. They called it an 'extra tropical hurricane'. It travelled slowly and building up until it started to move and came up fast. It was astonishing also that the bar never fell below 996. There is a lesson in this; in tropical waters a minor change or any deviation from normal may be serious. In the English Channel, a wind of force 10 would be unlikely if a low pressure centre was not down to 965.

What a magnificent vindication of 'Bluebird's design and construction. It was almost inconceivable that we had not lost our masts or suffered far more severe damage. How many people in

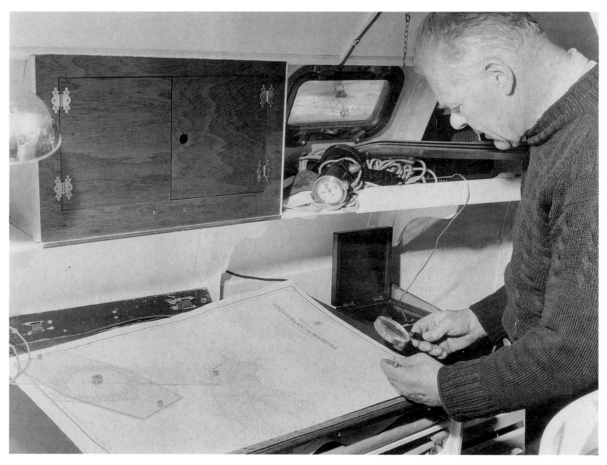

The Skipper in the chartroom.

the whole wide world have experienced a hurricane in a small yacht and survived to tell the tale. 'Bluebird' had done well and the design features justified. Four points were recorded: the stability curve would fall about halfway between that of a centreboard yacht like 'Doubloon' and that of a deep, single keel, ocean racer, cruiser yacht. The twin keel type correctly designed does heave to well, perhaps because the four leading edges of the two keels and two rudders, all in the fully stalled condition, create a more stable drift than a single appendage, while drifting rather faster may benefit the seas by leaving a larger slick to windward. If the balance and steering characteristics are as good as 'Bluebird's' under normal conditions, it is gratifying indeed that they are maintained up to force 12 with corresponding seas. I am now convinced that lighter displacement and a design with a clean wake, no quarter wave disturbance, and a short counter sawn off with considerable width of transom is an improvement in any weather as compared with the pointed stern and the finer lines of the former (1939) 'Bluebird', good though she was and is. Less water in heavy weather came aboard but this was due as much to higher freeboard as to the other design differences. The deckhouse, though modest in dimensions, strongly constructed and protected by heavy weather boards (which should have been rigged sooner) remains the most vulnerable feature. I have since rectified this and as a result of this experience, reinforced the construction and added perhaps 50% to the overall strength by adding permanent internal struts which are also functional as hand holds.

'Doubloon', about 40 ft length overall, 27.5 load water line, beam 10.8, draught 4.5 and with plate down 8 ft 6 in, has a displacement of about 10 tons in cruising trim with a ballast keel of 2.5. This gives a ballast D ratio of 25% as against 'Bluebird's' $33^1/_3$ and an ocean racer cruiser of typically 40 % or even more. 'Doubloon' was yawl rigged with a normal sail area of about 800 ft. The type is well known and successful for ocean racing and cruising and it may be considered carping or ungracious to suggest that the plate demands very strong and good construction, while the type is apt to carry heavy weather helm when hard driven to a considerable angle of heel and some examples are difficult to steer and control when running in strong winds or large seas.

Anyone who is interested and wishes to study this subject is strongly recommended to read K Adlard Coles' book, 'Heavy Weather Sailing'. 'Doubloon's' performance is discussed in chapter 18, 'Twice rolled over' and also the account by Joe Byars in 'Yachting USA', July 1964. This book was not published until 1967 and I regret that I did not know that it was in preparation and that Adlard Coles did not know that 'Bluebird of Thorne' had been in the same storm system and relatively close to 'Doubloon', however different the march of events and its results.

We were now a well-knit team. The three of us in the main crew were interchangeable in nearly every duty. Welded by experience, tested by stress and tempered by time. Roy Cook told me afterwards that this feeling was so strong he doubted whether he would fit in. He need not have worried; after a few days at sea he might have been with us for months. On the American coast, George and I had decided that we were anxious to be on our way home. Here emphatically we were on the way but the sense of urgency had departed, nevertheless we were ready for sea. Partly by luck and partly by determination on the last day in Bermuda, we achieved our sailing photographs and this gave me intense satisfaction. In the early morning of Tuesday, 19 May, we slipped away from Hamilton and the Commodore of the Yacht Club waved to us from his balcony as we passed out of the harbour. Roy Cook was with us, Jill Baty had remained in Bermuda, still trying to get a berth in the Bermuda Race, one of her great ambitions (and in this she succeeded). We tacked up a worn-out slipper on the bulkhead; this was a certain conversation piece with future visitors. Some men and most women asked about it sooner or later, "Ah! Wild nights in the Caribbean". For us it was a memory and tribute to the courage of that magnificent woman; always with some bits of sticking plaster somewhere on her person as she collected bruises, burns, cuts and abrasions. Her tendency to let the young and not so young know what they should or should not do, the intense arguments sometimes ending with, "I am not arguing but in my opinion...", once or twice leading the Skipper to intervene, "Jilly, no more opinions please".

The Voyage Home
The passage to the Azores was under fourteen days. This was fast by comparisons we knew of and we had feared the worst, as this passage has a reputation for light winds and calms at that time of the year. We had a struggle to get away from the Bermudas; head winds, baffling winds and squalls and eventually calms. Here we had the advantage of power and used it at full economy stretch, as it was so early in the passage. We came out of the calm on the right side and gradually the faintest of airs built up to a useful breeze in the best direction on our beam. For about seven days, we had almost ideal conditions; the swell was mainly slight, the sea was nil, the weather was delightful. We set 1,870 square feet of sail (112 square feet per ton of cruising displacement) and thus armed, achieved runs of 150 a day, while enjoying life and doing some varnishing and maintenance. In the long passages, it had become a point of honour for each man on his 'cook day' to produce something fresh and different for the main meal of the day. The Skipper was at his worst in the galley and the crew said that his idea of a sauce was something based on mashed potato.

We recorded water temperatures every day. There were considerable variations, but when the average declined, bucket baths lost their attraction. Roy Cook was a great success. He was enjoying this passage to the full and determined to extract the maximum pleasure, experience and gain the deepest suntan. The beam wind gave way to a threatened gale, but the wind drew aft and never exceeded force 7. As we neared the land, a navigational highlight was George and Donald achieving a cocked hat of $^1/_2$ mile with three star sights, within two miles of our DR position. This, we felt, would make even 'Vasco' sit up and think, and with this precision I was able under difficult conditions to glance at my wristwatch and say, "Time, I think". Then stand up, push back my oilskin hood and there was our light fine on the port bow, just visible within five minutes and $^1/_2$ mile of prediction. It was grand to close the bold land in a stormy dawn, blowing in with wind force 6, under the big genoa and the mizzen to within a mile of Horta. We had crossed the Atlantic for the second time. We remained here a few days. Roy Cook left us, as a convenient steamer service would enable him to meet his wife at Lisbon quickly and at reasonable cost. We missed him.

We thoroughly enjoyed this island and could not have received more kindness and a more genuine and friendly welcome from Martin Wolston and his family, representing Cable & Wireless, the Port Captain and the pilots. The passage to Ponta Delgade was achieved in 25 hours. There were only the three of us and had we seen the weather reports, we might have funked it. The weather indeed was a matter for disillusion. "Where", we said, "is the Azores high?" Local opinion said, "Three climates in one day. When Pico (the high mountain) is clear, it means trouble. When Pico has a cap, it means bad weather. When Pico has a band of cloud, it means bad weather and when you cannot see Pico, it is bad weather". There was mail from home and with it a card from John Franklin Evans. 'Tahiti' John and 'Kochab' were in Tahiti after a passage of 18 days from the Galapagos to the Marquesas. Well done!

At Ponta Delgada, we had a similarly genuine welcome and here I decided to do something as chance offered which we had never contemplated. The little motor ship, 'Ponta Delgada' was leaving to do a complete tour of the islands, including Corvo. We had been driving pretty hard, 5,000 miles in three months and only the last passage lay ahead. All of us were now conscious that the voyage was approaching its conclusion. We told ourselves not to take this last passage too much for granted and I think all of us felt the impending shadow of readjustment to problems on our return to England. So I thought a Skipper's celebration and a busman's holiday would be a good idea. The Port Captain took full responsibility for 'Bluebird', the pilots took charge of her, a member of their launch crew acted as watchman. Lance and cousin James were coming out in 3-4 days to join us, so we went off with no cares for a delightful eight days. With separate cabins, we had privacy after so long in close quarters. We had no cooking or ship cares; the Captain was charming and gave us the run of the ship, including the bridge and engine room. He made a practice of coming to our table for a chat each day, advised us about onshore excursions, arranged transport or guides and told us much about the islands. They made a good impression. Tourism almost unknown, adapting their economy as wine, fruit and cochineal might distinguish one island whilst another had

pineapples, cheese, meat and so forth. The climate, oceanic variable, humid and rather like the Scillies but warmer.

At length, we sailed for the passage home on Friday 19 June. The day before the weather had been lovely, the forecast had been excellent but that morning it was blowing force 6-7 from the north; a head wind. Off we went and sped down the lee of the island until we faced the open sea. It was very like an old English headland, accelerated wind, squalls off the high land, a filthy tidal sea and total discouragement. Do not sail on a Friday. Instead of heaving-to, changing to 'B' mainsail and starting the passage under rather grim conditions, we beat into Porta Cacao and anchored for the night in the lee of the island, while the squalls shrieked overhead. In the morning we were prepared under 'B' mainsail and intermediate genoa and sailed in earnest. The wind was now force 5. For two days we beat our way on the starboard tack, not leaving the Azores very fast and heading too much towards Newfoundland. We had an eclipse of the moon; very eerie and strange. One can imagine the effect on primitive tribes and the exploitation by witch doctors. We saw the last Portuguese 'man-of-war'. The flying fish had gone, but we saw one or two hardy turtles.

At length the wind died to be succeeded by a calm. "Is this the Azores high?" Apparently it was and for two days we made our way gently with a glass-calm sea, under power, recovering our position to a point B we had marked on the chart well north of the Great Circle course, but not as far north as the fruit schooners and Franklin Evans in 'Kochab' had practiced. We then proceeded on the port tack with sail to the big genoa, and with a few hours' exception when the wind freed sufficiently to use the mizzen staysail (though still just forward of the beam) and a few hours near Ushant when we used the engine again, we remained on the port tack for 7½ days. On this last passage we had a strong and congenial crew of five, so a continual headwind was of little moment. Overcast skies and cold misty nights brought out our unaccustomed sweaters and sleeping bags but 'Bluebird' must have smelt her stable. We averaged five to six knots with never a free wind and in spite of a rather foul bottom. It was lovely when dawn came up on the day mark of Gribben Head at the entrance to Fowey on Wednesday 1 July. George and I had both written home from America telling our people to licence our cars for 1 July; most appropriate. We were in fact, one month behind the original outlined plan for the voyage and this was the month accounted for by my operation. The second half of the voyage had been successful as a 'convalescent cruise'.

We had decided to enter Fowey because we all knew it and liked it and because Peter Pye had made it the end of his voyage; it would also give ourselves a chance to unwind and get some organizing done before we returned to Lymington. We could not have made a better choice. Two days in Fowey and the hospitality of the officers and members of the Royal Fowey Yacht Club, and the peace and quiet charm, made us realize that if only our weather were a little better, one must sail far to find anything more attractive than England. Perhaps a little less taxation and less 'profitless affluence'. We are a crowded island, but thank heaven we are still surrounded by a lot of sea. The passage up-Channel was routine and we returned to Lymington in the evening of 4 July. The voyage was over; it had been an experience none of us will forget or regret. It was well worthwhile and my personal questions had been answered satisfactorily. The new 'Bluebird' had proved herself. Thank you once (English) and thank you twice (American) to all my crews, particularly George and Donald who had shared the whole voyage. They had enabled me to achieve one of the ambitions of a lifetime. I believe they had gained much from the experience and it may stand them in good stead in the years to come. They were now men as well as seamen. In the first ten months of her existence, this 'Bluebird of Thorne' had covered about 15,000 miles in less than 100 days sailing time at $5^3/4$ knots speed. She had twice crossed the Atlantic and put her nose into more than sixty new places and islands and encountered an Extra Tropical Cyclone.

Chapter Twelve

So This Is Mare Nostrum

Malta

After such a voyage it is difficult to avoid a feeling of anticlimax when considering the plans ahead, but during the winter of 1964/65, there was much to do. We had rushed away across the Atlantic with quite an inadequate work up and trials and we had been extremely fortunate completing the voyage with no serious troubles and the minimum of minor defects. Inevitably we had come back with a notebook full of ideas and improvements. These had to be worked through, sorted out and as many as possible incorporated in the laying up and fitting out period. Some hold the belief that a yacht is not at her best until she had been used for five years by a devoted owner. It may also be true that there is never a moment when an owner has not got ideas. But in the spring of 1965, 'Bluebird' was probably as thoroughly tested and well worked up as many yachts have been after a much longer history.

I sought a new area for cruising and I imposed a twelve week limit to determine it. I had considered the Mediterranean and I had always said, "Time is insufficient and I can do that later or when I am old". Make haste young man it is later than you think! And so the plans were made for a fast passage to the Balearic Islands, what cruising we could achieve in the Western Mediterranean with Malta as the limit and the thought, "If I like it enough I can winter in Malta, if I dislike it too much I can retreat into the Atlantic". There was no difficulty about crew, the mere mention of the Mediterranean drew all former crews and had a magnetic effect on wives and daughters, but planning the mixture and the crew change was not easy.

With a departure in June, I hoped that the rigours of escape from the English Channel might be minimised, but the familiar news of an approaching depression as it came in from the west brought trouble. It was small however and centred at Brest so that we were able to lay Ushant on the port tack and when we had cleared that hazard in dirty conditions and bad visibility, we were able to lay a course down the Bay of Biscay to Cape Finisterre on the starboard tack. All this was uncomfortable and at dusk on the second day out, the sky was so unpleasant and some squalls were so nasty that a familiar debate ensued. "Is it

wise to carry full mainsail through the night? If it really blows we shall wish we had changed down. I should hate to lose time and find it unnecessary. If it were bad enough we could always hand the main and heave-to until dawn". We carried on; the decision was justified and improving conditions next day gave us a famous shove out across the bay.

We ultimately found a breeze that hardened into the Portuguese Trades. We made wonderful progress and a log entry "Perfect day, cool breeze, hot sun, little swell, regular sea, good visibility". We made about 6 knots down to the Berlengas. There were some thunderstorms and a wind up to force 6 across the Tagus entrance, and then the Trades steadied right aft. This was the moment for the spinnaker. What a wonderful sight. I wished that some heavenly chariot could have let me watch 'Bluebird' and photograph her chasing down the seas with the white crests and the white wake, and the blue and red spinnaker matching the hull colours and straining without a wrinkle to a wind force 6. The steering was exacting but not exhausting, the hull quivered as the breaking seas overtook the keels. Robert, the red-haired one, and 'Vasco' bet each other that they would exceed 25 sea miles in a three hour watch. 'Vasco' did 24³/4 - his best hour just, but only just, under 9 knots. 50 sea miles in six hours - magnificent!

The spinnaker was handed safely to the relief of the Skipper just before nightfall as we rounded Cape St Vincent in an awkward sea with many ships. The passage ended at Gibraltar, berthing this time at the developing marina. It would be an understatement to say that we were pleased; this time we had covered the 1250 miles in eight days, easily beating the former passage of ten days which itself had been quite good. We had used up the last of the rusty tins from the Atlantic voyage; there was a celebration dinner at the Bayuca and the first crew change. Roy brought his wife Pat for her first cruise in 'Bluebird'. This was it; the Mediterranean lay before us, how should we fare? We sailed with a Levanter declining, bad visibility, a head wind and a breaking sea, without sense or reason, which made the passage up the Spanish coast purgatory. Even those normally unaffected were seasick to some extent.

Off Cape Roldan, I was called on watch at 02.00 and as I turned out of my berth my feet found water. In a flash a sequence of thoughts entered my mind - "If the water is over the floor by my berth the forward bilge is full. It may be over the tank tops, if so

Right: Approaching Gibraltar - hard beat to windward.
Below: Palma.

the coffer dam is full and in that case the after bilge is also flooded. There must be tons of water in the ship, the leak could be uncontrollable. Call all hands, where is the nearest beach?" Our first experience in the Mediterranean had culminated in this moment. "So this is Mare Nostrum!" I said feeling bitter; but there was no leak only the forward bilge had flooded and that was cleared in about twenty minutes. The plunging in that awful sea had put so much water over the foredeck so frequently as to allow a ventilator, normally safe, to pass all this water below through the chain locker over a period of 24 hours. There is practically nothing that cannot happen once. A rather ragged crew assembled for breakfast but the sea was improving, though light wandering airs defied efforts to sail so it was the engine with the ghoster most of the distance from Cap de Palos to Ibiza.

Local cruising ensued in which electric storms drove us out of an anchorage at night and caused us to visit Santa Eulalia and there by chance we found the same aunt I had failed to trace in Torremolinos in 1963. A night passage to Andraitx and another crew change. Palma brought us to the start of the real Mediterranean cruising and this was marked by an unusual team. Mark and Susan, cousin James and Rose. We adjusted to the heat, and the mixture of boys and girls was successful. We found that the dinghy with the outboard motor made light of a load up to six people. It was cruising with small distances, little wind, siesta habits, much bathing and suntan and the attractions of the shore.

At Formentor, James and I harvested enormous clam shells up to 2 feet long. It was only later that we found these polished up attractively and were on sale to tourists. The night passages were almost more pleasant than the day. Minorca was less tourist ridden and a view of stepped beehive dwellings rather reminiscent of some in the Dingle Peninsular of south west Ireland. Susan, apt to be what might be called free and easy or scatty, had an embarrassing incident. Penetrating the market one day in something very short but which might suggest that there was nothing underneath, was almost mobbed and hustled out by a gang of angry matrons. We saw whales, sharks, porpoise and tunny but it was a delightful surprise to find so many of our old friends, the flying fish.

We sailed for the Cote d'Azur and made Portman, I'le Hyeres at dawn. In quite recent years this had been reported as a deserted cove. We found twenty-three yachts but that was a haven of peace in comparison with the crowded harbours we encountered later in the ten days on that coast. To some, this area must be a dream of heavenly bliss and judging by the numbers of yachts, this is a majority view. Not all of us were immune from the attractions and the fleshpots but the Skipper found the drawbacks outweighed the attractions. In one harbour with a very strong wind, I nosed up bow to quay with a kedge astern. This led to the Harbour Master dancing on his cap with Gallic rage and declaring in the manner of De Gaulle, "This is France; in France you berth stern to the quay; it is the law; I am the law; this is France". Wherever it was possible we anchored, preferring dinghy work, some motion and the occasional risk of having to clear out in the night to the alternative of squeezing into a berth, the often difficult manoeuvre of handling an auxiliary astern, the warps, the 'knitting' and the risk of a foul anchor. This was a real menace; we saw some first class tangles and heard that it was not uncommon to have many hours delay and sometimes the hire of a very expensive diver. When we anchored we were able to swing head to wind. This made our windsails effective and we were cooler, cleaner and quieter. It also made it possible to bathe directly from 'Bluebird'. In the ports, it was crowded to the limit, hot and smelly, with dust and dirt, noise and crowds, close proximity to one's neighbours and all too often the noise and exhaust fumes of their charging plants. The owner's parties in the luxury yachts may have thought that we were not very efficient paid hands and seldom spoke to us; the charter parties had no clue at all. By contrast the very competent professional skippers, once they realised that we were handling our own ship (and I hope not incompetently), could not have been more pleasant and more helpful, assisting us in every way with advice, information and berthing difficulties. We have pleasant memories of many of these chaps of several nationalities. To be fair, we did meet charming owners, some real enthusiasts and these included not a few who recognised 'Bluebird'.

In the Balearic Islands, feeding ashore had been indifferent to adequate, but good value. Here it could be anything from indifferent to first class but was all too likely to be completely ruinous. With very modest habits, we found that the cash costs were now £10 per head per week and I mentally compared this with £5 per head per week in the Bay of Biscay not many years ago. At Antibes, daughter Frances and her friend Mandie, joined with Kenneth, the old pirate who had not sailed with me for six years, and with this not very powerful crew we had three weeks in which we often encountered that other feature of the

Antibes

Mediterranean - sudden hard winds with little relation to sky, barometer or my experience. "Mistral" was the cry of dread to local yachtsmen and on the radio Cap Corse, "Mer agitee" was frequent. A hard blow kept us in Monaco, a pleasant fate and we sailed in fair conditions for a night passage to Calvi, but this ended sooner than planned as we charged in under full sail at over 8 knots in a sudden blow, making port at 02.30. The girls found this experience quite thrilling but I was glad and I think Ken was relieved when we were anchored with sail off her in Calvi.

Morning found us in a perfect berth. It was a magnificent sight; the port with the citadel above a great sweep of white beach, the dazzling colour of the wind blown sea (it was blowing force 8), and inland, the valleys, the foothills and the mountains soaring up to jagged summits piercing the blue sky. The flashes of white snow, still visible, seemed incredible in this heat. Catering was easy for four and Frances and Mandie thoroughly enjoyed the marketing. We lived well; meat and fish were often difficult, but

cheese was a good stand-by. Fruits and salads were compounded with great ingenuity from anything available; we could not have done better. In the next few days we worked down the magnificent west coast of Corsica. We alternated between calm and light airs and days with wind force 4 or more. In Ajaccio, it blew hard and we had the most difficult berthing exercise of the whole cruise. Round Cape Muro, there was a really nasty sea in wind force 6, and we were thankful to fetch up in Propriano. Here we had an amusing instance of the stern to quay nonsense. Some fifteen yachts came in. There was ample room for all of them to anchor; only three did so, the remainder played 'musical chairs' for the remaining berths, ahead and astern of the steamer.

We had a day of really delightful sailing to Port Servo in Sardinia. A day like this was glorious when we got it, and the passage through the straits and islands was interesting and varied. The fabulous development of this place astounded us, but it had been done with admirable taste and attractive architecture. Here we saw that fine ship 'Blue Leopard'; what a contrast to so many of the motor yachts. Again it blew hard and as we had lost some days, I wondered if I should have to modify our plans, but we made Porto Vecchio in fierce squalls with winds up to force 8.

Sailing on the 85 miles passage to Elba, we had infuriating conditions. First a sea so crazy that it was impossible to sail at all, followed by a usable wind force 3 on the beam but accompanied by a confused and broken sea that would not have disgraced wind force 6 and which reduced our speed to $2^1/2$ knots with the greatest discomfort so that we were forced to use the engine with full sail. In Elba we were instructed to berth stern to quay with our anchor laid out at right angles over four or five other cables. I refused and was allowed to lie alongside under protest for one night, after which we cleared out and anchored in the bay.

The passage down the Tuscan Islands was enjoyable with one call on the mainland at Ercole. Palmarola produced a spectacular limestone cliff and a cave through an island, passable in the dinghy, with wonderful colour effects. We enjoyed this stretch but there was little wind. Italian yachts were apt to leave their course and approach us waving and taking photographs. Incomprehensible until it dawned on us that it was a salute to 'Bluebird's' endeavour to sail with all her light canvas set. The yachts we encountered were invariably under power, often with awnings rigged, stern gangways cocked up in place and sometimes with no sails bent; no wonder slaves and convicts were chained to the benches of the galleys over so many centuries. Until the age of steam this system had its merits. The diesel engine had become the best sail in the Mediterranean.

Ischia was attractive and the centre for a complicated crew change which spread over a week. The toughest week of the cruise for me and, as I was wrestling with mail and business affairs each day, travel agents and in and out flights, everything was complicated. On four days we were sailing short-handed, including a circuit of Capri (the girls just had to see this and the Blue Grotto), and it involved berthing in Inschia three times, Porto Miseno twice and Mergellina once. Lance rejoined, George arrived and it was first time for Margaret. At the end of all this, I was anxious to depart with the feeling that the cruise was running down despite a fortnight with some 500 miles to go. George's first day was memorable. We had prepared him for calm, but we had a magnificent sailing day and several hours

with the Spinnaker set, feeling rather daring as we sped at 8 knots across the Bay of Naples, past Capri and down to Campanella Point. It was equally magnificent sailing in a strong beam wind with great squalls off the mountains along the spectacular coast of the Sorrento Peninsular, past Positano and into Amalfi. So far during this cruise we had been fortunate; we had never fouled an anchor nor had any incident with the 'knitting'. This was our undoing. Strong squalls, a surge in the harbour, a long, flat warp and the next moment it was round our propeller. We prepared to deal with this ourselves, but this was Italy! A gang headed by a dominant character appeared and took charge of the situation which developed in the manner of Grand Opera:

The Assembly:	Disaster! Disaster! What can be done?
The Crowd:	The line is fouled. It is round the propeller.
Leading Tenor:	Here is Pedro the diver, the diver for sponges.
The Crowd:	The warp must be cut and that man will be angry.
Leading Tenor:	There must be a reward. He demands his reward.
The Crowd:	Give him the knife, the very sharp knife.
Leading Tenor:	At your peril no motor or it is his doom!
The Crowd:	With the knife at great risk he may go to his death. He is gone - for how long? Pericoloso!
Leading Tenor:	Have faith in good Pedro and tend well his line.
The Crowd:	Behold he comes with ragged rope. The job is done, the ship is free. Success is sweet. All men are brothers.
Leading Tenor:	Now for reward and let us drink wine.

The crowd disperses shouting, drinking and singing, "The wine is good, the wine of Amalfi". (A prize for the first to set this to music). "That man" was not angry. The owner of the Sports Fisherman, despite his cut warp, visited us and we had a delightful evening. In our Visitors Book he wrote, "I am glad that a little accident make me happy to meet so nice people"; and so say all of us.

Amalfi was charming, very photogenic and we lingered next morning. A fair breeze lasted until nightfall and when it fell we handed all sail at dusk. With little swell we put up a riding light and turned in to sleep until 05.30. What a way to spend a night but no bad solution in this area if time permits. We came up to Stromboli in the early afternoon. At quite close range we were treated to a slide of hot ashes to sea level, noises like claps of thunder, jets of red gas for hundreds of feet and through our glasses we could see great gouts of rock hurled into the air, some of them rolling down the slopes glowing red; impressive as well as 'conspic'. We anchored at Panarea and spent the evening with a delightful character in a very interesting motor sailer who knew all about 'Bluebird'. He was an enthusiast and an architect. Over several glasses of 'Uovo' juice (George's expression), we produced a new design of twin keel yacht for Mediterranean conditions. This was most enjoyable and we were pleased with ourselves; "is he wise who tears up in the morning the design he roughed out overnight?" Our friend had gone, only our sketches remained.

Volcanic action is not far away in these islands. There were hot sulphur springs on a beach. We sailed over a subterranean mountain rising from the sea bed to 8 fathoms where no doubt the sea had washed off the soft ash of the volcanic cone. Isola Salina - volcanoes extinct and with a fertile slope; Lipari with millions of tons of white pumice rock; Volcan with a lunar landscape and little vegetation looking as if the lava had just cooled and with wisps of gas and steam on the cone. We were lucky to have a breeze to Sicily and after a long day we entered Milazzo by night. Next day we approached Messina. So fearful were the modern tales we had been told by Italian yachtsmen, so potent the spell of mythology and legends, that the crew threatened to deprive the Skipper of his red towel and to lash him to the mast like Ulysses. But alas, no sirens, no whirlpools; the whole affair was a distinct anticlimax. Sailing again from Reggio we encountered that now familiar horror - a shocking sea with practically no wind - but the coastline was magnificent with its twin features of enormous dry river beds, the highest mountains behind and most spectacular fortress towns and castles on eagle nest crags overlooking the sea. Strange to think that this rugged land was once described as "The soft under belly of the axis".

We only had time to visit Taomaina with the towering height of Etna, its plume of smoke clearly visible. We entered Augusta, a huge area of commercial port, only because we had a hard head wind. And finally Syracuse, a good place where we met 'Tanagra', a little motor sailer just out as a new ship from 'Bluebird's' birthplace at Thorne, and a replica of Pidgeon's 'Islander' in which an American and his Japanese wife had lived and voyaged form Japan over a period of eight years. This was in marked contrast with that most magnificent Italian yacht. We wondered whether that large and expensive vessel, immaculately kept by her paid crew, would in her lifetime do a quarter of the cruising mileage of the battered little yawl.

The last passage to Malta was a good sail and we changed as a wind freshened and headed from a ghoster to the big genoa which we managed to carry right into Sliema Harbour where we pushed our nose straight into a berth awaiting us. We had sailed 4,000 miles. We had made a considerable circuit in the western Mediterranean and I found it difficult to answer the question, "Do you like it enough or do you dislike it too much?" 'Bluebird' had acquitted herself well in an entirely fresh set of circumstances and we had enjoyed the experience but I hope I am not a grasping type and I was quite prepared to share the delights of 'Mare Nostrum". At that time, Malta had independence and was proud of it. She also had problems and they were serious and numerous, not least the future of the Great Dock Yard which had been our Mediterranean Naval base and now had to depend on commercial work. This was just working up nicely on tanker maintenance and repair when the closure of the Suez Canal had cut off much of this work. Beginning to see the possibilities of yachting, a marina was being constructed but when 'Bluebird' first arrived in Malta, the facilities and service behind this did not match the plans and it had not been foreseen that the construction of the marina would increase the effect of the surge from the Gregale, a dangerous winter storm which has always been uncomfortable and could be dangerous to a yacht moored at the marina. We experienced this in an autumn visit and had a night when sleeping was impossible. 'Bluebird' was snatching savagely at her moorings and it was quite impossible to get ashore until the wind had dropped. We suffered no damage; others were not so lucky.

Richard, a member of the Royal Cruising Club with whom I had sailed, was selling his yacht and he lived in 'Bluebird' for five months that winter. An admirable arrangement that suited both of us as 'Bluebird' was well cared for and much maintenance was done. I particularly enjoyed working with the Maltese. They were cheerful and ingenious and commanded an astonishing range of skills. Anything could be done if you worked with them, with a joke and a smile, but writing a letter from England and expecting results on time was not likely to be effective.

Eastern Mediterranean

The general scheme for 1966 was an exploration in the Adriatic with what cruising we could achieve in Greek waters within the time limits. A six day fast direct passage to Venice put us on the cruising ground and this was enjoyable and straightforward with more sailing than we had expected. Off the toe of Italy, tragic exhausted birds dropped in on us. Some remained aboard for the night and invariably died; the pathetic little bundles of feathers were found tucked away in unlikely corners. How small the margin between successful migration and death, an hour or two more daylight or light offshore wind could sway the issue. What tremendous losses there must be. Our most distinguished visitor was a handsome egret.

The best sailing was with a head wind force 4 under the big genoa across the Otranto Strait. The grim mountains of Albania came up and we dared not close the shore but put about to make back towards Brindisi and then north eastward again until we closed the islands of Yugoslavia at Mljet. We had decided to hold the eastern side of the Adriatic and the first view of the Yugoslavian coast encouraged us. Our course took us inside some islands; there were few fishing boats and small signs of life but the scenery was magnificent. On the fifth night out we had a good sailing breeze to take us across form the Yugoslavian coast near Pula to approach Venice at dawn. We picked up our light, lost it again and found ourselves in thick fog. We could smell Venice as we crept through a sea, covered with the most appalling ullage, some of which fouled our propeller. We crept in even more slowly under this handicap until we found the pier by sound and almost touch. It was prudent to anchor south of the entrance. An hour or two later with more light but fog still thick enough, we entered and groped our way to the Club Sportivo at St Elena. Here we were most hospitably received though the voluble and contradictory berthing instructions were typically Italian. 'Bluebird' remained in Venice for a month, partly with Richard and Ronnie caretaking; when we returned, all was well.

Christian came out for her first cruise in the new 'Bluebird'. The loyalties to the old 'Bluebird' were still strong but it was not long before she admitted that this 'Bluebird' had its points, that she could steer with a wheel and, during the following weeks, her opinion built up to the same confidence she had had in the old yacht with a completely flattering verdict on the improvements. Before we left Venice, there was a strong pro-Venice party headed by Frances in competition with the Skipper's pro-

'Bluebird' activities and this made it difficult to complete and sail on time. We had feared the bureaucracy in Yugoslavia but following advice from our Italian friends, we entered at Male Losinj, an island rather than a mainland port. No inventory of contents was demanded, only a list of certain equipment such as cameras and radios. A detailed itinerary was requested but our explanation of cruising in the islands was accepted loosely enough to leave us some freedom. There were prohibited areas and we marked them on our charts. The encounters involved in clearance lasted nearly three hours and were trying enough. Frances was a great help with languages, particularly German, which here and elsewhere was most useful.

From Male Losinj to Bar during the ensuing ten days, we covered nearly 350 miles on the Yugoslav coast. This included outer islands, inner islands, large and small sounds of every type, some mainland ports and some delightfully wild anchorages. Memory tends to pick out the high spots and on the mainland, Trogir was certainly a winner. This minute walled town displaying a veritable history of hundreds of years in stone and iron, every corner revealing some new delight. The inland fiord from Sibenik to the Falls of Kerka near Skradin was quite different from cruising on the coast. The great days of Venetian domination were evident and the winged lion insignia could be seen in almost every port on some of the ancient buildings. One evening in an island anchorage, we were received with charming hospitality and dignity by a family who corresponded more nearly to the old time picture of the Scottish crofter of the Western Isles. They had their boat, they caught their fish, they had their vines and they made their wine, and of course their olive oil. They had sheep, goats and chickens. They grew their vegetables and potatoes, and bees supplied honey. So far as we could see, the occasional sale of a good catch of fish would provide the only cash income which would be exchanged for flour, diesel oil, clothes and the very few necessary supplies from the outside world. When they visited the ship next morning they brought with them a generous basket of their own produce; the quality made our civilized living suffer by the comparison. We had some difficulty in finding from our stores items that they might appreciate and be unable to obtain. Our best export - Scotch whisky, was appreciated.

The weather and temperature were both delightful, the scenery varied and attractive and winds were mostly light and variable with only one hint of the dreaded Bora when it suddenly blew

force 8 for two to three hours in the night. Perhaps this was a 'Boradina'. As ever the larger ports were the most disappointing and we avoided them as far as possible, though Dubrovnik was inevitable as here George had to leave us before the end of the cruise and mercifully the attractive town is divorced from the commercial port of Gruz. George had been part of the ship with his accustomed ease, avoided sunburn with difficulty and plied his camera. Pat, on her second cruise, had managed to collect enough souvenirs to be an embarrassment for air passage home. Roy had been in charge of wines and had become expert in filling our wicker covered jar with the more drinkable of the local 'infuriators', but after one trial, "No more Slivovitch". Frances could usually be found with her nose in a book of languages, she rapidly improved in Italian and began to cope with Yugoslavian whilst Christian rediscovered the enjoyment she had had in former years.

A few years seemed to have made a tremendous difference to conditions on this Yugoslavian coast and our impression was more favourable than we had expected. Prosperity had increased, reconstruction had taken place, harbours had been improved and a more liberal attitude adopted to the outside world. If this was Communism it was a very free and easy brand, at least to the visitor from the outside world. In any main port we were greeted, directed to a berth alongside a quay, our papers dealt with promptly and returned without trouble. Information was readily obtainable and with a certain reserve, the people had striking dignity and good manners. It was well to make the first approach, the smile, the wave, the handshake and the greeting, but after that the thaw was rapid. We would cheerfully have returned and devoted more time to detailed exploration but this coast stood as one of the choicest cruising areas during our years in the Mediterranean; no wonder this area became so popular for flotilla cruising in later years.

From Dubrovnik with a depleted crew, we had to drive hard to make Corfu on time and this meant three nights at sea. We cleared from Yugoslavia at Bar where we encountered a yacht on charter which had belonged to Mussolini. Hard and persistent head winds impelled a long tack out to Italy and back again. The barrier of Albania was a restriction on course and progress. Friends in Yugoslavia had warned us, "It is bad", they said. We had heard tales of appallingly low standards on the one hand and a sinister infiltration by Chinese communists on the other. "Go down the middle of the Otranto Strait", our friends had said,

"and approach Fano Light from the west". We did not obey this literally though we were careful to keep out of any normal territorial waters and yet there were searchlights in the night. Had we been picked up on a radar beam? The searchlights did not reach us, we appeared to be just below their horizon. On the following night a sinister vessel without navigation lights shadowed us, following our movements as we tacked. This was uncomfortable. The vessel, similar to a large trawler in type, closed to some 200 yards, shone a powerful light upon us and made signals we could not read. At that moment a fast mail vessel, probably the Brindisi/Corfu Packet passed within sight to seaward, and whether on this account we do not know, but the unwelcome vessel then departed. While quite a good story to dine out on afterwards and lending itself to exaggeration, it was worrying enough at the time. It never occurred to us at the time but our unwelcome vessel might have been trying to warn us away from minefields! We remembered afterwards that two British destroyers had been sunk by mines when proceeding north from Corfu some years before.

After all this, we were thankful to reach Corfu again, one of the most attractive havens. Entering Greece, we received a practical form of ship's passport. How much trouble it would save if other countries wishing to encourage yachting visitors could adopt this system and avoid the tedious form filling in every separate port. It was strange to find the strong English influence and traditions and pleasant to find that our occupation had left a memory which was appreciated. Christian and I had two days on our own after daughter Frances departed on her own ventures in Austria and Germany, but Mandie joined again and Stephen and Dawn, both for the first time. Dawn was charming and made up for a lack of sea experience by erudition and entertainment. I remember her gracefully diving overboard for a swim and then confidently setting off down tide, which was running at $2^{1}/_{2}$ knots, completely unconscious of the fact that she would never be able to swim back to the yacht. Luckily somebody was watching and she was rescued by the dinghy. At the helm she preferred Stephen within call: "B, the little flag has changed sides, quick tell me what to do at once". The imminent gybe might or might not be averted but this was in light weather.

Mandie was strong and hardy, which was well because we passed into a period in which the wind exceeded force 6 in ten days out of fourteen. As well as her talent with 'Bluebird',

Mandie had a way with the Skipper. Her impassioned interest in yachts and a lively intelligence developed an exchange of thought which I valued. When we entered any port where there were yachts, Mandie would await an opportunity in the cool of the evening and would then say, "Skipper, take me by the hand please and lead me round this harbour telling me exactly what is wrong with every other yacht". She was never happier than in a blow and she was good at the helm. We said that she had her own little prayer:

"God's ancient young, 'tis thus I pray,
Send thy great winds another day
That I may speed this glorious yacht
Through those great waves in flying spray".

We had a 36 hour spell in Port Atheni on the island of Meganisi. This was a fascinating place and typical perhaps in giving us a feeling of the life in such an island. We walked up to the central village; the whole of the water supply had to be carried up a steep, very rough, stony track for a mile to the village. Much of this was done by women bearing various containers on their heads, the remainder by minute donkeys. The well was a dim insanitary affair from which the animals were watered also, and surrounded by a mess of mud, dung and urine. It seemed incredible to the Skipper that over hundreds of years nobody had thought that a little co-operative effort with ten or twelve men, with ten or twelve hammers doing a yard or two a day could have reduced that ghastly track to something quite reasonable. This led to quite a debate on primitive communities and their positive resistance to change, though the young men go away in ships and adapt themselves without difficulty to another life.

After leaving Port Atheni, we were having a lazy sail in wind force 2/3, intending to work our way to an attractive anchorage. The wind faltered, waffled a little in direction, died, and then a hard blue line appeared to the westward. There was white beneath it; within 15 minutes it was blowing force 6 and as our intended cove was 8 miles to windward, the Skipper decided to make Ithaca a weather shore and then make for Port Vathy. We were sailing at 8 knots under mainsail, intermediate genoa and mizzen; it was clearly time to hand the genoa. We did so but by the time the staysail was hoisted and the mizzen handed, it was blowing force 8. Alas for our weather shore. The Skipper should have considered the contours more closely. Vertical squalls tore down the ravines, and we were laid over at times to 40° or more;

a phenomenal thing to happen to 'Bluebird'. The Skipper feared for the gear under the strain, but everything held and we tore up to the head of the gulf in a series of wild swoops. Here we had hoped to find anchorage, better protected perhaps than Port Vathy, but the squalls were so terrifying that we dared not risk it. We handed the mainsail between squalls and blew into Vathy under bare poles with the engine ready to maintain command. When inside the harbour entrance, we saw that the quayside was exposed and the little enclosed port was full. A rapid decision was required and we anchored in a bay just inside the entrance to the port. This gave us partial shelter and the anchor held. There we remained for 36 hours while the wind howled and the squalls tore up the anchorage. Conditions improved next day and we landed in the dinghy to do our marketing; an unusual feature of this place was many butchers.

Two days and two islands later, the time had come to leave the Ionian Islands and we entered the Gulf of Patras. Both this and the approach to Corinth were to us more a stage to be passed than a cruising objective. The Skipper half regretted that we had not sailed round the Peloponnese, though it would have added some hundred miles to the programme. In these gulfs, desirable ports and anchorages were few, but we did get full value from a brief stop in Navpaktos, which was full of charm and the scene of a famous old Naval battle, and enabled a stay over for a day in Galaxidhion. From here we visited Delphi, going up by car in the very early morning and avoiding heat and crowds to our great advantage. We returned to the ship by 14.30 after a memorable excursion. In Greek waters, as in Yugoslavia, we assumed honesty and never closed or locked the ship. This atmosphere adds much to the pleasure of a cruise. We wondered whether we could have left 'Bluebird' thus in all English ports. A supply of English cigarettes formed the currency of reward and was acceptable always where money would sometimes be spurned.

The Corinth Canal is remembered for the entire absence of direction at the western entrance. We had not realised that all formality, payment and control centred on the eastern entrance. This important point was not clear from the information in our books. When at last we were permitted to enter, the narrow cut was airless and unpleasant in such great heat. We made only one port in the Saronika Gulf and before we visited Piraeus to verify that crew change at Zea would be practicable and to leave gas cylinders for recharging. The excellent brochures on yachting in

Greece were well written, attractive and encouraging. The authorities are trying hard to implement the facilities outlined, and with some success, but Zea was far from the promise of their brochure and it would be years before it reached the standard envisaged.

We still had a week before the crew change and decided to take a quick dart out into the Cyclades but this was "Meltemi here we come". Not a day without its rigours and under short canvas; memorable sailing from Souion to Kea. We did 8½ knots for two hours under reefed mainsail and intermediate genoa, 60° off the wind and in a sizable sea. The skipper's bare torso was thickly encrusted with glistening and condensed salt crystals when we entered port. Syros, that crossroads in the middle of the Aegean, with its ever present Loukoumi (Turkish delight) had the surprising apparition of a destroyer in a floating dock. We found caiques with exactly the same type of windlass used in the old Thames barges. We had to abandon a visit to Mykonos and Delos for fear that we might not be able to return to Piraeus in time for crew change. The return to Kea provided the most fantastic squalls in the lee of Yiaros, although we did not approach it at all closely. One afternoon under 'B' mainsail and staysail, we were making 5½ knots hard on the wind, force 8. The Skipper now said, "If it increases any more I shall heave to". At 15.30 the very time when by repute, the Meltemi will blow its hardest, the wind disappeared in 20 minutes and left us wallowing in a fantastic jumble of sea. "The winds are sure to baffle".

For 20,000 miles, 'Bluebird' had never reefed a sail but this was different. We had developed a counter technique known as the 'Meltemi rig'. This was to have either 'A' mainsail with a reef or to set 'B' mainsail and leave it set. The remark was heard, "They must have been sailing under-canvassed half the time", but that was not necessarily the case because we could set up to 1750 square feet with the small mainsail so the loss of 100 square feet hardly mattered and encouraged us to set bigger headsails and light canvas. We were surprised how efficient this was and the versatility it conferred. It saved a lot of work, valuable with a weak crew, and the crew's enthusiasm for sail changing was apt to diminish rapidly when the temperature rose into the nineties. The second visit to Kea and the life of that little corner intrigued us and we liked it.

After another crew change here we now had a strong team, all used to the ship and to each other, making life easier for the Skipper. As the first objective was the Sporades, we hoped that we should not have to punch 150 miles up north against a strong Meltemi. In the western Mediterranean the cry is, "Mistral, Mistral". Here it is, "Meltemi", and if there is repetition it cannot be avoided as it is the dominant factor in the seafaring life of the Aegean. We were fortunate and in four days reached Skiathos. Taking the bridge at Khalkis by night was an experience, though no great hazard. We had pleasant passages; the scenery and surroundings as we emerged from the Evvia Channel were attractive and the Sporades ranked high in our appreciation of the different groups of islands. Skiathos and its neighbours had charm and we enjoyed our time in those waters. We did not often feed ashore; a large number of our anchorages were in wild, primitive spots and far from any facilities, but it was a delightful change to go to sit out in the evening in the open and have a meal at a simple taverna, selecting our dish from the cauldrons bubbling in the background and drinking the Retsina wine, for which we quickly acquired tolerance and then a liking, considering it an antidote to olive oil and also a disinfectant. These meals were better than we had expected and, observing reasonable and ordinary precautions, we did not suffer from the dreaded stomach troubles. The cost for an adequate meal was perhaps 7/6d (now 38p) per head.

Panormos in Scopelos was a high spot; James found two wrecks. This was the cove figuring in Michael Carroll's book, 'The Gates of the Wind'. His vessel was there and the Mayor visited us with his family. It was hot, sometimes very hot, but we refused to fuss and considered that excess in the middle of the day was paid for by the lovely hours of the early morning and the evening when the changing lights and colours and the clarity of the atmosphere were so wonderful. The unclad sun-browned body has a wonderfully sensitive thermostat; it knows at once when it is cooler down below than on deck as the heat rises in the morning, and when the cockpit becomes attractive in the evening. And of course there was that lovely sea; bathing was marvellous; we had bucket baths or the deck house hose under way. Often in light winds, we would sail until it became calm, bathe until a breeze came again and so continue. This did not make for fast passages, only rarely were we uncomfortable and that was in harbour where we could not swing to the wind, the wind sail was useless and the water too dirty for the deck hose.

How varied the history and character of the islands. We discovered more and more. Some with an entirely different economy, way of life and occupation. An example was Psara. Here there appeared to be nothing whatever but a few goats on the land and fishing. This was the one place where we really saw fish being caught in quantity. Tales were told of a team of boats coming in with 30,000 kilos of fish in a night. We were given a bucket of mackerel or a few sardines or garfish as a matter of course. Excellent lobsters were obtainable at a reasonable price; a contrast with the disappointment of so many places where fish were not available, or very poor quality, or quite excessive in price.

It would be impossible in a cruise such as this, apart from the expenditure, to carry every available chart in every scale for all the places that one might visit. We found ourselves inevitably short of charts and on pretty small scale in some areas and carrying excellent charts for areas we had no time to visit. Another trouble is the names. It is all too common to find one sailing direction giving one name, the Admiralty sailing direction giving another, and a chart giving a third version (eg ancient Delphinium as a fourth version), while the map of Greece would give a fifth. It is not much comfort to reflect that Greek, Turkish, Venetian and Italian influence provide a logical explanation for this. The fact remains that it has a nuisance value to the modern mariner. It followed from this that we could not remember without reference the names of the islands that we had visited or were about to visit. The Skipper was all too apt to refer to 'that nisos' and this led to a light-hearted discussion as to how we would dine out on return on the impressive list of islands we had visited. It would be delightful to reel off, for example, Paxos, Antipaxos, Leros, Cosmos, Pathos, Syros, Cerebos, Scrapanto and Loukoumi. We had a few days of sailing in harder winds though not as hard or as unbroken as the previous experience and we were generally going downhill which made life much easier. What could be more enjoyable than 'Meltemi here we go', tacking to leeward through the islands under easy canvas in winds force 6, with the warmth, the sparkle and exhilarating sailing, while the engine almost went out of use for a few days. A welcome relief. We could now use our experience to avoid areas with dangerous squalls. So we worked down to Chios and to Samos with a view of the massive mainland peaks in Turkey. There was their ancient aqueduct, but for us, no water. A large charter yacht had filled for six hours and had emptied the cistern for two days.

The population of these areas must have been larger in former times. So many of the islands in the Adriatic and in the Aegean showed traces of extensive cultivation now abandoned. We debated the possible causes - climatic change, soil exhaustion or erosion, felling of timber, failure of fishing, wars or petulance, to say nothing of earthquakes. These were all possibilities without the modern trend of social change and education, making each generation less content with the conditions their fathers had accepted.

It was a lovely sail to Arki. This was quite a special place; the solitude and the peace, the view of near and distant islands and the fading of the colours through mauve to purple into dark, followed by the rising of a full moon and the realisation that for the first time we could see 'Bluebird's' complete shape projected on the clean sea bed of this enchanting lagoon as a moon shadow. Patmos and its monastery grew up fast as we sped across the wine dark sea with the wind again force 7 from the north. We were reaching the stage where we had seen so many islands and those who had been in the ship throughout had so many impressions that there was a tendency to stay longer and explore less, while the programme was not arduous and it should be quite easy to arrive at Rhodes on time for crew change. It was satisfactory to sail right in and up to our berth in Mandraki harbour. Rhodes itself was slightly disappointing in spite of the marvellous atmosphere of the old town. We had the impression it was rapidly becoming the equivalent to Palma in the Balearics in its tourist relationship to the Aegean islands. Our experience might have been unfortunate but to berth for three nights and take in fuel and water meant not less than five moves with their attendant handling of warps and chains and we nearly had a disastrous experience in the commercial port where an unmarked danger with great stones from a broken down quay lurked well off the quay only about 5 foot below the surface. Surely this should have been marked? Generally our impressions had been good. Only at Rhodes and Zea did the practice fall far, far below the write-up in the information brochures. But showing how misleading a single experience can be, the following year our experience was better, happier and very satisfactory. Rhodes corresponded to the Naples crew change last year; a longer period occupied with an attempt to catch up with mail and work. The office opened every morning as Margaret Bennett (the Skipper's secretary) had joined with the Skipper's burden of business papers.

We decided to leave Rhodes as soon as possible for Lindos and to do the crew change by car from Lindos in one day of multiple operations, which was achieved somehow against various difficulties. The Skipper was sad to see this team disperse. Rose had shown more devotion to the sun and sea than most of us and had become the 'golden girl'. We said that her colour could have been spread like butter, though spread is the wrong word as our butter had its own heat register and went liquid at about 95° despite our best endeavours with evaporation cloths. James had much expertise with diving. He delighted in bringing up strange objects for inspection and his winning number was a large shell with an octopus inside. This caused a sensation when it emerged and began its prehensile progress round the scuppers! With Anne, the skipper could conjure up memories of the West Indies, the ships and men they had known at English Harbour, where she had berthed for a time in 'Bluebird'. With three 'handmaidens' the standard of catering had been high, but taking a roster had meant that marketing was not a chore and nobody had become a galley slave. We had been nursing the anchor winch to spare the clutch; slow work on the hand lever or the much faster relay on the chain were equally unpopular with each successive crew as they faced the task for the first time. The Skipper, who had the unfair advantage of accustomed fitness, used to mutter, but strictly to himself, "Can't think why they fuss! Splendid exercise and so good for them!"

As we went east, there were fewer yachts and most of those we did encounter were on charter. Some were larger and older sailing yachts with modernised or cut down sail plan and a large diesel engine. It was at Rhodes that the Skipper felt a sense of the impending end to the cruise. The task of the return to Malta entered his consciousness, as had happened last year, the final stage was to be the Skipper with Lance Earle and one other - this time a young man who had never been in the ship before and had little experience. On Sunday, 7 August, we left Lindos and fetched up in an open anchorage south of Cape Sidro, calm and hot. It was just like life when a sailing breeze sprang up after we had anchored. There was but one habitation ashore and when we landed we were there received and they insisted on giving us drinks. The next day the habitual early start took us away from Rhodes and we had a good sailing breeze to Scarpanto. We came to anchor in Mkri Yalo. The description of Pegadia Bay had not encouraged us and the Skipper felt that we should be prepared for Meltemi at any minute and had led us to this anchorage. Was it a hunch? Was it just good chart reading?

At 02.00 the Skipper and Lance were on the fore deck veering more chain, adjusting the weight rope and preparing to let go the second anchor. The 56lbs weight down the chain had become standard practice in any anchorage, however calm, as a precaution against the sudden blow, and perhaps for this reason we had only dragged once, and that was by day after a lunch stop in ancient Delphinium. Thank heaven the holding ground was good and our position well judged. There was no abrupt high land to windward to promote squalls, but it was blowing upward of force 8 from west, north west. We had intended to sail by 05.00 but obviously this had better be the one day in seven on which we did not sail. With conditions unchanged at breakfast time, the Skipper prepared a vast list of jobs for the ship to occupy the day, as going ashore by the dinghy was quite out of the question, nor was there any visible attraction.

During the day the wind screamed past in squalls. We checked it with the anemometer periodically to satisfy ourselves. One or two people came to the bay to bathe, a shepherd took his flock out, whistling as he went. In the evening a sea bird called. The Skipper had rather feared this next passage, partly by general repute, partly by warnings from those experienced, and it looked as if the fears would be justified. We had studied the caiques with their accumulated local knowledge and it was clear that they had a better idea than we of when to sail, when to put into refuge, and what refuges to use. Their modern technique was a small steadying sail in strong winds with a diesel thudding at slow speed. There were times when we were impelled to copy this technique, particularly to make perhaps five miles to windward from a port to the end of an island before deciding what sail we could carry on our average course for the day.

Sailing in an area where one is seldom or never out of sight of an island is apt to breed the belief that shelter is always at hand, and this may be true when the weather is mild and it does not matter. How pleasant to enter some little bay, bathe, have lunch, a ramble ashore and a siesta before proceeding on your way. But when the Meltemi blow, all this is changed. To seek the smoother sea may be a mistake, the weather shore may be dangerous to approach on account of squalls. It is wise to study the contours and only use those with low elevations and gentle slopes; no bay not protected from the vital wind direction is safe. Quite a few of the island harbours are either unsafe to enter, difficult or impossible to leave, or hazardous within. Local knowledge becomes more and more important. Quite good anchorages may become untenable because the holding ground is not good enough in the squalls from different directions and there can even be a baffling wind on the weather side of a high island as the wind lifts to the obstruction.

Next morning at the break of dawn, we prepared for sea. We said the night had been a little better and the Skipper knew that we should get harbour jitters if we did not make an attempt this day. As we put out, the wind went up to force 8 and in the bay it was blowing due west right on the nose for our course. It was tempting to return but we were committed. As far as the western extremity of Kaso, conditions were not bad, our course was not too tight and the sea was reasonable, but when we headed out into the open, it was another story. The sea was both bad and an awkward length. Thank heaven the wind had sufficient north in it so that we could lay within 20° of our course, but even without the effect of current, likely to be adverse, leeway was bound to be considerable. It was a long, horrible, brutal plug and it took us eight hours to make Crete, some fifteen miles to leeward of our desired landfall. Margaret, who had never tackled this before, took her spell at the helm, drenched with spray and quite undeterred from inexperience, she perhaps imagined that this was the usual form for 'Bluebird'. By that time the Skipper was determined not to tackle Cape Sidero and its reefs in the dusk. Eventually we got our anchor down in Daskalia Cove. There was room for us to sheer to the gusts but not swing if the wind changed, so it was an uneasy night with frequent lookouts. It was impossible to tell the true strength of the wind as many of the squalls shrieked overhead leaving us untouched. This cove would have been quite secure if we had moored up to the shore at its head.

At the crack of dawn we again found conditions similar and, in this sea and wind, the short-cut through the reefs did not seem prudent, so we beat out on the port tack until we were clear and then went about and, with great thankfulness, put Cape Sidero astern an hour later. When we had done this, both sea and wind improved. The sea became more regular, the wind freed slightly. There is little more to say about that day. We added sail as we could, using the motor to maintain speed, tacking when we must, and so made Heraklion at 18.00. We were on schedule. Alas Margaret could only stay for a week but how she enjoyed herself. The harder it blew the better she liked it. An absolute natural, she could take the helm competently without any previous training or experience. She had graduated with credit

and took her place with so many others as another potential crew member. She departed to catch communications in Athens. We had put 200 miles astern from Rhodes and we could water, fuel and provision for the last passage.

We visited Knossos and this was easily the best of the antiquities we experienced, possibly because it was easier to recreate a picture of the life and the people. It is difficult to deal with archaeology as it is so much a matter of taste and time, but in general terms we all agreed on a few governing factors. Unless detailed study and enthusiasm was applied to reading up the subject, one ruin was apt to be like another and the enjoyment was closely allied to the ability to create a picture in the mind of what buildings were for, how they were used, and the life and social structure of the peoples. The result of all this in our case was to visit perhaps six outstanding sites on major excursions and to have what glance we could as opportunity offered of perhaps half a dozen lesser known ruins. This ignores the variety and excellence of the many castles and fortresses of later date.

We sailed at dawn with 520 miles to go. Until we cleared Crete it was the now familiar, "Just failed to make course, a tack to windward at each headland and use the engine with sail if it would significantly help progress". When we left Crete we settled down to sea-keeping routine and the skipper found, as ever, a lightening of spirit as the complications of the shore faded astern. What a wonderful sail we could have had if only the wind had been two or three points free. As it was, we could have sailed rather slowly on a course 30° from objective (with who knows what difficulty in recovering nothing at the end of the ride). Unusually for the Mediterranean, this wind lasted for sixty hours, declining at last into the more familiar calms and light variables of the western Mediterranean with the silly slop of sea. Such a handicap to sailing in light weather.

From the east, Malta is but seven miles wide. It may be invisible beyond ten or twelve miles with its low silhouette, its camouflage colour and a little haze; how unlike the islands of the Aegean. I believe it is not uncommon for yachtsmen to take a kick off from the toe of Italy, bounce off Cape Pasero in Sicily with a careful departure, and aim across Malta Strait, with its variable currents, as the surest way of making Malta. We had approached from 400 miles away, we did not want to overshoot and turned south. A few hours proved that we had been set back appreciably to the east during the last 400 miles, and to the south

The Skipper in the Caribbean.

A splendid schooner yacht, part of the Nicholson's charter fleet.

in the last 24 hours. We made a fresh course and in the afternoon a faint, barely imagined, pencil line appeared on the horizon. Two hours later, it was confirmed and so we came in to Malta at dusk, clearing customs in the Grand Harbour, and collecting a dead dog or some such object on the propeller so that we limped round to the marina going dead slow with the engine over-heating, but we had arrived. Friends were there to greet us, there was the familiar atmosphere, a known berth and procedure.

'Bluebird' spent the winter 1967/68 in Malta as before and with Jack still living aboard there was the prospect of a voyage and more care was taken in the work done and the preparations of such matters as overhaul of compass received attention. We sailed in May bound for Gibraltar but intending to make the return as interesting as possible by visiting the south and west coasts of Sicily, the coasts of Sardinia and Spanish ports, which would be new to us, though still including the Balearic Islands. I had to return home for a fortnight in June, which could most conveniently be done from Palma. These plans were carried out but the whole of the cruise to Palma was disappointing with such hard winds and much head wind. It was unseasonably cold and only in the latter part of it was the water warm enough to make bathing attractive. Richard, this one a youngster between school and university, was a good, keen hand. He was the only man we ever had in the Mediterranean who really caught fish from 'Bluebird' and it appeared to demand a rare devotion in which technique, skill and patience were blended. We also had Judy, the second daughter of Alfred and Beatrix, and she was a great delight to me as had been her sister Josephine and she entered the cruising life with equal success.

Sicily was relatively barbaric and the local name for dirty weather was 'Bourasco'. This was as nasty as it sounds and the same weather prevented us visiting as many ports in Sardinia as we had intended. The development of Porto Servo since our first visit in 1965 was quite startling. The season had not commenced and it was almost deserted, but the trappings of luxury yachting were working-up. Prices scared us away in 24 hours. The Straits of Bonifacio were as delightful as ever and this time better explored. We liked Bonifacio itself, berthing at the new Club which offered hot showers, still welcome, and we were proudly presented to a Vataire, recently installed and working! While we were there , France had a strike and even in this remote corner there was no post office service, no weather forecast, no paper and no telegrams. We had two gales before we reached Alghero

on the west coast of Sardinia. This was much more developed when we attained it by passing through the narrow and shallow gap in the islands after a grim night anchored off the convict settlement.

On passage to Port Mahon in Minorca, we had yet another gale so severe that we were hove to for some hours. The weather never relented until we reached Majorca where we were shocked by developments of mass tourism which had sprung up in only three years. Andraitx was the main base for local sailing while I was in England and well adapted to an easier life which all hands felt was earned after the rigours of the passages from Malta. While in Majorca, nephew John brought his wife Felicity, the sixth of the wives of my crew who had sailed with us in these 4 years. The Spanish coast was enjoyable with the better weather and the season warming up as water and bathing became more attractive. We had one last hard blow before we reached Gibraltar where we left 'Bluebird' in the marina until we could assemble for the final preparations before another voyage. This cruise, smaller and shorter than usual, was not up to the standard of enjoyment and again confirmed our preference for the eastern Mediterranean.

During the last four years we had sailed 10,000 miles and sampled the Mediterranean fairly thoroughly though without visiting Syria, Palestine or Egypt, or without any experience of the African coast. 'Bluebird' had done well in these waters and we had no trouble. Able to look after herself in hard winds, we had managed to keep moving in light ones, thanks to the large, light sails. The engine had been used about twice as much as we considered normal in waters outside the Mediterranean and had been satisfactory in every respect of performance, economy and reliability, while it had enough power to get us out when caught by a sudden blow in a dangerous harbour or anchorage. An ability to steer in reverse under power - an almost vital requirement when berthing stern to quay in the Mediterranean - had shown an ability in this respect far beyond most sailing auxiliaries; with enough nerve and taken fast enough she could be handled with great precision even in quite strong winds. In her we had suffered great heat and remained reasonably comfortable. If in these waters permanently, a fridge and a shower would be demanded and could have been installed. It is as tempting as it is difficult to assess the Mediterranean as a cruising area. It is too large to treat as a whole and some devotees would consider our experience too limited, but on our balance sheet it was so different from our previous experience that we should have welcomed a good assessment before penetrating its mysteries and that is the only justification for a verdict.

If we take out the Yugoslavian coast, the Ionian Islands, the Balearic Islands, the Sporades and parts of the Turkish coast, you have skimmed the cream off the milk. For the sailing man and sailing yachts, I shall incur wrath by the flat declaration that the Cote d'Azur and the Italian west coast are at the bottom of the list. For wintering, Malta is the better and Gibraltar possible if sterling areas are essential. With freedom of currency the choice is wide and without experience, it would be dangerous to recommend, but I should consider Ischia, Rhodes and Cyprus. How significant it is that the ancients and the modern gave names to all the dangerous winds in all parts of the Mediterranean. At least ten names come to mind headed by Mistral, Bora and Meltemi. The spring can be late, cool and rough. July and August are usually too hot for the taste of most Britishers. It may well be that September/October are the best months but our plans had precluded them.

We have said that the best sail for the Mediterranean is the reliable diesel engine as the worst feature for the sailing man is the prevalence of light wandering airs, often accompanied by an infuriating slop of sea and the sudden transition to violent wind, not always short lived. The winter gales in the Mediterranean can probably be as dangerous as anything in the world, excepting cyclones and hurricanes with their manifestation of tropical violence. There is a shortage of good bays, estuaries and anchorages. Too many small, dirty and crowded artificial harbours. There are few offshore dangers but these are frequently unmarked. In the sailing months there is little fog and the approaches to ports are usually safe and easy. Communication with England is swift and relatively cheap from Gibraltar and Malta in particular. A yacht in this area needs some rather contradictory qualities which have been indicated and perhaps the growing tendency is towards full powered and more luxurious yachts. The attractions of the coastal shore life are great and to those whom this appeals to, or with a special interest in archaeology, there are magnificent opportunities.

The last words are dangerous: "If you value the life, do. If you value the sailing, don't". We, and I know this view is shared by many other experienced sailing men, have left the Mediterranean with some relief. I shall never regret the experiences; I value all the four years we had in the Mediterranean and with my eyes wide open I would return if, and when, my plans and needs led me back again.

After a year's cruising in the Mediterranean, when it came to another even more successful season, I was searching for a way of presenting the account for the Cruising Club Journal without apparent repetition of the previous year. The thought struck me that our voyage had not been dissimilar to the 'Argonaut' in the ''Search for the Golden Fleece', immortalised forever in Homer's 'The Odyssey'. Why should I not write up the account of this voyage in the same manner. The word rhapsody came up in my mind and checking up in the dictionary, we found one of the meanings to be from ancient Greek - an epic poem narrated by the author. This vindicated the project and it became known as 'Skipper's Rhapsody'. In the interests of space, there follows four sections only from the lengthy poem.

Bluebird of Thorne, 1967, Minaret to Meltemi - Crete, Cyprus, Turkey, Aegean, Greece.

An odyssey of yachts and coasts, this tale
Of cruising round the eastern Med, in sail.
With men and girls joining, not quite as planned,
At four crew change points so that always manned
Fourteen there were - like actors on a stage,
Playing their part, then off as to a cue.
The Skipper, Twin Keel Balfour, Sheffield's son,
Jack Longsdon of that place in Derbyshire
Provided continuity throughout.
Much bastioned Malta with its cheerful sons...

...Venetian castle shattered on the height,
Climbed and explored before we shared that night
With passing fishermen, a simple meal.
Bread, olive oil and wine, fish grilled on coals
Of brush by their red boat, while Roseate Light
Declined on peak and velvet night descends...

...Rock tomb where Alexander's captain slept.
Bank that would not change traveller's cheque.
How can one reconcile the old and new,
Muezzin calls on Allah by loud speaker,
What faith Mohammed when the minaret
Protected by lightening conductor be?...

Left: Grand Canal, Venice

Below: Acropolis

Left: Galapagos iguana.

Below: Galapagos giant tortoises.

...When James departs in search of local wine
Do not expect his prompt return on time.
Service by one small boy who ran a lot
Rewarded Skipper's scale, "A Drach a trot"...

...Sunbathers have the foredeck, chosen place,
Girls horizontal can be left in peace
But Skipper standing back against the mast
Fondly imagines that his ample form
Was hidden by six inch duralumim....

...So back to Malta and M'Sida Creek,
More than three thousand miles beneath our keels,
While three score places we had visited,
In sixty -six our faithful anchor cast.
Intangible rewards, how can one seek,
Evaluate a thousand memories?

Water and air cooler this year than last,
And on the whole with quite a lot more wind.
The bodies brown the muscles in good shape,
With minds swept clean, ready to tackle fresh
Return to far more complicated life.
So staunch and sound is this our Bluebird ship,
Venture completed, carried out as planned,
No accident, no failure, safe to land.

Corinth Canal.

Chapter Thirteen

Half This Our World

It would be the supposedly British habit of understatement to say there had been a good deal of preparation; how does one decide what spares to take? A full outfit of tools is essential but where does one stop? A steel banding machine with stainless tape might be a life-saver in coping with broken spars. A wire pulley equally in case of rigging failure. It is impossible to foresee everything and sheer displacement limits what can be taken. What vital equipment requires a back up? This was provided for, sextant, chronometer and other equipment essential for navigation. Charts alone are a problem. Cost and weight are considerable and one cannot take the detailed charts for every port or coast one might visit. Other requirements will appear as the voyage proceeds. In contrast to the early days, inflatable life-jackets, safety harness, a life-buoy stern mounted, easily released by the helmsman, fitted with sea-water activated light, with quick attach and release clip, a life-raft and a semi-automatic 'Mayday' radio transmitter, operated by battery, was added as 'Bluebird' did not carry a radio transmitter.

We had allowed three weeks for final preparations in Gibraltar for our 1968 Atlantic passage and onward cruise and there were willing hands. Christian on the domestic side and in charge of stores and James, a volunteer, as he wished to film the start of the voyage (though neither of them were sailing on the Atlantic passage). The time was not too much for the tasks but meanwhile the Levanter blew and that is perhaps the least attractive weather at Gibraltar. The dank cloud hung over the Rock and when we went on the slip for a last and liberal coat of specially strong antifouling, we suffered from dirt and dust and we had not bargained for half burnt paraffin fumes from the jets taking off with an ear-shattering din from the runway only about 50 yards away. These fumes, combined with the dust to coat decks and rigging with a greasy film was as revolting as it was difficult to remove. We worked hard and such times pass quickly and are soon forgotten. Though tired and anxious to be away I had the happy feeling that 'Bluebird' was in good order and certainly in far better state than at the commencement of the Atlantic voyage six years earlier.

Yachts were arriving from the Mediterranean and from the European countries to the north to join a considerable number, most of them preparing, like ourselves, for the Atlantic passage and then when we were almost ready it blew a full gale from the west. Yachts in the torpedo pens had a bad night and some suffered damage. We could not sail. It is impossible for a small sailing vessel to force a passage out of the Straits to the west when she has to tack against such a force of wind and across the powerful and adverse currents running in from the Atlantic.

On Saturday, 2 November 1968, the west wind still blew strongly. At least two other yachts again postponed departure but we sailed, reefed down and determined to use all our cunning and the resources of both sail and power. We drove 'Bluebird' to her limit. It was a tough start and it was touch and go. We had tons of water on deck in the notorious overfalls and dusk found us just, but only just, able to make Tangier, which we had not intended to visit. We had made good only twenty-five miles from Gibraltar and to do this we had battled for eight hours and sailed fifty-five miles in the endeavour. Not for us that night the delights of the Casbah. We were exhausted but we had escaped. We had started a voyage and a voyage should have an objective but it is sometimes easier to define the objective in negative terms. No ice, no Cape Horn, no circumnavigation, no single-handed stuff and no publicity. What then remained? A desire to explore the Pacific and its islands in the hope that this would prove to be as much an escape and as enjoyable a venture as had been the Atlantic circuit of five years earlier.

"Whereas the said ship may venture over the seas... and touching the adventures and perils in this voyage. They are of the winds, the seas, men of war, fire, enemies, pirates, thieves, jettisons, letters of mart, surprisals, takings at sea, arrests, restraints and detainment. It shall be lawful to sail or stay at any ports or places wheresoever... Until the said ship with all her tackle, ordnance, apparel and merchandises shall be arrived at her destined port for twenty-four hours, in good safety... ". No, this is not Drake and the 'Golden Hind', it is an insurance at Lloyds effected upon "Bluebird of Thorne" - 20 ton, auxiliary yawl, whereof Lord Riverdale is Master-under-God. Words to stir the spirit of any skipper on a voyage to the far Pacific and its many islands, half a world away.

On this first passage to the Canaries we were four strong. The trusty Lance determined, after so many cruises, to do his first Atlantic passage. Derek, a new comer, equally determined to achieve his first seagoing passage in any yacht but particularly in

'Bluebird' and Mike, a nephew by adoption, only nineteen years, new and on trial in the hope that he might remain with me throughout the voyage until we reached New Zealand, which he wished to visit and where he had relatives.

Next day we left the Straits and entering the Atlantic, I had a strong feeling of relief and escape from the Mediterranean which was very real, however irrational, as we had enjoyed our experiences in the area. I had intended to stand well out into the Atlantic before making a direct course to the Canaries but head winds forced us down the African coast if we were not to add excessive distance and time while tacking westward. When two days out, however, we had a head wind rising to force 6 and, under short canvas, we tacked offshore for twelve hours and on shore for twelve hours again. Dawn found us becalmed in a large but oily swell within sight and sound of the surf crashing on the barren shores of Morocco. There was not a building, a man or even a camel in sight; just sand-coloured desolation. The log spinner had disappeared and the bent bracket indicated that it had been taken by something large, probably a shark. The first of our spares was broken out and put to use.

Again we made a new course for the Canaries and at the next dawn encountered a frontal line of black cloud stretching north and south as far as the eye could see. This threatened wind but after heavy rain the wind veered to north, north-west. At last we had broken out of an adverse weather system and we could set all sail and make good speed on our desired course to the objective. Celestial navigation became necessary and I was rusty after four years with little practice. During the day we overhauled a large ketch sailing on a similar course. This gave us great satisfaction but passing her at dusk we did not identify and lost her in the night. Next day the preoccupations of landfall and approach occupied us until we entered Las Palmas, Gran Canaria, after an interesting passage of just over six days, during which we had sailed 860 miles to make good 730 miles. We enjoyed a few days here. Derek departed and Roy and Dennis joined. What a pity that the harbour, in so pleasant a spot, should suffer from such appalling oil and filth, so much so that remembering Madeira I wished I had again made it the point of departure for the Atlantic.

Again a south westerly gale, unusual but just as unfortunate, delayed our departure by one day. Two yachts which had sailed returned somewhat battered and several others were awaiting more favourable conditions for departure. This is a place early in a world voyage where some ships come to rest, crews break up and depart and their voyages come to grief. We sailed with conditions still unpleasant but as we cleared the islands the wind came in hard from the north west and 'Bluebird' settled into her ocean stride and made a first day's run of over 150 miles. It was not long at this speed before we entered the north-east trades though they were weak and hesitant at this point. Throughout this passage my mind was occupied by comparisons with that of six years before. This time we had a strong crew of five, three of them yacht owners and potential navigators. All were interested and keen so that work was easy, my cares were slight and the chart room was almost red hot. With plenty of watchkeepers I decided to steer carrying rather more sail with the mainsail and one twin as against self-steering under the twin running sails. I was surprised to find that this made little difference to our speed. I should certainly adopt the easier alternative of self-steering on another passage.

I was glad to find that I enjoyed as much as before this, "one more passage in the north east trades", while all the others were achieving an ambition and were not disappointed. For Roy it was the second Atlantic crossing in 'Bluebird'. For Dennis it was the first and he was thrilled, "Thank you, thank you Skipper for bringing me into the lovely north east trades". There were other differences from the former passage; this time we sighted man-made Sputniks in the heavens and it was easier to receive time signals from B.B.C. and W.W.V. with its nasal chant, "When the tone returns the time will be...". When six days out we had a wind force 7 but, with some reduction of canvas, continued at unabated speed. On many occasions we had massive squalls and always the difficulty in judging whether they would prove to be harmless and short-lived or whether they meant business and could become dangerous. It was perhaps more overcast than normal and this was confirmed by later comparisons with other yachts. Those a week ahead and a week astern of us reported an easier ride and more regular winds. At a position approximating the mid Atlantic ridge, we crossed a mile of confused sea exactly like the tidal water off a headland in the English Channel. Could this have been a submarine volcanic disturbance?

I had intended a course sweeping further south than before but running before the wind tended to force us into the same path so that the comparison showed a remarkable conformity between the two passages. Life was regular and happy. Fresh food lasted well.

A novelty was Gofio, a partially roasted and flavoured maize meal, reputed to have been the staple diet of the ancient and extinct Guanches of the Canary Islands, as a complete food stuffed with vitamins. But after trials only the Skipper appreciated this experiment. Cala do Flor, a long lasting cheese, was more popular and we had some of the best and largest avocadoes I had ever seen or tasted. I did not know that Gran Canaria grew these and also mangoes, lichees and other exotic fruits.

No Atlantic passage is uneventful and this one was no exception: one afternoon on my watch off, I realised that we had only about 250 miles to go. I was turning things over in my mind before drifting off to sleep and it occurred to me that Mark and Susan should be flying in to Barbados at that time. Dropping off to sleep by day is sometimes aided by a book that soon falls out of one's hand. A call from the watchkeeper, "The squalls are bad; I am nearly 90° off course. Do you think we should gybe?" I come on deck, study the conditions and decide to hang on during this watch. I think the wind may return to its former direction after this line of squalls. I put my head down in my berth and I am almost asleep again. Another call - "Skipper, you said you wanted a sight and there is a gleam of sun". "Quite right", I said, and I am on deck with the sextant standing by for half an hour but without success and when it is hopeless I put my head down for the third time. I need that sleep and this time I really drop off.

A crash. I am instantly awake thinking that the running sail boom has smashed. I can feel that the ship is doing 8 knots; the wind must have increased and, reaching the cockpit in seconds, I find a badly-shaken watchkeeper and the others turning out. In an exceptionally bad and sudden squall the wind had fluked round 30° and the man at the helm had been caught out with an involuntary gybe. Of course there was a strong boom guy but in that sea and wind force 6 or more, it had added to the pressing strain on the boom and one of the wishbones had sprung. This should not have happened but there it was. All hands to hand the mainsail. Not easy in that force of wind from astern. Secure the boom and investigate the damage. My thoughts are racing. The damage can certainly be repaired within our own resources to complete the passage and this would have applied even in mid Atlantic and the task would be easier owing to the banding machine I had brought for just such an emergency. But meanwhile it is blowing hard, dusk and a dirty night threatens, our position is known and there is no risk of running into land. Decision follows. With all secure, hand the running sail, set No.

2 jib and we will carry on tonight under headsails. I order the kettle to be put on and all hands to tea.

I tell the watchkeeper, who is feeling bad, "I should probably have been caught out myself". I hear young Mike remark, "The Skipper swears at me when something trivial happens. Now we have smashed the main boom and he says, 'we will have a cup of tea'". Next day the repair is made so that we can set the reefed mainsail should we need to do so on approaching land, but in this strong wind we are making over 6 knots. A fix is obtained and a trial on the R.D.F. confirms the bearing; though this is comforting I regard it only as a check. The cry goes up, "Land ho!" Great excitement ensues. There are guesses on our relative position and a temptation to alter course. I have had this so many times that I announce firmly, "I am putting my head down, call me in about an hour when we can really see and get some bearings. Meanwhile do not alter course but you may go 10° to starboard if the indications confirm". There is a strong wind and a big sea. An hour later it all comes up as it should have done. The familiar low lying land of Barbados with the small islands just visible in relation to the low land stretching out to the south east point.

We round this point fairly close to the coral reefs and begin to smooth our water. At this point it is well to check and clear everything during the approach. The anchor has to be brought up and shackled on, gear stowed and everything possible is done so that we are not in a mess on arrival when we may be invaded by health authorities, customs and police. The yellow quarantine flag goes up to the crosstrees. We have no courtesy flag for Barbados. While all this is done we sail along the coast identifying marks until we can head up into Carlisle Bay, sail into a suitable anchorage and down goes the hook. We have arrived and I am thankful another Atlantic passage is behind us, this time in twenty days. Not bad but with good regular trades 'Bluebird' could have done better. The formalities are easy and pleasant and when they are over Roy, Dennis and Lance go ashore by dinghy. Returning three hours later they have air berths booked for departure and have made contact with Mark and Susan. We are to join them for a good shore meal that evening. Next day the three stalwarts departed, all with a sense of achievement and this experience behind them, hurrying back to wives and families, jobs and a more normal life.

While in Barbados for a few days of pleasant relaxation the boom repair was made good but I had already decided to make

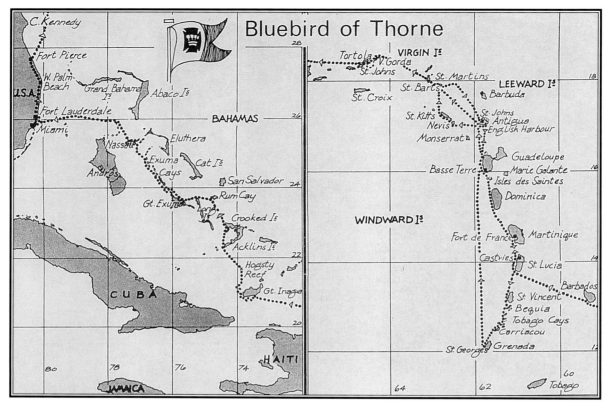

Track chart - Bahamas.

up new booms in Grenada. The original ones had suffered seven years, mainly in the tropics and would now be suspect. I realised that I could improve the design and ensure that the weather did not get into the glue joints by using a glass-fibre covering. In planning this voyage I had regarded six weeks cruising in the Windward Islands of the West Indies more as a family holiday than a part of the venture and we approached it in this spirit as we worked up the familiar chain of islands from Barbados to Antigua and down again to Grenada with the crew, all family and friends, visiting places well remembered and exploring many new anchorages. I had wondered whether it would be so enjoyable on this second occasion or whether developments in the area might have spoiled it for our tastes. I enjoyed it as much as before and I had to admit that all the tourist development had its compensations in making life easier in some ways for the cruising yachtsmen. The number of yachts

had almost doubled. Hotels and air-strips now existed or were projected but the quiet anchorages remained, the trade winds blew and we found that we had a host of friends and saw many well remembered yachts. Christmas in English Harbour was just as good as ever and the hospitable Nicholsons, with their great party in the powder magazine, as much appreciated. Again there were twice the number of yachts compared with six years before but another generation of young Nicholsons was growing up in the expanding activities.

The yacht charter game had changed and extended. There was now competition from hotels, some of them offering package holidays combining shore luxuries with sailing activities. The successes and rewards of chartering seemed now to be gained by the larger yachts, impeccably equipped, maintained and handled with special regard for the personality of the Skipper and, as much

Left: In the Caribbean.

Below: Windsail over fore hatch for ventilation.

or more so, that of the Skipper's wife. Phil and Plat joined us for their second West Indies holiday in 'Bluebird' as my family scattered and we started south again with a manoeuvre in the harbour to circle the new 'Wanderer IV' and give Eric and Susan Hiscock a chance to photograph 'Bluebird' under sail. This encouraged full sail to the large genoa but outside the harbour we found a really strong trade wind. For the third time we improved our passage to Deshayes Bay by averaging 8¼ knots in a considerable sea with the speed log surging up to the 12 knot stop. Christian thoroughly enjoyed steering under these conditions and Phil Allen quietly observed to the Skipper, "I don't know whether Christian or 'Bluebird' deserves greater tribute but I find this most impressive". The trades continued strong and courses were more to windward than we had expected. We carried a reef in the mainsail for a week and with the invaluable small genoa we made many fast passages between the islands. Usually there were yachts in every anchorage and occasionally special incidents or memories such as a remark from a passing citizen, "It's gotta be a famous yacht, it's in my magazine!"

We liked Martinique and the French atmosphere. Nowhere else had the womenfolk so proud and beautiful a carriage. Bequi and its schooners were the prelude to the lovely Grenadines but everywhere there was development. The nice Palm Island, where swamp, mosquitos, land crabs and wild goats were the inhabitants six years ago now had an airstrip, a water catchment, power plant, hotel and attractive villas, presided over with competent charm by the same nice Caldwells whose indomitable voyages in the yawl, 'Outward Bound' had led them to put down roots in this haven. We could not remain in contact with the steel bands and the calypsos of this area without our own reaction and so the Skipper and Mike produced words and music for a 'Bluebird' calypso which helped to enliven our evenings when we exchanged visits with other yachts. Some of these were slightly scurrilous allusions to people:-

Christian in her comfy bunk
She sleeps an awful lot
Complainin' when she come on deck
That's it's far too hot
Woe is me -
Shame and scandal in the family.

So at last to Grenada for slipping, the new booms and other work, while Christian and the Skipper flew home for a spell of hard work before continuing the voyage.

"Grenada, Nutmeg Isle of Spice,
Bluebird' remains where life is nice.
Back to England cold and fog,
Work and taxes, life's a slog".

Grenada/Panama

I flew into Grenada, tired but with the satisfaction that stems from doing the utmost in a limited time, and joined 'Bluebird' at Prickly Bay. Grenada had served well and the crew had enjoyed themselves. Slipping and all the main jobs that had been done by the yard were satisfactory if expensive. The crew had worked hard also, but there was a tremendous list to complete before we sailed and this occupied a week. The charter season was in full swing and it was fascinating to study the many yachts, old and new, some of them large by modern standards, with a trend towards fibreglass, trimarans and catamarans becoming evident. 'Havfruen' came in. The Hiscocks sailed and then: disaster! Bartie had arrived with a damaged knee (South Africa), a damaged back (England). Almost electrocuted by a defective drill, he then crashed from a scooter, and though X-rayed to prove no bone was broken, his shoulder was so dislocated that it was unserviceable for eight weeks. He was cut to the bone on knee and elbow with numerous other abrasions, so that we feared he might not heal in the tropics. Daily dressings, mostly by Anne, were effective and he recovered.

We departed one Sunday morning making all sail to a brisk trade wind. It was a testing passage. The Skipper had to assess and work in the new crew, try out a five-man watch bill and check the work on 'Bluebird' together with the improvements we had made ourselves. Two days out we sighted the Hermanos Islands, a check on our navigation. We drove the ship hard. We had quite enough wind astern, rising to force 7: a rousing ride for two days before it eased to force 4. Life was then comfortable. We stripped and repainted the dinghy. The wind fell light; we set spinnaker. Is this a cruising sail? It did good work and was handed intact. We achieved more than 1,000 miles under sail in a week. Not bad, but no record, though preferable to landfall in the Gulf of Panama with a wind force 8. Glass calm, a little engine, and then a light wind with which we sailed between the breakwaters at dawn, astern of 'Carmania' and came to anchor on the flats close to 'Wanderer IV'. Eric and Susan had arrived the day before. It

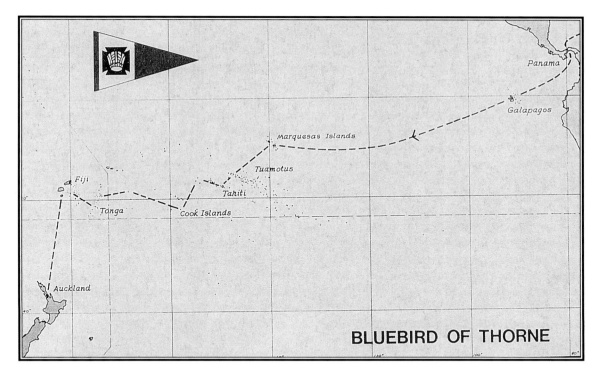

BLUEBIRD OF THORNE

Above: Track chart - Panama to New Zealand.

Right: Grenada.

181

had been a satisfactory passage. Ship and crew were proved; we were ready to tackle the broad Pacific.

But first the Panama Canal. This is no place to write an analysis of tribulations, paperwork and difficulty. It is better and also correct to record the efficiency of the canal system, the friendly help of the officials and the yacht clubs at Colon and Balboa. We passed a week that was an enjoyable experience as a whole, in not too trying weather conditions. The actual transit of the canal was exciting. We did not commence the passage until 14.30 with considerable doubt whether we should not have to remain in the canal overnight (at considerable extra cost), but we were fortunate and went through with two 70 foot Mexican shrimpers, whose crews handled the shore lines while we secured to them. It was quite the easiest possible drill for us. Our pilot was delightful, and, encouraged by him, we sailed across Gatun Lake at speeds reaching 9 knots. He then called for power and our faithful Gardner gave us 8 1/4 knots with ambient water and air temperatures both over 90º; an outstanding performance. In the dark we surged through Culebra Cut to arrive at the locks, still with our Mexican friends, much to the astonishment of their pilot, who with good-humoured badinage questioned, "Say, is that thing nuclear, or what is the secret weapon?" We went down the locks into tidal water, under the great bridge and secured to a yacht club buoy at Balboa. The passage had taken 7 1/2 hours, a normal full-powered ship schedule. Our pilot was delighted. "When I have my yacht I guess she's gotta have twin keels".

If it is the business of a yacht to visit islands, she must first leave the mainland - and what a struggle that can be! We sailed on Tuesday, two days later than intended. We had topped up to the limit with water, fuel, stores and gas, but a sobering thought - in spite of all our endeavours we were without any assurance that we should be received or given facilities at any island of any nationality for more than 5,000 miles ahead. This passage has an evil reputation. Sailing vessels have failed to leave the Gulf of Panama and staggered back to Balboa short of water and demoralized. We were lucky. After an uncertain few hours, a fine breeze gave us 150 miles to clear the Gulf and leave Cape Mala astern. It was a thrill to feel that at last we faced the wide Pacific.

One morning a US Navy Sky Warrior located us as a reconnaissance exercise. How incongruous! That fantastic machine costing £1 1/2 million, consuming on this one mission 15 tons of fuel - 'Bluebird's' total displacement - was flashing overhead at 300 mph taking photographs of our 6 knot progress. Never a dull moment! We caught a shark, quite a large one, his power was terrific. We got him alongside, subdued him, hoisted him on board and killed him. A successful exercise, but we hoped we would never tangle with a larger specimen. Edible? Yes, we tried, but there was no enthusiasm. Our wind had gone; we faced the reality of this passage. Days of glass calm, slight lazy swell and wandering airs never more than force 1. We saw numerous turtles but resisted the temptation to catch and eat them. 'Bluebird's' power radius had been designed to traverse the windless areas of the world. This was the pay-off. At 5 knots the faithful Gardner was so economical that we could have steamed as much as 1,250 miles. Without power we should have faced as much as three weeks of frustration. If any sail would draw with or without power it was set. So we wandered slowly across the vast bowl of sea under a burning sky with high humidity and the vertical sun beating down on a gasping helmsman at midday.

One night we encountered a fantastic tropical storm. There was little wind, but spectacular lightning, and it rained so hard that the cockpit filled against the drains. We topped up our tanks; we cleaned ourselves and our clothes. The air was so full of water it seemed difficult to breathe. No meridian altitude was now possible and we had some overcast skies with strong and uncertain currents. We should have sighted land one morning. Nothing! The Skipper recorded some real anxiety in verse and song :-

"Oh island in the mind
Why are you so hard to find?
Are you ahead or are you behind?
Or is it just that we are blind?

We sailed slowly all day on a safe course towards the islands. In the late afternoon, a combined sun and moon shot gave us a more reliable fix and on that our courses brought us to a correct landfall soon after dawn next day. A breeze came in and we sailed into Wreck Bay to anchor near Diogenes. Gene and Shirley Watson had made a similar passage of nine days from Panama.

Galapagos Islands

Wreck Bay was not impressive. We were protected by a reef, but still the swell rolled the yacht, smashed on the shore and surged at the jetty. There were a few decrepit fishing-vessels, one of them almost sinking, an ice plant inoperative, a jetty broken up, oil tanks empty, and the village a somewhat sleazy collection of shacks with a rather dark-skinned Indian type of Ecuadorian, and a lot of dirt and flies. Resources were minimal. The storm we had encountered had washed away a reservoir and carried away the pipeline so that the settlement had no water. The last ship had forgotten their supplies, including flour. There were a few eggs, a little fruit, early oranges - and little else.

But, and a big but, there was the naval detachment, sixty-eight strong. The commander had been recently appointed and William, a naval officer and number one, was quickly our friend. He spoke perfect English, learned from enthusiasm and to relieve boredom during his long exile in these islands. We were befriended and made welcome. England and the English are accepted by tradition of Darwin and the 'Beagle'. We were granted some fuel, which involved a complicated exercise in seamanship, handling 40-gallon drums from depot to jetty, jetty to sea, to yacht, hoisting aboard, siphoning to tank and return, all in a big swell. All this under cover of darkness as this was an illicit operation. We were thankful that there was no damage or injury. With 'Diogenes' we organised a combined expedition to traverse Kicker Rock. The commander and his wife honoured 'Bluebird', William went aboard 'Diogenes', and we exchanged some crew to facilitate photography. It was not a good day, but fortune smiled. The sun broke through as we approached Kicker Rock. This was a fantastic experience. There is a cleft 400 feet high right through the rocky island. It is only about 15 yards wide, quite sheer, and the water is deep. In line ahead the two yachts traversed this cleft. It seemed that our cross-trees must foul the cliffs or a surge of swell make us sheer bodily into the rock face, but all went well. It was quite unique. We returned to our anchorage twelve miles away without incident, landing the commander and his wife, who had been variously protected by an assortment of ship's garments and fortified by Avomine so that the worst had just, but only just, been averted.

We sailed to Santa Fe, anchoring at dusk between a chain of rocky reef and island and the mainland. It was a barren but odd landscape, all rock and great spiny cactus plants of peculiar form almost tree size and with reddish papery trunks. In the morning an iguana swam past the ship, obviously disconcerted by our anchor chain. A photographic expedition went off to the islands. We were stalking seals from pups to great bulls. Iguanas were on the rocks and brilliant red crabs with one or two strange birds. It was a fascinating experience and all the fauna were tame and

confident. One seal playfully lifted our dinghy anchor and started to tow it away. Anne was sitting on a rock with two seal pups at her feet while their mothers flirted and dived in the water at little more than touching distance.

It was a pleasant sail to Academy Bay, Santa Cruz. This place gave us an entirely different impression as compared with Wreck Bay. There was a white community, they were building a Nascent hotel, the Darwin Institute, and the Angermeyer family with their pet iguanas. The two Angermeyer brothers had been refugees from Hitler's Germany and had sailed out to escape persecution. Eventually putting down roots in the Galapagos, one of them had become quite famous for his skilful paintings achieved solely with his fingers and tubes of oil paint. I have one of them which he did for me in fifteen minutes on an old box lid. A quite amazing art form. In the port were five yachts and the 'Cristobel' carrier. This vessel, the only and most irregular link with the mainland, looked exactly like the ship that brought the rebels in a film of a South American revolution. She had a reputation of total unreliability.

One rule of travel is that you should have been there at some other time; so with the Galapagos. This was the Alneno, the year the Humboldt current swings away, the equatorial current slips in, the water temperature is 8° too high, the air temperature 10° too high, the humidity quite awful, and exceptional rainfall is encountered. For this reason the track to the highlands was pronounced impassable and the mosquitoes were truly dreadful. It was little comfort for us to realize that life could have been much pleasanter. This situation influenced us in making a limited circuit by cutting out visits to the northern islands. It would have been a struggle in any case to return against contrary winds and strong north-going currents. One can understand Darwin's fascination with the distinctive varieties of birds and mammals, such as flightless cormorants. Mans' depredations in this unique paradise have been horrific. The old whalers took away the giant tortoises by their hundreds as a welcome addition to their food supply. The effects caused by man's introduction of goats, pigs, dogs, rats and so forth have wrought havoc with the food supply, livelihood and reproduction of the indigenous fauna.

We visited Islas Plaza, where the seals and sea-lions were larger and more numerous. So tame were they that we had fun bathing and playing with them. We sailed with a fair wind to Baltra and took a hair-raising narrow pass between rocks with soundings down to 10 feet. Safely through, we came on the wind to Berero Bay. There was nothing ashore. No droppings, no signs of life, no fish, but we were shaken by the sight of a giant ray followed by a killer whale which circled 'Bluebird'. Other islands now in view appeared similar when inspected by binoculars. We were in misery with hordes of mosquitoes during the night.

We sailed direct to Post Office Bay in Santa Maria Island, beating 100 miles to windward in light winds against the current, so that we arrived at night, heaving to until first light before entering the bay. It was a satisfactory anchorage; wild, deserted, with no feature except the famous barrel with the names of many yachts. There was a bird's nest on top with eggs within. We left a record of our visit carved on one of 'Bluebird's' sail battens. We posted our mail (which was ultimately delivered by a yacht via Ecuador) and made ready for the long passage to the Marquesas. The Galapagos had been a worthwhile addition to our tally of islands and an experience we would not have missed, but the wild life is the main attraction. None of us would have wished to remain after our experience of thirteen days.

Galapagos/Marquesas

When should we find the south-east trades? We were lucky. After two days of uncertain weather, but never without a useful wind, we reached the trades. Bright sparkling days, cooler nights, lower humidity as well, a swell that did not worry us, no sea that really mattered, but best of all our speed gave us an apparent wind exactly on the beam. We carried out kites setting from 1,250 to 1,950 square feet. Our angle of heel was seldom 20° more often not more than 15°. Little roll gave us a comfortable and easy motion. We began to compare this with the north-east trades of the Atlantic and every comparison was in favour of the south-east trades. And speed – how we were sailing! 'Bluebird' was designed for this and she took advantage of it. Should we hand the ghoster at night and set the big yankee in case the wind might increase? Should we hand the mizen staysail? Or would she stand everything? The reaching staysail, our least used sail, came into action and was set for days. We worked up to a best day's run of 192 miles. The best week was 1,184. Cautiously we began to think of passages we had heard about twenty-two to twenty-eight days. At this rate we might even crack eighteen. Life was delightful.

Often challenged to describe what a typical day is like in the middle of a long Pacific passage the Skipper remembered the Rhapsody from the Mediterranean and again attempted to write this in the manner of Homer's Odyssey.

But what is the reaction of the crew to times like these? Some find themselves predominantly looking back to what they have left behind, others may be anticipating what lies ahead. One may be failing to adjust to watch keeping, is short of sleep, bad tempered and unhappy but one or two, a lucky few, like myself find the middle of an ocean passage when all is going well, a time of mental, physical and spiritual exaltation. One of the high spots in life that make it all worthwhile.

There was the day of the dolphins; in one day we had six strikes by these lovely fighting fish. We caught two of them, which was all or more than we could cope with and they were good to eat. But the excitement of these flashing fish-azure, aquamarine, emerald and gold-as they came alongside, fighting to the last! A wonderful sight, wonderful colours and streamlined shapes. Equally thrilling was the day of the porpoises-mammals this time. A large school, perhaps a hundred of the largest we had ever seen, came and stayed with us for three hours, playing around the ship so closely that they were almost rubbing our plating. So close that we could speak to them, we could hear them squeak, we could see the expressions in their eyes, we began to recognize individuals. One with a ragged dorsal fin, one with a scar on its head, another with a sore eye. And even more extraordinary, if you put your ear to the plating below their talking was so loud and clear that James was able to take a sound recording, possibly the first that has been obtained from a yacht in the open ocean. Needless to say, the photographers were busy.

Perhaps this was too good to last. Despite the probabilities of the routing chart, the wind drew aft and decreased, becoming less effective, while we no longer held our desired Great Circle course. Our worst day's run was only 86 miles. Morale declined as did all chance of a record passage. It was time to make a decisive change. Up went the big spinnaker (it had been repaired in Grenada), set on the twin running booms clear of all rigging. No need for racing tactics here! It pulled us along as nothing else could have done until we had more wind. Five days and nights and then force 4/5. We had intended to hand the spinnaker at noon, but we were too late. A tear developed and it came to hand again needing extensive repairs. Morale had suffered another blow. Anne had been unwell and was ordered off watch with a temperature and a nasty pain at the load waterline. The Skipper was worried; Pyrexia and possible appendix? We could only use pain killers and penicillin. What other care could we apply? The more powerful antibiotics were held in reserve, as no clear symptoms showed.

Our distance was decreasing steadily and we had entered the third week at sea, but we were still far out. This time the Skipper had no regrets when we sighted Ua Huka, a significant landfall at a distance of forty miles. We passed the craggy peaks of this magnificent island in the dusk and closing in with light winds and the engine, came up to Nuka Hiva in the night. A good moon enabled us to enter Taiohae Bay and come to anchor. We had completed our longest passage in less than twenty-one days.

An Epic Trek

It has been said that the business of a yacht is to visit islands: if so what happens to a yacht and her crew if these islands are of paramount importance to the voyage. An experienced member of The Cruising Club said to me, "Of course you must plan a voyage. If there is no plan it is all too easy to fall into longer and longer periods in different and attractive places so that the purpose of the voyage is lost and may never be completed, but," he continued, "while avoiding this error it is well to include rather more than less time in different places and particularly islands, to obtain the true enjoyment of a voyage".

When we reached the Marquesas group of islands in French Polynesia, I realised that this was an important point, a sort of watershed in the voyage to New Zealand. We had passed the halfway point, we had covered the longest of the Pacific passages, it was our first visit to a group of Polynesian islands and for all these reasons we spent more time in this group than we might otherwise have done and at our first port of call there was yet another factor; Anne, who had been gravely ill on the long passage, had been kindly received by a group of Roman Catholic nuns. There was no doctor but under their ministrations she made an almost miraculous recovery and was able to rejoin 'Bluebird' and thoroughly enjoy the remainder of the cruise to Tahiti. I may well have more to say later about Anne and her story.

We had been received with great courtesy and charm by the French Governor when we had no official entry to French Polynesia and as is often the case, we should technically have gone to a larger and more important headquarters to obtain entry in the first place. We found later that the French had suffered greatly, particularly in Tahiti, from the numbers of people whether from yachts or for other reasons who tended to sink into the life, maybe go 'native' to some degree and remain indefinitely. For this reason they had brought in a regulation that you were denied entry unless you had a return ticket and could satisfy them or deposit funds which would enable you to return whence you came at their option. As I remember it my 'American Express' card was accepted together with other resources and we did not have to actually deposit funds and so the Governor had sent our particulars to headquarters, no doubt with a recommendation that we seemed to be a good outfit, and in due course he received a reply and informed us that we had been granted entry and could pick up our papers later at headquarters; this was of course a welcome relief.

After a few days when we had found our way around, realised how delightful the atmosphere was, caught up with the few jobs that had accumulated on passage, I had an idea and announced one day, "I suggest that tomorrow we have a quite different day. Would it not be a good idea to scatter, get away from each other and do our own thing?" This was discussed and well received. In due course someone said, "What are you going to do Skipper?" And I replied, "My memory tells me that Joseph Conrad once deserted a sailing ship here and lived for a time with the natives in the Haapai Valley on the other side of this island. I have made an enquiry and been told that there is a good track so that I shall not lose my way. I have no map but the dividers on the chart say that the island is some eight or nine miles across and finally I have been shown where the track starts at the back of the village". So next morning I got up early, made a good breakfast and started at dawn carrying but a small knapsack with a few cans of fruit juice and a minimal bite. I had a good, stout pair of walking shoes. Behind the village there was a considerable range of mountains, this is well shown in a film which James Templar made called, 'Trade Winds to Tahiti' which was shown on the BBC with considerable success. I both wrote some of the script and participated in the action and it is now translated into a video so that we can readily show it at home. It is one of the delightful memories of the voyage.

I found the track, it was well graded but the ascent was longer and more formidable than I had expected. At the summit there was a breathtaking view that I shall never forget and after a brief breather I descended down the other side of the range with the valleys of the interior of the island; lush, tropical growth, but alas, as so often in Polynesia, everywhere deserted villages, evidence of a once fine people maybe five times or more numerous than the often rather dispirited and seemingly purposeless native community that now remains. So the track wound on, quite delightful until I came to another considerable ascent. I tackled this believing that when I reached the summit the other side of the island would be in sight and the Haapai Valley before me. Not so, though it was a lesser range than the first, when I reached the summit there before me was another stretch of valleys and behind them a further range of mountains quite as formidable as the initial one from my starting point. Undaunted I continued my way until at last I attained the summit of this range and there the welcome sight again of a magnificent view, though not so spectacular as the other side of the island, and the quite large and important Haapai Valley before me with some habitation in sight. I descended reaching plantations and cultivation and so came to the village where I received a splendid welcome. There were but three or four Europeans but everybody turned out to greet me. I suppose that to them an unknown stranger was almost a 'little green man' descending from outer space. A welcome assured, my sweat soaked shirt and shorts washed out and put on again wet to dry on me in this climate and then one of the Europeans approached me and said, "I have recently received a new engine for my launch, I have been waiting for this for about a year, my previous engine was hand-starting but this one has a self starter and electric wiring with a battery and I don't know how to connect up the circuits, could you help me?" This sort of thing was quite typical and so I said' "Lead on". We walked about a mile down the valley and there was his launch with the new engine. I was able to fix him up quickly and without difficulty and we returned gratefully and I was given lunch. I didn't eat much but the non-alcoholic drink was welcome and then my hosts said, "While you are here you should see our Tiki, it is supposed to be quite famous and of archaeological importance as proof of an early stage in the Polynesian migrations. This is a subject of great interest to me and I had seen or had examples of Tikis from New Zealand, in the north-west of South America, right through to the well-known Tikis of the Maoris in New Zealand. So again it was, "Lead on". The son of one of my hosts led me about two miles up the valley and there was the Tiki, very fine and interesting. I think a Tiki might be described as a sort of fertility symbol with a resemblance which may be symbolic only to the female human figure.

On return to the village, I glanced at my watch and said, "I must now make my farewells and depart". At this there was a chorus, "Surely you are not returning today, you must stay and we will look after you". I replied that I must return as I had told the crew that I would be back that night and if I did not do so, it would cause consternation and so in an atmosphere which might be described as, 'Sooner you than me', I set off up the mountain. It would be easy to make a long or a short description of the next three or four hours, the way was familiar and one finds that the return along a track that one has explored for the first time seems shorter on the return journey but I knew what lay before me. I didn't press my pace keeping to an easy long lasting stride but not being tempted by what would have been welcome stops every now and then and so at long last I was ascending the last range of mountains. About halfway up I lost my footing and fell, rolling a short distance down the steep side of the mountain. I was not hurt, it was just annoying but I then found and I remember my surprise that I had great difficulty in crawling up the few yards to regain the track. It was a warning and for the first time the thought that I might fail entered my head. The remainder of that ascent was a grim ordeal, I only just made it and when that magnificent view opened up in front of me I sank exhausted. I relaxed, sipped my last half can of fruit juice and I suppose almost passed out for half an hour or so. Then my mind became alerted, I realised a new danger, in about an hour the swift tropic night would descend and it would be dark. I could not then descend that track, I had got to make it now. Then a more terrible warning, I was unable to stand up, and only solved this problem by crawling to a small tree and by clasping this and using my arms I got to my feet and stood there leaning against the tree and taking measured deep breaths and saying to myself, "It is all downhill, you have only got to keep on your feet and just keep moving". If I had spent the night out, there would have been no great harm in that climate and in that location I should not have been beset by mosquitoes but with no food and more important no drink, I should surely have been incapable of movement by the morning. In the whole day I had seen no more than two lots of travellers on the track and if I were not rescued fairly speedily there could have been only one outcome. Somehow I made the descent, it was not the agony of the last ascent but it was touch and go and when I struggled out into the village street just as the light was failing, I saw the assembled crew who had been getting worried and wondering what to do. They hastened to me and as helping hands arrived I collapsed at their feet. They manhandled me bodily back to 'Bluebird', there at my direction I was stripped of my sweat-soaked clothing, laid out on the deck and they poured continuous buckets of sea water over me while a large, nourishing, hot drink was prepared. Into my berth propped up just enough to enable me to drink comfortably, I slowly ingested a large quantity of that life giving fluid.

We had been invited by the Governor to dine with him that night. I urged the others to go bearing my apologies and with some reluctance they did so. My excuses were gracefully received by the Governor and when they explained he said, "I am understanding you correctly when you say that Lord Riverdale walked to the Haapai Valley and back today?" And at this assurance, lapsing into French he said, " Mais sans doute, c'est evidement il doit être maintenant completement epuise", (but evidently and without doubt he must now be completely exhausted). He went on to tell them that when he made an inspection trip to the Haapai valley, he would ride over one day on his horse and even if his duties did not demand this he would stay at least one night, thinking it well as he said, to rest his horse before making the return journey over the mountains.

When the crew had departed I sank down with a really delicious sensation, it was peace, no more anxiety, no more stress, no more effort, no more will power, I could drift into unconsciousness without a care in the world. It was fifteen hours before I came to the surface, had a good meal and resumed life. I was stiff, I was not fit for any exertion but I was completely recovered and there was no ill-effect. Discussing it with the others, we came to the conclusion that the distance had of course been much greater than the straight line my dividers had measured on the chart and in the Haapai Valley to the launch and to the Tiki had added some five miles, I had probably covered not less than thirty miles. But more importantly from sea level to sea level, back and forth across that island, I had ascended and descended some 10,000 feet. Fit you may be but you cannot take walking exercise on a long sea passage and this was the tropics with considerable heat and humidity and finally in a life not without dust and heat and with many adventures, I don't remember ever before reaching the point of total exhaustion. I never took account of this but I was 67 and I suppose I had not quite got the reserves of power and endurance that I had possessed 30 or 35 years before.

Storm in the Tuamotues

I had looked forward with special interest to the group of islands known as the Tuamotues, they are included in French Oceania, but they are remote, distinctive and less developed than the Marquesas and far less than Tahiti and its surrounding island group. We were not to be disappointed, dozens of islands scattered over hundreds of miles, nearly all of them coral based, sea level and with a life that has changed little since Captain Cook's time. The population density is low, the way of life extremely simple and the economy minimal, with a small production of copra, coconut palms, pearls - almost fished out, leaving a small harvest of pearl shell, often restricted to one area of the extensive lagoons each year. The communication by primitive craft between the islands and a visit perhaps once or twice a year by a 'goelette', a schooner from Tahiti which now of course will have a diesel engine as well as sail and this we were to find, not a regular service but something that might arrive as and when it happened. At the first island we visited, we secured to a little jetty in the Pass. We had a natural, friendly welcome from all, any house was open to us, we were beckoned to enter and offered a drink or a meal. In this atmosphere, I threw 'Bluebird' open to the islanders and they would flock on board, an interested and chattering group, there might be perhaps up to fifteen at any time. They were intensely interested, enquired about everything, fingered everything, but nothing went missing. As far as we could tell, the social life on the islands was almost idyllic; there was a chief, more a sort of headman and he exercised some sort of authority which was expected. There was no sign of any crime, nothing like police, minimal bureaucracy, virtually no trade, perhaps one little store and children arriving in a quite haphazard manner, often with the father indeterminate or away from the island, would be cared for impartially by everybody. The language was what I call 'fractured French', there was no indigenous written language. We were presented with shell necklaces, fish for our needs and taken out to be shown their methods of fishing and diving in the lagoon. When we wished for a little privacy, it was only necessary for me to shout, "Tout a terre, nous sommes fatigues, je veux dormir", (everyone ashore, we are getting tired, I want to sleep), and off they would go a happy, chattering group. They had a sort of 'pound' gated from the sea, in which they could keep fish or sea products for use at will. Things could happen which were pure farce; have you ever been swimming underwater and looking up, seen a pack of about a dozen dogs, all purposefully swimming above you in one direction? The village dogs, like ourselves, choosing the moment of slack water in the Pass, had decided to go

Above: Tolati – our splendid Tongan pilot.

Above: Robbie with one of his speared fish.

Left: Opua - our first anchorage in New Zealand - a triumphant moment.

Below: Maori dancers.

on a foraging expedition along the atolls across the Pass from the main village. On one occasion in the Pass, Anne got tangled with a moray eel which resembles the conger eel and is quite formidable. We rescued her, slew the eel to cook and eat some of it, quite delicious. As the bulk of it was of no use to us, we threw it overboard and as it drifted up the Pass on the current, there was a sudden flurry and fight as the sharks rushed in to compete for a portion; as we had been bathing in that very spot only an hour or two before, there was what might be called a rather thoughtful look on the faces of the crew.

You may ask what did we contribute to the life of an island like this? It was very simple; first of all the interest of the yacht and conversation with strangers; a tin or so would be a welcome gift, luckily I had had the idea and had brought quite a supply of needles and these were a very welcome present for the ladies, while the men valued fish hooks of different sizes which I had also brought and the children loved the sweets, something they had never seen before. In addition, we were asked to help with any pieces of equipment which were not working or broken-down. Sometimes they would borrow our tools, sometimes they would ask our help but one overriding feature of one particular island, there was a splendid woman - she would be aged I think about thirty, and quite exceptional in that unlike so many of her sisters, she had not married or produced casual children. She had trained as a nurse in Tahiti, she could read and write and her English was perfect. She had dedicated herself to caring for the health of the people; she had a hut which was used as a clinic; the French Government gave her a supply of drugs and bandages and equipment once a year and thus equipped, she was the sole medical resource for about 500 people and had to cope with any emergency which might range from a diving accident, a foot gashed by an axe, a broken bone, child birth and any illness that might strike. I drifted into the habit of having a chat with her nearly every day; we would sit on a log in the shade of the palm trees, looking out over the Pass, away on our left the dark blue tropic sea, white flecked as waves broke in the trade wind. Across the Pass, palm trees and atolls, and on our right the wonderful lighter colours of the varied depths in the lagoon, behind us the huts of the village and the wind making a soft rustle in the palm fronds at the heads of the trees above us. We covered many subjects and both enjoyed learning something of the life and culture of the other in such different settings. But on one occasion I remember something tremendous, the Polynesians of course had no written culture and not thus burdened had remarkable memories and learned the past from folklore handed down from generation to generation. She could relate her ancestry for some thirty generations, and after explaining this she went on to legends of her race. There was the story of treasure brought in by pirates and hidden in the lagoon. This traditionally was guarded by an enormous shark and there was the story of some Americans who came to seek it, failed to find it and lost some of their equipment in attacks by the shark, and then she talked about their relations with Tahiti: "When we were strong and we thought that they were weak, we would raid them, and when they were strong and they thought we were weak, they would raid us and you might say why was there not peace between us but *voyez-vous*, we were not the same as the people of Tahiti because some of our ancestors in the distant past came from the east". My mind leapt into action, here at first hand in the legends of her race, was confirmation of Thor Heyerdahl's theories on the migration from South America by balsa rafts in to what became Polynesia; simply marvellous!

Yes, if you are wondering, there was a mutual attraction, it was mainly of the mind as I have related; she was not strikingly beautiful but a lovely, well-built Polynesian woman with fine features as well as a splendid mind. Recollecting this, I realised that had I stayed longer, almost inevitably our relations would have become much more intimate. Then, as our departure drew near, I was taken on one side by the chief; would I take some letters and mail to Tahiti? Yes certainly - and then a serious request. His wife had recently given birth to a baby boy; the infant was very sick and would almost surely die without skilled surgical attention far beyond the powers of my friend. I think it was a dangerous case of congenital hernia. Would we take his wife and the infant to a much larger island centre some hundreds of miles away where there was a doctor and a hospital? I gave this serious thought and reluctantly felt that I must refuse and my reasons? I didn't want my freedom of action curtailed as I hoped to visit one or two more islands before making that centre or going on to Tahiti; that I would have bypassed, but what if the woman were incapable or sick, how could we care for her and the child? What would be the reaction of the French authorities to us taking passengers, and far more serious, what would happen if she and the child should die? In the French manner, we might be accused of 'crime passionelle', but the final and most serious reason of all was that storm or shipwreck might prevent us reaching the desired island. I explained all this to the chief; it was received with calm understanding and dignity, accepted, and our friendship remained unimpaired. And so at last we departed, seldom have I felt such regret at leaving. We made one or two more island calls as I had projected, very similar if not quite so attractive and varied. In the lagoon of one, I met a shark socially; swimming round a coral head one way, a shark about 9 feet long swam round the other way and there we were eyeball to eyeball. I kept quite still, feeling this the best policy. We regarded each other steadfastly for a moment or two with mutual respect and then we both went on our separate ways. Then the passage to the island centre where there was a doctor. I was now anxious to reach this as Barry was in trouble. Starting originally with bites of the 'no no' fly in the Marquesas, these had become infected; his ankles were a real mess and threatened with anything from tropic ulcer to septicaemia. That passage, as was my practice in those waters, was to leave with a good light in the late afternoon, make the night passage with one or two doglegs so that in that area of coral reefs and uncertain currents, we would never be within twenty-five miles of the coral and so to the morning where we could approach our objective again with a good light for entering the Pass, but it was not to be. During the night, the barometer fell, the wind changed and increased and in the morning it was blowing a gale. We were but eight miles from our objective. I was beginning to be doubtful whether the unknown Pass would be safe to enter, but I had an escape route; if I turned to starboard, I could weather the coral reefs at the end of the island and reach clear water, but just as I was thinking this, the wind increased again and changed direction; it was now blowing force 9. I certainly dare not risk the Pass and my escape route was closed as it was now to windward; what to do? We were almost embayed but our best chance was now to go about and try to escape round the other end of the island which lay in a curve about twenty-five miles long. We still had to make to windward but we could lay our course, we were literally fighting for our lives. It was a tremendous challenge for 'Bluebird', reefed right down at our limit for sailing and with a tremendous sea, we battled on. Occasionally I would run the engine at slow speed, any increase in speed would have risked shipping dangerous solid water, but if it kept our progress a little steadier and reduced leeway slightly, that would help. I am not going to attempt to describe that passage, those who have had such an experience can imagine it well enough; to those who have not, I doubt if a description could convey the situation, the physical effect, the motion and the anxiety of dealing with an almost unbearable stress which lasted until the late afternoon when with a tremendous feeling of relief, praise for 'Bluebird' and satisfaction, we had cleared the last horn of reef stretching out from the corner of the island and could bear away and soon were in calmer water behind the island where we could heave to with plenty of clear drift to leeward, until the storm blew itself out next day. But then there was no question of going back to windward and beating around the island again, there was only one option, the direct passage to Tahiti. This was in normal pleasant conditions with but one clear, delightful memory. In the light of morning, I saw just visible on the horizon, the tops of the mountains of Tahiti which must then have been twenty-five miles away. We closed in, entered the easy and well marked entrance and secured to the well-known Quai Birhachim, anchors out, solid warps astern to the rocks, landing by dinghy; many other yachts, ranging from those so run down and unlikely that you wondered how they had ever arrived, to larger, well-found and even luxury vessels. The promenade with many people passing to and fro, the palm trees and behind them the busy thoroughfare with much traffic. Barry went straight to hospital with no questions asked and just in time, where with proper and skilled attention, his ankles began to mend. We spent a day padding around, the Harbourmaster, Police, Customs, Immigrations, absorbing the now unaccustomed busy scene and preparing for the delights of Tahiti; this another story but word reached us that the 'goelette' which had been expected at our island in the Tuamotus had been wrecked in the very storm that we had survived. No lives were lost, all managed to get ashore over the reefs on to an uninhabited atoll, where they survived as best they could until they were discovered and rescued some weeks later, and so alas I fear that that poor infant must have perished, but how, sadly, my forebodings and misgivings had been justified.

Wonderful Tahiti, very French, very expensive but a delightful atmosphere. From here I flew home to deal with my affairs leaving the yacht in the charge of my nephew John Hope who had joined and Anne. Alas a cable announced that she was in hospital with a tumour on the brain, believed to be inoperable but thanks to the splendid co-operation of Quantas airlines, she reached home and to her sister but died a few months later. Dear Anne, a splendid woman and I shall always be so thankful that I enabled her to realise one of her life's ambitions to sail across the Pacific.

Above: Copra - The economic lifeblood of the Pacific.
Right: Landing at Pitcairn.

I rejoined 'Bluebird' and an incongruous moment; we were due to leave Tahiti when a friendly neighbour invited us on board to hear a recording of the first moon landing. What a contrast behind our method of progress and this modern miracle.

The outer islands near Tahiti are in many ways superior in the attractions and we then had a long fast passage to Aitutaki, an out island of the Cook Group of Isalnds where we later visited the principal island. Each group of islands could almost be a chapter in itself but we must hurry along our passage to New Zealand, calling at Nuie, Ongia Ngdriki, where we managed to scrub 'Bluebird' with only five foot of tide and saw the wonderful native catamarans scudding across the lagoons at about 15 knots.

Tonga, one of three visits recorded elsewhere, the Lau Group, Fiji, Colin Phip and designing the 95 foot 'Tau' which will appear later. The great Astrolabe reef and the final passage across the notorious Tasmin Sea to New Zealand, without a storm this time and a wonderful moment in my life when like those first Polynesian voyages in their canoes from Hawaii whose first sight of New Zealand, like our own, was a long, low distant cloud named by them with the delightful word, "Aiotaroa", and our first nights anchorage in Opua Bay with a wonderful sunset and the realisation that I had sailed half this our world covering some 15,000 miles from England.

Above: Second 'Bluebird of Thorne' on 28 day Pacific passage.
Right: A welcome addition to our diet.

Chapter Fourteen

My Sailing Life ~ 1970 to Date

Three Simple Questions

When in New Zealand with its charming people, I think you have to attune your mind slightly to their way of thought to get the best value. It is not surprising that their outlook differs slightly as they are a small population in two large islands and at the other side of the world. Auckland boasts a higher proportion of its population concerned with yachts than any other place in the world except perhaps Stockholm in Sweden and as a result you may there encounter absolutely anybody from any section of society and yachts from just anywhere in the world, whilst any tourist visitors to Auckland will most certainly visit the marina. At anytime you may meet a Prime Minister, a Trade Union Secretary or a craftsman.

An example of this was my dear Josephine, a distant relative and life long friend; now elderly, a little frail but bright and active, had the Union Jack hoisted on her flagpole on 'Bluebird's' arrival in New Zealand and when I went to visit her, one of her first greetings was, "And how was the dear Queen when you left her?" Tuning my mind as it were to this, I realised that she envisaged the voyage out from England in the yacht as taking no longer than other methods of transport and because I had a title she imagined that I would be in constant attendance on the Queen and, as it were, having lunch with her once a week. There was a delightful sequel to this: it so happened that the Queen did pay a visit to New Zealand whilst we were there and quite naturally, as I have indicated, she was taken to see the marina. There, noticing our Blue Ensign, she stopped by and had a few words with us so that I was able to go back to my dear Josephine and report that the Queen had indeed flown out from England and come to enquire how we were faring in New Zealand. This was taken as perfectly natural and appropriate, just in fact what she would have expected the 'Dear Queen' to do.

So it was that one day when I happened to be alone in 'Bluebird', pottering about doing odd jobs, I noticed a man pacing up and down and examining 'Bluebird' from all angles with great interest. There was nothing specially remarkable about him. He was good looking, maybe middle-aged, neatly dressed, but it was the whole air of intent that got my attention. So when he passed again I called out to him, "You seem very interested in 'Bluebird', would you like to come aboard?" He accepted with alacrity and when he was in the cockpit I said, "There must be some reason for your intense interest?' His reply was somewhat astounding. "I have travelled up from Invercargill in the South Island because I heard that you were here and I wanted to examine 'Bluebird' and, if possible, have a few words with you". It might be well for those who are not acquainted to say that this would be equivalent to a yachtsman, in say Lisbon, travelling to look at a yacht at Lymington in England. A slight sense of foreboding as I said, "You had better come below". When we were seated in the saloon, I said, "Perhaps you had better tell me the whole story". His reply, as unexpected and unusual as his previous statement, went thus, "I have built a yacht, the hull is almost complete but then a friend of mine came back from a voyage, he had seen your 'Bluebird' in Tahiti, he had seen her plans and he had had a talk to you. He was so impressed and he so impressed me that I have decided to remove the centre keel of my yacht and complete her with twin keels like your 'Bluebird'". I think my heart must have been somewhere in what is called the pit of the stomach as I tried to think of a way out of an impasse. "What is the construction of your yacht?" I asked, thinking and expecting that it would be wooden planking on wooden frames. Had this been the case I could have said that it would be wiser and safer to complete the yacht as designed and intended and that I could not possibly recommend the alteration proposed. But his reply came, "The yacht is of welded steel construction". My instant thought was that the impossible had been removed by one notch. Reeling somewhat mentally, I said, "I suppose you have brought the plans of the yacht?" "Oh no!" He replied, "I did not think that they would be necessary. You see I only want your answer to three simple questions". With real trepidation and with my heart sinking further, "Would the questions relate to the twin keels?" "Yes", he replied. "I had better have the questions", I said. "How large should they be, what shape should they be and where should I put them?"

The dull thud you might have heard would have been my heart coming to rest on the sole of the saloon. Now I was really up against it, this was the crunch. I realised that if I turned him down, which is what I should have properly done, he would not understand, he would have been bitterly offended and he would never forgive me. Then the overriding thought came up in the mind; this is New Zealand, it could only be New Zealand, I have got to 'have a go', and so I got out paper, my drawing instruments and we had a long session; question, sketch, more questions, more sketches, figures, dimensions, until gradually I had built up a picture that he said was his yacht and which made sense to me. It was a nice vessel, about 40 foot overall, a cutter; there was nothing about it I disliked; there was much about it that I did like. I did not ask who was the designer, that would not have been tactful. In New Zealand you do not go to the designer of the yacht you want to build and pay a modest fee for permission to build to that design and a set of plans, oh no! You just fall in love with some design you have seen in some yachting periodical, you enlarge the plans to the best of your ability and even with a distinct lack of ability, just bash away and build it yourself. Not surprisingly results are not always predictable. I think I have related elsewhere one example of this and it has happened to me.

Again attuning my mind to his way of thought I realised that he had envisaged two, large, thick plates of steel from which he would cut the shape of the twin keels. He would then proceed to edge-weld them to the hull, what I could only describe as, 'some bally where, some bally how'. Other factors may have been just trivia to him; complete re-disposition of the ballast was required, an entirely new rudder design was necessary and a drastic alteration to the structure of the yacht to enable the twin keels to be attached and to absorb the entirely different stresses that they would impose. The answer to the question, "how large", was not now difficult and "what shape" was not too difficult but the "where shall I put them", involved not only the vertical angle but also the angle to the centre line and involved the foil form of the keels, symmetrical or asymmetrical and the degree to which they carried ballast and how this also was to be designed. I did my best and after a long session, clutching an untidy roll of papers, he departed with profuse thanks, to start his long journey back to the South Island.

I sat back, my mind in a turmoil and had a large dram of the malt whisky I kept on board for special occasions. I might not have earned this but I needed it badly and I think I deserved it.

As I tried to relax I felt like Gypsy Lee, the fortune teller, with this character in front of me and my crystal ball. What should I see as I gazed into its depths and what would my answer be? "I see you in a yacht, I see you sailing far across the sea", might have been my vision. Or would it have been, "I see you surrounded by water, it grows darker and darker as disaster descends". Eventually I stowed the whole episode away in one of those convenient recesses at the back of the mind where things are out of sight and unnoticed but available for recall whenever required.

About a year later, in England, a long letter arrived. It was from New Zealand and, as is their custom, the name and address were on the reverse. It was the builder of the yacht. I confess a moment of real trepidation, mounting almost to fear, and I had to nerve myself to open that letter and read it. As I did so a warm glow that was both mental and physical spread over me; a feeling I can only describe as analogous to sinking into a lovely hot bath after returning wet, cold and exhausted from a long day's abortive stalking in bad weather in the Highlands of Scotland. It was a long letter but it could easily be paraphrased, "I completed my yacht in accordance with your instructions". The word 'instructions' gave me a nostalgic shudder. "When the yacht was fitted out I went for a trial cruise up the coast with my family. The yacht sails beautifully, she handles perfectly and I am absolutely delighted with her".

God was in His Heaven, I could give thanks, feeling that there must have been some degree of divine intervention to have succeeded against such formidable odds, and so somewhere along the coasts of the lovely South Island of New Zealand, there is a nice twin keel yacht, unusual certainly, as few yachts can have been completed by removing their centre keel and attaching twin keels, but this yacht is unique, absolutely unique, there cannot be another in the whole wide world that was designed by answering 'three simple questions.'

Preparation for a voyage

I think that our hurricane experience indicates the importance of preparing a yacht for a voyage and there are references to the difficulties one may encounter. I could write a chapter on this but it is so governed by the size and type of yacht and other factors and so involved with design and technical requirements that it is best omitted.

Your crew is absolutely vital unless you sail single handed for a variety of reasons. I shall try to condense this vast subject as far as possible and with one or two aphorisms. "If you find a good crew, marry her". There is great truth in this as many of the most magnificent voyages have been achieved by man and wife teams and I must mention lifelong friends and sailing acquaintances,

Peter and Ann Pye and Eric and Susan Hiscock. Sailing is one of the sports in which women can vie with men on equal terms and wonderful feats such as: sailing round the world single handed have been successfully achieved by women.

On my voyages it was not unusual to find a yacht abandoned or laid up because their voyage had come apart at the seams; this was seldom due to the vessel itself, almost always due to a bust up of some sort with skipper and crew. It could be money or it could be something quite stupid; remembering always that sharing in a yacht is one of the greatest tests of personality that life has to offer. I have sailed with more than 100 people, boys, girls, men, women, family and friends, people introduced to you by someone you know well and perhaps the sons of members of the Royal Cruising Club. How difficult it is to summarise all this experience; another aphorism: "do not voyage with anyone with whom you have not successfully spent a month in a small yacht". My preferred crew for an ocean voyage would be four people; myself, aged perhaps sixty, my nephew John, a wonderful back-up aged about forty, and two young men perhaps after university or maybe one woman. There are some I should not ask again, there are some who would not sail with me again, there are none with whom I did not part with on friendly terms; I never had any form of mutiny or desertion. Many young men who came to sea with me for the first time became my sea sons and kept in close contact with me for the whole of their lives. There are similarly five sea daughters headed by Jilly Baty my hurricane girl; if I sent a telegram to her - "bad news, come", she would be with me within 36 hours, take charge of any situation and see me through any of life's hurricanes.

I had my own watch-keeping system based on three hour periods, (I did not use self-steering gear feeling it better for both safety and morale to maintain watches) and so arranged that each night you had a different watch and every third day you were cook/housekeeper without day watches and on a further third day you had an all night in with no night watch. This system was so successful that it had been quite widely adopted by others.

A Circuit of Islands

On 19 May 1971, 'Bluebird' sailed from New Zealand, bound for Nuku'alofa, Tonga. She was in very good order and everything except the echo sounder was working. Behind these simple statements there had been a tale of, 'Blood, toil,

sweat and tears". We sailed out four strong but Ian and Robbie and Jo had not sailed with me before. Jo, a fiery woman, was one quarter Maori, a school teacher with a perhaps exaggerated opinion of her knowledge and importance. Ian and Robbie were both competent and could navigate, The whole passage was in difficult weather, mostly under reduced sail and with much headwind. We had problems. Could we make enough to windward to weather an ugly detached reef off the south west corner of Tonga? If so would it be safe to skate along with reefs under our lee for ten miles and then run up the channel to Nuku'alofa? I set a limit. If in 45 minutes it was not clear that we could weather the reef, then we must run and heave to in the lee of the main island. 'Bluebird' made it. The sea became the problem. We rigged heavy weather boards and took all precautions. Several times Ian, then at the helm, shouted a warning, "Look out! We shall be swept", but each time with a convulsive wriggle, 'Bluebird' rose and we had no heavy water aboard. If this and the channel became too dangerous I could still have run down the far side of the island to heave to in the same place as by the other route. But all went well and by noon we were anchored by the Queen Salote wharf. A very rough anchorage it was but how welcome after that dramatic arrival as the climax to nine days and 1,100 miles sailed. Here in Tonga, we had our friends from two years ago and a wonderful welcome.

Ian flew away on some Honolulu/San Francisco mission. Christian and Robert, delayed by the wedding of Robert's sister, now flew in. Robert had sailed with me from Fiji to New Zealand on the previous voyage and with knowledge from maintaining 'Bluebird', was a tremendous asset, while Christian's experience took over all the cares of catering and civilised living off my shoulders. It was time to review plans. Originally I had been faced with a difficult task in outline planning for this voyage. The main objective was a more leisurely and detailed exploration of Pacific Islands than had been possible when voyaging to New Zealand. I had eventually fixed limits, not east of the Tongas, not north of Samoa, not west of the New Hebrides. There was a new factor, if we delayed a few days in Nuku'alofa, and what could be more pleasant, a Tongan seaman and pilot might be seconded to us for a week in the Haapai Group. Meanwhile we had collected reports and impressions indicating that Samoa, involving 500 miles of sea passages, might not be good enough value to warrant the time and distance. An all hands conference voted, "Cut out Samoa and spend the time on the Tongas".

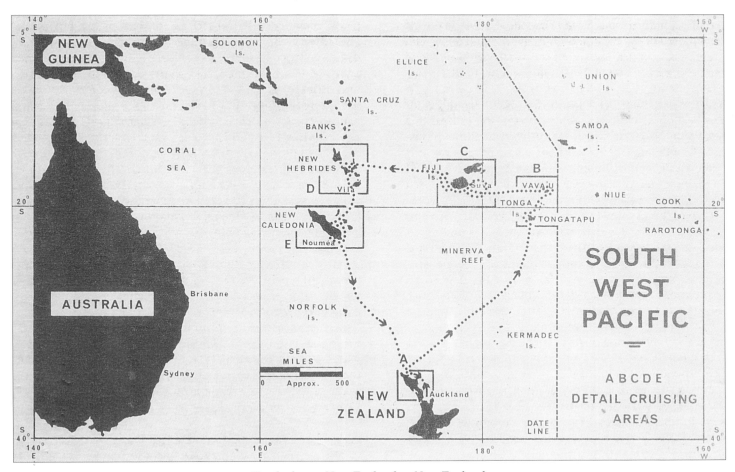

Track chart - New Zealand to New Zealand.

We never regretted this decision. Tolati joined us; a tough grizzled Tongan of sixty-two, he became family friend and adopted us in the most charming manner. His brother was the hero who had saved seventeen lives by building a boat out of a wreck and sailing 800 miles after spending 100 days on Minerva Reef. We had seen the boat in which this epic had been achieved (See book: The Minerva Reef). I have visited Tonga on three occasions in my voyaging. You can now fly there from Fiji and there is a wharf which cruise ships can secure. I should have no difficulty in writing an extensive chapter on the Tongan group of islands but must restrain myself and mention just two or three things to convey I hope the atmosphere. Tonga has never been conquered, it still had a royal family and a constitution not unlike England after the Magna Carta. When Queen Salote, greatly beloved, was in England for the coronation of our Queen, it was I think Noel Coward who said when asked who the little man was at her side, "That's her lunch".

In an interview with the King, I found myself discussing the possibility of buying broken car springs and converting them into agricultural implements for use in Tonga.

A group of yachtsmen from Australia were expelled from the country, the charge being, "A nude bathing party within view from the royal palace on a Sunday morning".

And finally what could be another chapter in itself, the wonderful Talati, a Tongan pilot seconded to us on leave by my friend the harbour master. On one occasion when enclosed in a narrow channel amidst the coral reefs, the wind changed and it became necessary to shift our anchor. "If you get the chain in, I will start the engine" I said. "No engine", was the firm reply from Talati. He then went forward, looked round, carefully dropped over the bow, went down the chain, picked up the anchor and went some 30 yards to lay the anchor. He then came back on board with a big smile to say, "Okay Skips I fix".

We had found that the Tongans in general, both men and women, had great natural dignity combined with almost courtly good manners. This made them less gay than the Polynesians but they had natural charm. When we had to say farewell and he took a passage from Pangai back to Naku'alofa, he embraced me with tears in his eyes and Mrs Skips (as he called Christian) and I were not ashamed to feel similarly affected.

It was quite a shock to return to our own methods of navigation and we nearly made a mess of our next passage to Vavau but emerged unscathed to beat into this quite different but entrancing group of islands with the contrasts of high bluffs, low ground, fiords and extensive reefs. Our swimming, snorkelling and skin diving had much improved. Robbie, the best diver and spear gunner, brought us many fish and with this and a line from 'Bluebird' when sailing, we averaged fish every second day; a very welcome addition to our diet. The villages supplied coconuts, bananas, paw paw, the occasional pineapple, taro and bread fruit. Like most Europeans, our team were not very keen on the starchy and rather tasteless vegetables which formed the basic diet of the population.

After a month, it was time to leave the Tongas. We did so with regret, we had been happy there and felt that our decision to cut out Samoa had been fully justified. As we left Vavau we went through a front and very unpleasant it was. When this had cleared after about eight hours, the weather gradually became more like the south east trades. We decided to break the passage to Suva, the port of entry, by calling at Ongea N'driki in the Lau Group. For this purpose, our pump became strategically unserviceable and our engine filters were logged as requiring a symbolic change. Luckily we were coming from an area free from rhinoceros beetle towards an area already infested rather than the reverse. As there was a dangerous off-lying reef, we hove to a prudent twenty miles off until dawn before proceeding too close. For miles right round the island, we skirted great thundering reefs, the roar of the breakers constantly with us. The great seas cresting up and crashing on the reef were an awesome sight. The colours were fantastic under the bright sun and a spray haze drifted over the lagoon which we finally entered by the Barracuda Pass. We used two anchorages off the deserted island and did an extensive reef crawl on the outer reef at low tide. The whole area was so beautiful that it became a high spot in our memories and our solitude was enhanced rather than spoilt by a visit from the most cheerful and friendly group of Fijians who sailed across from Ongea Leuv in their picturesque takias. These were the primitive dug out canoe with single outrigger and a palm leaf, mat sail, changed end for end when the whole craft reverses direction to put about or gybe. When we sailed, the remainder of the passage to Suva was dull and rather slow, in light winds.

As soon as we had cleared we went across to the Bay of Islands and anchored off the Trade Winds Hotel where we had a wonderful reception by Colin Philp and his family. I was fascinated by Colin's yacht, 'Tau', the 95 foot steel hull was complete. This promised to be the largest twin keel yacht in the world. She was clearly a 'Bluebird' derivative and influenced by my work with Colin on his design two years before. Arthur Paterson joined us and we started out on a circuit of islands to the south and east which might extend to three weeks and cover 600 miles. The first objective was Kandavu, the great system of reefs, lagoons and islands enclosed by the Great Astrolabe Reef. This time we spent five days in this area, penetrating as far south as Kennedy's island. This involved miles of reef dodging with a man at the cross trees. Some channels were intricate and narrow, some had beacons. It was made the more difficult as strong winds and bad weather affected the light and colour by which one must detect coral heads and judge the depths. Anchorages were difficult to find as the sheltered inlets, where the water was dark or cloudy, were apt to be over 12 fathoms or under 6 foot in depth.

I was able to visit an old friend on Ndravuni Island, he laid on a ceremonial Kava party for us: as you progress across the Pacific, customs change as well as the Polynesians and the languages and

Above: An unexplained stonehenge type structure in Tonga.

Right: St Christopher - the only means of contact between Tolati's island and the main islands of the Tongan group.

so as you approach Fiji, you encounter the Kava ceremony. This I found reminded me of the Finnish Sauna in that it was an almost religious ritual. What then is Kava? It is a root of a plant and it is prepared and made into a drink, traditionally by being chewed by the women who spit the resultant juice and saliva into a bowl, some water is added and it is left for a time to mature though I do not think that it ferments. Now to the ceremony: When you visit an island you will be summoned to attend a party given by the chief and including the tribal elders; women are not usually included but serve and wait. A little wooden cup is dipped into the bowl, the chief says a few ritual words and drains the cup. It is then passed round from one to another, no doubt in some precedence but the visitor is given the cup after the chief. There are a few ritual words said by all and this continues until the bowl is empty. And what are the effects? When you stand up afterwards, you are not drunk as from alcohol but you do feel what is best described as a little fuzzy and a little wobbly. Your tongue, mouth and lips have lost all feeling as if they were paralysed. Not unnaturally we were somewhat terrified by the lack of hygiene, not only what virus or infection might result from the spit but also, goodness knows, whether the water itself might not be deadly. There is perhaps some antiseptic element as we never suffered any dire result. As we progressed east of Fiji, this becomes even more important and warned and alerted by our friends in Fiji, we purchased in the market a considerable quantity of Kava root and presented a ritual tribute from this store whenever we were invited to a ceremony.

We made a night passage to Toyota in very threatening weather but we found ourselves standing off and on for two hours in strong winds awaiting the light for entering the pass. In that wind we did not go to the usual anchorage but found a sheltered bay, this was a very happy choice as the coral was marvellous and a party of children welcomed us with song. Arthur had made us a coral viewing kit from a plastic basin and perspex. This was a great success and became known as 'Uncle Arthur's magic dragon box'. Next day a party of women came fishing, they wore little goggles, their normal clothes, a basket of bait for their catch tied round their waists. Their faces were darkened with charcoal to reduce sun glare and they stayed in the water over 5 hours fishing over the reefs, returning cold and exhausted with a very meagre but widely assorted catch. They cooked part of their catch on the beach over a coconut fire and in this we joined before they set off for a five mile walk over the hills to their homes.

Our next passage was again at night to an uninhabited island in another reef system, here we had great success fishing with the spear guns. We were now in the Exploring Isles. We entered a great lagoon by the Tongan Passage used by an invading force in their canoes hundreds of years ago. So we came to Loma Loma, one of the most attractive and friendly villages in our now extensive experience. We explored a gorgeous lagoon completely enclosed and sheltered behind a barrier of tricky shoals and reefs before making a long passage through the reefs to a most attractive series of anchorages in another Bay of Islands. Really bad weather kept us here for three days and for this reason we had to cut out two other islands we had intended to visit. John, my nephew and well-tried crew member, was awaiting us in Suva, to which we returned by a direct passage in very hard weather but we made 150 miles in 24 hours, severely testing the stomachs of the crew. This circuit south and east of Fiji had taken three weeks and had been most enjoyable with many beautiful and interesting anchorages though we had never had good or settled weather. We anchored off the Trade Winds Hotel and relaxed for a few days, completing our programme in and around Suva. The Fijians were gayer and more spontaneous than the Tongans, the women and girls in particular laughing more readily. They were invariably friendly and hospitable, there was never any difficulty in making contact. So often I have been asked the difficult question, "Where in all your voyaging, if you wanted to get away from it all would you choose to live and sail?" The answer is of course subject to so many things, to age, finance and so forth but I have little doubt that a part of my heart would be found in the islands of the south west Pacific, centring perhaps on the Lau Group of Fiji.

John joined and Uncle Arthur departed, bitterly regretting that he had to return. We sailed again, this time bound for Lautoka but visiting Mbengga, Vatulele, several other anchorages and some islands in the Yamanuccas. Vatulele had given us the trickiest pass we had yet tackled. Creeping through in dead smooth water, the surface like glass, we threaded our way within feet of coral heads and with little depth to spare. The crew at the cross trees and on deck were so thrilled by the magic underwater world of coral and fish, sharks and turtles that they forgot to be frightened while the Skipper and John were tense with concentration until we reached unobstructed areas of the lagoon.

A strong fair wind gave us a flying passage into Nandi waters and we caught a fine fish as we went in through the pass. We had now moved into a different weather pattern, drier and less affected by the mountains of Fiji. It was a change for us to see this way of life, we found it unexpectedly attractive and even as passing visitors we were made welcome and given help and many facilities. One of the most idyllic days of the whole cruise was spent at Mana Island, a paradise guarded by a very tricky passage through the coral with right angle turns which 'Bluebird' could only just negotiate. Lautoka is a sugar port with ships taking out 400,000 tons a year. Here we cleared from Fiji waters with no difficulty and with permission to cruise in the Yassawas before leaving for the New Hebrides. We entered this area with high hopes and considerable apprehension as we had heard that it was fabulously attractive but very hazardous as there were no charts, with shallow soundings and unmarked reefs scattered broadcast (Captain Cook had not penetrated further than here). We had managed to obtain land survey maps and friends had marked these with routes and anchorages they had used. We now tackled as a normal procedure the intricacies of coral navigation and pilotage that would terrify the yachtsman unaccustomed to these perils and which might have daunted us at the outset of the voyage. We found that though great care was needed the difficulties were not much greater than those we had already encountered.

Perhaps the most beautiful anchorage was inside Nanuya Levu Island, where we remained 36 hours. Here we had the remarkable experience of a full double rainbow as a rain squall passed in the afternoon, followed an hour later by an inverted rainbow which must have been formed by reflection. This was a moonbow and neither I nor anybody I have met had ever seen one. We found that the more remote islands, far as yet from tourist penetration and which had never seen a yacht before, were delightful to a degree and we were welcomed in these villages with friendly enthusiasm. We made ceremonial gifts of Kava to the island chiefs and sometimes endured the Kava drinking ceremony. Here again the feast and the gifts of shells, though fruits and vegetables were scarce. We speared fish and the spiky crayfish, walked on the dazzling beaches and hunted for shells (in the Pacific voyages, Christian had developed an enthusiasm for shells and under her inspiration we had amassed a really beautiful collection). With now more practised care, we swam and snorkelled in the warm waters under a brilliant sun. Reluctantly we sailed, crossing the last reef in Fiji waters ten miles from the shore; we were on passage for the New Hebrides some 600 miles away.

It started well with light fair winds which we turned to good account by setting the ghoster and the mizzen staysail. Progress was less effective when the wind went aft and we had to set running sails. The weather then deteriorated and as we approached the New Hebrides, an interesting situation developed. The barometer was falling and any serious change is potentially dangerous in the tropics. The sky was solid, the sunset ugly with great black areas and a greenish light between. As night closed in, there was almost continuous lightning in every direction. The wind ranged rapidly from 0, with the yacht barely under command in the swell, to force 8 at the onset of squalls which may hit or miss and usually provide blinding rain. This tropical rain may be at a gasping rate, three times as heavy as England ever knows. Thank goodness the yacht was reefed down and well secured and the squall situation could be dealt with by handing or setting the small genoa and the mizzen, leaving her under reefed mainsail only at the height of the squalls in which the wind may change direction violently with the yacht running off temporarily in any direction. Thank goodness sights during the day had given a reliable fix. Luckily there were no coral reefs immediately adjacent. A deep rumbling noise may have been thunder or the eruption of an active volcano about thirty miles away. No land had been sighted before dark and it is a matter of judgement under these conditions whether to close, if possible, when twenty miles off by dead reckoning from the last fix, as unknown currents and the many changes of course may have made the position doubtful by up to seven miles. We then saw the volcano with the glow from the spouts of molten rock lava flow and the clouds of steam and smoke plainly visible. (It's habits were unknown and I thought an appropriate notation in the log might be, "Beware, showers of molten rock"). Imagine us anchored one evening off a large island with an active volcano, of which we had heard missionaries may have made contact with natives on the shore but the island is unexplored and unknown. The crew wanted to go walking ashore but I was reluctant and discouraged them by singing, "You may go awandering along some mountain track, but if you do, take care, you might well not come back".

We have been told, but the sailing directions do not confirm, that it is here possible to clear into the New Hebrides. This is our first experience of the Condominium, known quite affectionately as the Pandemonium, where British and French flags fly side by side in jealously guarded equal size and elevation. Happily for us the British are mainly dealt with by the British and one friendly

Left: The lovely sailing catamarans.

Below: Colin Philp's 'Tau' - at 95 feet, the largest twin keel yacht in the world, she had sailed at 15 knots.

British Police Official, combining in his duties all roles except Customs, clears us in ten minutes in one office. An example that might well be learned in much larger and more sophisticated ports. Santo offered us many surprises. The anchorage and the dinghy landing were appalling. We had strong winds. We here encountered Pidgin English, very necessary as there were nine native languages in an island 80 miles by 40 miles. French is also an advantage and there used to be Spanish influence due perhaps to the discovery of the island of Quiroz. We had moved into racial groups more akin to Papua and New Guinea and in remote areas tribal customs remain with bones in the nose, decorations of dog's teeth necklaces, pig's tusks and the great mambas have a genital area covering which is spectacular. No doubt a useful protection when jungle bashing with no clothes, but perhaps also to frighten the enemy or develop the 'bigger boy gets better girl' approach. In the island of Pentecost there is the fantastic diving to earth from high towers with vines on the ankles, this has been well documented and is becoming commercialised. We could not stay for a big display to be held on 4 September. The cost of living was about two and a half times that in England and this hurt badly as it was the middle of the US dollar crisis. The one bank would change nothing except small limits daily in Australian travellers cheques; only John had a few of these. We were brought beef, a great treat. We visited a Japanese fishing enterprise from which sixty vessels operate. 20,000 tons a year of frozen fish, mainly tuna, are sent away to Japan and the hard working efficiency of this station was most impressive. We all felt that there was no chance whatever of anything we had seen in the islands, including New Zealand, competing against this operation.

The anchorage became untenable and we departed thankfully for the well protected Berrie Bay. This anchorage was pleasant but for three days, hard wind and squalls, force 6-8, dead on the nose for our course to Malekula did not encourage us to start another passage. There was good walking ashore through coconut plantations which were well tended in contrast to the haphazard operations more usual in Fiji. Cattle grazed the grass below the palms and here we found the remarkable coconut-eating crabs and, with the experience of the difficulty in penetrating the coconut husk, we could appreciate the enormous power required by these crabs in opening the husk and feeding on the meat. The coconut is life; we counted twenty-seven uses of the coconut palm and its products and there may well be many others which we did not know. To many, the islands' copra is the only cash crop with which they can pay for any

Top: Coral reef spectacular.

Above: And there were shells.

requirement from outside. The price of copra had been $100 a ton but we learned that it had crashed to $60 a ton; this would be a disaster affecting the whole way of life directly or indirectly of every man, woman and child in the south Pacific.

Another yacht came in; Robin and Ian Singleton had been living in and working from their little self-built vessel for four and half years, mainly in New Guinea and they were a mine of information on native customs and the islands generally. One of their exhibits was a necklace of human teeth, they assured us that they had not removed these from the previous owners but apparently they were the much valued examples of success in tribal wars. They also had an almost complete command of Pidgin English and many examples of this were quite delightful. I remember them one evening reciting in Pidgin, the story of 'Little Red Riding Hood' as told by the missionaries to the native children. "And Lila Red Pala had no fright more. That dog, that big dog, that big long dog, that big long, big-toothed dog, that big, long, big-toothed bad dog, he done die finished". On our last evening, we asked the plantation manager if he could get us some meat. His answer was unexpected. Seizing a rifle, he mounted a tractor and cruising the plantation, selected a nice young beast which was shot and cleaned. An hour later there was a macabre scene on 'Bluebird's' after deck. In the light of two torches and dripping with blood, Robbie and the Skipper skinned and butchered the whole back-end half of a cow, still warm and twitching. There were eight mouths to feed and on a combined cooking and eating for three meals, we did our best to see nothing was wasted. It was at this point that we celebrated something I considered unique; my seventieth birthday, in command of my own yacht which I had designed, in the remote islands in the South Pacific.

The passage to Port Stanley in Malekula was a hard beat with reefed mainsail. Here there was another surprise; the headquarters of the British District Agent was so smart and well set up that it gave the effect of 'The sun never sets on Government House'. A little thatched guest house bore a sign, "A home from home, bed and breakfast, £1.7s.6p"; Prince Philip had spent the night there on a visit to the islands. Another long head wind day brought us to Port Sandwich, a most attractive anchorage abounding in fish. From here we walked out to a large Roman Catholic Mission which was instructive and we managed to get some bread, a rare treat.

Again we had a head wind, force 6, to Epi Island and a rather open anchorage in a sandy bay. Next day there was less wind and we had a smashing sail with full mainsail and the big genoa still on the wind but on course and making 7 knots for seven hours to a spectacular entrance through an island gap. Tricky sailing and a beat brought us to anchorage in Port Savannah. We caught a beautiful 30lb fish in the last fifteen minutes. The sail to Vila was interesting and took longer than we had expected. Vila had been an objective for quite a long time. We found it attractive with a predominantly French atmosphere. There were several yachts and we felt that we had returned to civilisation. John left us here to fly back to Australia. He left a gap and we missed him. The New Hebrides deserve and demand more time but in our brief experience, in the weather prevailing, we found them less attractive than the Tongas and the Fujis. The north had also been hotter and more humid. After a pleasant 3 days, we left with regret bound for the Loyalty Islands and New Caledonia. The passage did not develop as intended, a calm start tempted us to make for Tana, another island with an active volcano but by midnight when half way there we were enveloped in a hideous set of heavy squalls and head winds to force 8. Next morning a rather battered crew realised that Sandal Bay on Lifu Island in the Loyalty Group was now the best objective but could not be made before dark. There was no virtue in speed so we sailed for seventeen hours still on the wind in big seas and strong winds, making 3 knots under staysail and mizzen only. This was the most comfortable answer to the problem, comfort of course being a relative term only. The landfall came up at dawn as intended but it was afternoon before we anchored in complete shelter at the head of the great Sandal Bay.

Life is full of contrasts at sea and an evening start to make Tyo Pass at dawn was frustrated by too little wind from too far aft. It was midday before we entered but the murk and overcast skies were so threatening that we were quite lucky to identify our marks and enter the reef system before frightful thunderstorms swept down. We now had three days sailing right round the south end of New Caledonia and inside the reef system for 100 miles. Tides were strong, at one point we were almost stationary in a tide running up to 4 knots against us. It had been quite a struggle when we made Noumea at last after two night anchorages and securing at the Yacht Club found many friends and the largest collection of yachts since we had left New Zealand. The local yachts were predominantly high power speed boats with inboard-outboard engines, rather suggesting that the hierarchy in the great nickel enterprise ran them as status symbols, the higher echelon having the fastest boats with the largest engines. The prices here were terrifying and, with our diminishing funds towards the end of the cruise, it was a case of essential supplies only. The yacht club amenities were, in contrast to the wild and deserted areas we had traversed and the parties with our fellow yachtsmen, appreciated as a change; so were frequent fresh water showers on the quayside. The aquarium was magnificent; there was truly an amazing variety of fish and it was here that we reluctantly said goodbye to the wonders of the coral seas.

We spent two days sailing to the Isle of Pines and coming on deck in the morning at the first anchorage the scene was so like the western islands of Scotland that it made one gasp. The whole of the New Caledonian coast had offered magnificent scenery but this particular anchorage could have been in our own 'Caledonia', stern and wild. There was even a light which simulated heather on the hills, the air was cool and crisp and walking ashore we found bracken in the undergrowth. In contrast we picked a welcome basketful of lemons. Next day it was a touch and go decision whether to sail or remain. With forty-five miles to go through reefs, scattered as if shaken at random through a pepper pot and a rising wind, already force 6, we could have met trouble particularly had the visibility deteriorated. This was an occasion for very short sail with help from the engine and, using this without shame, we made fast and successful passage to the Isle of Pines. We hoped to have two days swimming, snorkelling, sunshine and rest in this highly recommended resort before tackling our last passage. Alas, the wind screamed past, never less than force 6 and it was cool, a sweater was welcome by day and a rug at night. The sea temperature was 72°F which felt chilly to us after the warmer seas further north. There was a sense of sterner things to come and a reluctance to tackle the stormy Tasman although all hands were ready to return to New Zealand. We could not afford to dine ashore at the holiday hotel but a surprise awaited us ashore. A charming English family picked us up and invited the five of us to a delightful dinner and an evening of entertaining discussion which relaxed us and took our minds off ship's affairs and the coming passage. This passage across the Tasman Sea to New Zealand would be more than 1,000 miles and I knew from Cruising Club records and friends who had circumnavigated the earth that it had been recorded as providing the worst weather encountered in their voyages. I'd also heard it said you will not go a month in the Tasman without both gale and storm.

On Thursday 16 September at 10.00, we took our departure from Ile Inferno with an offing from the reefs surrounding the Isle of Pines. It was a tough start and we were well reefed down. The desired course was south east and the wind was force 5-6. The wind was east to east north east with a horrible sea. Draw a veil over a period of endurance for two and a half days. It was cold, it was rough, the sky was menacing but 'Bluebird' had made 121 miles in the first 24 hours and 131 on the second. We felt that this was no mean feat for ship and crew in these conditions. On the morning of the third day the wind fell away rapidly, an hour's calm and then the wind came in and settled about west south west. It soon reached force 5 and we had another 113 on the log. The wind rose steadily, force 6, force 7, force 8, in squalls. Heavy rain and an even more ominous sky led me to an instinctive feeling that there was worse to come. We had picked up New Zealand radio but the static was so bad that we could only catch odd words. It had not increased our comfort to hear of a storm 990 millibars, deepening and extending between us and the North Cape with winds of 55 knots. We set about preparing for a dirty night, the heavy weather boards went up round the deckhouse and in the companionway, the deck was cleared and everything double lashed and secured above and below. Sail was reduced until only the close sheeted staysail remained but at last we could run on course making an average of 4 knots. The man on watch wore a harness as the sea was enormous; below we were more comfortable than we had been when thrashing to windward. We had warps ready to stream but this was unnecessary. The next day, four days out with another 106 on the log, wind and sea were declining. More sail was made, the wind worked round to south, south east and baffling conditions obtained so that the fifth day our plot only gave eighty-five miles made good.

We had managed a satisfactory fix by sun sights every day though these had been difficult to take with only the odd glimpse of the sun through cloud and great seas obscuring the horizon. On the sixth day the winds were westerly, we were still on course and we had made another 130 on the log. In the early hours, we even had some pleasant sailing with the full mainsail and large genoa but this only lasted for four or five hours before we were again reefed down and driving the ship hard with winds south west up to force 7 or more in the squalls so that we had our best day's run of 164 miles. These were the conditions under which we first sighted New Zealand just after dawn on the seventh day.

Top: The rescue boat from Minerva Reef
Above: Christian, O.A.P. Seaman first class, Tasman tested.

We had changed ship's time, advancing our clocks one hour and at 05.30, Cape Brett, our intended landfall, was sighted right on the bow. There was general excitement and joy, we were back to Aotearoa, the land of the long white cloud. We were tempted to make the shelter of the attractive Bay of Islands close at hand but carried on through a difficult day with sail constantly up and down as the squalls were often force 6 but in periods of sunshine in between, we might only have force 3. The night approach to Auckland ended with the wind south west force 2 and some engine to maintain speed with sail until we anchored in Auckland harbour at 04.30. It was bitterly cold with a temperature of 42°F and we had a hail storm. After the tropics it had been necessary to have to struggle with layers of heavy duffle and oilskins to go on watch. To add to our discomfort on this passage, everything was damp; not from the sea or rain but from the humidity of the driving winds. It had been a testing passage and we felt a special tribute was due to Christian, our 'OAP' (old age pensioner as she called herself) for whom it had been her longest and roughest passage. Christian was really proud and pleased when the young crew presented her, on arrival at Auckland, with a carefully inscribed certificate on genuine parchment, "OAP seaman first class, Tasman tested". We had sailed 975 miles in seven days, 17$\frac{1}{2}$ hours.

A check with the met office in Auckland was interesting. A plot of the storm curves and movement against our daily positions showed that we had been very lucky just missing the worst of two storms. The one referred to earlier had developed to a barometer low of 980 millibars and had swept over the North Island just south of Auckland. Winds had reached 75 knots and 100 had been reported in the notorious Cook Straight.

I was reluctant to end the voyage and return to the cares of another life but Christian and I both felt it was time to return home as we had been away from England for nine months. The voyage had been a tremendous success, an experience we shall never forget or regret; beyond this I was thankful that we had returned with 'Bluebird' intact and without incident. In 5,500 miles of sailing, visiting fifty islands, making a hundred anchorages and through countless reefs, perhaps the most testing voyage of my career in navigation and pilotage, we hit nothing we had intended to miss and had missed nothing we had intended to hit. All the crew members had enjoyed it and I was grateful to them. We had suffered no serious ill health or accidents and Robert, another of my 'sea sons', had become fully competent in celestial navigation. 'Bluebird' as ever had met every challenge with credit. The R.C.C. Challenge Cup was awarded for this voyage.

At three score years and ten, I had a prolonged discussion with Christian about our future including of course my sailing life. Christian with her usual devastating logic came up with this, "We can never do a more enjoyable voyage, so far you have been able to do everything yourself and you have a wonderful record. The day will come when you depend on others and you will not enjoy it so much and you may fail. Finally young men will not want to come with you". I remember this hurt like hell, it was so true and so penetrating and it was the deciding factor in the decision to sell 'Bluebird'. I sold her as I had sold the first 'Bluebird of Thorne' without any difficulty, to Dr Howard Hilton of Washington U.S.A. He and his brother sailed her from New Zealand to California; his report reading, "What we did not know about voyaging, 'Bluebird' taught us as we crossed the Pacific". I had gained another friend. I was not to know how my sailing life would continue but happily I was to sail at least 15,000 miles in the next twenty years.

A Catalyst
In 1976 when I was nudging 75 years of age I thought that whether I realised it or not I was missing 'Bluebird' and sailing voyages, so when my long-standing friend in America, Tom Watson, came up with a projected Pacific voyage, I was thrilled. I suspect that it was a rather critical moment in his life also - after a heart attack, caused I think by the high way in which he stressed himself but luckily not serious and from which he made a good recovery. It had triggered two changes in his life; he had relinquished his position in control of IBM and after a trial and finding he liked it, he had turned from ocean racing to cruising in a sailing life which I think was as important to him as it was to me. Typically he was making thorough preparation for the projected voyage, accumulating and reading a library of information on the area, studying the weather patterns, the winds and the storms. He remembered that I had done a similar voyage in 'Bluebird' so he contacted me and flew to England to stay for a few days. Apparently he was sufficiently impressed with the briefing I had prepared for him to invite me to go as a crew member on the voyage. Not surprisingly Christian was not so thrilled with this idea but consented when Tom said that he needed me as Pacific advisor and coral pilot. I received from Tom Watson a list of the books that one might read in advance and a splendid sea bag with my name emblazoned upon it. This was a hint on the kind of baggage one would be allowed and what amounted to an order not to bring hard luggage. Imagine the stowage problem in a yacht if eight people turned up with an assortment of hard suitcases!

I think this is the point at which one must say something about the yacht. Palawan, an island in the Pacific, impressed Tom when he was a pilot with the American Air Force in the Second World War and as a result all his yachts had borne the name 'Palawan'. There had been three ocean-racing yachts which he had skippered in many of the important ocean races of the world and with considerable success but this was the fourth 'Palawan', a cruising yawl of 40 tons displacement, 68 feet overall, 18 foot beam, 7 foot draught without her centreplate, and designed by Sparkman and Stephens. Tom, knowing that I had successfully designed and produced my own yachts for cruising, sent me the full design and specification of the new 'Palawan' and asked for my comments. Without attempting to assess the lines but with a feeling that I should have deleted some of the elaborate high technology, modern electronic and mechanical equipment, I came up with one suggestion: a Hundested adjustable pitch and feathering propeller. Rather to my surprise this suggestion was adopted 'nem con' and I think added perhaps one knot to the yacht's average speed under sail by eliminating the bulk of the drag from the sizeable propeller that serviced a General Motors 180 h.p. diesel engine. It also improved the efficiency of propulsion under a wide range of conditions ranging from motor sailing in a calm sea to bashing into a strong head wind and sea under power alone. The accommodation for the yacht had been worked out by Tom and Paul Walther, Tom's personal skipper, in a barn with full scale mock-ups.

So the great day came at last. I flew out and joined 'Palawan' at Balboa at the western end of the Panama Canal. 'Palawan' had been brought down from Maine by Paul, his wife Barbara, a married couple who were friends of Tom, and Dave Flannigan a yacht professional from Camden, Maine. The married couple had departed and so I was welcomed by Paul and his wife as Tom and the remaining crew had not yet arrived. This was I think a rather happy circumstance as I could settle in, learn my way about the yacht and make my number with Paul. I found later that he was noted for making instant decisions about people and fortunately we both had an instantly favourable rapport which was to stand me in very good stead throughout the voyage. There was another happy circumstance; by pure chance my second 'Bluebird of Thorne' was on passage from the Panama Canal from west to east in the course of a voyage from Seattle on the west coast of America, to Annapolis on the east coast and I had a happy day aboard exchanging news with my friend the present owner, Dr Howard Hilton. The next day Tom flew in with the rest of the crew and there was also a vast store of high-grade meat and the like for the deep freeze. So to the crew: I learned from Paul what this was to be and I could not help some reactions. One was, how should I react to being a crew member in a large yacht with no less than three others who could take command, when I was so accustomed to being sole skipper in charge of my own yacht? How should I react to the men, all American, some fifteen years younger than I and, even more so perhaps, to the three girls some fifty years younger? Finally what would this large crew of Americans make of what must inevitably be a somewhat 'odd bod', a single, elderly Brit? As soon as all was settled and the gear dealt with, we sailed and the great voyage started.

The first passages, to Cocos Island and then on to the Galapagos, were as expected; hot, rather calm and with a good deal of engine. Cocos, a reputed treasure island, was interesting but not as out-of-this-world as we had expected as we there encountered two interesting yachts and an expedition headed by the son of the well-known mariner, Jacques Cousteau. In the Galapagos, Ecuador had clamped down on visits from yachts; apparently there had been troubles of some sort but Tom had overcome this difficulty by enlisting the help of the Darwin Institute and secured his 'laisser passer' by agreeing to take two scientists of the Institute on a tour of the islands. This made ten on board. It was a pretty tight squeeze but we all agreed not only were they very nice people but one was an expert in the marine and sub-marine life and the other an expert on fauna and we learned much that we should never have achieved on our own. With them we did some 500 miles and visited many islands. The final call was to Post Office Bay where in a barrel the whalers of the last century used to deposit letters home when outward bound to be collected by east bound whalers returning to Boston on the north west coast of America. There was a batten with 'Bluebird's' name carved upon it with records of many other yachts and for the second time I posted letters in this unlikely spot to be delivered without fail by east going yachts.

We now started one of the great Pacific passages - from the Galapagos to Easter Island but on the first day we had some bother - the gearbox failed. Skilled work by Paul and Dave found two tubes in the gearbox oil cooler which had leaked allowing salt water to penetrate the gearbox. This was thoroughly washed out with changes of oil and all seemed well but there were to be repercussions. Now to what I consider the greatest sail of a lifetime. When we had picked up the south east trades, we went swinging away over the ocean seas with the wind just aft of the beam, a full sail and for a week we achieved well over 200 miles a day, nudging 1500 sea miles in a week - a magnificent experience in a magnificent yacht with the day and night passages an equal delight. Tom got a little uptight about the navigation, trying to find a speck in the ocean at the end of some 2500 miles, but this was achieved without any drama.

In contrast to the magnificent sailing experience, it is time to say something about the crew. Tom himself was a strong and complex character. Perhaps his strongest characteristic being a constant attempt to challenge himself in a wide field of endeavour. He still flew his own converted Air Force jet, reaching speeds of 600 m.p.h., and I had flown with him in this. Jimmy Madden was sixty years plus, an old friend of Tom's who had skippered his own ocean-racing yachts. Now a little frail with a heart condition, he was one of the nicest men you could ever meet. He never put a foot wrong, he would never say an unkind word; a charming companion who drove himself almost too hard as he was normally the navigator. Jimmy Madden's daughter Anne was very much in the same mould but I shall have more to say about her as I came to know her much better later in the voyage. Ellie Wright was in her early twenties and had sailed with Tom before. She had a very good brain, intelligence and intellect. Her task was to write a series of articles for a magazine back in America. She had some sea experience and Tom had a very high regard for her. Finally Carter Christenson; about nineteen years of age, of outstanding beauty, quite a strong character but rather scatty and resisted direction. I found her unpredictable and could make no assessment of what her future might be. Her sea experience was nil and she had been invited by Tom's daughter Helen who would join later. The girls were assigned by Tom to night watches with me - I think he considered that

I was the best person to handle this situation, interest them and instruct them so that they could better play a useful part in the running of the yacht.

So to Easter Island; I think it is rated as the island which is at the greatest distance from any other land in any direction. Its civilisation and past is still something of a mystery. Water and fuel presented some difficulties here which were overcome. At our anchorage there was some swell and 'Palawan' rolled a good deal. Paul and Dave invented and constructed what was known as the 'flip flop', a contraption which considerably reduced the roll. In came a modern jet bearing Tom's wife Olive, his sister Helen and his daughter Helen. They all stayed at a hotel, Tom moved in with them and we all spent a happy week exploring Easter Island. Sadly and unexpectedly Jimmy received news that his brother was dying in New York, so he took Olive Watson's return ticket and she joined 'Palawan'. Tom's daughter Helen, whose agreement to come on this cruise had given him great delight, also joined. What effects did these changes have with a total now of nine including five women? 'Palawan's' accommodation was somewhat stretched and as a result there were changes. So far I had shared the after cabin with Tom. If any ocean voyage in a yacht is a test of personality perhaps the ultimate is to share a cabin for a month and how happy that we both emerged from that test with credit and mutual pleasure. There was only one answer for me - I moved forward and shared a small two berth upper and lower cabin with Anne Madden. This could have been another personality test but she was calm, reserved and capable, warm-hearted, sweet tempered - very much a reflection of her father. Here again it gives me delight to say that I think our six weeks or so together, with an age difference of fifty-six years, was a complete success. Tom's daughter Helen: tall, very slim, good looking, affecting way-out provocative clothing, she was also a somewhat complex character. I found myself forming the opinion that she had the experience of life of a woman of twenty-seven while her mental age was more like seventeen. A rather hazardous combination you may say and making it just as difficult, but in a different way, to predict her future as in the case of her friend Carter Christenson.

So after all these changes we sailed again, a good sail on quite a long passage to Pitcairn, the 'Mutiny of the Bounty' island. At Pitcairn we encountered another aspect of Pacific voyaging. As in many other islands, there is no safe anchorage and a yacht visiting the island may have difficulty when the crew must split, one party going ashore while the other party on the yacht standing to and fro for any odd anchor. There is a potential danger here if the party on the yacht is not strong enough to handle her in bad weather and there could be dire consequences. In 'Palawan' there was no such difficulty and we could go ashore in batches in a sturdy surf boat whilst at the last moment, turning to port round a rock to the only rather precarious landing. We had a delightful welcome and after a ride on the back of a Japanese motorcycle over a rough track up to the village, we were taken individually into different homes and so had the experience of seeing exactly what life was like. The island is the eye of New Zealand and the young tend to drift off there but the present inhabitants are full of charm and earn some ready money by receiving tourists from ships and by selling artefacts and carvings while the agriculture and natural produce of the island suffices for modest living.

Away again and another longish passage to a group of French islands where we entered a vast lagoon and made our way, a somewhat tricky passage with broken indication marks, to a calm and sheltered anchorage off Mangareva; our first for many weeks. I was reminded of the Marquesas, another group of French islands and here also one had the impression of a once vigorous and splendid people reduced to quite small numbers of rather dispirited inhabitants. In this case apparently the major damage had been done by a half mad missionary but even now they had more modern troubles. The vast lagoon on which they depended for their living had become contaminated and the fish could not be eaten. This was a case of 'non-proven', but inevitably it was linked to the atomic experiments which the French had carried out on the island of Mururoa Atol. The main thing I remember about this island was that Paul and I took off one day and explored the island, walking, climbing, scrub-bashing and even swimming around headlands, returning exhausted at dusk but with a feeling of satisfaction. I think we both got something out of our systems with this epic venture.

So to the Tuamotus, to me one of the most fascinating group of islands in the Pacific with tremendous memories of my own and new experiences to come with this voyage. We could not stop at many islands and it was quite a task for Tom and I to decide which we should visit and which we should omit. Our choice resulted in one fairly sophisticated island and one virtually uninhabited island, where my coral pilotage was perhaps most

Right: 'Happy holidays with Phil and Plat Allen in their 43ft cutter 'Talulah' in both the Mediterranean and the Caribbean.

Below: 'Palawan' near Tahiti.

useful. Nevertheless I was learning still - this was the first time I had sailed with radar and as in 'Bluebird', I had made a rule never to be nearer than ten miles off a coral reef at night. I found though that with 'Palawan's' radar, I could see surf breaking on a reef two or three miles away so that one could make an approach to one's objective and enter the pass in the light made at dawn. At the uninhabited island, visited only occasionally by parties gathering coconuts to make Copra, Carter Christenson produced a simple play and we spent an unusual day rehearsing and acting our parts. I was the bold bad raiding chief who came in and captured Carter, a native princess. Tom said that the video of this visit was not nearly as funny afterwards as it was at the time, when it gave us a carefree and happy day.

Back to the crew relations: as this second part of the voyage, with different crew, developed, I felt that Tom was getting far too uptight and worried about the changing friendships of the various crew members. I thought that everything was going as well as could be expected but he was at times quite worried, fearing perhaps that he might be accused of having favourites and could they be right. In retrospect it has occurred to me that with my rather detached point of view I may not have known half of what was going on between the others.

So at last we headed for Tahiti, a significant changing point in the voyage. There we anchored at the famous quay in the company of so many other yachts; anchors out ahead, mooring ropes astern to the rocks and landing by dinghy. Some yachts in splendid order, some run down, some with crew troubles, some at the end of their voyage with every shade of nation and numerous contacts, particularly for the girls. I of course knew the island but it was a great pleasure to go round again. I'd had many experiences but for me this was the end of the voyage as I, with Tom and Tom's sister, flew back to New York from whence I came home. After our departure, with Paul in command, there was a delightful tour of the Society Islands. Tom rejoined for a cruise to Fiji and then flew home. From Fiji to Maine, some 12,000 miles, Paul and Dave skippered with a crew of Tom's friends. The entire cruise had finally totalled some 25,000 miles in about fifteen months - what an achievement! Tom Watson was later awarded the Premier Cruising Award of the Cruising Club of America for a whole array of cruising voyages and it would be quite apparent from this account what an important chapter in my sailing life all this had been at a particularly significant time. How had my anticipation worked out? I had enjoyed every moment, I had never lost a day

but what of the reactions? I can quote I think from Tom Watson's excellent book, "Log Book for Helen", opinions both complimentary and critical. Tom recorded that he never regretted inviting me to join 'Palawan'. He considered me a great seaman and my nautical advice was always sound. After nine weeks and 9,000 miles I left the ship with the admiration and respect of all the crew but there had been times where Tom found that I tended to double guess him. Yes I did tend to imagine I was the Skipper at times, yes I did tend to compare this voyage with mine so I had earned the reaction, "This is 'Palawan' not 'Bluebird'. I did tend to reminisce too much and I was a disaster in the galley which Christian had warned Tom about so I was excused galley duties but they said this was compensated for by my willingness to tackle anything else in the yacht at any time. I wasn't a success at the games they played like charades to keep the younger members of the crew amused in the long tropical evenings but a firm friendship with Tom had ripened. What in all had my part been? My role as Pacific adviser and coral pilot had been full and I forget now whether it was in some notes I wrote for the Royal Cruising Club or Tom who brought up the word 'catalyst' but it was agreed by him as he wrote in his book, that I was a catalyst - a constant unchanging friend who was available at all times to every member of the crew being independent of any and every reaction or interaction between the other members of the crew.

In the later years following the Pacific cruise, Christian and I had several happy voyages with our friends Phil and Plat Allen in their yacht 'Talulah', sometimes in the Mediterranean, sometimes in the Caribbean.

The World of Twin Keel Bluebirds
Everybody knows the oft quoted aphorism, "lies, dam lies and statistics", but I find equally and perhaps more useful, well informed guesstimates are, if not generally accepted, a useful way of summing up a situation. So when I think back over 70 years or more and I ponder on the record of the 'Bluebirds', I find it so astounding that it is worth recording in its own right.

The first 'Bluebird', launched in 1924, is still going strong and over 70 years old. She has had 8 owners, 4 rigs, 4 decks, 4 engines, 4 dinghies and lost a rudder in an argument with a barge. She may have done some 30,000 miles and has had one stranding on the Scharmhorn Rif where she was pulled off by a fishing boat. There was a period when owner Commander Gandy, when yachts with a 24 foot water line were admitted for junior ocean racing, put a false cone in the stern to achieve 24 feet and did some ocean racing with her. In his words, "No triumphs, no disgraces and a lot of fun". She is now owned by Fons Bleyendaal who is devoted to her, extremely proud of her and with Jan, an equally enthusiastic friend, has done a marvellous job of restoration and maintenance without which she would not be in action today. In her 68th year she cruised from Holland to Falmouth and back and I have a photograph of her sailing off the White Cliffs of Dover. In 1994, I had an invitation to sail in her on her 70th birthday. I was 93 years of age but looked forward to the day. I admit that I take great pride in the fact that something I created with my own hands 70 years ago was so good that it has not only survived but also deserves a page in the log of yacht design history. I think you will agree, there it stands and I am proud of it.

We now come to the second 'Bluebird', the first 'Bluebird of Thorne' built in 1939. She is still going strong after 56 years and she has had 3 owners and is now in the Channel Islands, in good order and has had a new engine and some internal alterations. She may well have done 50,000 miles. and is now owned by Michael Allo and based in Jersey.

The third 'Bluebird', the second 'Bluebird of Thorne' launched in 1963, is now in Seattle and is still going strong. She had one stranding on the Californian coast and was picked off the beach by a mobile crane. None of the yachts have had accidents; the only personal accident was when I broke my back in the Irish Sea. There have been no paid crews of course, no pilots except my story of Taulati and Tonga and no rescues by lifeboat. If one now adds, 'Curlew of Walney' - a 'Bluebird' in all but name, which Ken Flather launched in 1955 and is still in action, she has had three owners and she may well have done 40,000 miles. And so we come to what I find astounding; the three 'Bluebirds' total over 150 years and have probably covered more than 150,000 miles and I myself have probably sailed a similar distance.

In the 1950's with the explosion in yachting and numbers of yachts, the designs attributable to my 'Bluebird' multiplied extensively. At a boat show at Olympia you might find forty examples; I didn't approve a lot of them and I still divided them into yachts with bilge keels and twin keel yachts. I was told at one point that 45% of the market in small cruising yachts was now of this type and a yacht users information poll produced a majority in favour of this type of yacht. I saw in the future with the opening up of Russia the possibility of a greater, round European voyage from the Black Sea to the Baltic or Murmansk. This has now been done by an Englishman and justifies my conception which I translated into a design called 'Duo', worked up with John Lewis and published in the Yachting Monthly, but this yacht has not so far as I know been built. I have always kept my work purely amateur and have had great rewards from the interest and pleasure which has resulted. My later designs have cruised the world and I read a paper on the design of twin keel yachts to the Royal Institution of Naval Architects in 1967. In the bibliography, there are numerous references to my work.

You would not expect professional designers to rush into print or go about saying what they thought of a new idea like twin keel yachts. One exception, Robert Clark who was really coming from amateur to professional, did produce an interesting design called 'Buttercup'. She was so clearly 'Bluebird' designed. She later made a successful crossing of the Atlantic.

Jack Giles, a foremost engineering yacht designer whom I came to know quite well, told me after many years, that he had done some model experiments on twin keel yachts but he did not tell me what his findings or conclusions were. He later designed a twin keel yacht for the Westerley Company which was well received and successful. The Westerley Company was started by one, Fred Rayner, and while I couldn't possibly claim to have had anything to do with the launch of this successful company, it may be true that if Fred Rayner had not happened to meet up with me and 'Bluebird' at Beaumaris, where he was quite fascinated and had extensive discussions on the design, he might not have started the Westerley Company and I well remember his successful twin keel design 'Centaur', which was one of their early models. He did tell me that he had in fact a dilemma. Westerley were marketing centre keel yachts and these included their fastest and more sporty, racing types. Whilst the twin keel yachts were intended to be for cruising and rather more sedate, Jack Giles found, however, that in some conditions his twin keel design was beating their more sporting versions.

Jack Giles designed one other twin keel yacht, this because he was heavily leaned upon by a friend who wanted to try some experiments. As I remember it the yacht had experiments with rig, hull and keels which contain complicated plates intended to maintain the same centre of lateral pressure whether they were down or half up. Alas as others before him have found, it is a

Above: John Lewis with 'Logic'

Above: 1924-1994, the same yacht, the same man, just seventy years between.

mistake to try too many experiments at once and this character died before he got it all sorted out. The yacht came into the hands of a retired Group Captain whom I had met. He came to me and told me that he was dissatisfied with the yacht but felt it had potential and what did I advise. Could I resist such a challenge - oh no! Scrap the plates, redesign solid twin keels. The rudder was an ugly, narrow, hoisting blade affair. Scrap this and as the yacht had considerable weather helm, I stuck my neck out and advised twin angled and asymmetrical rudders. This brave experiment worked well; the rig and other questions he sorted out for himself and so at the end of the day he had a useful yacht that satisfied him and was a worthwhile member of the twin keel society.

In the 1980's I had what I called a treble chance; sailing in all three 'Bluebirds' in the same year. 'Little Bluebird' in Holland, the first 'Bluebird of Thorne' from the Channel Islands to France and the second 'Bluebird of Thorne' from Ireland to Lymington - fantastic!

Where Do We Sail From Here
As I approach the last decade of a voyage from my memories of an important and enjoyable sector of my life's activities for eighty years, I may have contributed a not unimportant element of innovation and development. This interest has not ceased and I might be tempted at this point to set down some ideas towards what I should now produce if I were contemplating a new voyaging and cruising yacht for myself, or recreating 'Little Bluebird' with today's knowledge and materials. In the 1920's, the designer went to his drawing board with nothing more special than a few graphs, splines and weights, a little instrument for measuring areas and a slide rule. Today the designer would be hopelessly handicapped if he did not command extensive computer-aided equipment and recourse to all the sophistication of the modern test tank technology. I have discussed this with my friend John Lewis who, younger than I, has so equipped himself and adapted to it and I am amazed at what he has revealed, but I received some comfort in discussion with him when he agreed that the designer still requires artistic flair and imagination as well as knowledge and experience. I am tempted to try to further illustrate this by a simple statement: When I was designing a yacht in the 1920's, I had perhaps two or three options for every function contributing to the design of a yacht; today the designer has not two or three but ten or twelve options for all the same functions and the increase in knowledge and technology is never ending.

All this is of little importance compared to the people. I am convinced that every generation will produce men and women who just want to go to sea, who just have to sail and when all is said and done, what does it matter how they do it and what their equipment may be provided that they derive pleasure from it and a sense of achievement and satisfaction. The winds will not have changed, the seas will not have changed and man's capacity for enjoyment will not have changed.

I have said earlier and elsewhere that I have a complete faith and belief that there is something beyond this life and I like to think that perhaps if one has behaved oneself, one might be granted an ability to look back and to see what is happening, more particularly in the elements that one has enjoyed in that spell on earth. If so, it might be granted to me to see twin keel vessels of the type I invented, still wayfarers on the seas and oceans of the world and maintaining a mounting memorial to this seaman who is also a hunter, of whom it could at last be said:

*"Home is the sailor home from sea
And the hunter is home from the hill".*

Four twin-keel designs

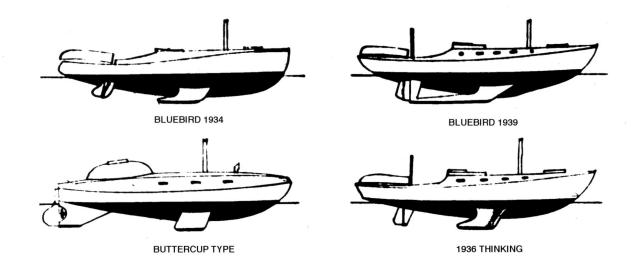

BLUEBIRD 1934

BLUEBIRD 1939

BUTTERCUP TYPE

1936 THINKING

TWIN KEEL YACHTS—DEVELOPMENT OVER 45 YEARS

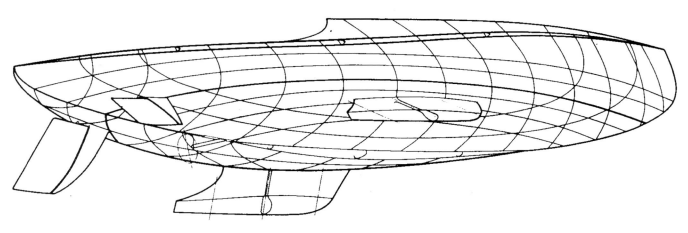

Fig. 1. 'Bluebird', 1924

John Lewis's isometric drawing.

'Duo' - a design by Lord Riverdale and John Lewis.
This was intended to be a yacht which would cope
with inland waterways and seafaring or a possible
round Europe voyage including Russia.

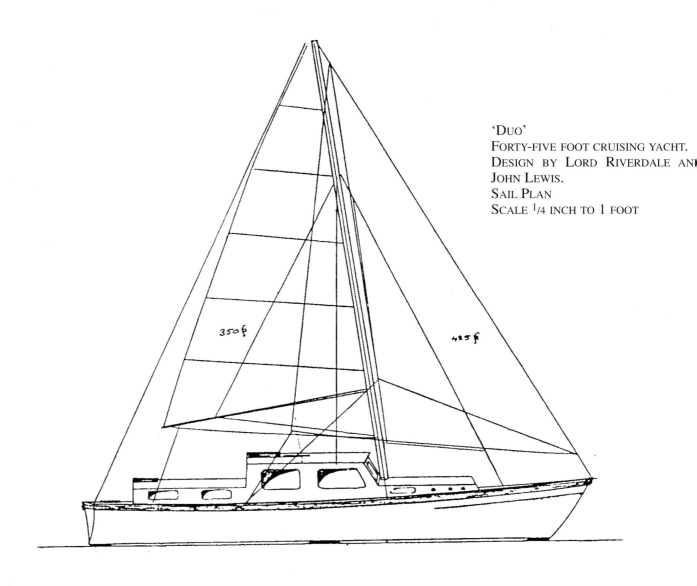

'DUO'
FORTY-FIVE FOOT CRUISING YACHT.
DESIGN BY LORD RIVERDALE AND
JOHN LEWIS.
SAIL PLAN
SCALE $\frac{1}{4}$ INCH TO 1 FOOT

350f

425f

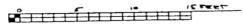